VALENTINO

BY IRVING SHULMAN

NOVELS

The Amboy Dukes ⎫
Cry Tough ⎬ A Trilogy
The Big Brokers ⎭

The Square Trap
Children of the Dark
Good Deeds Must Be Punished
Calibre
The Velvet Knife

SHORT STORIES

The Short End of the Stick

BIOGRAPHIES

The Roots of Fury
Harlow
Valentino

VALENTINO

By Irving Shulman

Trident Press New York

1967

PN
2287
.V3
S5

Library of Congress Catalog Card Number: 66–12335

*Published simultaneously in the United States
and Canada by Trident Press,
a division of Simon & Schuster, Inc.,
630 Fifth Avenue, New York, N.Y. 10020*

Printed in the United States of America

ACKNOWLEDGMENTS

*Permission to quote from the following
is gratefully acknowledged:*

FIRST PERSON PLURAL
by Dagmar Godowsky: The Viking Press (1958)

THE SHEIK OF ARABY and
THEY NEEDED A SONG BIRD IN HEAVEN
and reproducing the cover from
THERE'S A NEW STAR IN HEAVEN TONIGHT:
Mills Music, Inc. (1926)

A DREAMER'S THOUGHTS:
The Daily News (1926)

For
Judith Crist
Who is critic enough to know

AUTHOR'S NOTE

I arrived in Los Angeles on Labor Day 1947. Shortly thereafter I went to work as a screen writer, during which time I was fascinated by the back lots of studios and all the other behind-the-scenes aspects of film making. To my surprise the life of people affected and motivated by movies, as described by Nathaniel West's novel *The Day of the Locust* (1939), was a modest delineation of reality. This was borne out to me many times, but the most dramatic incident occurred in 1950 when I had the opportunity to visit a little apartment-temple to the memory of Rudolph Valentino. The temple was the private property of a lady not at ease in this world. The holy place, its artifacts, and the dithyrambic declamation of its curator, which alternated its verse praise of Valentino with a violent fishwife's denunciation of all the false high priestesses who dishonored the memory of the Great Lover with their fraudulent claims of election to his favor, so impressed me that I incorporated this visit and a description of the shrine in my novel *The Square Trap* (1953).

The shrine and its heady priestess stimulated my interest in Valentino, what passion he had inspired in females, and I began to collect material related to him; in 1959 I rewrote the relevant chapter in *The Square Trap* to make it a short story "—Your Hands Entrap My Quivering Heart" and included it in a collection of my short stories which was published under the general title of *The Short End of the Stick*.

My interest in Valentino as an authentic socio-cultural phenomenon continued and in the preparation of this biography I was assisted by collectors in Los Angeles, San Francisco, Washington, D.C., and New York who made available to me their

Valentino collections; public and professional libraries also made available their holdings. The private individuals who assisted me prefer to remain anonymous; what they had to say about Valentino was certain to be resented by the professional keepers of the myth whose big fat mouths froth at the use of published photographs, printed materials, and citations that can be documented.

In addition, I must note that in the summer of 1964 I was scolded by a group of oviparous females of both sexes, who among the intellectually underprivileged of Hollywood are much admired. The tips of their brown noses aquiver, they chided me for not liking movies. I deny their silly charge. I don't like bad or poor or bathetic or maudlin or silly or stupid or banal or pointless or meretricious or wearisome movies; nor do I like movie magazines, gossip columnists, or any of the truck with which these lickspittlers are associated. To compound my heresy, I hated *The Singing Nun* which starred Debbie Reynolds, and after seeing this movie I can only conclude that Louis B. Mayer is alive in Argentina.

But even if I didn't like *all* movies, I submit that a comprehensive abjuration of this soporific would place me in the company of many perceptive men and women of good purpose, all of them able to distinguish fact from fancy, reality from myth, history from legend, religion from idolatry, substance from imitation spun sugar; for they are beholden to intelligence and not to stupendous colossal stupidity even when it is presented with a cast of thousands and is—Lord, help us—popular and profitable as an entertainment.

IRVING SHULMAN

"APPENDIX FROM MORONIA"
PREJUDICES, SIXTH SERIES (1927)
H. L. MENCKEN

By one of the chances that relieve the dullness of life and make it instructive, I had the honor of dining with this celebrated gentleman in New York, a week or so before his fatal illness. I had never met him before nor seen him on the screen. . . . I began to observe Valentino more closely. A curiously naive and boyish young fellow, certainly not much beyond thirty, and with a disarming air of inexperience. To my eye, at least, not handsome, but nevertheless rather attractive. There was an obvious fineness in him; even his clothes were not precisely those of his horrible trade. He began talking of his home, his people, his early youth. His words were simple and yet somehow very eloquent. I could still see the mime before me, but now and then, briefly and darkly, there was a flash of something else. That something else, I concluded, was what is commonly called, for want of a better name, a gentleman. . . .

I incline to think that the inscrutable gods, in taking him off so soon and at a moment of fiery revolt, were very kind to him. Living, he would have tried inevitably to change his fame—if such it is to be called—into something closer to his heart's desire. That is to say, he would have gone the way of many another actor—the way of increasing pretension, of solemn artiness, of hollow hocus-pocus, deceptive only to himself. I believe he would have failed, for there was little sign of the genuine artist in him. He was essentially a highly respectable young man, which is the sort that never metamorphoses into an artist. But suppose he had succeeded? Then his tragedy, I believe, would have only become the more acrid and intolerable. . . .

Here, after all, is the chiefest joke of the gods: that man must remain alone and lonely in this world, even with crowds surging about him. Does he crave approbation, with a sort of furious instinctive lust? Then it is only to discover, when it comes, that it is somehow disconcerting—that its springs and motives offer an affront to his dignity. But do I sentimentalize the perhaps transparent story of a simple mummer? Then substitute Coolidge, or Mussolini, or any other poor devil that you can think of. Substitute Shakespeare, or Lincoln, or Goethe, or Beethoven, as I have. Sentimental or not, I confess that the predicament of poor Valentino touched me. It provided grist for my mill, but I couldn't quite enjoy it. Here was a young man who was living daily the dream of millions of other young men. Here was one who was catnip to women. Here was one who had wealth and fame. And here was one who was very unhappy.

ACT ONE
UNITED ARTISTS PRESENTS
A FRANK E. CAMPBELL
PRODUCTION

The Great American Funeral

ACT ONE: SCENE ONE

That Monday morning, August 23, 1926, the best the *Daily Mirror* could offer was a banner headline—VALENTINO DYING—and a full-page still of Valentino taken from *The Son of the Sheik*, and captioned "The Sheik's Picture Coupon." For five cents, to cover mailing costs, the *Mirror* would send a five-by-seven glossy of "Valentino in his Ahmed Ben Hassan Sheik costume" to any fan wishing to take advantage of this public-spirited offer. Hundreds of thousands did.

Since there were at least several million dollars tied up in *The Eagle* and *The Son of the Sheik*, the phone wires between New York and Los Angeles were soon commandeered by less hysterical executives of United Artists, bravely facing up to what until then had been a traditionally catastrophic problem: moving pictures starring dead actors and actresses played to empty theaters. The superstitious public apparently believed it was indecent to watch dead people perform in their full vigor, to see men and women officially dead and properly buried engaging in such dramatic activities as the preliminaries to the heavy-breathing courtships which preceded conception, maturation and birth. But the time had come to educate the public upward; a strong effort had to be undertaken for the good of continued economic growth, investment and the industry's future. Despite the ruthlessness of death, a consistently healthy appreciation in keeping with the widespread bullish optimism of American free enterprise had to be maintained.

Fortunately for the press, the picture business and industry at large, the American public was robust, vigorously adolescent and eager to worship new anthropomorphic golems or deities created in its own image. Americans are a thrifty people and, paradoxically, generous. They would now assist United Artists in the profitable elevation of its new god for domestic and foreign worship.

At the hospital, the sober announcement of death had been delivered to the assembled press corps by Joseph Schenck, chairman of the board of directors of United Artists. Haltingly, his voice breaking, and pausing occasionally to pat the arm of a weeping nurse or aide, Schenck at last managed to announce that the romantic star had lost his brave battle, then went on to say that he had lost a friend, the industry had lost a star and the world had lost a lover. But—take heart—heaven had gained an immortal.

Frank E. Campbell, funeral impresario par excellence, had already offered the honors of a deluxe Campbell funeral—absolutely free unless United Artists Corporation or the Valentino estate cared to compensate his Funeral Church. Furthermore, Campbell suggested, the pomp and circumstance of such a funeral might serve to keep Valentino's current pictures alive. Perhaps *The Eagle* and *The Son of the Sheik* would not have to be canned and shelved in vaults, where they, like their star, might soon become dust. Instead, they still might be shown with profit.

In all such discussions, Campbell had been ably assisted and seconded by Harry C. Klemfuss, an optimistic publicity man of great ingenuity. Why should United Artists suffer business misfortune because one of its most valuable assets had died? If Valentino had heeded the Angel of Death, who could better roadshow this dramatic event than Frank E. Campbell, whose organization was geared for maximum exploitation? If the Gold Room at Campbell's had been good enough for Anna Held, Vernon Castle, Oscar Hammerstein, Olive Thomas *and* Lillian Russell, it was certainly good enough for Valentino. The House of Campbell was awarded the funeral and began to prepare for a gala holiday of death.

Relieved of all funeral responsibility, Joseph Schenck was able to turn to more important matters. Mr. Schenck telephoned William Randolph Hearst to thank the newspaper and motion picture magnate for his sympathy and suggest ways in which the Hearst press might help UA recover its investment in Valentino. The *Examiner*, it was decided, would carry an editorial elegy the very next day. "The Whole World's Loss" was agreed upon as a heading and a grateful Schenck thanked Hearst and invited him to the New York services, since the place of the entombment had not yet been decided upon. That would be up to Valentino's brother, when he arrived from Italy. Hearst appreciated Schenck's invitation and was of the vigorous opinion that the body of Valentino belonged to Hollywood. His newspapers, he added, would stress this.

But there was more urgent business: it was imperative to make new prints of *The Son of the Sheik* and rush them into the movie theaters if United Artists hoped to profit from the publicity attending Valentino's funeral. Schenck hoped the Valentino estate might prosper from this, since the actor had died deeply in debt. It seemed inconceivable that a man could squander a million dollars in one year and have nothing to show for his efforts, but Valentino had accomplished this impossibility. With some comfort Schenck reflected that United Artists had shown foresight in insuring the star's life.

Campbell and Klemfuss could no longer delay the arrival of the principal in what they were increasingly convinced would become the most successful attraction on Broadway. They pleaded with journalists to leave, for they had to prepare the Funeral Home, but the reporters were reluctant to go. The impromptu bar was good and they did not trust Campbell—yet they dared not ignore Harry Klemfuss' observation that they would be scooped by other newspapermen at the hospital when Mr. Campbell went there for the body. So warned, they rushed to the hospital. But earlier that afternoon Frank Campbell's funeral coach had driven to the private entrance on West Fifty-first Street to take custody of the body, which had been placed in a large wicker hamper and moved to a small auxiliary warehouse some buildings removed from the Funeral Church.

Hospital personnel told the reporters that Mr. Campbell had clucked sorrowfully that the star had had to suffer such an indignity for even so short a part of his final journey. To improve appearances Campbell had covered the hamper with a heavy gold cloth. A member of his staff had taken several photographs of the transfer and these would subsequently be released to all the newspapers.

While the body was being removed, a death certificate had been prepared by Dr. William B. Rawles, the chief resident surgeon, under the actor's real name—Rodolpho Guglielmi. His correct age was recorded, and the major causes of death were described as "ruptured gastric ulcer and general peritonitis." Septic pneumonia and septic endocarditis were listed as contributing factors. Dr. Paul E. Durham, who had been in constant attendance upon Valentino, suffered a cardiac seizure and was promptly hospitalized on the premises. A medical bulletin issued that night stated that Dr. Durham was suffering from nervous exhaustion but was not critically ill.

Meanwhile, back at the Funeral Church, more and more of the spectators who had kept vigil outside the hospital began to arrive, along with police to keep them in order. This gathering was soon enlarged by the many who had read the afternoon papers or listened to the radio, which spoke increasingly now of Campbell's, and they remained to discuss Valentino, mutability and what had *really* killed the Sheik. After the dinner hour people began to arrive from the large apartment houses on Central Park West, Riverside Drive and West End Avenue. Soon Broadway, from Sixty-fifth to Sixty-eighth Streets, became impassable for vehicular traffic.

Would Jimmy Walker appear? Would Doug Fairbanks, speeding homeward from Europe, and Flo Ziegfeld appear at the parlors? Was the Army really going to fly Pola Negri to the funeral in an airmail plane? The night was warm and soon ice-cream and soft-drink vendors appeared to service the curious. The crowd certainly now numbered more than ten thousand, many of them strangers to the neighborhood, and police were having difficulty in maintaining order.

That night, at the film laboratories, men began to work around the clock to produce scores of new prints of *The Son of the Sheik* and other Valentino films. In constant touch with the situation, United Artists' executives began to feel an increasing confidence in the ringmastership of Frank E. Campbell. With things going so well, the ceremonies might be prolonged for a week, possibly for two. Was this possible? Valentino, after all, was not Abraham Lincoln. But Lincoln had died more than half a century before and was mourned by no more than half a nation; although he had been a great humanitarian, he could never have been called a sheik.

In Hollywood, all work on *Hotel Imperial* had been suspended. Miss Pola Negri, prostrate with grief, had been chauffeured to her bungalow at the Ambassador Hotel, where she had authorized Charles Eyton, a close friend, to make the following statement to the press:

> Just before he left for New York, Mr. Valentino had told me that he and Miss Negri were to be married as soon after January 1 as their picture work permitted—which was later confirmed by Miss Negri. They planned to spend their honeymoon in Europe. Throughout the morning Miss Negri spoke again and again with heartbroken sobs of the tragic shattering of their romance. "I have lost not only my dearest friend," she said, "but the one real love of my life." She insisted on going to the home which Valentino had been building for her, now nearly completed, and into which both had poured their ideas for the ideal home they planned to occupy after their marriage. She spent more than an hour at the beautiful shrine of her lost romance, a pathetic and heartbroken figure.

Mr. Eyton terminated the conference with a plea of sympathy for the tear-bathed star. Soon she would have to undertake a long, sad pilgrimage, and in their sympathy—he knew—she would find strength.

ACT ONE: SCENE TWO

The first daylight hours of Tuesday, August 24, 1926, were hot and oppressive. Most of the morning papers forecast rain, which perturbed Frank E. Campbell and his loyal staff, but everything was put into full gear to insure that the laying out of Valentino would be the most impressive in the history of necrolatry. The same process that had been used to keep Enrico Caruso presentable was employed. Expert cosmeticians and a skilled barber plied their scented arts. And Mr. Campbell himself chose the custom-tailored, backless, formal evening wear and complementing sartorial niceties which would make the dead actor as impeccably clad as the Man in the Arrow Collar.

There had been a feeling among the staff that great funebrial history might be made if Valentino were consigned to rest in one of the movie costumes he had made famous. An Arabian

9

burnoose was ruled out immediately but Frank Campbell telephoned Joseph Schenck to ask if United Artists would object to Valentino's being buried in the costume of a gaucho or matador. It was too bad, Campbell stressed, that there was no distinctive national Italian dress, save that of an organ grinder or a Black Shirt, and since neither of these seemed truly romantic, why not bury Valentino as a gaucho or a toreador, with a black shirt livened up by touches of red and gold? It could only improve Latin American relations. But Schenck had rudely vetoed the suggestion and hung up on the grief director.

To enhance olfactory responses, the Gold Room was perfumed with a light, fragrant incense, and Campbell's most lavish treasures and genuine marble sculptures were tastefully arranged around the draped catafalque. Although the ravages of illness had been cosmeticized into a semblance of repose, it was still possible to see the drawn lines of pain around the mouth and eyes of the departed. So the chapel lights were arranged to shadow what the final illness had done to the idol of millions of women and young girls. Potted palms and luxurious ferns were arranged around the catafalque; a single red rose in a gilt bud vase supplied a touch of color behind Valentino's head. At a small altar, a statue of the Virgin was framed by scented candles, a tooled volume of the Vulgate Bible and a rosary. Because floral offerings had not yet arrived in quantity, appropriate bouquets and wreaths were moved in from Campbell's florist shop next door.

Mr. Campbell seemed pleased with what he had wrought and telephoned Joseph Schenck to invite him to a preview showing. Mr. and Mrs. Schenck were informed that important persons would be made welcome from two in the afternoon. The public would not be admitted until six that evening. Mr. Campbell then suggested to Mr. Schenck that there might be certain incidental expenses relating to the proper care of members of the press and distinguished guests, and would United Artists resist being billed for them? It was only an afterthought, Mr. Campbell pointed out, but certain radio broadcasts and evening newspapers had made public that an insurance bonanza of a million dollars would be paid Mr. Schenck as the beneficiary of certain Valentino policies.

Indignantly, Mr. Schenck replied that United Artists Corporation, not *he*, was the beneficiary. It sounded very much like communism, he added, for Mr. Campbell to suggest that such corporate foresight be penalized. To minimize such rumors of wealth through death, he intended to announce that there had been only two hundred thousand dollars in insurance. He hoped the arrangements made with Mr. Campbell by United Artists would be honored. Yes, small bills would be acknowledged by his office—United Artists was not tightfisted—but he hoped the bills were not—and he repeated this several times—to include any charges for illegal creature comforts. For hot-weather refreshment, nothing was better than iced tea.

As a superior mortuary merchant, Mr. Campbell knew when to terminate conversations with the living. He thanked Mr. Schenck for his understanding and invited him to visit the parlors at will. He reassured him again of conservative financial outlays, and regretted that news accounts had exaggerated the amount of insurance due the corporation.

To assure the fans of its noble grief and orchestral lamentations, the movie industry could rely upon Miss Louella Parsons and other filmland reporters, but in New York the extent of the public's emotional instability would have to be proved by the little people who made the stars—or so the movie magazines and columns told them. Would the little people prove that they too could deify a dead film star? It would be more than the industry, with all its money and ballyhoo, had ever been able to accomplish for one of its own.

By six, on the morning of August 24, the first pilgrims to Campbell's mecca of mourning debouched from the subway stations near Broadway and West Sixty-sixth Street. The weather was still warm and the humidity gave definite promise of discomfort. Signs of rain were increasingly evident, and some decided to return home for umbrellas while others planned to buy them as soon as neighborhood stores opened. The crowd around Campbell's soon numbered five hundred but order was easily maintained by three policemen and a Campbell's usher, who good-naturedly informed these early birds that the Funeral Church did not intend to open its doors to the general public until six in the evening. In refutation of this announcement, dozens of people waved copies of the *Journal*, whose headline boldly announced that Valentino had wanted his body viewed.

The crowd continued to swell through the early-morning hours. A policeman telephoned the West Sixty-seventh Street precinct for reinforcements, because disputes were erupting everywhere over who had arrived first, who was shoving too hard, who was stepping on whose feet. Still, for the most part the throng was cheerful as its members talked animatedly about their loyalty to Valentino, his wonderful pictures and which were their favorite roles. This cheerful mood was tempered only by some discussion of the strange circumstances of Valentino's death.

Newcomers continued to arrive, and many of them carried Thermos jugs, sandwiches and collapsible camp chairs. Newsboys and shoeshine boys appeared in strength and neighborhood urchins raided the local stores and markets for wooden boxes and crates, which they sold for quarters to those in the lines. As the crowd swelled and the supply of boxes diminished, the price rose to as much as three dollars. People from nearby apartment houses began to sell fruit and sandwiches. A bustling trade in soft drinks, ice cream and lemon ices developed; platoons of frankfurter vendors exhausted their stock.

At noon the crowd, by the most conservative estimate, numbered more than ten thousand and it became increasingly difficult for the dozen policemen—ten on foot, two mounted—to control it. Patrolman William C. Wood again telephoned the West Sixty-seventh Street station to urge acting Captain Hammill to send reinforcements.

A slight diversion was provided by the arrival of a floral offering from Sophie Tucker. Bouquets and wreaths also arrived from Princess Karneska de Charrow, who claimed to have played opposite Valentino in *The Cossack's Daughter* (did she refer to *The Eagle?*), Constance Talmadge and James R. Quirk, the editor of *Photoplay*. But the crowd approved most the four asters left by a little girl who was unable to spell her name for the reporters.

Police officials throughout Manhattan were soon notified that at Campbell's the crowd was threatening to turn into a mob. Every uniformed man who could be spared was to be held in readiness. Police strength was now about fifty patrolmen, assisted by a dozen more on horseback, who used their mounts to keep the surging mob from taking over completely. From their horses they kept repeating that the doors of Campbell's might not open at six and everyone had best go home. But this was greeted by hoots, jeers and obscene gestures.

The first arrivals had been women and girls, but more and more men had now joined the crowd. The average age of the boisterous mob seemed under thirty-five and reporters remarked on the increasing number of men sporting bolero jackets and gaucho hats. Many also wore balloon trousers, spats and the slick hair and long sideburns made popular by Valentino. As mourners they presented a strange assembly.

When it became evident to the officers that the mob could not be dispersed, police efforts were undertaken to at least bring some order into the spreading chaos. Pushing, threatening, cajoling, using their clubs to move the crowds, the police finally succeeded in forming rough lines almost a block in length and cleared a small area before Campbell's for the reporters and photographers. But the mob continued to expand rapidly, en-

larging its perimeter. The front ranks pushed until both uniformed men and horses were compelled to retreat. Time and
again the mounted policemen rode into the crowd in an attempt
to force it off Broadway and into the side streets.

Soon after two o'clock, to the delight of the police officers, it
began to drizzle. Minutes later it was raining steadily and the
more than fifteen thousand people now massed in the vicinity of
Campbell's chanted in unison for the doors to be opened. Those
fortunate enough to be near the doors of the chapel or its plate-
glass windows began to beat their fists against the bronze and
glass as they demanded admission. Additional squads of police
arrived, along with several police sergeants and lieutenants, led
by Captain Hammill, and pushed their way through and managed to enter while the officers already there beat back the
crowd.

Within the parlors, Frank Campbell and his associates were
told the mob was out of hand, and whatever arrangements had
been made for important visitors to view the dead actor between
the hours of two and six would have to be called off. Once the
doors were opened, people would have to be admitted on a first-
come basis. After a hurried face-saving consultation between
Campbell and Klemfuss, they agreed that the doors should be
opened within ten minutes, which would give the police a little
time to restore a semblance of order. There were by then almost
twenty thousand people clamoring to get in. The sidewalks between the subway stations at Fifty-ninth, Sixty-sixth and Seventy-
second Streets were unable to accommodate the influx, and all
north- and southbound traffic on Broadway was choked to a
standstill, as was crosstown traffic between Columbus and Amsterdam Avenues.

Psychologically blind, emotionally drunk, intoxicated by
steamy human contact, increasingly defiant of the impotent
police force—the mob, transformed into a human juggernaut,
stormed the doors. It shouted and screamed and cried out in a

masochistic ecstasy that transmuted pain into joy. Step by step, three of the policemen gave ground until with a mighty surge the mob trapped them against the large plate-glass window. Then, as if it were a giant wave, it paused, gained a crest and broke against the policemen until the glass shattered, raining razor-sharp shards over the struggling policemen and the screaming mob.

Three policemen and two women fell through the broken window. Others lay stunned or unconscious, as the crowd continued to surge forward. To save the fallen, three mounted policemen charged desperately at the crowd until it fell back. Several men and women were trampled by the horses' hoofs as they attempted to duck under the animals' bellies.

At that moment the front doors of the Funeral Church opened and in the first mad rush the police officers detailed there were swept along with the milling crowd that knocked over potted palms, chairs and other furniture. Lamps fell and were trampled as the mob pushed toward the Gold Room, where Valentino lay. George Ullman, Valentino's manager, attempted to block them, as he shouted at the police to close the gates of the chapel. In the mounting confusion, yowling men and women clawed at each other, kicked and spat and struck out blindly, as they hurled themselves forward. They did not seem to hear or care that men and women were being dangerously trampled as they surged into the Gold Room and toward the catafalque, where for several terrible moments it appeared as if the draperies and casket might be spilled to the muddy carpet.

Police, attendants, even some reporters and photographers fought to expel the mob. At last they succeeded. Outside, along Broadway and in the adjacent side streets, the police wielded their clubs and charged on foot and horse until at last an area around Campbell's was cleared of all but the wounded. A hundred policemen formed a long line with clubs at the ready to hold back the cursing mob.

More than a hundred people had been injured. Women wept, and cried that they had been felt up or robbed. Mothers were separated from their children, and the pavement outside the wrecked Funeral Church was littered with umbrellas, women's shoes, purses and torn clothing. A small lost-and-found was established but at midnight there were still dozens of unclaimed articles, among them twenty-eight different shoes. To add to the hopeless disorder, the rain continued to fall steadily. People began to fight for shelter under the few umbrellas, and individual sorties, with handles or tips of umbrellas as weapons, were increasingly waged against the police.

What confused the officers and inhibited their decisions were the circumstances of disorder. Most of this swarming mob was made up of people who had never before been and might never again be connected with any disturbance. They were not here to lynch, burn or protest but to pay last honors to a movie idol. They had come because the newspapers had said that Valentino wished his body to be viewed by his fans. Small radio stations in and around the city were also entreating their listeners to pay personal homage to the dead star, to dedicate one day of their lives as a tribute to the actor who had given them so many hours of love, affection and enjoyment. And several Italian-language stations carried little else but funeral dirges and eulogies about Valentino. These stations urged, as an act of national pride and religious grace, a pilgrimage to Campbell's.

A sort of field hospital was set up in the funeral home for emergency medical attention, and the more serious cases were removed by ambulance to nearby hospitals. More women began to faint, and hysterics increased in number. It was decided then to close the Funeral Church until four o'clock, in the vain hope that the continued rain would dilute the strength of the mob. But such attempts were frustrated because news of the riot had spread throughout Manhattan, and thousands more appeared, all willing to endure extreme discomfort, rough handling, even danger, at the remote possibility of getting a quick look at the dead actor.

For perhaps three-quarters of an hour the police managed to keep the rioters in check while the debris was swept out and Valentino's body was removed from the Gold Room. The carpets had been muddied by the mob, who had made profitable use of its time by sacking the parlor for souvenirs and mementos— flowers, leaves and ferns had been stripped as if by locusts. Outside, on the street, people vied in an orgiastic exploitation as they displayed a flower, a petal, a leaf, a tassel or fringe. Thereafter they would hoard these souvenirs as if they were national treasures. And there had been other depredations as well— people on the crowded sidewalks demanded police help, for their pockets had been picked, their purses rifled. But there was not time to take inventory of such losses or record complaints, because good news suddenly pepped up the mob. Campbell's was ready to open its doors again. The bewildered policemen braced themselves for action.

Valentino's body had now been placed in a silver-bronze, glass-enclosed coffin in a smaller room on the second floor, placed at an angle on the catafalque. Valentino's head was turned to give mourners a three-quarter-profile view, and from here mourners could be directed down an emergency stairway to Sixty-seventh Street. Police ranks were further reinforced. Through megaphones police officials harangued the mob to maintain order, go home, be patient: everyone who behaved and cooperated would see Valentino.

At three-fifteen, the doors were reopened and the mourners were hurried upstairs, past the coffin and then down the back stairs. For some minutes there appeared to be order outside, but soon the rowdier elements in the crowd began to rush the police lines. Once again the police had to give ground. The mob smashed the store window of the Brown "Drive It Yourself" Automobile Company on the corner of Broadway and Sixty-sixth Street and overturned one of Mr. Brown's Ford cars parked at the curb. More persons were trampled and one young girl was felled by a horse. She was rushed to Knickerbocker Hospital. Dozens of women fainted; more mothers reported that they had lost their children.

Among the celebrities identified in the afternoon crowd was Mrs. Heenan, mother of Frances "Peaches" Browning, who was married to "Daddy" Browning. The life of Peaches, age sixteen, and Daddy, who was fifty-two, was being featured by the Hearst press along with "My Honeymoon Diary," a "piquant recital of exciting adventures amidst the magnetic enticements of love and riches." Mrs. Heenan gave her autograph and promised her daughter's as well to anyone who would have them.

Four more times during the afternoon the mob regrouped and each time it was driven back by the mounted police, now under the direct field command of Captain Hammill, who swore that in twenty years' experience he had never seen such a crowd. For unruliness and for its complete failure to realize the need for some order, it was without equal. "This crowd has the real mob spirit. . . . So many of them are morbidly curious that they won't go home."

This statement given to the press, Captain Hammill telephoned for added reinforcements, then ordered Campbell's doors closed again because he wished to rotate his men and give some of them a chance for a little rest. Members of the fire and sanitation departments finally appeared on the scene, and most of the broken glass was swept away. After a quarter hour's respite, the doors were again opened for homage. Police and the reporters noted that once people were inside, the demeanor changed, they became quiet and meek; but "outside the building an air of hilarity and hoodlumism prevailed."

People were packed so tightly around Campbell's and had become so truculently determined that no latecomers would usurp their places that it became increasingly dangerous for anyone to attempt a breakthrough. Thus it was the crowd rather than the police that repelled assaults between four in the afternoon and six that night. This helped to speed approximately five thousand people past the body on display in the second-floor room of Campbell's. Most people did not attempt a leisurely look; those who did were moved on by a police officer. Later, officers revealed that although people were respectful, they appeared to be curious rather than unhappy.

Police methods were deplored by Mr. Campbell, who was spiritually offended by the gruff, impatient tones of the policemen on duty. Such impatience was not in keeping with the polite tradition of the house, so Harry Klemfuss telephoned a private-detective agency for a large squad of men trained to combine authority with courtesy. The police officers welcomed their assistance and shrugged off Mr. Campbell's statement that the private detectives were there "to give the police a lesson in funeral suavity."

However, the relatively peaceful interlude of late afternoon came to an end at six o'clock, when the more than twenty thousand turbulent rubbernecks besieging Campbell's were augmented by men and women freed from the bondage of earning that day's bread. A fresh, strong, fun-loving tide of men and women poured into the streets around Campbell's and police officers braced themselves to stop this new horde at Sixty-sixth and Sixty-seventh Streets. Once more the police failed.

The crowd's spirit was best summed up perhaps by a young lady from Brooklyn. She had arrived at Campbell's at one in the afternoon, had been pushed, buffeted and shoved in every direction, had endured four hours of pelting rain without benefit of umbrella or shelter and finally had fainted. Luckily she had collapsed at the feet of a policeman, who had quickly determined she was not a malingerer and carried her into the emergency ward of Campbell's to be treated by Dr. Leandro Tomarkin of 52 West Sixty-eighth Street. After Johanna Berg was revived she was permitted a long three-second glance at the dead Latin's profile.

Dr. Tomarkin estimated that more than a hundred people had been treated in the emergency ward by six o'clock, when Captain Hammill again telephoned Police Commissioner McLaughlin to requisition at least another hundred police. This would bring the total to two hundred and fifty. The Commissioner approved the requested reinforcements, then decided to visit the scene and see for himself whether the situation had been exaggerated. Commissioner McLaughlin was taken through the crowd on foot, for it was impossible to get his official automobile into Broadway between Sixty-sixth and Sixty-seventh Streets. After a short, angry conference in the Funeral Church, Commissioner McLaughlin ordered the doors shut until seven-thirty, during which time the police were to attempt to clear the area and get traffic moving. The police acted with new determination, their morale raised by the appearance and direction of the police commissioner himself; the crowd was driven back, recontained and forced again into a semblance of order.

"Why don't you be a man and let me in?" one woman shouted to one of the police.

"Why don't you be a lady and go home?" the officer retorted.

With astonishment, the *Herald Tribune* reported that the woman responded by lifting her umbrella and bringing it down on the man's head.

Working manfully, the police and their volunteers succeeded in forming a queue which must still hold some sort of record. The line, which was estimated at thirty thousand, four to eight abreast, started at Broadway and Sixty-sixth Street and extended eastward to Columbus Avenue. There the line ran for two blocks northward along Columbus Avenue, then westward again, for two more blocks on West Sixty-eighth Street, to the entrance to Campbell's. There it was thinned to two abreast.

By nine-thirty Commissioner McLaughlin had ordered another

fifty officers to assist at Broadway and West Sixty-eighth Street, where the weary men in blue were meeting strong resistance in their efforts to thin out the crowd. Two of the men on duty in the parlor, Barth Fruery and John Ackerman, told reporters that many of the girls were "repeaters" and they wondered aloud at the foolhardiness of youngsters willing to endure so much for so little.

From seven-thirty until midnight all vehicular traffic on Broadway between Fifty-ninth and Seventy-second Streets was diverted to Columbus Avenue, and the police estimated that during these hours there were at least eighty thousand people in the area. From nine-thirty on, the mood of the crowd became more resigned and less defiant, and mounted officers had little trouble in using their horses to maintain order. People were now passing the coffin at the rate of a hundred and fifty a minute, or nine thousand in an hour. This did not slacken by midnight, when there were still more than twenty thousand concentrated in the streets.

Within, the monotony was relieved by an occasional young extrovert who would fall to her knees at the catafalque and attempt to embrace it. Other young ladies kissed the side of the coffin or the hem of the fringed cloth. One bolder, more imaginative soubrette clambered atop the catafalque to press her lips to the glass lid just above the lips of Valentino. She was hustled out of the room, cheered on by the admiration of the others in the line.

Miss Lola Pierce, then appearing in a Broadway production, and by her statement Valentino's former dancing partner, became hysterical when she saw the body and was assisted, sobbing, to a taxicab by friends. Reporters noted that she was one of the few professional people to have come to Campbell's. Mrs. Alfred E. Smith, Jr., also made a brief appearance and left.

The dark, wet streets were, if this was at all possible, now more crowded than ever, and Mr. Campbell summoned ranking police officials to announce that he was not closing the doors at midnight. To do so would be shirking his civic duty, for "there were many women who worked at night, or in the early morning hours, who soon would be going to their jobs and might have no other opportunity of seeing the body. . . ."

But the police had had enough of Mr. Campbell, his aides-de-camp, his establishment, his solicitudes and disquisitions for the living as well as the dead, and they told him so. Captain Hammill announced that his men were physically and emotionally exhausted and he refused to answer for the consequences if he had to hold them on duty another four hours. Mr. Campbell was ordered to close his doors at midnight, and reluctantly he complied. The doors were locked and placed under the guard of private detectives. Wooden barricades were set up to protect the windows, and with some difficulty the hooting, weeping, jeering mob was dispersed and driven from the neighborhood.

However, shortly after midnight the doors of Campbell's were reopened when a group of five uniformed men made their appearance. The leader identified himself as Guido Valenti of 145 West Forty-fifth Street. Mr. Valenti, who claimed to be a relative of Valentino's, informed Mr. Campbell and the interested reporters that he and his men represented the Fascisti League of America. Italian Premier Benito Mussolini had cabled Phaon de Revel, chief of the Italian Fascisti in the United States, to place a laurel wreath from the Italian Government: he also had requested the Fascisti to serve as a uniformed honor guard at the bier. With impressive solemnity the wreath was placed—it bore the legend "FROM BENITO MUSSOLINI"—as the Black Shirts took up their stations. Both the honor guard and Mussolini's wreath were photographed for the morning papers.

Mr. Campbell was delighted. Mr. Ullman, too, was impressed. Such sympathetic honors from the Italian dictator might inspire Calvin Coolidge to do as much. At the very least he could send an American honor guard of soldiers, sailors and marines. Certainly Warren G. Harding, who had been a honey, would have done so.

The funeral services for Valentino at St. Malachy's Chapel—properly known as the Actor's Chapel—were scheduled for Monday, September 30, which gave Campbell and his showmen five more days for the gala presentation. Meanwhile, the Fascisti stood guard, newspaper presses worked overtime and Pola Negri's wardrobe trunks were packed with three thousand dollars' worth of exclusive widow's weeds. After all, she had to be as well dressed as the man who lay in Campbell's casket. Their public, the little people who created stars and deities, demanded it.

ACT ONE: SCENE THREE

The hours after midnight of Wednesday, August 25, provided no rest for the mortuary and motion picture executives charged with keeping the Valentino image alive. If they had speculated about publicity and the extent of the public interest, the initial response was so heartening that the concern shifted from How much news can we get? to How much news do we want? The New York *Daily News* had devoted its only editorial to Valentino, the immigrant boy who by making good had once more proven the American tradition of rags to riches. The editorial had applauded Valentino "as one of the few truly great actors," but had leavened this with the observation that "he had probably passed the apex of his fame when he died." Campbell's and United Artists were going to prove the *Daily News* wrong.

Wire-service bulletins assured the corporate executives that the newspapers of every major European capital were devoting a good share of their front pages to the story of Valentino and his untimely death. Parisian newspapers paid tribute to Valentino as an artist and for "his faculty of bringing the flavor of romance into the lives of people." By the following day every cinema in Paris able to book *any* Valentino film did so. The theaters reported overflow business and while women waited in the lobbies for admission, they stood in rapt reverence before blowups of Valentino and wept.

These were good primary press and booking reactions, but opinion among the United Artists executives was divided over the news value of a London suicide prominently exploited by the tabloids. Miss Peggy Scott, a twenty-seven-year-old cabaret performer and chorus girl, and reputedly a cinema actress, had been found dead of poison in the bedroom of her West End flat. Miss Scott had expired in her bed, surrounded by autographed letters and photos from Valentino. A suicide note addressed to a friend confessed that Valentino's death was too much to bear, so she had decided to end it all. When interviewed by the police, a friend told how Miss Scott had met Valentino "while he was holidaying at Biarritz, had greatly admired him, and that at one time there had been a rumor of romance." Also, Miss Scott had always worn a photograph of Valentino inside her dress. It seemed not unlikely that there might be more such lamentable incidents.

To the lounging reporters in the funeral parlor, Mr. Schenck made public a telegram of tribute just received from Los Angeles and signed by John W. Considine, Jr., Charles Chaplin, John Barrymore, Buster Keaton, Samuel Goldwyn, Ronald Colman, Vilma Banky, Henry King, George Fitzmaurice, Sidney Franklin, Fred Niblo, Mme Fred de Gresac and Abe Lahr. Reporters were also informed that Alberto Guglielmi was sailing that morning from Paris on the *Homeric*. Mr. Campbell and Mr. Schenck had received identical cables from Alberto requesting postponement of the funeral services until his arrival. He would agree to a requiem mass before he landed on American soil, but traditions would be violated if no member of the family was present at the funeral. Queried about the final resting place of his brother, Alberto had refused to commit himself.

Italian newspapers had also published interviews with Valentino's poor Castellanetan relatives, whose sorrow was tempered with joy because they were convinced they would share in the dead actor's estate. A cousin of Rudolph's, identified only as Maria, did not believe that Valentino had left a will because as a south Italian he would have been superstitious about such documents. Furthermore, she and the others rejoiced that he had "died with two friars at his bedside and firmly believed the matrimonial adventures which, with his frequent divorces, had so horrified his relatives, would be forgiven." Maria did not believe the various women he married were really his wives; as he was a Catholic, there was no validity to any union following divorce. According to this voluble cousin, the body would be returned to Naples in a silver coffin and proceed in great procession to Taranto for a magnificent state funeral and burial.

It was quickly ascertained that these plans did not have Alberto's approval. Rather, the late actor's brother declared that he had found no fault with Miss Negri's statement to the Hollywood press: "I am going East with one hope in mind, that Rudolph's brother will decide to bring the body here."

Such civic-mindedness pleased Frank Campbell, who envisioned a funeral train at least equal to Lincoln's and making a considerably longer journey. The only untoward note had been Alberto's rather embarrassing statement to reporters:

"I can't understand Rudolph's sudden death," he had exclaimed, on the point of tears. "He always kept himself in perfect condition by daily calisthenics. He was thirty-one years old when he died, and I never knew him to have a sick day in all that time."

Rumors were still thick in New York that Valentino had been murdered. The previous day's rehash of these shooting or poisoning rumors by the Chicago *Tribune* was certain to receive the widest circulation throughout the entire Midwest, and the gloom thickened when Chicago friends of Valentino's telephoned Joseph Schenck to inform him that the *Tribune* had also published the home-town reaction to the death of Valentino, and these impressions were being snapped up by dozens of papers, among them *The New York Times*.

In short, the little village of Castellaneta in Italy was indifferent. The *Tribune*'s correspondent had found only one family, that of Angelo Maldarizzi, in mourning for the village's most famous son. And when he had been shown a movie-magazine photograph of Valentino's birthplace, Maldarizzi had laughingly informed the reporter that the building had been considerably improved upon. At Rudolph's birth, it had been the humblest of cottages. In 1926, the only association of the Guglielmis with Castellaneta was the village graveyard, where Rudolph's sister lay. His mother was reputed to have been buried in France and his father in Taranto.

To this uncomplimentary account had been added the information that the Vatican's *L'Osservatore Romano* had commented critically on Valentino's death and found no occasion for joy in "his need for two priests at his bedside." Editorially, *L'Osservatore* scored his popularity with silly girls and impressionable women "as a sign of the decadence of the times" and unhappy proof that most people sought the solace and satisfaction of mundane values at the expense of the spiritual.

What would happen, Schenck and Campbell suddenly thought, if the Church in the United States acted likewise? The projection was gloomy and financially dangerous until someone remembered that Valentino had received a Catholic's last rites at the Polyclinic Hospital. Surely the Church could not go halfway and stop; Valentino had received the Church's sacraments; *ergo,* he would also receive a Catholic burial. Still, it was decided to investigate this matter cautiously. A Campbell delegate was assigned to visit St. Malachy's later that morning to sound out its clergy.

But perhaps the most vexing problem of all was the projected transcontinental visit by Pola Negri. Adolph Zukor, in New York, had received a telephone call from the studio in Hollywood: "Pola is overwrought and she's heading to New York for the funeral." Zukor had advised putting a nurse and publicity man on the train and gave strict orders that Pola was to guard her statements to the press. Obviously, Paramount intended to make Pola's sad pilgrimage more important than Valentino's demise.

As she was herself an important maker of news, publicity for Pola could not be watered down, especially since her presence would add luster to the ceremonies and thus increase the earning power of the two hundred prints of *The Son of the Sheik* ordered by Joseph Schenck. Nevertheless, a reasonably fair ratio of importance, even if it involved self-sacrifice on the part of the living, had to be observed. Valentino could not speak for himself; Pola could make as many statements as she wished. Obviously some system of checks and balances would have to be established. Schenck gave firm instructions to both Campbell and Klemfuss: no matter what Miss Negri intended, she was to be offered every assistance—so long as her activities were subordinated to the image of Valentino. To emphasize this no-nonsense attitude, Schenck informed them that there were creditors to whom Valentino owed substantial sums of money and it would be disgraceful if the dead actor had to be declared in bankruptcy because his publicity had been eclipsed.

Miss Negri had intended to leave for New York on Saturday, August 28, but a New York friend had wired her that so late a departure would deprive her of her starring role at the Valentino services, scheduled for August 30. So despite the pleas of Charles Eyton and other Paramount executives, she booked a compartment on the Santa Fe for Wednesday, scheduled to leave Los Angeles at noon. Bravely defiant, scorning the concern of her physician, Dr. Louis Felger, and the pleading of Paramount officials that she remain until Saturday, when principal photography on *Hotel Imperial* could be completed, she dressed herself in black, attached a black veil to her hat and made ready for departure along with her many trunks, her secretary and a trained nurse, Adelaide Valencia.

A seasoned campaigner, Pola refused to pose for photographs. "I do not wish to advertise my grief," she said.

Rock Island officials notified her of the instructions they had received from the Santa Fe to make her trip as comfortable as possible. To eliminate the bother of a train change in Chicago on Saturday morning, they intended to transfer the car in which she was traveling directly to the New York Central. News of such unheard-of railroad cooperation was coupled with a rather ghoulish announcement by Rock Island officials. They explained that Valentino had bought a round-trip ticket from California to New York and that his manager, George Ullman, was in possession of that ticket. They went on to say that they had given orders to honor the ticket in transportation of the body if it was returned to Hollywood.

During the wee hours of Wednesday morning, at George Ullman's insistence, the catafalque and coffin were moved downstairs to Frank Campbell's private office. These arrangements were not only attractive to the police authorities, but the removal from the second-floor room to Mr. Campbell's office gave the honor guard of Black Shirts a rest as well. Until six in the morning, while the Fascisti were diverted elsewhere, the interior of the Funeral Church hummed with unusual activity.

Some days later, James R. Quirk, editor of *Photoplay*, confided to close friends the astonishing news that because of Ullman's fears that through some act of vandalism the body be desecrated, it was decided to remove Valentino's body and substitute for it a male store dummy, topped by a hastily molded wax head of Valentino. It was, considering the pressures of time, a reasonably good likeness. Another precaution was effected by attaching the coffin to the catafalque against the wall of the office so that it could not be overturned. Should people comment on the abnormally smooth and glossy features of the figure in the coffin, it would no doubt be attributed to either the severity of Valentino's final illness or the arsenical poisoning the *Daily News* had hinted at in its provocative headline: RUDY POISONED?

The story below the headline had confidentially told its readers that "there flew along Broadway yesterday sinister reports that Rudolph Valentino . . . came to his death by arsenic poisoning." The rumors hinted at both jealousy and revenge as the supposed motive, and Ferdinand Pecora, the assistant district attorney, said that if such reports "came to him officially, he would begin an investigation to sift their verity." Indeed, the Associated Press thought the rumors sufficiently important to quote Pecora in full: "If any responsible party brings up any proof tending to show the commission of any crime the matter will receive the official attention of this office regardless of what it may involve. We are not going off on any rumor or idle gossip that goes around the town. If we did we would have no time for the legitimate affairs of this office."

Such rumors that Valentino had met with foul play were to persist for many years. It was widely believed, moreover, that certain physicians and certain officials of United Artists, if they so desired, could have named the person or persons responsible.

Campbell and Klemfuss, having catnapped on sofas, were

awakened to learn that Dr. Sterling C. Wyman, of Flower Hospital, had arrived to supervise the emergency clinic which hospital authorities had decided to continue at Campbell's. After Dr. Wyman was admitted and made welcome, he told Mr. Campbell that when other doctors and nurses arrived for duty, they would be favorably impressed to find a medical man already there. A careful examination of the room used the day before was made by Dr. Wyman, who suggested that facilities closer to Mr. Campbell's office would be more appropriate. His suggestion was accepted and Campbell employees assisted him in the arrangement and placement of required furniture.

By eight in the morning people began to arrive in number but sufficient police were on hand to maintain order. Mrs. Jean Commo, 150 East Third Street, who identified herself as a native of Castellaneta, brought a bronze cross that she wished to lay on the coffin. Floral wreaths of impressive size were received from Lois Wilson, Mildred and Harold Lloyd, Nellie and Mae Savage, Marilyn Miller, Constance Talmadge and other luminaries. June Mathis sent a wreath of roses, and a larger wreath of roses bore the card of Irving Berlin and his wife, the former Ellen Mackay. Dahlias and roses were the tribute of Samuel Goldwyn; Mr. and Mrs. Schenck identified their blanket of yellow roses and orchids as the gift of "Norma and Joe." Charlie Chaplin sent a wreath of orchids with a card: "To Rudy, whom I loved as an artist and a friend." The floral pieces were banked around the bier to cast their shadows on the coffin, but Premier Mussolini's wreath was accorded the place of honor.

Knowledgeable reporters of the café and theatrical scene were unable to identify one woman with a spray of gladioli who was readily admitted, so they interviewed her after she left. Isabel Clough, it developed, was just a plain person who had observed that people with floral tributes were admitted immediately to Campbell's, and bought herself some posies at a nearby shop. "I figured this would be a good way to get in," she told the press. "I have always admired Valentino, and I thought I might buy him some flowers so that I could get in to see the body right away."

By nine that morning, although it was raining heavily, the police estimated there were nearly ten thousand people waiting, and the lines grew. When the doors of the Funeral Church were closed late that night, it was estimated that ninety thousand people had passed in line. Although police duty during wet weather is never enjoyed by a policeman, in this case the only regret was that it had not rained harder, for all police officials agreed that good weather might have doubled the number.

Police officers were pleased to note that the disorderly excitement of the previous day did not prevail; the crowds moved swiftly along the carpeted areas of the parlors and obeyed the admonitions that forbade them to pause anywhere, except for a moment at the coffin. It was quite dull until in the early afternoon a volunteer organist, who introduced himself to Mr. Klemfuss as H. E. Hall, seated himself at a recently installed pipe organ and played appropriate melodies of *triste*, unrequited love, mourning and eternity. Many women were moved to tears; others had to be admonished not to applaud the impromptu concert. Most believed the organist was yet another evidence of Mr. Campbell's generosity, and vowed to recommend his establishment to their friends and families.

But real excitement was generated in and out of the Funeral Church when Mr. Campbell announced that he had received a telephone call from Jean Acker, Valentino's first wife, asking to view the body of her former husband in private. Immediate plans were made to halt the lines when she arrived. Shortly after two in the afternoon, Jean Acker, her mother, Mrs. Margaret Acker, and a cousin were guided through the crowd after they had posed for photographs. The doors of the Funeral Church were closed and all other visitors were hurried past the coffin.

Reporters heard, and later reported, that Miss Acker was ill with sorrow. In a brown raincoat, blue suit, brown shoes and stockings, and a small brown hat, she approached the bier, gazed intently at the body and burst into a dollop of tears. Her mother and cousin then helped her to an upper-story room, where she was able to compose herself before meeting the press.

"I was in the room next to him when he died," she said. "I had just been reconciled to Mr. Valentino. We had always retained our love for each other. At least I have, and friends have told me he had also. My affection for him has always been of a motherly or sisterly nature. Three weeks ago he gave me a beautiful picture. This will help me to keep my memory always fresh."

She sobbed again, but composed herself enough to reply to a reporter's inquiry asking whether Valentino and she had intended to remarry.

"I cannot say whether we would have married again," she said. "I didn't think it would end this way."

She discussed the problems of burial and told reporters she would attend Monday's services but had no opinion as to where Valentino should be interred. "I think Rudolph would prefer to lie near his father and mother, but he was so young he never thought of death."

Overcome again by grief, Miss Acker rested on a couch as her mother told reporters that Jean contemplated a return to the stage.

Although the departure of Miss Acker and family made possible the resumption of public homage, George Ullman expressed increasing dissatisfaction over the attitude of the crowd. He made allowances for gaiety on the long lines, where police were better prepared to cope with people in a happy mood, but within the solemn interior they showed little reverence. Acting as if they were contestants in a beauty parade, most of the women primped themselves before they entered Mr. Campbell's office, where they joked aloud, laughed irreverently and chatted quite amiably about trivia. The bolder of the men and boys attempted to pick off a leaf or pluck a flower to present to some girl in the line. If successful, the gift was accepted with a shrill squeal of delight.

Requests for solemnity were greeted by giggling and snickers. Impudent girls approached the organist and ordered him to pep up the music. Several Shebas actually requested that he play "The Sheik of Araby." Time and again Ullman told Campbell and Klemfuss that more good would be done Valentino's image if men were stationed at the front doors of the parlor to instruct people in the traditional solemnities of mourning deportment. Ullman's advice was ignored.

The most newsworthy crisis of the day was the arrival of an angry delegation from the Anti-Fascist Alliance of North America, led by Pietro Allegra, its secretary, who protested the presence of the Fascisti and demanded the immediate removal of the wreath and offensive honor guard. It required a detail of ten policemen under a sergeant to forestall violence between the rival groups. The room was cleared, but not before the Anti-Fascist leader loudly read several Associated Press dispatches from Rome.

They stated: (1) official representatives of the Italian Government knew nothing about any American Fascist honor guard; (2) the American organization was *not* acting on instructions from the Italian dictator, who (3) had not ordered a wreath placed on Valentino's casket. However, as a diplomatic hedge, the government spokesmen in Rome explained "that Fascist organizations abroad have broad powers to act in such matters without need of authorization from Rome."

Campbell officials read the newspaper dispatches carefully, noting that "officials were unwilling to discuss what honors would be shown the dead actor until it is learned definitely whether the body will be brought to Italy for burial," and concluded that at best, if Valentino was buried in Italy, the rites would receive only semiofficial recognition. This was not good enough for Campbell or United Artists, who were resolutely determined that the funeral be accorded only the highest honors and recognition.

Already disappointed over the Italian Government's denial of the American Fascisti, Campbell was about to make some statement to strengthen the claims of the native Black Shirts when he was beckoned aside by publicity man Harry Klemfuss. In a hot whisper Klemfuss informed him that although the American Fascists were authentic, the wreath had come from Campbell's own flower shop, and Klemfuss himself had hired the local Fascists and coached them in the military formalities to be observed as they stood guard at Valentino's bier.

Mr. Campbell was only momentarily disappointed. Poise regained, hands clasped under the tails of his claw-hammer coat, he judged the honor guard quite effective. Furthermore, the Italian Government had not completely disavowed the wreath; who knew, might not the Italian Government, if it liked the publicity, come around to sponsoring the honor guard?

In English and Italian Mr. Allegra and his committee spurned a generous invitation to partake of good liquid cheer; instead, they continued to protest to everyone the presence of the Black Shirts. With weary patience a police lieutenant suggested that it would be best for Mr. Allegra and his followers to leave quietly before they were kicked off the block.

Later, from his headquarters, Allegra fired off a telegram of protest to George Ullman. In due time Ullman received the wire and told reporters he intended to ignore the Alliance's demands.

"I'll pay no attention to that," George Ullman said. "Here's the way it was: I considered the offer of the Fascisti to guard the bier as a gesture from Mussolini himself. It was almost official recognition from the Italian Government. The Anti-Fascisti, if they exist at all, do so only in America. There are not any of them in Italy. I'm not going to pay any attention to what an

American organization does. As far as Rudy being treated out-rageously in Italy is concerned, that is not true. Why, he and General Nobile, the North Pole flier, were as thick as could be, and Nobile is a sort of right-hand man to Mussolini. There were some demonstrations against Rudy's films in Italy but they were all by a bunch of hoodlums."

That Rudy had been sympathetic to Fascism and its leaders was corroborated by Anthony M. Ruffo, Jr., Acting Mayor of Los Angeles, who told a *Herald Tribune* reporter that "Valentino was a Fascist and had told him Mussolini 'had done wonders for Italy.' " Mr. Ruffo, who issued his statement in Atlantic City, said he had seen the actor shortly before his death.

If the Anti-Fascists were outraged by the honor guard of Black Shirts, Dr. Sterling C. Wyman was not. Indeed, he had thought the uniformed men added solemnity and an elevated style to the proceedings. Dr. Wyman was so enthusiastic about such military honors that he left the infirmary for Broadway, where he searched the lines until he found two charming young ladies, who assured him that they were movie actresses. Dr. Wyman introduced himself as the physician in charge of the Valentino infirmary; the young ladies identified themselves as Carmen Lopez and Anita Hoffman of 241 West Forty-second Street. Both had not dared to hope for more than "a peek at Rudy's body," but Dr. Wyman rushed them straight to the bier and installed them as girl members of the guard of honor. They stood guard for two hours, envied by everyone.

Misses Lopez and Hoffman were such attractive adjuncts to the honor guard that in the opinion of expert critics of the Broadway musical comedy, the tableau was worthy of Ziegfeld. To compensate the girls for their time, Dr. Wyman promised to introduce them to Pola Negri and to speak about them with important motion picture actors and executives *after* the funeral services. Dr. Wyman also invited the girls to join him for a late supper after he closed the clinic. The girls were just thrilled.

Harry Klemfuss and Frank Campbell were so impressed with
Dr. Wyman's intuitive understanding of showmanship that they
urged him to represent Campbell's as official physician throughout the transfiguration. Aware that he was being called upon to
render unto Caesar, Dr. Wyman agreed to put aside his busy
practice and serve.

From late afternoon far into the night, lines of people were
processed through the parlors. However, when George Ullman
had to fight his way through an unruly mob at the corner of
Sixty-seventh Street, he decided that the continued presence of
such churls in the area of Campbell's could only turn good
publicity into bad. In addition, the festive air was making a
mockery of mourning. Without consulting executives of United
Artists or the Funeral Church, he decided to inform the reporters
that this was the last day the public would be welcome at the
bier.

His decision was reinforced by the return of Mr. Allegra with
Luigi Quintillano, editor of *Nuovo Mondo*, an Anti-Fascist publication. Both announced bluntly that the continued presence
of the Black Shirts had aroused the strong resentment of every
Anti-Fascist in the United States. Again they insisted that the
guard be removed and warned of trouble if their ultimatum was
ignored. They were escorted from the premises by police officers.
Although they had lost two skirmishes, the battle was still to be
fought. Allegra and Quintillano vowed to return in greater
strength, and George Ullman realized the time had come for an
announcement to the press.

"This has gone far enough," Ullman told reporters, then explained that even loyal employees of the Funeral Church had
told him the solemn occasion had turned into a farce. "From
midnight on, Valentino's body will be viewed only by friends and
associates under my personal supervision. The lack of reverence
shown by the crowd, the disorder and rioting since the body was
first shown, have forced me to this decision."

He also announced that contrary to Mr. Campbell's plans for "a grand procession down Broadway, 800 autos, autos laden with floral pieces, motorcycle policemen riding ahead and about the hearse, airplanes strewing flowers along the line of march," Monday's funeral procession to St. Malachy's would consist of only the hearse and one or two limousines for the closest of friends and business associates. There would be no procession, parade or other exciting hippodramatics.

The police officials and men in charge of the private detectives were alerted, and every effort was made to speed more people through the chapel. The two-second pauses at the bier were cut in half and an increasing number of people complained that they had been given the bum's rush. Among the late-night visitors were Mr. and Mrs. James J. Corbett. The former heavyweight champion and his wife were permitted to enter immediately when they showed their cards to police officers. They stayed only long enough to glance at the body and to shake hands with Mr. Campbell.

Evening newspaper headlines informed the crowds that Douglas Fairbanks and Mary Pickford had returned that day from Europe on the *Majestic;* both said they were deeply shocked at the radiogram from Joseph Schenck which had informed them of Valentino's death. But to the disappointment of the crowd, which had seen few celebrities that day, Mary Pickford decided not to come to the Funeral Church. Douglas Fairbanks also said that he preferred "to remember Valentino as he last saw him, alive." Both, however, agreed to attend the funeral.

The absence of important celebrities compelled the press to root out smaller lions, and Mrs. Richard Reese Whittemore of Baltimore, widow of the recently executed notorious bandit and murderer dubbed the "Candy Kid" by the tabloids, was recognized in the line at about nine that evening. Margaret "Tiger Lil" Whittemore was still in mourning. In her widow's weeds, so correct for this occasion, she told the reporters that she had met Valentino when he had come to Baltimore to judge a beauty contest in which she had appeared. Now she had come to New York City to pay her respects.

Another notable was Miss Nellie Savage, who told the press she had appeared with Valentino in *A Sainted Devil* and *Monsieur Beaucaire*. Miss Savage was accompanied by her sister Mae, and they were pleased that their floral offerings had been placed quite close to the bier.

The lines now moved more rapidly than the seconds of the clock, until at eleven-thirty the word was quietly passed to all the men guarding the parlors or controlling the crowds that in ten minutes the line of mourners would be cut off at Broadway and Sixty-eighth Street. Between seventy-five thousand and ninety thousand people had already viewed Valentino's body, but there were still more than five thousand pilgrims awaiting their turn. The police moved rapidly to weed out the thin line from Sixty-eighth Street to the front doors of Campbell's so that no more than two hundred people would be admitted before midnight. As hundreds of mourners realized that they had waited for hours and were not to be rewarded by a peek at the Sheik, their voices rose in a roaring chorus of imprecations. Shrieking defiance, they pressed in against the police, who stood with arms locked and clubs at the horizontal to ward off the first shock of contact. As the mob struggled to break through the police line, a troop of mounted policemen rode out of the side streets to take the crowd from the flanks and rear.

Men, women and children scattered, for they were neither prepared nor organized to resist such cavalry maneuvers. Thrown into panic, the crowd broke and raced across Broadway until they reached Lincoln Square, near Campbell's, where the lights had been shut off. There they were repulsed by another double line of police officers, who engaged them as the mounted officers rode in to scatter the disorganized forces.

Disorder sapped the strength of the mob and, screaming their disappointment and vowing they would return in the morning to kill the dirty cossacks, the last of them fled. Suddenly the normal street sounds of midnight prevailed along Broadway, punctuated by the groans and tears of frustrated men and women. The disappearance of the crowd revealed that at least three hundred foot patrolmen had been in the vicinity of Broadway and Sixty-seventh Street.

A special detail of twenty detectives escorted the Fascisti and their memorial wreath to Fascist headquarters at 145 West Forty-fifth Street, where several detectives stayed the night to protect them. And at midnight, George Ullman ordered the coffin sealed. He then gave orders to everyone that the coffin was to remain closed until the funeral, when it would be opened only if Alberto Guglielmi wished to glance upon his departed brother.

ACT ONE: SCENE FOUR

On Thursday morning, August 26, most metropolitan newspapers carried an advertisement from Campbell's Funeral Church:

> We wish to announce that normal decorum and dignity now prevail at the Frank E. Campbell Funeral Church.

> *Death is the port where all may refuge find,*
> *The end of labor, entry into rest;*
> *Death hath the bounds of misery confined,*
> *Whose sanctuary shrouds affliction best.*
> EARL OF STERLING

That same morning, readers of the New York *World* complained in their letters to the editor of the shame that had struck their city, the ignorance that lamented the demise of an actor as it continued to dismiss as inconsequential the passing of Charles

41

William Eliot, president emeritus of Harvard University. Dr. Eliot had been granted scant attention by the tabloids and minimum lineage by the Hearst papers outside Boston. As Heywood Broun of the *World* wrote in his column: "Dr. Eliot is likely to be remembered among the great men of his day, while the fame of Valentino was a passing thing."

The New York *Herald Tribune* also commented editorially on the riots, the vulgarities and carnival excesses of the past Monday, Tuesday and Wednesday, when "normal decorum and dignity" had not been in evidence at the Funeral Church. Titled "A Force To Be Reckoned With" the editorial concluded that "the film . . . a 'low-brow' form of amusement . . . never will have such tremendous power to awaken thought as it has to arouse emotion."

So uncompromising an indictment of bathos did not find favor with the Hollywood bashaws, whose belligerent and bellicose reactions to constructive censure had already become historic and traditional. Was it Hollywood's fault that the American public preferred Rudolph Valentino to Charles William Eliot? This was a free country where men and women had a freedom of choice. And—the cinema tastemakers and their press panderers pleaded—how could anyone criticize adversely an industry which from its inception had contributed so much to the national ignorance? The movie magazines, Hollywood's trade press and its scribblers were actually unconcerned that most literate people and literate journals considered the industry and its product to be substantial evidences of intellectual strabismus, that such critics thought of Hollywood as an aesthetic joke, where emotional rubble was used to produce tasteless junk. Such highbrow evaluations did not embarrass or discomfit the movie studios or their moguls; they were quite aware that most people in the United States were semiliterate and suspicious of, even hostile to, intelligence. A lofty silence was the best rebuttal to the literate word; full steam ahead with the funeral, which already had received more publicity among the people who counted than could be bought with a million dollars.

Finally, the carping editorial could be dismissed with a tolerant snap of the fingers when it was weighed against the really good news just received at Campbell's: fears that Valentino might be denied a religious funeral had proved groundless. Catholic authorities had decided that Valentino was entitled to a requiem mass and burial by the Church. True, he had been married and divorced twice, but these occasions had been contracted and dissolved by civil courts; therefore, in the eyes of the Church, which did not recognize the validity of such contracts, Valentino had been neither married nor divorced. Furthermore, canon law stated that if a Catholic confessed sorrow, begged forgiveness for his transgressions and swore to abjure sin, he could receive the Church's pardon. Valentino had seen a priest and made a confession before he died. He had received the last sacraments. He was entitled to a Catholic funeral.

St. Malachy's had acknowledged some protests and there was talk that an official Catholic publication in Brooklyn intended to align itself with the editorial position of *L'Osservatore Romano* and strongly condemn Valentino as an outstanding example of prideful worldliness cut down in his prime. But St. Malachy's approved the use of its facilities.

Valentino's sealed coffin had now been returned to the Gold Room, where it was to remain closed until the arrival of Alberto. Reporters were ushered into Frank Campbell's office where George Ullman, in a measured voice, gave them the news of the day.

To the best of his knowledge, Ullman emphasized, Valentino had never known the Peggy Scott who had committed suicide in London. No matter what Miss Scott had written, or her friends said, Valentino had never been acquainted with or in correspondence with Miss Scott. Autographed photos of the star, of course, had not been difficult to obtain.

Honorary pallbearers were to be Joseph M. Schenck, Adolph Zukor, Marcus Loew, Hiram Abrams, Will H. Hays, Nicholas Schenck, James R. Quirk, Michael Romano, Frank Mennillo, Douglas Fairbanks, Sidney Kent, Richard Rowland, Rex Ingram and Mal St. Clair. An invitation to serve as honorary pallbearer had also been extended to the Italian Ambassador in Washington. A reply had not been received.

The *Homeric,* sailing from Cherbourg, was not due to dock in New York until Tuesday or Wednesday, so Ullman had requested permission from New York City's Commissioner of Health, Dr. Louis I. Harris, for an extension that would permit Alberto Guglielmi to attend his brother's funeral. Commissioner Harris had issued a permit "extending for forty-eight hours the time that Valentino's body may remain unburied after the church services on Monday."

Interrupted by several reporters, who told Ullman that it was not yet eight and already more than five hundred people were in the line outside the Funeral Church and what did he intend to do about them, Ullman repeated his resolve to keep the morbidly curious on the street. Even sincere admirers, unless they were known to him, would be refused admittance.

"I know it would have been Rudy's wish that the public—his public—be allowed to see him in death," Ullman explained. "But I had no idea that the public would act as it did. When I came to the Funeral Church yesterday, it struck me that people were acting disgracefully. They showed the most gross irreverences. Women and girls laughed. And some men, you would have thought, were going to a picnic or three-ring circus. I am sorry they were allowed to see him at all. It was a shock to me. Out of respect to my dear friend, whom I loved, I could do nothing but stop it. For this reason no others will be permitted to enter the Funeral Church."

Ullman regretted that some true friends of Valentino had hesitated to visit Campbell's because of the unruly mobs and their outrageous demonstrations. These sincere mourners had been content to send flowers and to present themselves at the church services. Other friends would not attend the services because they preferred to remember Rudy as he was in life, a robust, joyous boy.

A telegram and two cablegrams were delivered to Ullman and he shared them with the reporters. The telegram was from Pola Negri and had been sent from Hutchinson, Kansas: "THE BEST THAT I CAN DO IS TO PLEAD WITH THEM, BUT I HOPE I CAN MAKE MR. ULLMAN AND ALBERTO, RUDOLPH'S BROTHER, REALIZE THAT HIS FRIENDS IN HOLLYWOOD HAVE THE FIRST RIGHT TO ASK RUDOLPH'S BURIAL THERE, WHERE HE BECAME FAMOUS AS AN ARTIST. I WILL NOT ASK IT, HOWEVER, FOR MYSELF."

Another paragraph begged Mr. Ullman to meet her at the Hotel Ambassador when she arrived in New York City, and to keep the press away because of her grief.

Ullman was informed by the reporters that Pola had collapsed in her stateroom when she had been shown a newspaper with a "picture showing the dead actor's body reposing on the bier." He made no comment.

The first cablegram, from Alberto aboard the *Homeric*, revealed that Maria had wired Alberto her approval for burial in Hollywood—unless Rudolph had willed otherwise. She had found the suggestion of William Randolph Hearst to bury their brother in the film capital honorable and worthy; her approval was now a matter of record. Ullman believed that Alberto, who had spent seven months with his brother in Hollywood, would also approve the film capital as the most appropriate site for a Valentino memorial, now in the initial stages of planning.

Alberto's cablegram pleased Ullman more than the one from Valentino's second wife, Natacha Rambova. She ordered a floral tribute in her name to be placed on the casket, and added, "It is my wish that he be placed in the Hudnut family vault," located in Woodlawn Cemetery, the Bronx. This impertinence was overshadowed by Natacha's concluding bombshell—she wished the body of her former husband to be cremated.

Ullman was shocked. "I'm quite sure it will not be done," he said emphatically. "Between the funeral services Monday morning and the arrival of Mr. Valentino's brother Wednesday, the body will rest at the Campbell Funeral Church or in a receiving vault. I think it should be buried in Hollywood, the only appropriate resting place for the body of Valentino."

Coincident with the services, Joseph Schenck announced that the Motion Picture Producers Association had ordered all work to be halted at every studio and picture location in California at 10:00 A.M. Monday morning for "two minutes of silent tribute to Rudolph Valentino." The MPPA was happy to announce that this was the first time in the industry's history that so great and singular a tribute had been planned for a former member. In addition to this silent tribute, an earlier memorial service would be conducted at the Hollywood Breakfast Club, where one of Valentino's horses, with inverted boots in the stirrups, would be led by Norman Kerry, Emmett Flynn and George Fitzmaurice to a vacant seat at an open-air horseshoe table where a floral horseshoe had been placed to honor Valentino's memory. Before a photograph of the actor draped in mourning, a prayer would be offered, then a soloist would sing "Adieu." The Orpheus Four would finally render "Lead, Kindly Light" and "Nearer, My God, to Thee," after which a bugler would blow "Taps" for the departed horseman.

Pressed by reporters for details of the Valentino memorial, Ullman asked James Quirk to explain this project to the press. Quirk told the reporters of two movements to build memorials, one in Hollywood and the other in Chicago. The drive for the Hollywood memorial had been launched in New York, Quirk explained, by a committee of three who had elected him treasurer and chairman; Joseph Schenck and George Ullman were the other members. "A permanent memorial to Rudolph Valentino is

the purpose of the Rudolph Valentino Memorial Committee. . . .
The form of the memorial will depend entirely upon the amount
of subscriptions received. It was decided that no subscription
for more than one dollar would be accepted, as it is the purpose
of this committee that this memorial should be one expressing the
love and sentiment of many people rather than one expressing
the love and affection of the few. Any subscription from five
cents to a dollar will be gratefully accepted. It is the idea of
the committee that whenever this memorial is decided upon
it should be located in Hollywood where the late star lived and
made his successful pictures, believing that Hollywood is the
mecca toward which all lovers of pictures turn their eyes." The
committee could be expanded, Mr. Quirk added, and would
soon be organized in corporate form. Meanwhile, donations
should be sent to the Rudolph Valentino Memorial Committee
in care of James R. Quirk, 221 East Fifty-seventh Street.

In Chicago, five of Valentino's personal friends, among them
a judge and an assistant state's attorney, Michael A. Romano,
were reported to have filed articles of incorporation to build
another memorial in a city park. Mr. Romano had arrived in
New York on Wednesday. At Campbell's he had "bent and
kissed the glass on Rudy's face, and fell on his knees and
prayed. . . . Hundreds of people kissed that glass yesterday.
It had to be wiped off constantly," Ullman stated.

It was also reported that the village of Castellaneta had relented and intended also to erect a memorial.

To conclude the press conference, a spokesman for Mr.
Schenck announced: "The death of Rudolph Valentino has had
no apparent effect on the shares of the United Artist Theatres
Circulating Company stock, which handles moving pictures for
independent producers and the Valentino pictures. The stock,
which is an exceptionally slow mover in the market, sold on
the New York Curb yesterday at $100 per share, which was
unchanged from the last sale."

The reporters dispersed to file these intelligences and Ullman continued to resist the opening of Campbell's doors. Officers of the Funeral Church were disappointed, but police officials, who feared a revival of the mob spirit, were delighted. If further viewing of the body had been permitted, the dry, clement weather might have brought as many as a quarter of a million people into the area of Lincoln Square.

Outside the Funeral Church the police officers announced to the assembled mourners Ullman's decision to bar the public. The business manager was booed and vilified by the crowd, but praised by the officers as they worked with vigor to disperse the thousand or so mourners who had formed lines. By nine in the morning at least a hundred policemen lined the east sidewalk before the Funeral Church.

Pedestrians were ordered to keep walking and were even refused permission to pause to peer into the windows. Persistent idlers, who had begun to saunter up and down the block, were warned to leave Broadway or face arrest. Men and women who insisted they were friends or business associates of Valentino's were escorted to the front doors and permitted to enter only after they were duly recognized and approved by Ullman.

On previous days flowers had opened the doors of the Funeral Church; now such ploys failed. When young girls and women approached, hoping to part the doors by the pleasant scent of their store-bought or home-grown bouquets, the offerings were accepted by the attendants who refused to admit the donors. Several bouquets were reclaimed, but this was rare. Some fans, more determined than others, gained entry when they attached themselves to a group that had been approved by Ullman. A few women tried the fainting routine and were permitted to lie unattended for several minutes; then they were revived by the prod of a nightstick.

Still, men, women and girls continued to linger in the area, but because they contented themselves with occasionally walking up and down the block, the police treated them with tolerance. Floral tributes arrived in yet greater numbers, the cluster of a hundred and fifty American Beauty roses from Gloria Swanson particularly exciting admiration. But this tribute was soon overshadowed by the delivery of a nine-foot standing wreath of larkspur, asters and roses from United Artists, which was so bulky that volunteers helped to carry it into the parlor and managed to sneak a quick glimpse of the closed casket before they were ushered out. This ruse, too, worked only once. The largest individual floral tribute was an urn of gladioli ten feet high. It was sent by an unknown, A. E. Kundred of Goshen, Indiana, and the urn was so large it could not be taken through the double doors of the Gold Room.

Then, to the consternation of the police and the delight of reporters and photographers, who had already begun to complain about the day's dullness, a squad of Black Shirts appeared to resume their vigil. This brought shouts and imprecations from several open windows in a nearby building, and a group of Anti-Fascists boiled out into Broadway and also demanded admission. Patrolmen kept both apart while they denounced each other volubly, making the insulting sign of horns to identify the opposition as cuckolds. Police officials demanded that both groups be ousted and told not to return. George Ullman agreed and, assisted by a police lieutenant, he conciliated both factions by swearing that neither would be permitted to take any part in the funeral ceremonies. The Anti-Fascists complained that they at least should receive equal time as a guard unit, even if it were for only ten minutes. But this demand was rejected.

After the rival groups left, Ullman told the reporters he had "permitted the Fascisti to stand guard only because I thought Rudy would have liked it. He was always afraid Mussolini did not approve of him, and this seemed like proof that there was no basis for that fear." Lest this would seem to make Valentino a lesser hero, Ullman quickly qualified his statement by adding,

"Rudolph had a superstitious fear of the Fascisti, but he wanted to be friends with them. I did not ask them to place a guard about the casket, but I did ask them to leave."

The rest of the day was relatively quiet. The only newsworthy event was the arrival at Campbell's in the evening of twenty-eight emigrants from Castellaneta, who carried a wreath of oak leaves, palms, valley lilies and orchids. As a group they entered the Gold Room and remained there for about twenty minutes, during which they recited prayers. Several of the women affected hysteria and one lady fainted. She was revived by Dr. Wyman.

Also that evening Joseph Schenck announced that an insurance check for $200,000 had been received from the Missouri State Life Insurance Company, and checks for $125,000 were being forwarded by the Canada Life Insurance Company and the Northwestern National Life Insurance Company. Frank Campbell was naturally disappointed; Joseph Schenck had told him that at most United Artists would collect $200,000, and $450,000 had already been received. Although he believed more firmly than ever that Valentino had been insured for a million dollars, Campbell merely sighed philosophically. He had agreed to bury the actor without fee and he would keep his word.

Louella Parsons devoted most of her column for Sunday, August 29, to a nose-out-of-joint discussion of: "WILL FANS BE TRUE TO VALENTINO[?]." Of *The Son of the Sheik* Miss Parsons observed:

> There is still a matter of some 6,000 contracts in this country and nearly that many abroad to be considered . . . to recall *Son of the Sheik* from the screens of the world would not only be an enormous loss to United Artists . . . but certainly not what Rudy would have wished himself. While it is the height of bad taste to capitalize on death and to bring back old films, there is no reason to expect United Artists to withdraw *Son of the Sheik*, which has not yet been released throughout the country. Even with Rudy's enormous popularity and the unanimous delight of the movie patrons wherever the *Son of the*

Sheik was shown, I doubt very much if it will be a profitable venture. That morbid curiosity and interest that is so much a part of human nature has not in the past extended to the player who had [*sic*] passed on.

The chagrin and gloom engendered by Louella Parsons—who had stabbed some of her best friends in the pocketbook—were relieved by the news that at the twenty-second annual convention of The Grand Lodge of the State of New York of the Order of the Sons of Italy in America, held at the Hotel Biltmore, the delegates had stood and remained silent for three minutes to honor the memory of Valentino.

Despite this signal honor, it was increasingly evident, by the volume of letters of protest to the editors of responsible newspapers, that there was a smug, superior, pharisaical class of men and women who refused to identify themselves with the hippodrome that had been playing for almost a week in the vicinity of Campbell's Funeral Church. Its origins, roots and WASPish mythology did not seem to require participation in the god-making process which the foreign bourgeoisie and lower classes found necessary to assure themselves of their very own sympathetic pantheon. To the ordinary man and woman in the street, Hollywood's temples and stars were the new faith. Nevertheless, there seemed to be a minority of conservative Americans who were still content to be served by their old-time religion.

On Saturday evening, the floral tribute of yellow roses and orchids sent by Norma Talmadge and Joseph Schenck was removed from the casket and replaced by a pall of roses sent by the grieving movie queen Pola Negri. This composition of four thousand blood-red roses, which Pola offered as a proof of love, cost two thousand dollars. The size, however, was more impressive than the cost; the carpet of blooms was eleven feet long and six feet wide, and through its middle "*Pola*," in Spencerian script, was worked out in white buds.

A Los Angeles *Times* correspondent waxed elegiac as he described Pola's arrival in Chicago where, "in the loneliness of her private car she mourned today over the fragments of her starred dream—a film career crowned with a picture of herself and Valentino starring together, then a happy marriage, love, and children."

At Chicago there had been a three-hour layover before Pola's Pullman car was attached to the Twentieth Century Limited. During that time her drawing room was besieged by reporters, who, insensitive to grief, shouted their questions through the outside window or the door.

For religious reasons, had Rudy felt that his marriage to Jean Acker, his first wife, was binding in a spiritual way?

"No, no, no. It is not so," Pola replied. "Everybody on the Coast knows it is not so."

Would she take his body to Hollywood?

"I will try. I will do my best."

Was it true that Valentino and she had planned to make a picture?

"We were to have made a picture together," she replied, "which was to have been the final one of my career. Then we were to have settled down."

By now Pola had become so distraught that her publicity man, S. H. Neal, begged reporters to leave his client alone. Did they want her to become so ill she would have to abandon her journey to New York and miss the funeral?

Thomas Meighan, also a passenger on the train, assured reporters that Pola was weakened and hysterical. "I asked her to rest with Mrs. Meighan and myself at our place at Great Neck, Long Island," he said. "She promised she would unless she returns West with his body."

George Ullman, his wife and entourage were at Grand Central Station at ten-thirty Sunday morning to meet Pola. Again, as throughout the difficult days of the past week, Ullman was sur-

rounded by photographers, reporters and the morbidly curious.
"I hope there will be no crowds, no demonstration at the
station," he said. "Pola wired me and asked that I arrange for
her to escape interviewers. I'm sure her grief is too profound for
her to speak of this boy's death. He was to have met her here."

Miss Negri had by now realized that her floral offering was
rather large and conspicuous. Therefore, she had wired that it
be destroyed and replaced by a smaller, more modest creation
costing five hundred dollars. Clad in deep mourning, she was
greeted at the steps of her car by Mr. and Mrs. Ullman. Black
enhanced her exotic beauty, her pale countenance, green eyes
and red lips. Sheltered by the Ullmans and Dr. Sterling C. Wyman, the actress was assisted to the upper level of the station,
where the eyes of the curious stared as news cameras flashed.
Indignant at this attention, Pola began to weep hysterically.

Many descriptions have been written of her arrival in New
York, but none equals the reportage of Micheline Keating for
the *Daily Mirror* of August 30. It carried the arresting headline:

POLA   FAINTS,
           FAINTS,   FAINTS

Miss Keating's remarkable account of Pola's progress is worthy
of extended citation:

> Yesterday brought Pola Negri to New York to attend the
> funeral today of her great lover, Rudolph Valentino.
>   Pola is heralded as the screen's greatest emotional actress.
> Anyone who saw her yesterday won't doubt it. Our regret is
> that the kliegs and cameras were missing. No acting Pola will
> do upon the screen will compete with the performance she
> gave before the mob of morbid curiosity seekers who haunted
> the portals of the Grand Central.
>   As the Twentieth Century drew into the station Pola, dressed
> in her specially designed mourning costume (costing $3,000
> according to her press agent), emerged from her dressing

room. Pola, the actress. Pola, the emotional, Pola the Slav. Pola was everything she has been reputed, and a little bit more, for some reason best known to herself.

A weeping Pola, resting upon the arms of her maid and Mrs. George Ullman, stepped through the train gateway to her waiting audience bunched in excited, neurotic groups under the star-domed station.

Pola saw the people.

Pola hesitated.

Pola screamed. Pola fainted. She did it well. Why shouldn't she—this great emotional star?

Water.

Pola revived.

Pola screamed.

Why not? There was that mob of the morbid hanging upon every gesture.

Still screaming, Pola was guided to a waiting car. The car carried her to the Ambassador. The same hotel where her reputed fiance spent the last of his carefree days.

Pola entered the lobby.

Pola fainted.

Pola fainted into the arms of her maid and Mrs. Ullman.

It is fortunate for the great star that her maid and Mrs. Ullman were there. The floors of the Ambassador, like all other floors, are hard when fallen upon. More water. Pola felt better. Pola was taken up to her suite on the third floor. Five floors below Rudy's.

The blinds were drawn. The great star demanded that. She desired darkness for her sorrow. Well, why not? Racked from her emotion, she fell limply into a chair. Well, why not? Who wouldn't be tired after half an hour of screaming?

Somebody said the press was waiting to see her. The Polish importation threw her hands imploringly forward. "The newspapers," she cried. "Why? Why won't they let me alone in my sorrow?" Well, why not?

Pola is left alone with her sorrow until 1 P.M. Then Pola emerges from her sorrow long enough to call a taxi to take her to the bier of Valentino. The taxi is cancelled. A few minutes later another is called. That also is cancelled.

Pola wants to go.
Pola doesn't want to go.
Pola is having hysterics.

Fortunately for everyone, Dr. Wyman, a modern Hippocrates, stepped forward to lead Pola to a sofa before he administered two aspirins. In quiet, measured tones he comforted Pola and explained that unless she contained her grief he would have to advise that she neither visit Campbell's nor attend the funeral. In the presence of sympathetic friends and the knowledgeable physician, Pola regained her composure.

While Ullman telephoned for a limousine to take them to the Funeral Church, Dr. Wyman told reporters that as long as Pola was in New York, she would be in his care. He would be at her side on Wednesday when the *Homeric* docked and she went aboard to meet Alberto Guglielmi. The good doctor continued to make himself useful: He answered telephone calls, shunted aside the cynical, bold and curious, and corroborated his confidential statement to the press that Ullman had told him "there was no foundation for the talk of an engagement between Rudy and Pola. Ullman, he said, remarked 'if there is any engagement then Rudy and I knew nothing about it.' " However, Dr. Wyman informed the reporters, it would be inadvisable at this time of agonizing stress to pursue this delicate personal matter with Miss Negri.

Pola was hurried through the crowded lobby of the Ambassador and there was an even larger crowd to welcome her at the Funeral Church. There were at least twenty policemen on hand to maintain order, but as soon as the limousine containing the Ullmans, Dr. Wyman and Pola drew up, the crowd broke through the thin police lines. They rapped on the limousine windows and shouted rudely that they believed or did not believe the stories of her love for and engagement to the departed

Valentino. Aided by several police officers, Frank Campbell made his way to the limousine and motioned the chauffeur to drive around the block to a private entrance where Miss Negri could be spirited into the Funeral Church.

With Mrs. Ullman at her side, Pola entered the Gold Room, stood quietly while the heavy lid of the silver-bronze casket was raised, and through the unbreakable glass looked down at the face of the real Sheik. For about five minutes she stood rigid as if in a catatonic seizure. Then she faltered, and had to be supported by Mr. Ullman and a funeral attendant until her composure was regained. She asked leave to pray and, kneeling before the bier, recited the Litany of the Dead, moaned wretchedly and collapsed on the carpet. It was a half hour before Pola could thank everyone for their kindnesses.

Recovered and seated on a small sofa in an antechamber, she glanced at the questions submitted in writing by the reporters who were waiting outside, and through George Ullman made the following reply:

> I am happy that everything has been made so lovely for Valentino in death. We were really engaged to be married but the fact that we both had careers to follow accounts for the delay in our wedding plans.
>
> My love for Valentino was the greatest love of my life. I shall never forget him. I loved him not as one artist might love another, but as a woman loves a man.
>
> I loved the irresistible appeal of his charm, the wonderful enthusiasm of his mind and soul. I didn't realize how ill he was or I would have been here before his death; he kept the seriousness of his illness from me.

The reporters demanded to know if Valentino had been aware that he was engaged to Pola, and one enterprising interrogator brought to Ullman's attention Dr. Wyman's statement that there had never been an engagement. Ullman refused to discuss the matter, chiding the man for being irrelevant and irreverent at a time of mourning and overwhelming grief. He would only say that five hundred tickets had been issued for the Valentino rites, and services at St. Malachy's would begin Monday morning at eleven o'clock. The number of mourners would be six: Miss Negri, Jean Acker, Norma Talmadge, Mrs. Nora Van Horn, half sister of Natacha Rambova, and Mr. and Mrs. Ullman.

ACT ONE: SCENE FIVE

There is a row of old-law, weathered-brick apartment houses across the street from St. Malachy's Church on West Forty-ninth Street between Broadway and Eighth Avenue, and on Monday morning, August 30, their entryways, stoops, windows, fire escapes and roofs were choked with spectators, many of whom had paid a fee for such vantage points. Although the funeral was scheduled for eleven o'clock, police had been on the block since eight that morning, closing the area to all vehicular and pedestrian traffic. The banning of vehicles had presented no problem; keeping pedestrians off the street was another matter. It seemed that everyone had come to shop in the little neighborhood stores adjacent to or across the street from St. Malachy's. But an order to close the shops took care of that. Although the crowds knew they would not be permitted to attend the services, their appearance in large numbers was balm to Frank Campbell, Harry

Klemfuss and especially United Artists, who were delighted with what the mortician had accomplished.

Despite Louella Parsons, who had based her Sunday column on precedents—the deaths of Wallace Reid, Barbara La Marr and Olive Thomas had compelled the shelving of their films—theaters in three key cities fortunate enough to have prints of *The Son of the Sheik* and *The Eagle* were reporting unprecedented business. In one theater alone receipts amounted to two hundred thousand dollars. Never before had Valentino's films grossed such sums. Everyone wanted to see the young Italian gallant as he cavorted, courted and kissed, and it was estimated that if the trend continued, the dead actor would net about twenty-five thousand dollars a day. Forty days of such grosses would bring into his estate a million dollars. In the past five years Valentino had earned about five million dollars but had spent every nickel of it. What he earned posthumously would, to the joy of his creditors, probably pay his debts.

By ten o'clock almost everyone with a card of admission to St. Malachy's had entered the church. The crowd had expressed its delight by cheering the arrival of Douglas Fairbanks, Gloria Swanson, her husband the Marquis, Madge Bellamy, George Jessel, Marilyn Miller, Bonnie Glass (one of Valentino's first dancing partners), Hope Hampton and Major Edward Bowes. Now the crowd was anticipating the arrival of Miss Negri. But she was still at Campbell's in the care of Mr. and Mrs. Ullman and Dr. Sterling C. Wyman, who were joined by Miss Acker, her mother and her cousin, Edith Acker. The crowd outside the Funeral Church now numbered more than three thousand.

At ten-forty-five the coffin, with its new coverlet of roses, was borne from Campbell's by professional pallbearers, flanked by the honorary pallbearers. In the first car behind the hearse were Pola Negri, Mr. and Mrs. Ullman and Dr. Wyman. The second sheltered Miss Acker and her party. The third bore Mary Pickford and Norma and Constance Talmadge.

The progress of this modest cortege was preceded by twelve motorcycle policemen, who managed to turn back the few sorties of those who broke through the police lines and attempted to touch or kiss the sides of the black hearse. Stoppages were few as the procession drove south on Broadway and Sixty-eighth to Forty-ninth Street, because more than two hundred and fifty policemen had been mobilized along the curbs to restrain the sightseers. Even so, the crowds had impeded the progress of the hearse and limousines; it did not arrive at St. Malachy's until about ten minutes past eleven. The Reverend Edward F. Leonard, in his black cope, stood at the door of his little church to await the body; at his side were the Reverend Joseph Congedo, a crucifer and acolytes. Within, the pews were filled with five hundred men and women, most of whom were known to readers of movie magazines.

The place of honor behind the coffin as it was carried into the church was occupied by Jean Acker, assisted by her mother. This seemed highly significant to the tabloid reporters, and the groundlings on the curb. The two ladies were followed by a heavily veiled Miss Negri, fortified in her despair by Mr. and Mrs. George Ullman and Dr. Wyman.

Dr. Sterling Wyman sat himself in a nearby pew. All the ladies in the funeral limousines wept as they entered the chapel; all were weeping when they departed. Just before the benediction, Dr. Wyman assisted Miss Acker when she was overcome by emotion and collapsed in a faint. During the services Miss Negri leaned forward with her head bowed and several times she swayed and faltered as if she were about to faint.

Texas Guinan and two of her entertainers sat in a rear pew and sobbed so loudly that they caused widespread mutterings of disapproval. One of the girls was identified as Ruby Keeler. More distressing was the expulsion of two tabloid photographers who had secreted themselves in the church the night before to take forbidden photographs. One was discovered in a confessional booth. The second, Izzy Kaplan, an employee of the *Mirror*, had shown greater ingenuity by hiding in the choir loft.

According to the account by Frank Mallen in his memoir of the *Graphic*, Izzy had been discovered because he could not resist lifting his voice with the sextet as he took photographs of the ceremonies. Mallen also related that the Marquis de la Falaise de Coudray, the husband of Gloria Swanson, had ousted Kaplan from the choir loft and dragged him down the staircase to the church door. There Kaplan was unceremoniously kicked down the stairs. In the fall from church to sidewalk, both his camera and the exposed plates were smashed.

Another interlude was provided by Nicola Abrazze, of Brooklyn, who identified himself as a barber and boyhood friend of Valentino's in Castellaneta. After the ceremonies, as the coffin was being borne up the aisle, Mr. Abrazze (who had sent *him* a card of admission to the church?) threw himself toward the casket in a frenzied demonstration of impetuous Latin emotionalism. "Good-bye, Rudolph! Good-bye, my friend," he wailed in tones that all but drowned out the church organ. "I will never see you again."

Abrazze was captured by the ushers, who attempted to assuage his grief with a strong stimulant, but Abrazze freed himself and during his brief liberty began to lament again. "He's gone. He's gone!" He was finally overcome and forcibly removed.

To avoid the risk of a demonstration by the crowd of thousands still lining Broadway, the funeral hearse and limousines were rerouted to Ninth Avenue. Within ten minutes the cortege had returned safely to Campbell's, where the honorary pallbearers lined up behind the coffin as it was carried from the hearse to the Gold Room.

Miss Negri and the Ullmans did not remain at the Funeral Church for more than a few minutes because Dr. Wyman ordered the actress—for the good of her health and her obligations to her art—to return to her hotel suite, where she could rest and recover from her traumatic ordeal. The good doctor had suggested absolute quiet and seclusion but Miss Negri would not hear of this, insisting instead on scheduling a news conference. After the reporters were made comfortable and all photographers were removed, Miss Negri was helped from her bedroom into the drawing room of the suite, which was so filled with flowers it was difficult to locate the furniture. With a regal nod Pola approved a sob sister's itemization of her black georgette dress, sheer black French chiffon hose and black pumps. Against the gold-and-blue taffeta of the divan, her pale features, dark hair and dress made for a startling contrast. For about a minute Pola wept, then, red-eyed and tear-stained, but brave of manner and voice, she challenged the reporters. The ladies and gentlemen of the press, she said, had treated her harshly and with deliberate malice in an attempt to make her a target for ridicule. Why did they refuse to recognize her as a sorrowing woman deserving of sympathy? Why were their newspapers so cruel?

Exhausted by the vigor of her accusations and the sorrow she had suffered, Pola sank into the cushions of the divan as George Ullman placed an icebag on her forehead. Pola shifted the bag to her eyes and when she felt better Ullman handed the icebag to the maid and helped adjust the pillows behind the star's back.

Suddenly Pola was overcome by a wrenching sob. Hands outstretched, fingers splayed, she keened and appealed to the reporters for understanding. "If you newspaper people knew what was in the bottom of my heart, you would not be so cruel to me." Pola sobbed again as she dabbed at her eyes with a miniature square of dampened lace. "Here, here is a letter," she exclaimed as she reached for her purse. "A letter from Dr. Meeker. I am going to read it to you."

Although her voice broke often, she read slowly and without assistance:

DEAR MISS NEGRI,

I am asking Mary Pickford, an old friend and patient of mine, to deliver this to you as I had to leave for my camp in Maine before you could arrive.

About 4 o'clock Monday morning I was sitting by Rudolph alone in the room. He opened his eyes, put out his hand and said: "I'm afraid we won't go fishing together, perhaps when we meet again, who knows?"

This was the first and only time he realized he would not get well. He was perfectly clear in his mind. He gave me a message for the chief—Mr. Schenck—and then said:

"Pola—if she doesn't come in time tell her I think of her."

At this point Miss Negri was again overwhelmed by tears. Then, as George Ullman asked if she wanted help with the letter, she clutched it to her bosom, recovered most of her voice and continued to read:

Then he spoke in Italian and went into his long sleep. I feel an obligation to get this message to you.

Yours sincerely,
HAROLD D. MEEKER

"That was his last message to me," Pola sobbed, and made no effort to wipe the tears from her wan cheeks. Then she stood, once more the queen and star. "I can't answer any questions. My secretary or Mr. Ullman will be glad to talk to you."

A nurse and Miss Florence Hein, her secretary, helped Miss Negri to her bedroom. When Miss Hein reappeared, she was unable to add anything except: "We can't get Miss Negri to eat. She hasn't said anything at all. She hasn't asked for any mementos or keepsakes but one. That is the great portrait of Valentino as a Spanish gentleman painted by F. Beltran y Masses, which hangs in his Hollywood home. Miss Negri wants to take it with her to her château at Reuil-Seraincourt, where she has a chapel. She plans to make a shrine there."

Miss Hein also told the reporters of Pola's certainty that

Alberto Guglielmi would join her on the train which would bear Valentino's body to Hollywood. In this sad entourage would also be Mr. and Mrs. George Ullman and several members of the United Artists Company who had been very close to Valentino. James Quirk might also make the trip.

Reporters asked Dr. Wyman if he would accompany Miss Negri when she returned to California, and he replied that his practice, too long neglected, required him to remain in the East. However, because rumors of Valentino's death by foul play still persisted, Dr. Wyman distributed to the press fifty-seven copies of a memorandum from Dr. Meeker. The memorandum detailed Dr. Meeker's medical report on the ailment that had killed Valentino, and the treatment employed in an effort to save his life. Attached was Dr. Wyman's notation wherein he certified his concurrence in Dr. Meeker's diagnosis and treatment.

In the circulation war among the tabloids, the device used to gain readers was less news and more headlines. The *Graphic*, however, undertook original approaches to the Valentino story. Whenever and wherever possible, the *Graphic* concentrated on exclusive coverages beyond the ability and resources of all other papers. So when a self-professed medium telephoned the *Graphic* that during a trance he had seen Valentino in heaven, the *Graphic* immediately faked and published a photo showing Valentino, in a white togalike garment, being welcomed to heaven by a female spirit of matronly appearance. Valentino's right hand covered his breast and the fingers of his left hand were raised in a signal later to be identified with Winston Churchill. According to Frank Mallen's book on the old *Graphic*, the background used was a composite made from "a movie still of an army of souls crossing the river Styx."

This composograph created a sensation, and it soon became known on the ectoplasmic circuit that the *Graphic* was sympathetically receptive to communications from the spirit world.

Within hours another medium visited the *Graphic*. He announced that because of a finer tuning into the ether, he could not only corroborate Valentino's residence in heaven, but had also witnessed with what friendly enthusiasm Valentino had been welcomed into the land of eternal bliss. Indeed, the first to welcome Rudy, the first to extend a hand of friendship and to offer a guided tour of that blessed place, was Enrico Caruso.

If there are skeptics who doubt that Caruso was in heaven, because of that Italian gentleman's reputation for wine, women and not-so-operatic song, these skeptics are immediately referred to a popular American ballad composed in 1921, the year of Caruso's death: "They Needed a Song Bird in Heaven (So God Took Caruso Away)."

> *They needed a song bird in Heaven*
> *To sing when the angels would play—*
> *So God told the angels where one could be found,*
> *They came and they took him one day—*
> *He's gone to that sweet land of sunshine*
> *Forever and ever to stay—*
> *They needed a song bird in Heaven*
> *So God took Caruso away.*

The composite of Valentino and Caruso depicted both in robelike togas, but unencumbered by Sunday halos or wings. Mr. Mallen noted that although many readers of the *Graphic* were pleased to have their newspaper verify that the abode of the blessed was the residence of both immortals, there were some who found fault that the *Graphic* composograph had chosen to portray so many souls who were quite obviously not wearing brassieres.

The *Graphic*'s next communication to its readers was an article headlined "VALENTINO'S GHOST CRIES FOR AUTOPSY, SAYS MEDIUM." To prove to doubting Thomases, if there were any among the paper's psychical readership, that the article was not

a fiction, it was by-lined by the medium, now identified as
Nicola Peccharara.

> The spirit of Rudolph Valentino is crying for revenge.
> It would bring to justice that guilty person, whose hand
> administered the treacherous potion that laid the body low.
> For Rudolph Valentino was murdered—slain over a beauti-
> ful woman via the poison vial.
> I know only too well. For each night the spirit of the great
> lover hovers over me, begging and pleading that I aid in
> bringing the murderer to account.
> Last night this strange wraith, whose very presence tortures
> me, explained the entire crime. It conveyed to me those last
> few hours of sensuous pleasure before the ugly monster of
> jealousy laid the actor low.
> There had been a party. The scene was in a fashionable up-
> town apartment. Beautiful girls were there. And wine, wine,
> wine. Valentino was enamoured of one of the maidens. She
> clung to him, refusing to leave his side even at the earnest
> solicitation of her affianced and the star himself.
> Then came jealousy.
> Valentino was urged to take one more drink. He succumbed
> to the coaxing and drained the poisoned contents of a cup.
> And now his spirit demands revenge.
> It torments me continually, demanding an autopsy to prove
> that its body was turned to dust through one who had been
> trusted.
> At night, when I close my eyes, the grim specter appears to
> inflict weird torture on me because the man has been allowed
> to go the way of all dead without an attempt to determine
> what speeded him along that dark road.
> It scratches my hand, clutches at my heart and foments my
> brain into a turmoil.
> "See that justice is done or I shall haunt you for eternity,"
> it cries.
> Call it psychic phenomenon, or any name you will, these are
> facts and I stand ready to prove them by a seance before any
> reputable body of scientists.

This direct, first-person communication from another place

15165

had two things going for it. One was that for at least four years
Valentino had believed in and participated in seances. The other
was that this was exactly what everyone already believed, anyway.

Nor did it hurt when Barclay Warburton, Jr., the host of the
party at which Valentino had become "ill," departed for parts
unknown the minute he left the sanitarium where he had taken
refuge shortly after Valentino entered the hospital.

Then Mike Li Calzi, the cabdriver who had pickd up Valentino and Miss Marian Benda at four-thirty in the morning at her
apartment and driven them to Warburton's apartment on Park
Avenue, came to the *Graphic* and reported that Valentino had
been in the best of health then. The ride from 145 West Fifty-fifth
Street, where Miss Benda lived, to Warburton's apartment on
Park Avenue had taken at most fifteen minutes; yet at five
o'clock Valentino had been removed from the Warburton apartment on a stretcher and transferred to the Polyclinic Hospital.
That Valentino had been well when he called for Miss Benda
at dawn was also corroborated by Frank Gross, the elevator
man in her apartment house.

These items were welcomed by Bernarr Macfadden, who
fired off a signed editorial: "Why Should Valentino Die?" Mr.
Macfadden wrote:

> An expert in natureopathy [*sic!*] has already pointed out
> what he considers to be many blunders made in the treatment
> of this great Italian star, but we believe that *the whole truth
> and nothing but the truth* should be supplied to his friends in
> reference to the original cause of his difficulty. . . .
> There have been many rumors as to the first symptoms as-
> sociated with his condition and verified statements as to where
> he was at the time he was attacked with this serious illness had
> not been furnished to the public.
> His friends are entitled to know the complete details, and
> beginning tomorrow, I have asked the editorial staff of this
> paper to *make every effort to get at the absolute truth of the*

various dramatic details associated with the tragical death of this great star. From day to day the facts that are brought to light will be published for the benefit of our readers.

Valentino is gone, but his spirit and his fame as an actor will live for long years to honor his name and his country.

This impassioned editorial appeal for the truth prompted an ambulance driver at the Polyclinic Hospital to tell *his* story to the *Graphic:*

Answering an emergency call from Dr. Durham, I arrived at the Park Avenue address Sunday morning. Entering the drawing-room of the luxurious apartment, I saw a young man, dressed in a flowered lounging gown, writhing in pain on a divan. When Dr. Durham and I helped him to his feet he clutched at his sides and moaned in agony. We helped him from the place, supporting him by putting his arms about our shoulders. We put him in the ambulance. Dr. Durham cautioned me not to delay by allowing the patient to converse with anybody, but to speed to the Polyclinic Hospital, where he would meet me. He followed in another car. As I drew up before the hospital, he arrived. An intern helped us take our patient upstairs. That was the last time I saw him. I did not know until later that the man I had brought to the hospital was Rudolph Valentino.

Meanwhile, Frank E. Campbell had turned over a disquieting letter to the New York City Police Department. Postmarked Jersey City, the letter was taken quite seriously by some metropolitan police authorities.

SIGNOR FRANK CAMPBELL:
Some of us who are dynamite workers in Dover and Hackensack and other towns, are going to get you if it takes all our lives. I belong to the Black Hand of Italy.

You took the body of our beloved Guglielmi from the hospital and had it for a advertisement exhibition. You let the Americanos see it. You took Guglielmi's body out and put another one in for the people to see it.

Letters in a similar vein were received by the Polyclinic Hospital, the Ambassador Hotel, the Italian Consulate and the New York offices of United Artists Corporation. In language too strong to bear reproduction, the letters vilified all Americans, but especially doctors, nurses and mortuary personnel.

Police became increasingly concerned and inquired of Mr. Ullman how soon he intended to remove Valentino's body from New York. When they were informed that this would probably take place September 2, they wished for that day to come and depart.

The *Homeric* was due to dock on September 1. Pola Negri appeared early at the foot of the West Seventeenth Street pier. As the giant liner sailed through the Narrows and into New York Bay, she and her party left their limousines and proceeded slowly, behind police escort, to a cleared space on the pier. Pola, clad in becoming black, was assisted by Mrs. George Ullman. Dr. Sterling Wyman bore an Italian flag with crepe bows at each of the corners.

The *Homeric* was secured to the ways, the gangplank was lowered and Miss Negri's party made their ascent to the ship's deck, but not before Pola told newsmen: "You know how I have suffered. I had a collapse this morning."

Alberto, clad in a black suit and gray hat, stepped forward. George Ullman was shocked; Rudolph's brother had lost at least twenty pounds. His anguished features were unmistakable evidences of his sincere shock, bewilderment and sorrow over his brother's untimely death. To most people Alberto's appearance was a surprise. He was only five feet six inches tall, of swarthy complexion, and had a rather bulbous nose. He had little of his brother's handsomeness; still, there was a family resemblance.

Pola kissed Alberto three times. Their tears mingled as they embraced, and as the passengers aboard ship closed in on this little drama, the principals all but disappeared from view. From the pier, the only way one could locate the group on the ship's deck was by the flag borne bravely by Dr. Wyman. After Pola, Alberto and their party disembarked, the police temporarily lost control over the crowd on the pier. In the resultant confusion the crush became so great that the customs inspectors could not process Alberto's luggage, so it was arranged for one member of the party to stay behind, while Pola and Alberto hastened to the Funeral Church.

Alberto was permitted several minutes alone with the body of his brother before the casket was sealed for all time. Then Father Congedo of St. Malachy's assisted Alberto to a private room on an upper floor of the building, where his prayers were heard only by the priest. Upon his return, Alberto met the press. His halting statement was translated by an Italian member of the party for the benefit of the reporters.

"My brother belonged to America," Alberto sobbed. "His resting place shall be in California, which he loved. My sister Maria feels that way about it, too. It had been indicated to me clearly that all America loved my brother and wants to keep him. I could not help but accede to America's wish. In doing this I am acting from my heart and not from any desire for publicity."

After the formal award of so consequential a gift, Alberto told reporters that "as his own tribute to his brother he had adopted his name and would pass it down to his children." To substantiate this intent, he had been identified on the *Homeric*'s passenger list as Alberto Valentino-Guglielmi, and he would be pleased if the press referred to him as such. "I hope to perpetuate the name of Valentino," he continued, "by getting the permission of the Italian Government to permit me to use it for my middle name."

This raised a number of reportorial eyebrows. In an autobiography, first published in *Photoplay,* it had been established that Valentino was part of the family name. If the younger brother had been entitled to its use, how could this normally primogenitive privilege be denied the elder? Why indeed did Alberto have to petition his government for a right already established? At any other time this matter might have been a subject for intensive interrogation, but the reporters were interested in something closer to the American dream.

"Do you think your brother was engaged to marry Pola Negri next January?" Alberto was asked by the *Times* reporter.

"Probably it was so. I know they were very fond of each other."

On September 2, at six-thirty in the evening, Alberto, Pola, Mr. and Mrs. George Ullman, Frank Campbell, Harry Klemfuss and W. H. Hull, manager of the Funeral Church, made ready to depart on the Lake Shore Limited for Chicago. Two special cars had been engaged—certainly far more space than Valentino's return ticket warranted—but plans for a solemn funeral procession through the Chicago streets with the body had been canceled. The stopover in that city would be limited to the time it took to switch the connecting cars to a Southern Pacific train headed for Los Angeles.

The first Pullman car would accommodate members of the mourning party and those members of the press willing to make the journey. The second would carry the dead actor's body and its floral tributes. Several papers had estimated that at least fifty thousand dollars in flowers had been displayed at Campbell's Funeral Church, and advance intelligence from Chicago indicated that all the flowers assembled to decorate the chapel where Valentino's body had been scheduled to lie in state would now be moved to the railroad station for impromptu services during the four-hour stopover.

It rained again late Thursday and there were only smallish knots of spectators outside Campbell's as eight pallbearers carried the coffin to the hearse. If these hardy onlookers expected to see Pola, they were disappointed, for she had been met at the Hotel Ambassador by Dr. Wyman, who was increasingly recognized by the group closest to Valentino as their surrogate. Dr. Wyman helped Pola into his car—which bore a Police Department emblem, for he was an honorary police surgeon—and, disregarding traffic laws and stoplights, he drove her to the Forty-third Street side of Grand Central Station.

Meanwhile, the hearse drove to the Forty-fifth Street baggage entrance, where porters maneuvered the two coffins—one encased in the other—onto a baggage truck. The outer coffin was silver bronze, the inner one gold bronze. Across the top was placed a tapestry of cloth of gold and a floral offering from George Ullman and his wife. Photographers popped their flashlights and employees gathered to watch the truck load onto an elevator that would descend to the train platform, where Mr. Campbell and the pallbearers stood guard until the train was ready to receive it. George Ullman, Alberto Valentino-Guglielmi and Pola Negri refused to grant interviews or sign autographs, but Miss Negri had given Dr. Sterling Wyman an authorized statement for the press.

"On the eve of my departure for California, I wish to take this opportunity to express my most sincere thanks to my many dear friends in New York who have offered me their sympathy in this dark hour of my sorrow. It is a great consolation to know that the last remains of my beloved will find a resting place in California, the spot where he rose to fame and spent so many hours in the home he loved so dearly."

With this statement Dr. Wyman distributed more copies of Dr. Meeker's analysis of Valentino's illness and his own concurrence. Asked once more for his evaluation of Pola's claim to Valentino's love, which had been strongly reinforced by Alberto's affirmative statement, he cryptically observed that he was better acquainted with cardiology than matters of the heart. However, he did add that although he considered himself a close and good friend of Miss Negri, he believed she was exaggerating the strength of Valentino's affection.

Mr. Campbell now stepped forward to the center of the stage and with many a handshake and statement of gratitude, gave to each of the reporters who had been covering the tragic events a personal coffin plate of brass with the recipient's name and birth date and a blank space for a terminal date. With each went a gift certificate that could be redeemed for a first-class funeral, without charge, at the House of Campbell.

At that moment, the station platform was invaded by a group of angry men and women shouting accusations in English and Italian.

"Rudolpho has been murdered!" one man shouted, waving his fists in the air.

A woman shrieked, "He has been poisoned!"

"Foul play! Let's avenge him!" screamed an excited girl, her pretty face flushed with emotion as she exhorted her cohorts to capture the coffin so that an autopsy could be held. A riot was averted when detectives and special police hastily grouped themselves around the coffin as reporters dove into the crowd to interrogate the frustrated vigilantes.

Mr. Ullman told a reporter from the *Times* that no autopsy would be held; the printed memorandum that Dr. Wyman had distributed several days before, and again within the past hour, should have served as "a means of quieting rumors which have been spread during the last few days to the effect that Valentino was a victim of poison or violence."

New York officials, police and the New York Central were glad to see the train depart. But the *Daily News* suggested to its readers: "While Hollywood waits, follow the train bearing Rudolph Valentino across the continent. For the reception at Chicago and other developments, read tomorrow's pink and other editions. . . ."

ACT ONE: SCENE SIX

In Chicago the heavens wept all day Friday. But the unpleasant weather did not deter the estimated throng of fifty thousand who crowded into the La Salle Street Station. The entrance to the train shed was so solidly packed that police doubted if another person could have entered. Souvenir hawkers were in evidence everywhere with mementos that duplicated the gewgaws which had been sold in New York City, with the exception of Rudolph Valentino Sculptured Wall Plaques that had been heavily advertised in the New York *Daily News;* these had been created by Jean Del Val, who was identified as a "noted artist and sculptor." The advertisements had pointed out that the "faithful likeness has won the admiration of all of Valentino's closest friends, and they come in one and two dollar sizes."

The crowd realized it could not hope to see the body but

would have settled for a glimpse of the coffin and the principal mourners. Most people never saw either, and the only persons permitted to visit Miss Negri or Alberto comprised a committee that represented the Chicago Valentino Memorial Association. Judge Berelli, chairman of the committee, presented the association's tribute—a broken wheel composed of five hundred roses, gladioli and lily blossoms that stood eight feet tall.

Members of the committee gave the secluded mourners an oral account of the funeral services held in the Trianon Ballroom. More than two thousand persons, about 90 percent of them women dressed in deep mourning, had attended. Intertwined American and Italian flags had framed a statue of Valentino, and after he had been prayed over by a priest, a Protestant clergyman and a rabbi, they had eulogized him as an "ideal for American youth" and a "beloved impersonation of the spirit of romance."

Mr. Campbell and Mr. Klemfuss of the Funeral Church congratulated the representatives of the Valentino Memorial Association for their devotion, and Mr. Campbell assured them he had been in favor of a prolonged stopover in their fair city, but that the schedule had been set by others and his hands had been tied.

Shortly before the train departed, Katherine Ochsner Rast-Elliott, a pretty nineteen-year-old girl who was unfortunately crippled, brought a little bouquet to the station to which was attached a card: "To my beloved Rudy. My heart can only express its love and grief with flowers and a prayer that you may rest in peace."

Katherine had stood for three hours in the rain until George Ullman had noticed the pretty mourner, accepted her bouquet and personally escorted her to the bier.

All the Hearst Sunday papers featured a full-page posthumous article by Rudolph Valentino, which the Boston *Advertiser* headlined "WHY MARRIAGE WAS A FAILURE IN MY CASE," and the Los Angeles *Examiner* bannered "VALENTINO'S OWN STORY OF LOVE FAILURE."

A boxed note informed readers that the "article was written by Valentino two days before he left Los Angeles on the trip to New York that culminated in his death . . . and reveals with amazing frankness why his marriage with Winifred Hudnut (Natacha Rambova) was such a ghastly failure." The article, which maintained a high emotional pitch, insisted that when a wife competed for accomplishment in the same career area as her husband, any marriage was doomed to failure.

At the conclusion Valentino observed wryly:

> Perhaps this account of my second wreck on the reefs of matrimony will give the lie to the line which has been tacked on to me—that I am "a great lover," both on and off the screen. I suppose it is intended for a compliment, but I do not relish it.
>
> I wish above everything to be known some day as a great artist, and am working earnestly to be given a picture which will demand something more than a physical performance and I want to be ready when the time comes. After all, a man gets tired of being talked about and written about as though he were a professional "handsome man."
>
> For this reason I need to concentrate on my work and plan for my future as never before. And what may happen is on the lap of the Gods. However, I must admit that I am not insensible to the charms of the fair sex.

Male reporters on the funeral train noted that Valentino ruled out the possibility of a happy or enduring marriage where husband and wife practiced the same career; moreover, the article made no mention of any new romance in Valentino's immediate future. How did Miss Negri choose to answer these statements?

Pola never once lost her composure.

"We were never formally betrothed," she told George V. Buchanan of the International News Service. "We did not believe in formal engagements. Last April we frequently talked of our plans to marry and our close friends knew of our love. We decided that our private life belonged to us and we did not want to make publicity of it."

When she turned to Alberto for confirmation, he nodded. "Yes," he said, "Rudy had many loves. Pola was his last."

"Was this his greatest?" Mr. Buchanan asked.

"Ah, that I do not know," Alberto answered dolefully.

What the press never reported to the papers was that this transcontinental wake was provided with wassail in sufficient quantity to have floated it across the country. Whenever stops were made, mysterious strangers would load mysterious cases aboard the train that kept everyone so euphoric that a literary reporter wondered if he were not aboard the Celestial Railroad described by Nathaniel Hawthorne. It is even recorded that at El Paso a mysterious coffin was taken aboard and when it was opened it was found to be chockablock with high-proof nutritives smuggled across the border from Juárez.

As the Golden State Limited approached the California border, George Ullman devoted himself to plans for the rites to be conducted on Tuesday, September 14, at the Church of the Good Shepherd in Beverly Hills. To avoid the large crowds which Mr. Campbell fervently hoped would welcome the entourage in Los Angeles, he had planned to have the body removed at the Richfield Station in Pasadena by the undertaking firm of Cunningham and O'Connor, who would whisk it to their parlors at 1031 South Grand Avenue in Los Angeles, where no one, however great or important, would be permitted on the premises. Then on Tuesday morning six hundred guests would be admitted to the church solely by invitation to participate in the requiem mass, after which the body would be taken directly to the Hollywood Cemetery, where a sizable police cordon would bar sightseers and maintain order. Only persons bearing invitations would be permitted to enter, for it was remembered that when Barbara La Marr had been buried in February of that year, the public had so overrun the cemetery that the official funeral party had been unable to get anywhere near the grave.

But another unique problem confronted Ullman: Valentino had not owned a plot in the Hollywood Cemetery. True, there were massive plans for a memorial designed by Matlack Price, a local architect who had worked feverishly to complete his plans by August 30, and these scale drawings and interpretations had already been published in *Photoplay*, a periodical long devoted to the architecture of divine afflatus.

The architect envisioned a heroic necropolis of classic neo-De Mille pizazz—a natural "trysting place for lovers . . . a graceful half circle of columns standing serene and dignified against the dark background, and curving toward you like welcoming arms held out and within that half circle that architects call exedra, would stand a great figure of the *Sheik* . . . to invite moonlight and starlight meetings under the two pergolas that run across the ends of the terrace . . . all . . . raised ten feet or so above the street level, as any important monument should be, on a grass embankment, with broad stairs inviting the passerby up to a terrace of Spanish tile. In style this simple half circle of columns is Roman. . . . In detail, the palmette capital on the columns is suggested in place of the conventional Corinthian type—a bit of symbolism of the desert in memory of the Sheik. There are eight columns and at the base of each is planned to incorporate in the design low relief panels, six of these to show Rudolph Valentino, in costume, in his six greatest roles: 'The Four Horsemen,' 'The Sheik,' 'Blood and Sand,' 'Monsieur Beaucaire,' 'The Eagle,' and 'The Son of the Sheik. . . .' The design is to welcome and charm, like youth itself, and to create a setting for living romance." How lovers could utilize the monument for "moonlight and starlight meetings" after the cemetery gates closed at dusk was unexplained.

These grandiose plans were immediately approved by the

Rudolph Valentino Memorial Committee. Still, where were they going to bury the Great Lover? Then June Mathis, who had given Valentino his first chance in *The Four Horsemen*, proved her generosity again by offering the facilities of her family crypt at Hollywood Cemetery until an appropriate memorial for the actor could be erected.

Certain now that Valentino would be buried, Ullman published the list of honorary pallbearers—Cecil B. De Mille, John Barrymore, Douglas Fairbanks, William S. Hart, Mack Sennett, Louis B. Mayer, Harold Roach, Harry Langdon, Manuel Reachi and Charles Eyton.

On Monday morning, when the Valentino train arrived in Los Angeles, the New York papers carried headlines of almost unbelievable comic relief:

The *Daily News:*

POLA'S DOCTOR EX-CONVICT

The New York Times:

DR. WYMAN EXPOSED AS FORMER CONVICT

Man Who Took Active Part in Valentino Rites
Identified as an Impersonator
CALLS ULLMAN HIS "FRIEND"
Served Term for Wearing Naval Uniform as
Escort to Princess Fatima at White House

The *Herald Tribune:*

"DR. WYMAN," AID TO VALENTINO'S
MANAGER, ADMITS JAIL TERMS

Ullman's Representative, Who Indorsed
Medical Report, Indignant at Exposure
as Ex-Convict; Signs $1,000,000 Checks;
Once Had "P.D." on His Auto.

For the next four days, during which Valentino eulogies, obsequies and interment were major news in the West Coast newspapers, New York papers delighted in articles about Dr. Sterling Wyman, who had added Valentino's mourners to the long list of people he had duped.

If Ullman, for one, felt that he had been a mark, he was not alone. What about Dr. Meeker, whose medical diagnosis and regimen had been approved by "Dr." Wyman, and the administrators at the Metropolitan Hospital, who had sent interns to Campbell's when Wyman had telephoned the hospital and identified himself as "house physician for Campbell's"?

New York City roared, congratulated itself on so "sterling" a citizen and demanded more details about "Dr." Wyman. Of course, all the New York papers reported it fully. To start at the beginning, the "doctor" had graduated from P.S. 18 and Eastern District High School, both in Brooklyn. He had then matriculated at the College of Political Science at Charleston, South Carolina, where its honored faculty granted him a degree. He himself had had a Phi Beta Kappa key struck off, perhaps his first deception. He next had enrolled at Oriental University, Washington, D.C., an institution but recently closed because its dean and president, "Bishop Dr." Helmuth P. Holler, had been removed from his presidential study to a federal penitentiary for using the mails to defraud. It appeared that the Post Office Department had looked unkindly on the activities of Oriental University for offering degrees in haircutting, chicken feeding and paperhanging, along with degrees in law, medicine and philosophy, and at a cost of twenty-five dollars, hardly enough to cover the cost of the diploma.

Prior to this matriculation "Dr." Wyman had had some experience in psychiatry, for he had been confined as an inmate at Dannemora State Hospital for the Criminal Insane from October, 1917, until April, 1919. Apparently he put it to good use, for he had talked well enough to dupe Dr. Lorenz, the famous surgeon, when he visited America.

And when the Princess Fatima of Afghanistan, with a large entourage and an emerald in her nose, had engaged a lavish suite at the Waldorf, Wyman had appeared in full-dress uniform to extend the official greetings of the United States as "Lieutenant Commander Ethan Allen Weinberg." Gallantly he had offered the Princess his services, and when Fatima had expressed a desire to meet President Harding, he said he could arrange it. And he had. But after being welcomed with the Princess at the White House, Weinberg fell afoul of two Secret Service men, who penetrated his masquerade. Their testimony was instrumental in rewarding him with an eighteen-month sojourn in the Federal Penitentiary at Atlanta, where Weinberg captivated young society ladies of the city who were doing social service at the penitentiary. He also assembled a variety of disguises too baffling to mention.

After George Ullman and his party had departed for Los Angeles, Wyman installed himself as the personal representative of Mr. Ullman at Ullman's office at 1440 Broadway, and represented him in the District Attorney's office over the demands raised in some quarters for a Valentino autopsy. He might have succeeded in this masquerade had the name of Dr. Sterling C. Wyman not nudged the memories of several reporters.

Mr. Ullman immediately disavowed "Dr." Wyman, who now interviewed the press in his Brooklyn apartment, where his mother could not keep him from talking freely. He admitted cheerfully that he had billed Miss Negri for a thousand dollars for medical services and that he had been paid. He complained, however, that his "enemies" were determined to destroy him and his good reputation by constant reference to his retreats at Dannemora, the Elmira Reformatory and the Atlanta Penitentiary.

During the interview, Wyman made reference to his lectures on medical jurisprudence, which he had given before learned bodies at well-known universities. However, he found it difficult to remember the names of these universities, and though he claimed to have obtained a law degree in 1923 from the Hamilton School of Law in Chicago, he could not produce his diploma, though he did produce a document which bore his name and resembled a medical diploma. However, he placed a sheet of paper over the name of the school. Queried about the attentions he had given visitors to Campbell's, to Miss Negri and even to Ruby Keeler, one of Texas Guinan's showgirls, Wyman dismissed these patients with a laugh. What knowledge was required to administer aspirin and smelling salts to hysterical or fainting women? The reporters were hard pressed to remember a more engaging impostor.

The next day Wyman also elaborated on his relationship with Ullman. He claimed to have known Valentino's manager for some years and had offered his services to that good man after he had begun to suffer great anguish of mind over Valentino's illness and death. Ullman denied all this curtly, disassociated himself completely from "Dr." Wyman and ordered him removed from the office in New York. After all, he had more important work at home.

ACT ONE: SCENE EIGHT

The Golden State Limited hove into the Richfield Station outside Los Angeles shortly before three in the afternoon. Before Miss Negri left her compartment, she placed a large sheaf of yellow roses on the coffin. Then she fell into the arms of Marion Davies, who had boarded the train earlier that day at San Bernardino, and was led to a limousine whose rich appointments included a nurse and genuine physician. Alberto and the Ullmans rode in another car, and as both followed the hearse to the funeral parlor, a motorcycle escort preceded them under full siren. Many cars joined the impromptu cavalcade, hoping to get a glimpse of Pola Negri and the other notables, and at the mortuary several hundred spectators, most of them women, had anticipated the arrival of the coffin. Tears of welcome and lamentations of sorrow arose as if on cue and a number of women attempted to rush the hearse and Miss Negri's limousine, but a police guard prevented any major disorder.

Reporters followed the coffin and notables into the mortuary, where attendants informed them of the discovery of a young girl who had secreted herself in a closet the night before. She had been reprimanded and sent home; the premises would be searched regularly until the funeral on the morrow. All the studios would be closed for an hour next morning when a solemn high requiem mass would be celebrated once more over the body.

In the early morning of September 7, Valentino's body was taken from the mortuary to the Church of the Good Shepherd in Beverly Hills. Passersby on their way to work paused for a moment as the coffin was loaded into the gray hearse, and long before ten o'clock a crowd had begun to gather across the street from the church. About two hundred policemen were on duty but they had little to do because the spectators were unusually well behaved. Rarely did an officer have to escort some man or woman back to the sidewalk.

As impressive cars drew up before the church, the knowledgeable men and women in the crowd solemnly identified the stars as they hurried to the church doors. Many wept as they left their limousines. At last Reverend Michael J. Mullins entered the sanctuary, and quiet filled the church as the mourners composed themselves for the services. Father Mullins was assisted by a master of ceremonies, a deacon and a subdeacon charged with the supervision of the altar boys in their white-and-purple vestments.

As the strains of an oratorio pealed forth, Pola Negri, her features covered by a black veil, was assisted down the aisle by Alberto Valentino-Guglielmi. They were followed by Mr. and Mrs. George Ullman and important officials of United Artists. This group sat in a front pew close to the casket, which was entirely concealed by flowers. Light clouds of incense rose from the altar as the priests chanted mass. Then Richard Bonelli, an opera star identified as a friend of Valentino, lifted his voice from the choir gallery to sing "Ave Maria" before Father Mullins prayed for the repose of Valentino's soul.

Thousands of people lined the streets from Beverly Hills to Hollywood. At the Hollywood Cemetery, where reporters estimated the crowd at more than seven thousand, police were out in force at the one open gate. A lane of flowers extended from the mausoleum door to the crypt, where Father Mullins and the altar boys waited to complete the ceremonies. Cameras clicked incessantly to record every nuance of the ceremony and a gentle rain of blossoms fell from the skies as Paul Whittier, the air officer of the Beverly Hills Police Department, flew over the cemetery and dropped thousands of flowers. They covered the ground with a bright, fragrant carpet. The crowd was pleased. Messrs. Campbell and Klemfuss, take notice!

The pallbearers carried the magnificent coffin through the bronze doors of the crypt to the niche where Valentino would rest temporarily. Then for the last time Father Mullins recited a blessing as Pola Negri cried aloud. Alberto wept, too, and just before the marble slab was lifted into place, Alberto pressed his cheek against the coffin, kissed it and whispered farewell.

It would be a weary exercise to list the Hollywood notables at the funeral or to describe their floral tributes. Touched they were when onlookers sang Jimmy McHugh's emolliental memorial— "There's a New Star in Heaven Tonight"—as if it were a hymn.

One afterthought. In *From Under My Hat* (1952), Miss Hedda Hopper recorded a rare anecdote that she attributed to Joseph Hergesheimer, whose bungalow at the Ambassador Hotel faced Pola Negri's.

> From his bungalow Joe watched Pola emerge in deep mourning, with the veil thrown back so newsreel cameras could record how she faced going on living with bravery and fortitude.

Shots were taken. One cameraman yelled: "Pola—the light's not good on your face—will you do it again?"

"And," Joe reported to me with awe, "darned if she didn't! It's the only time I ever saw a retake on mourning."

ACT TWO
THE IMMIGRANT AS
A YOUNG MAN

To secure wealth is an honorable ambition. . . . Money is power.
Every good man and woman ought to strive for power, to do
good with it when obtained. I say, get rich, get rich!
  RUSSELL H. CONWELL, *Acres of Diamonds* (1888)

MIRAGE
Happiness—you wait for us
  Just beyond,
    Just beyond.
We know not where.
  Nor how we shall find you.
We only know you are
  Waiting, waiting,
    Just beyond.
  RUDOLPH VALENTINO, *Day Dreams* (1923)

ACT TWO: SCENE ONE

The legend of the messiah is common to all cultures. Occasionally the myth becomes a reality, and so it did in Castellaneta, in southern Italy, for there, on May 6, 1895, Rodolpho Guglielmi, the messiah of romantic love and burning passion, was born. His mother, Beatrice Barbin, to whom was later granted the virtues of a madonna, may have been a French citizen before she married Giovanni Guglielmi, a practitioner of veterinary medicine in Castellaneta.

Where Giovanni received his veterinary training is unknown, but his experience and the knowledge gained through practice were adequate for the treatment and care of the domestic animals of his region. His occupation lifted him above most of the citizens in the impoverished community. His small house had once had its front wall painted, there was a division of three rooms within the house, and part of the roof was tiled—all proofs of his influence and wealth.

Beatrice, the Guglielmis' eldest child, died at the age of eight. She was followed by Alberto, Rodolpho and Maria, all of whom survived. Giovanni died in 1906 and left his widow to fill the functions of mother, ruler, judge and disciplinarian. In relation to their neighbors, the family still lived reasonably well. They had black bread on the table almost every day and their income permitted Beatrice Guglielmi to provide simple schooling for her children.

Alberto and Maria accepted this change in parental authority, but Rodolpho never could reconcile himself to his father's death. At times his mother's authority took no stronger form than a reprimand or scolding, but she never hesitated to call in a male relative to dispense discipline with fist or stick if she judged her youngest son deserving. Soon enough the boy learned to obey, at least in her presence. But inside he was deeply hurt and bewildered.

Like any boy in Castellaneta who could be spared from work in the fields and whose family had some ambition for him, Rodolpho received some little early instruction in reading and writing from the village priest and from several elderly spinsters or widows, who were likely little better than illiterate. Often he missed his lessons because he found adventures in the hills and caves of Apulia more exciting than dull books. Besides, he did not enjoy having his ears tweaked for his failure to apply himself.

In later life Rodolpho claimed to have attended the Dante Alighieri College in Genoa between 1906, when his father died, and 1908. Italy is filled with such colleges, which graduate their pupils with a *licenza di scuola elementare*—about equivalent to a sixth-grade diploma. But the Dante Alighieri College at Genoa is no longer in existence and its records have disappeared. He also claimed to have continued his education at the Collegio della

Sapienza, an elementary military school for doctors' sons in Perugia, and that he had been on the school's soccer team. This school, too, is no longer in existence. There are snapshots showing Rodolpho in school uniform, but a number of expert photographers are convinced these are crude composites, the angle of the head being not quite right for the posture of the body. Also the paper on which they were printed was not of European manufacture.

The truth probably is that Rodolpho's mother, distraught at her son's intractability, only wished she could have afforded to send the difficult boy to a boarding school, for he appears to have been a village scourge, constantly at odds with all adults. He refused to go to confession or even attend church. He was arrogant. He spat, cursed, fought; he raided every orchard around the village and refused to work. Sometimes, in desperation, his mother locked him out of the house. When she did so, he threw rocks at the front door and more than once broke the shutters. He seemed determined neither to become a peasant nor to learn a trade.

After Valentino's death, the Chicago *Tribune* dispatched a correspondent to Castellaneta to interview the handful of people who had known him as a youth. They remembered him only as a troublemaker, a runaway who disappeared for days at a time, sometimes to turn up in some Taranto jail, charged with vagrancy.

The mother despaired. She attempted through tears, prayers and discipline—laid on her son by a stick wielded by a male relative—to make him learn some trade or apprentice himself to the land as his forefathers had done, even to study enough to become a lay brother of the church. She got nowhere. What Rodolpho wanted to do, he did not know. He hated Castellaneta, its stony fields, its dull resignation to poverty, and as he entered his teens he spent more and more time idling on a hillside or wandering through the streets of Taranto, where he became increasingly adept at filching food in the markets and avoiding apprehension by the police.

In 1910, when Rodolpho was fifteen, or so the Hollywood version of the story goes, he was enrolled at the Royal Academy of Agriculture in Santo Ilario Ligure, a small village above the Mediterranean near Genoa. But even in his official autobiography, a frothy catechism of pink icing whipped up for *Photoplay* magazine, Valentino did not reveal how long he was there, though he claimed to have received an agricultural degree, a *licenza di scuola media inferiore*, roughly equivalent to a secondary-school diploma. But records from the Royal Academy also no longer exist.

What was there to do in Castellaneta for a teen-age rebel at war with every facet of his environment? Nothing but to continue his warfare with the community, its folkways and traditions, or to resign himself to its despair and abject poverty, the blunted viewpoint of the average peasant whose horizon was his boot tops. Time and again he pleaded with his mother for sufficient funds to establish himself in Taranto. Time and again he was ordered by his mother to reconcile himself to Castellaneta. Violently, tearfully, he insisted that he be permitted to become part of a larger world, where a man could earn his living in some other way than digging into the earth or licking the boots of a priest or landowner. He did not demand riches, luxury or power—only the opportunity to see cities, their streets and shops, and the houses of the rich. Unable to accommodate himself to a belief in an inheritance in heaven, when as one of the poor and meek he would be given his share of the earth, Rodolpho would reply that in the end all the earth he expected was a spadeful to cover his face.

After one violent rage that could not be quieted by a heavy-handed beating from one of his relatives, Rodolpho's mother capitulated. Tearfully, with many prayers for his safety and a formidable number of admonitions concerning his conduct, she entered into correspondence with some Castellanetans who had escaped from the village to New York City—that El Dorado across the wide ocean—and when they agreed to receive her son and teach him the ways of the New World, Mrs. Guglielmi agreed to his emigration.

On December 9, 1913, Valentino sailed as a steerage passenger. Though he had shed the required tears, he had left without regret, looking forward to a richer, fuller life of excitement and high adventure. He might still work with his hands, with his back and feet, but he would no longer be on his knees like a peasant grubbing in the hostile earth. Sewn in the lining of his threadbare coat were the addresses of the two Castellanetan families who would receive him in New York, and one American dollar.

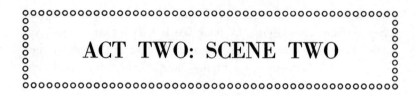

ACT TWO: SCENE TWO

Standing on the third-class deck, where the steerage passengers had been permitted to gather once the ship had sighted the Statue of Liberty, Rodolpho Guglielmi got his first glimpse of America. From his place at the prow, pressed against the railing and able to endure the cold because of the sheets of heavy paper under his shirt, he saw Ellis Island, the gateway to his brave new world. Vividly he remembered how he had begged, sulked, refused to go into the fields or seek work in Taranto, until his mother had finally agreed to borrow the money to get him out of Castellaneta. He recalled how, as he walked away from his home, he had turned to spit at the town, where slops were emptied into the streets.

By rights it was Alberto, the eldest son, who should have gone in his place. Suppose the immigration officers asked if he had an elder brother? Would they ask why Rodolpho, rather than his brother, had come to the United States? There was no one to meet him at Ellis Island, and if he was permitted to enter the United States, how would he find his way around this overwhelming city? There was one man from Genoa, whom he had met on the ship, only twenty-three, but at least he had been to America before. Of all the Italian immigrants he had met in the steerage, only this Genoese, in his dark suit and derby hat, looked to him like an American.

He claimed to have lived in New York and then moved on to Atlantic City, where he had been a barber in a prominent boardwalk hotel. He had prospered and decided to return to Genoa, where his American dollars would enable him to marry a woman somewhat above him in class, whose dowry, combined with his dollars, would enable him to live forever without working. But misfortune had overtaken him; on the voyage back, he had met a beautiful Frenchwoman in the ship's lounge. She had invited him to her cabin—and what a woman she had been! —and later she had asked him to join some of her friends in another cabin, all titled gentlemen and ladies, most of them French, who spoke knowingly of Cannes and Monte Carlo and the Parisian boulevards. They had honored him by including him in their card games, and by morning he had lost every cent he had saved except for one lucky twenty-dollar bill that he had always kept in his right shoe.

So he had landed at Genoa, not so rich, but much wiser. One look at the city had convinced him that to live there forever was something he could not do. He had worked hard and in less than a year had saved enough to return by steerage to the United States. When he was with this Genoese, Rodolpho felt calmer. His friend told him not to worry; they would clear the immigration officials together and he would take Rodolpho to the flat where the Castellanetans lived.

How amazed Rodolpho was when he got there to find a

kitchen with matching chairs, an enamel-top table and an iron stove that warmed every corner of the room. There was gaslight in every room, a toilet in the hall shared by only four families, and two faucets in the kitchen sink—he had never imagined so wonderful a thing. And next to the sink was a boiler heated by gas. Hot water came through a faucet!

How the Castellanetans laughed at his wonder. Everything was so busy. There were streetcars and buses and wagons and automobiles. But they were glad to have him, glad to hear him tell of friends and family left behind in Castellaneta, and they howled their approval after he had prevailed on his Genoese friend to tell them about the Frenchwoman and how her confederates had taken him.

Ten years later, Valentino adopted the story told by the Genoese to explain why *he* had settled in the United States.

The young immigrant was reluctant to live for long in the slums of lower Manhattan, and shortly after his arrival, once he had gained sufficient confidence to travel on the elevated lines and subways, he moved into a room on West Forty-ninth Street with another Italian family. There he remained for approximately five months while he learned rudimentary English. During this time he supported himself with odd jobs as messenger, dishwasher, janitor's assistant and clerk in an Italian grocery. None of these jobs pleased him, however, and he was frequently unemployed. But small remittances from his family in Italy were sufficient to cover his dollar-a-week room rent and purchase enough food and red wine to sustain him.

New York was as exciting as he had dreamed it would be. But in the midst of these granite towers and streets filled with elegant women and well-dressed men, he was desperately lonely. New York was no place for someone whose English was all but nonexistent. If he asked directions and could not make himself understood, the person he addressed would hurry off. Some evenings as he walked by himself or sat in his small, musty room, his eyes would fill with tears as he thought of his mother, his brother and sister, and, desperate with homesickness, he would long to write to his mother, confess his errors and ask her to rescue him from this place where even the Irish policemen were contemptuous of Italians. How strange it was, he raged to the Italian family with whom he lived, that of all the immigrant groups in the city, the Italians should be relegated to the lowest economic and social rungs. His landlady and her husband would shrug, curse everyone who was not Italian, and advise him to stop worrying about how people felt about him and apprentice himself to a good Italian bricklayer or baker. That way he would learn a fine trade and be able to marry and support a wife. Once he had a wife and children, he wouldn't have time to be concerned over such nonsense.

Spring brought pleasant weather and in June of 1914, Rodolpho found employment as a subgardener on the Long Island estate of Cornelius Bliss. He had sworn never to live off the soil but this was somehow different, for on the Bliss estate Rodolpho discovered his true purpose in coming to America.

He had been rebellious in Castellaneta because he would not accept a poor and socially predetermined station in life. Here in the United States he discovered wealth and the wealthy. From the moment he set foot on the Bliss estate, he became passionately absorbed in a study of rich people; he dedicated himself to aping their ways, to becoming like them—and, eventually, one of them. The rich held their heads at an arrogant angle and walked with assurance, as if the touch of their foot gave them possession of the land. The rich laughed easily. They saw only what they wanted to see. The rich devoted themselves to the pursuit of pleasure, and the greatest pleasure, as Rodolpho observed, was the pursuit and conquest of women. One day, he would be rich.

How, he did not know, but it would come. Until then he would devote himself to learning. And with this discovery, Rodolpho no longer felt foreign. His English was poor but did not foreign noblemen also have accents?

Rodolpho enjoyed his work on the Bliss estate. He observed secretly and later, in the privacy of his room, practiced. Then one day he was discovered by the ground superintendent imitating the activity on the tennis court from behind a grove of trees, and he was discharged.

When he returned to Manhattan, he practiced what he had learned. His improved manners impressed his Italian acquaintances, but the only immediate employment he could secure was with the Parks Department. Although he had to mow lawns, prune shrubs and perform other tasks assigned to this class of laborer in Central Park, it provided him with vantage points from which to observe the prosperous and elegant young men as they rode by in the company of beautiful young ladies on horseback. At night he straddled a stool in his room and pretended he was riding a fine horse. With one hand controlling his mount, he gestured with the other and practiced telling amusing stories to imaginary company.

Then came a black day. His superior, who generally delighted in tormenting him, assigned him to the most degrading of jobs. He was given a burlap bag, a stick with a spike on the end, and set to picking up loose papers and cigarette butts. But because he thought the people he admired most were laughing at him, he quit and accepted employment as a gardener on a New Jersey estate. Here, in addition to receiving a small salary, room and board, he continued his concentrated study of the rich.

It was possible for him to save a little money. Still, he longed for the city, and at the end of August he quit and rented a two-dollar-a-week room in a tenement near the Williamsburg Bridge. He frequented midtown Manhattan, however, which seemed to offer the best opportunities for a young man who did not want to be a peasant or a laborer and gravitated naturally toward the cheap dance halls and cabarets where the flashier of his countrymen congregated. And here Rodolpho became increasingly adept at the popular ballroom dances—the maxixe, the American and Continental tango, the Castle Walk, the Hesitation and Airplane waltzes.

He was always gregarious. He liked to have people around him, to be in the company of men and women having fun, and he found the dance halls and cabarets to his liking. They offered him an opportunity to get to meet American girls and through them improve his English. Their free-and-easy attitudes fascinated him. They were so different from the women of Italy. In Italy a woman was content to walk with a great load on her back while her husband rode the donkey. But here, in America, the new woman demanded social equality. Bold, aggressive, assuming male prerogatives of speech and action, she was uncompromising in her demands for a single standard of behavior. The American woman was exciting and free and attainable.

At the cabarets, she came to dance and chose partners she had never seen before. There were many establishments where she paid such partners for dancing with her, dismissing them if they displeased her, and if she left the dance floor for the casual hotel bedroom, the choice again was hers. By 1912 such cabarets were an established part of New York's night life, and the favorite playgrounds of the young social set of Manhattan.

The most famous were Maxim's, Delmonico's, Bustanoby's and the Ritz Grill. With the importation of the tango from Europe, the larger cabarets employed two or more orchestras. One might play for the professional entertainment and ordinary social dancing, the second for the tango. Such cabarets were famous not only for their physical appointments and the quality of their cuisine, but also for their male tango dancers.

These dancers were expected to be of a Continental appearance and had to provide their own evening clothes. To change from afternoon dansant garb to more formal wear, they were provided with small dressing rooms. Within a very short time Rodolpho realized that if he were going to practice the social graces, this would be as good a way as any. He rapidly became proficient enough as a dancer to seek such employment. Soon he gained a reputation as a pleasant young man able to put almost any woman at ease and make her seem more beautiful and graceful than she actually was.

Such male dancers were referred to as gigolos, even by the women who danced with them, and to the average American male they were pariahs with effeminate manners, heavily brilliantined hair and an oily manner. Out West, ranchers shot coyotes and other varmints; in New York City, good Americans punched gigolos. Rudolpho returned their contempt with hatred and began even to dislike American women—a dislike which he never relinquished or modified. Their freedom no longer delighted him, for in their emancipation they used him as a commodity, to be bought, exchanged or discarded at whim. He became convinced that American women were more shallow, selfish, willful and unfaithful than the women of any other nation.

American women were more masculine than most men and the unnaturalness of this attitude, the boldness of their sexuality, seemed an affront to him. He began to reject their invitations to meet them after the cabaret closed and instead practiced his dancing until he became so professional he had hopes of qualifying as an entertainer. He applied for employment at the better cabarets and Maxim's added him to its staff of dancers, who gave ballroom-dance exhibitions and doubled as instructors.

Although he no longer considered himself a gigolo, he was still compelled to dance with rich American women of all ages. They were impressed with his foreign accent, sensual eyes, good manners and grace on the dance floor, and for added stature he changed his name to Rodolpho Di Valentina and claimed to be of a great and noble house fallen into ruin. The scar on his right cheek? Once, outside of Paris, he had met an opponent on a field of honor. And queried as to why he had not returned to Italy to fight against the Central Powers, he spoke mysteriously of diplomatic missions or told the ladies in his arms he had applied for American citizenship because of his love for this nation. He delighted in stories so easily invented, enjoyed their impression on the gullible women who shivered deliciously as he murmured phrases of love and brushed their ears with his lips.

It was a wonderful way to make a living, but what he enjoyed most was the warmth of Maxim's kitchen where the staff laughed at the clientele and he was fed delicacies supposedly reserved for customers. Never in his life had he eaten so well, and with reluctance he would leave the kitchen to return to the dance floor. The headwaiter observed nastily that he was gaining weight; the dancers at Maxim's had to be as slender as guardsmen. Rodolpho took to wearing a corset.

In the infrequent letters he wrote to Castellaneta, his enthusiasm for the United States, especially New York, was almost blasphemous. He considered the American city second only to heaven, and as he became more confident of his place in the richest, most sophisticated and metropolitan of all American cities, his bitter memories of Castellaneta lost their hard, abrasive edges. Soon he would look back with kindness, occasionally even with nostalgia, on the primitive town where he had been born and lived for eighteen years before his escape to the New World.

Within several months Rodolpho became one of the most popular dancers at Maxim's, a reputation which delighted him especially as it became known that if he deigned to dance with a lady, his standard tip was five dollars, although ten dollars would make him happier. He was increasingly in demand by the bejeweled ladies who came to Maxim's, and began to receive gifts of appreciation. Surrounded by the waiters and kitchen help, he would open these finely wrapped packages and read aloud the enclosed cards. They made everyone around him laugh as proudly he would display the choice silk shirts, toiletries and other expensive trifles. These gifts of favor compelled Maxim's to reward him with an even larger salary and to grant him special privileges. He demanded more accomplished dancers as his professional partners when he demonstrated the tango and popular ballroom waltzes and they were furnished him.

By this time Rodolpho was an accepted and fairly popular member of the cabaret set in Manhattan. Increasingly welcomed backstage, he watched musical shows from the wings. Whenever Mae Murray visited Maxim's she danced with Rodolpho, and soon included him among her circle of friends. And then one evening Bessie Dudley, a handsome colored dancer who trouped with Ken "Snake Hips" Johnson, asked Rodolpho to wait for her after her theater performance. It was she who introduced him to Bonnie Glass.

Bonnie was a winsome brunette of aristocratic profile whose real name was Helen Roche. In her home town—Roxbury, Massachusetts—she had been considered one of the local beauties and no one was surprised when she eloped with Graham Glass, a Harvard undergraduate and scion of a fine family. Their marriage lasted three years. After the divorce Bonnie had come to

New York and achieved a reputation as an outstanding photogenic beauty who was also an accomplished performer. Bonnie had been the dancing partner of Clifton Webb, but they were dissolving their act and Bessie Dudley believed Rodolpho could be Clifton's replacement.

Bonnie auditioned the young Latin dancer, concluded he was sufficiently professional to appear with her, and offered to start him at fifty dollars a week. Aware that he was being presented with a real show-business opportunity, Rodolpho hesitated only because this was less than half what he earned as a dancer at Maxim's. But Miss Glass was considered a headliner, and more important, the New York police, in a sudden turnabout, were frowning upon cabaret dancers. Even at Maxim's there had been scenes on the dance floors and at the tables. Police pressure, stimulated by the disagreeable persistence of influential reformers, had already succeeded in shutting down many of the cabarets. Graciously, Rodolpho accepted Bonnie's offer.

He opened with her at the Winter Garden. Later they performed at the Palace and other Keith houses in the New York area. As an established headliner Bonnie earned far more than her new partner, an economic injustice which soon began to rankle Rodolpho. Time and again he attempted to reason with her, to point out that he deserved more money, but Bonnie laughed off his complaints, and told him to leave the act if he was dissatisfied. After she took over the basement of the old Boulevard Café in 1915 and opened it as the Montmartre, however, she doubled the young Italian's salary to a hundred dollars a week.

Later that year, Bonnie closed the Montmartre and for a short time toured the Keith vaudeville circuit with Rodolpho. Upon their return to New York, she opened another cabaret, the Chez Fisher, on West Fifty-fifth Street. This business venture also proved successful but shortly, in the spring of 1916, Miss Glass closed the cabaret and announced her engagement to Ben Ali Haggin.

Bonnie told Rodolpho that Haggin was a painter but the

newspapers informed him that Ben Ali was worth at least ten million dollars. Rodolpho was stunned. The sum was enormous, almost beyond his comprehension, and with awe and disguised jealousy, he began to question Bonnie further. She suddenly displayed a prim, tidy aloofness and unusual reticence about discussing her groom. And she reacted with considerable annoyance when he asked if Ben Ali had a marriageable sister.

At liberty, a condition never enjoyed by an actor or entertainer, Rodolpho signed with the William Morris Agency and was booked into the Old New York Roof at Broadway and Forty-fifth Street, where he performed with several different dance partners at a hundred and fifty dollars a week. But luck continued to favor him. Joan Sawyer, who had graduated from her Gus Edwards "School Days" act, asked him to audition and hired him as her partner. Miss Sawyer was one of the few exhibition dancers who still commanded a good salary. When working cabarets, she insisted upon a percentage of the cover charges, which brought her income to a minimum seven hundred dollars a week.

Although Rodolpho was flattered at Joan's appreciation of his skill, he was disappointed over her flat refusal to cut him into her percentage. Standing against the fireplace in her living room, he could not help but admire her calm assurance and beauty. She was a classic brunette with soft dark hair and a fine aquiline nose. Quite impersonally, she buffed her nails until they gleamed as she expressed her surprise at his lack of comprehension. *She* was hiring him; his nervy concern over her earnings and the silly suggestion that he share in them proved how much he still had to learn. If she had been angry, if she had sworn at him, Rodolpho would have understood. But her calm, contemptuous rejection was deeply disturbing. Before he could find the appropriate words—for he was still having trouble with his English in times of stress—she wondered aloud if it might not be wiser to employ a less ambitious partner, who would be willing to contribute something to their act before he asked for a raise?

Her eyes challenged him to do the obvious: to curse her and stamp out of the apartment. But his training as a gigolo proved useful. He erased the tightness around his lips, compelling himself to smile before he laughed gracefully and strode across the room. Dropping to one knee, he took Joan's hands, brushed her nails against his lips and kissed her palm, then swore by God, country and mother that Joan was the dancer he had always wanted to work with. They would be good friends and she could transform him from a competent dancer to a true professional.

He despised himself for wheedling and begging, but controlled the impulse to slap this pretty but greedy young woman. The William Morris office had been enthusiastic about this opportunity to dance with Joan Sawyer; the waiting rooms of agents were filled with dancers fully as competent as he. By exercising strong control, he continued to talk happily about their future association until Joan Sawyer nodded and said that she was no longer angry. But would he please leave now? His presence was distracting. She wanted to look her best because she was expecting a guest.

The imperious tone of her dismissal was not lost on Rodolpho. Indeed, it made him aware that she had not been taken in by his sudden reversal. If she had seen through him, the only conclusion he could draw was that his manners still required polishing, his anger better masking. Whenever he had a moment, he practiced facial expressions before a mirror.

He danced with Joan Sawyer in the better night spots and theaters in New York City, Philadelphia and Washington. Upon their return to Manhattan after one such tour, Rodolpho boasted to his cabaret acquaintances that Woodrow Wilson had been in the audience at Washington and had enthusiastically applauded as he had led his partner through their waltz pantomime.

ACT TWO: SCENE FOUR

Then suddenly, one day, to Rodolpho's dismay, Joan Sawyer canceled their bookings, dismissed him and denied him admission to her hotel suite. When at last he managed to reach her by phone, Joan told him, in a voice so cold it froze the receiver in his hand, to forget her address, her name or that he had ever known her. The De Saulles affair, of course, was the reason.

Jack De Saulles had been a gridiron great, captain of the Yale football team in 1901. His father had been a major on the staff of Confederate General Polk and his entire family had distinguished social connections. In 1911, as a representative of the South American Concessions Syndicate, he had visited Chile, where he met Senorita Bianca Errazuriz, at her mother's immense estate at Viña del Mar, a suburb of Valparaíso. Bianca was the daughter of a woman so beautiful she was known as "the star of Santiago," and her beauty was held to be its equal.

Shortly after this meeting, Jack and Bianca announced their engagement and were married in Paris in December, 1911. Jack De Saulles returned to the United States and became well known in the business world as a member of the real estate firm of Heckscher and De Saulles, with offices in Manhattan. He also took an active interest in politics and, with his close friend William F. McCombs, organized the Wilson College Men's League, which grew to 72,000 members and actively campaigned for Woodrow Wilson's election. For his political work in Wilson's behalf, De Saulles was offered the post of Minister to Uruguay, but turned it down because he wished to devote himself to his real estate business. Jack De Saulles and his wife were handsome, popular and wealthy. They were frequently seen both in the sedate restaurants approved by the older social leaders and in the noisier, not so selective cabarets and clubs which provided entertainment for a younger and more restless social group.

According to Mae Murray's version of events, Jack had become enamored of her but she had kept their relationship platonic. Frustrated by Mae's resistance to his blandishments, De Saulles began to abuse his wife and made no effort to conceal his affairs with other women. In desperation, because she was lonely, unhappy and despondent, Bianca De Saulles began to frequent Maxim's, where she became acquainted with Rodolpho Di Valentina. From this point, personal interpretations of events and relationships differ dramatically.

Mae Murray claimed that Bianca and Valentino were in love, but that Bianca feared to bring divorce proceedings against her husband because he had a violent temper and would strip her of her huge fortune. Valentino swore, when he gave his version, that Bianca had no direct knowledge of her husband's infidelities, and as a friend who felt sorry for the unhappy lady, he had determined to manipulate Jack De Saulles into committing an indiscretion which would enable Bianca to sue him for adultery, the only grounds for divorce recognized in New York State.

On July 27, 1916, Bianca De Saulles sued her husband for divorce and named Joan Sawyer, Rodolpho's dancing partner, as corespondent. Principal witnesses against De Saulles were Annie Curtis, a cook recently employed by Joan Sawyer, Julius Hadamak, Jack De Saulles' former valet, and Rodolpho Guglielmi, who was identified by the New York press as a former dancing partner of Joan Sawyer.

On the witness stand Valentino talked freely. In fullest detail he told the court how he had escorted Joan Sawyer to De Saulles' apartment. He also claimed to have seen them together at the Narragansett Hotel in Providence, Rhode Island, and described how Jack and Joan had shared a drawing room to and from New York City.

With weighted irony Lyttleton Fox, the attorney for Jack De Saulles, asked if he did not consider that in giving such testimony he was doing his partner an ill turn?

"No, I don't think so."

"Are your relations friendly with Miss Sawyer?"

"They were friendly the last time I saw her. I don't know now. I volunteered to testify here."

On September 15, 1916, Bianca De Saulles was granted her divorce.

Ten days earlier, on September 5, shortly after Rodolpho's testimony had helped influence the court to grant a divorce to Bianca De Saulles, members of the New York City vice squad raided an apartment on the east side of Seventh Avenue between Fifty-seventh and Fifty-eighth Streets, near Carnegie Hall. There they arrested Mrs. Georgia Thym, the lessee of the apartment, and "Marquis" Rodolpho Guglielmi. The police officers had maintained an observation of the apartment for several weeks and, as reported by *The New York Times*, had acted "on information given by a witness in Narragansett Pier and a well-to-do New York businessman, who said he had been victimized." Assistant District Attorney James E. Smith, who led the raid on the apartment, informed a reporter for the New York *Tribune* that the well-appointed apartment with its heavy draperies, plush furnishings and large, suggestive oil paintings was "one of a number of places where blackmail has been practiced on wealthy New Yorkers."

An attempt had been made to serve Mrs. Thym with a subpoena, but this had failed, so the assistant district attorney had decided to accompany Detectives McGlynn and Duffy on their assault of the apartment to make certain that Mrs. Thym was served. The detectives pounded on the door and called out that it was useless for anyone to attempt an escape by way of the fire escape, since the entire building was surrounded.

Bolts were withdrawn and when the door opened the detectives were greeted by a nattily dressed young man whose attempt at nonchalance was not overly successful. When he was asked the whereabouts of Mrs. Thym, he replied that she had been out of town for three weeks. The detectives made it quite clear that they did not believe this and, still blustering, the young man told them that if they didn't leave he'd call the police.

At this moment Assistant District Attorney Smith stepped from the shadows and in a tone of surprise greeted the young man by name. "Rodolpho," he asked, "what are you doing here?"

The young man attempted to shut the door but Detective McGlynn's big foot prevented this. "Rodolpho hasn't been here since last May," the young man replied. "Now beat it."

As Smith later informed reporters, the detectives had preceded him into the apartment, where one of them had discovered Mrs. Thym hiding in a bedroom. Protesting their innocence and making reference to important public officers who would be outraged at their arrest, the two were bustled without ceremony to the assistant district attorney's office. Asked to elaborate about the questioning, Smith refused to comment beyond an admission by Rodolpho Guglielmi "that he is a bogus count or marquis, and he had made statements which, if true, are of immense importance in this investigation. He is a handsome fellow, about twenty years old, and wears corsets and a wristwatch. He was often seen dancing in well-known hotels and tango parlors with Joan Sawyer and Bonnie Glass."

To those who may be astonished at the assistant district attorney's emphatic condemnation of a wristwatch, let it be said that prior to our entry into World War I, such timepieces were considered as irrefutable proof of the wearer's moral degeneracy, far worse, indeed, than wearing a corset.

After this statement, the "marquis" was introduced to the members of the press but declined to answer questions. He asked permission to telephone a friend and, when it was granted, called police headquarters and asked to speak with Second Deputy Commissioner Frank Lord.

"I'm in bad, Frank," he said over the phone. "I wish you'd come down and help me out."

After the call the "marquis" informed the prosecutor "that he had dined with Deputy Commissioner Lord in the 'domino room' of the Café L'Aiglon, in Philadelphia, when Joan Sawyer was with the commissioner. He said Mr. Lord remained in Philadelphia three weeks on that occasion."

The reporters, smelling a bigger and better story, hastened to interview the deputy commissioner, who denied, then admitted that he knew the "marquis," though he couldn't recall where he had first met him. This admission made, Lord denied ever dining with Guglielmi in Philadelphia, and offered to take any oath suggested by the reporters. Yes, he had been in Philadelphia on one occasion with a party of friends, and Guglielmi had later entered the café and danced with Joan Sawyer.

"I would find it quite difficult to remain away from New

York for three weeks, as this fellow charges," Lord told the reporters. He added that he did not number liars and phony nobility among his intimates. "This afternoon he called me on the telephone and said he was Rodolpho. I didn't know him until he finally added that he was Miss Sawyer's dancing companion. Then I remembered who he was. I told him I was unable to help him."

After the arraignment, both Mrs. Thym and Guglielmi were ordered held as material witnesses. A ten-thousand-dollar bail was set and, unable to post it, both were taken to the House of Detention.

Ten days later, on the very day Bianca De Saulles was granted her divorce, Rodolpho Guglielmi was charged with "Misdemeanor, white slave investigation." His police file was numbered E4127. This file is still on record with the New York City Police Department, Bureau of Criminal Identification, but there is nothing in the folder, not even a disposition, to indicate whether Guglielmi was found guilty. Georgia Thym's folder is also empty. The New York City Police Department maintained two copies of records: those in the Records Room and those at the Bureau of Criminal Identification. All records in the Records Room prior to 1930 have been destroyed, those in the Bureau of Criminal Identification are supposedly complete. Yet both files are empty, and a perusal of *The New York Times Index* for 1916 and years thereafter reveals no disposition of the case, although the *Index* had noted Guglielmi's arrest in 1916 under "NEW YORK City, *Police Dept.:*—Graft Investigation."

The Guglielmi records could have been mislaid. But others relating to Valentino have also disappeared, which suggests that at some later date, probably between 1921 and 1923, when *Photoplay* published his "official autobiography," records that might have embarrassed the actor and the studio were removed from their folders. We must infer that (1) other biographers of Valentino were unable to account for Valentino's activity in 1916, or (2) they have consistently altered dates to conceal his unfortunate arrest and indictment. One, Beulah Livingstone, had Valentino arrive "in the screen capital of the world, in September, 1915." Robert Oberfirst, a more recent biographer, conveniently has Valentino in San Francisco in 1915. And Jane Ardmore, in her biography of Mae Murray, had Valentino "framed" by Jack De Saulles in 1919, when Miss Murray was filming *The Delicious Little Devil.* As Miss Ardmore relates Miss Murray's version of Valentino's plight, his testimony in the De Saulles divorce trial is moved from 1916 to 1919, a problem since De Saulles had been shot and killed by Bianca De Saulles on August 3, 1917.

Moreover, in her efforts to keep her dates consistent, Miss Ardmore had Valentino visiting Mae Murray on the set while she was acting in *Fashion Row* and he was starring in *The Young Rajah,* and telling her that Bianca had just killed her playboy husband. By this Miss Ardmore increased the span to five years, for *The Young Rajah* was filmed in 1922, five years after the death of Jack De Saulles, and Valentino was by then already married to Natacha Rambova.

For the rest of his life this arrest plagued Valentino and he made numerous but unsuccessful attempts to have mention of it expunged from *The New York Times Index.* After Valentino's death, an article by Herbert Howe, "The Last Days of Valentino," recalled that "at the height of his fame, the world kissing his hand, he could not forget the three days he spent in the Tombs prison of New York on a false charge. Pathetically, he showed me clippings retracting the libel. The retraction was small compared to the headlines that had damned him. He told me how he had been framed when he was the dancing partner of Joan Sawyer. I know he told me the truth."

If Valentino told the truth and there was such a retraction, no trace of it remains. And Stanley Walker, in *Mrs. Astor's*

Horse (1935), says of Valentino: "It was in this period, according to the records of the New York Police Department, that he became known as a petty thief and blackmailer."

Nineteen seventeen was a black year for Rodolpho. On November 19, Bianca De Saulles was to go on trial for the murder of her husband. Rodolpho realized it might be wisest to remove himself from New York before that date. He was not a citizen, nor had he applied for citizenship, and he could be declared an undesirable alien and deported to Italy. When he heard from a fellow dancer that a lightweight musical comedy, *The Masked Model*, would attempt to play its way across the country to San Francisco, he auditioned for a part and was hired for seventy-five dollars a week and traveling expenses.

Before he left, he attempted to communicate with H. A. Uterhart, who had been retained to defend Bianca De Saulles. The attorney curtly refused to see him and through his secretary explained that the case for the defense would be strengthened in direct ratio to Guglielmi's distance from the Nassau County courtroom. His presence would only revive interest in an old scandal and might prejudice the jury against the defendant. Mr. Uterhart later had his client acquitted of the charge against her.

With indifferent success, the traveling musical comedy played to small houses until it reached Omaha, Nebraska, where closing notices were posted. Luckily for the cast, there was enough money in the kitty to pay for day-coach tickets to New York. Rodolpho took his and exchanged it for a ticket to San Francisco.

Friendless, unknown, Rodolpho was greeted by two suspicious San Francisco detectives. Ignoring his efforts at friendliness, they frisked him for weapons and demanded that he give an account of himself. Fortunately, he had bought a San Francisco newspaper; he turned to the play advertisements and told the suspicious detectives that he had come to San Francisco hoping to appear in the Bronson Baldwin musical *Nobody Home*. He had not definitely been promised a job, he said, but when *The Masked Model* had disbanded in Omaha he had decided against returning to New York. Members of the defunct company had suggested that he go to San Francisco, give their regards to Baldwin and try for a place in the show.

Still suspicious, the detectives wanted to know what he intended to do if the Baldwin production couldn't use him. Rodolpho wiped his face with a handkerchief and told the detectives he had been trained as an agriculturist and would attempt to find work in one of the Italian vineyards. The actor's distressed sincerity made an impression on the detectives, especially when he explained that he had to look and dress as he did because he was a tango dancer. And he was overcome with joy when the *Nobody Home* company was able to use him in the chorus line to replace a dancer the stage manager believed to be defecting to Hollywood.

In the fall of 1917, Eddie Foy and the Seven Little Foys were playing San Francisco. One of Eddie's sons, Bryan—Brynie to his friends—took a busman's holiday and attended a matinee performance of *Nobody Home*. Among the dancers he observed a young man of agility and grace. After the performance Brynie went backstage, where Bronson Baldwin introduced him to the "count," for all Italian performers were called counts. The young men liked each other immediately and Rodolpho was flattered when Foy, whose reputation as a headliner was fully established, congratulated him on his dancing.

Nobody Home had been scheduled to close in three weeks and Rodolpho was nervous about remaining in San Francisco. After a performance one night he was introduced in the Palace bar to Norman Kerry, a young and increasingly successful movie actor. Kerry spoke enthusiastically about the opportunities for personalities in moving pictures. If one made a mistake, the scene could be shot again; one didn't even have to learn lines. The camera didn't emphasize the histrionic ability of an actor; what it did was record his personality. If the camera liked the actor's personality, success was assured, and the rewards could be fabulous.

Rodolpho was sold. All he needed now was a place to stay in Los Angeles and someone to introduce him to the moviemakers. Fortunately, the Eddie Foy Show was also closing in San Francisco and was booked to reopen in Los Angeles. Brynie Foy invited Rodolpho to come along and stay with him in his rented apartment on Sixth Street near the Elks Club.

ACT THREE
THE YOUNG MAN AS
AN ACTOR

THE SHEIK OF ARABY

I'm the Sheik of Araby.
Your heart belongs to me.
At night when you're asleep,
Into your tent I'll creep.
The stars that shine above
Will light our way to love.
You'll rule this land with me,
The Sheik of Araby.

LYRICISTS: Harry B. Smith and
Francis Wheeler
COMPOSER: Ted Snyder
PUBLISHER: Mills Music, Inc.
(1921)

ACT THREE: SCENE ONE

In Los Angeles his resources were whatever small sums of money he could cadge from Norman Kerry, who had greeted him with enthusiasm, and from Brynie Foy, openly amused that the money he borrowed was used to buy fancy neckties and cheap stickpins. And like every other unemployed actor in Los Angeles, by late afternoon Rodolpho was to be found at the Alexandria Hotel bar, at Fifth and Spring Streets. Five o'clock was the cocktail hour, and the free hot ham sandwiches were many an actor's supper. In the rococo lobby with its elaborate crystal chandeliers, ornately carved furniture and marble columns, producers clustered on the "million dollar" carpet to discuss big if-deals, and in the bar, directors, actors and actresses gathered to talk shop. The atmosphere was informal, even friendly, for cutthroat business maneuvers were usually undertaken in New

121

York. Everyone was reasonably well dressed and conversation was animated.

Through Norman Kerry's influence, Emmett Flynn had used Rodolpho as an extra in a ballroom scene in *Alimony,* whose leading lady was Josephine Whittel. For this he had earned the standard five dollars a day—less than he had generally received for dancing a set with a lady at Maxim's only three years before. No matter how sanguine he attempted to be about his situation, no matter what reserves of Latin optimism he drew upon, his prospects in the picture business seemed dismal. Life had become a begging for favors from arrogant little men, accepting handouts, cadging drinks and living off the free-lunch counter. These indignities convinced him he would have to turn again to dancing if he wished to obtain even a small measure of personal respectability.

Foy and Kerry were still being kind to him, but the time had come for him to stand on his own. He auditioned at Baron Long's Watts Tavern, a roadhouse frequented by some of the movie set, and was hired to dance the tango with Marjorie Tain. Thirty-five dollars a week was an indignity, but it was more than he could hope to earn as an extra. Besides, he received billing on the posters outside the tavern and in the fliers distributed in the streets by small boys.

For several weeks Rodolpho danced there, polishing old routines and working on several new ones. Then Brynie Foy telephoned a tip: Katherine Phelps, a dancer of some reputation, was to open a dance act at the Maryland Hotel in Pasadena and was looking for a partner. He had recommended Rodolpho, and Miss Phelps, who knew he had danced with Bonnie Glass and Joan Sawyer, was willing to pay him seventy-five dollars a week. He gave immediate notice, and at the Maryland Hotel opening, his assurance, grace and Continental mannerisms pleased the Pasadena socialites. Some of them were equally impressed by the coat of arms on a cigarette case he had bought in a San Francisco pawnshop.

At last he was able to move into an apartment at Grand Avenue and Fifth Street, just a short walk to the Alexandria. Steady employment renewed his confidence; the better salary enabled him to replenish his wardrobe. He was also able to pay for his own drinks at the bar and even occasionally buy one for an indigent extra.

The talk at the Alexandria turned more and more to the increasingly large sums of money the stars were earning. Mary Pickford had started at five dollars a day in 1909 for Biograph, when Marion Leonard was the highest paid star in the business at seventy-five dollars a week. By 1917, Mary was earning more than half a million dollars a year and had not yet reached her top. William Farnum had boosted his salary from a thousand to ten thousand a week. Billie Burke had once been paid forty thousand for five weeks' work. Stars were buying mansions on Adams Boulevard; chauffeur-driven Rolls limousines and sporty foreign tourers were in their garages. Some were even buying yachts.

A break in pictures often came overnight. The opportunity was always present; the break was just around the corner. The business was big, growing so rapidly that expansion plans were obsolete before they were completed. More and more pictures meant more and more stars.

On one such late autumn afternoon in 1918, Rodolpho met Emmett Flynn, whom he had not seen since his day as an extra in *Alimony*, and Flynn greeted him warmly. More important, he told Rodolpho that Hayden Talbot had just completed his script for *The Married Virgin* and had expressly suggested him to Joseph Maxwell for the part of the villainous Italian count. The role was his if he wanted it. Flynn was astonished at the young dancer's hesitation. But Rodolpho, always sensitive about his background, was reacting to the not unnatural fear of being cast as a slick foreigner—a treacherous gangster, foul blackmailer, disreputable gigolo. On the dance floor, in evening dress, he was a hero; to appear in *The Married Virgin*, to accept fifty dollars a week for work in an unsympathetic role—why should he be enthusiastic? Yet Rodolpho thanked Flynn and took the part. To play a Latin villain, whom the American audience would hate, was humiliating, but at least it would get him in front of a camera.

The Married Virgin was made under the direction of Joseph Maxwell, but the completed picture was not released because the cameraman and his crew had not been paid for their services and through court action were able to prevent the film's distribution. After this double disappointment Rodolpho next appeared in *A Society Sensation*, made at Universal by Paul Powell. Carmel Myers was its star and so assured of her position that she could afford to be tolerant to Rodolpho as he jockeyed himself into several good scenes before the camera. Actually, Miss Myers thought Di Valentina amusing and got him a twenty-five-dollar-a-week raise when he appeared with her in *All Night*, which was also released in 1918. *All Night* was not a notable success and failed to bring Rodolpho the acclaim he hoped for. Was he forever to be catalogued as a heavy, limited to portraying suave, sensual gigolos who thought of nothing but sex or blackmail? During the next months he turned down two or three thankless roles because they reminded him too forcefully of his last days in New York. But economic necessity finally compelled his acceptance of a few French Apache and small-time-gangster parts.

With such credits he would never achieve stardom; still, he was in the movies, meeting people and managing to get along. And 1919 started off as a better year because Mae Murray, whom he had known in New York, helped him get bit parts in two of her films—though he had to take a salary cut to a hundred dollars a week. In *The Delicious Little Devil*, directed by

Robert Z. Leonard for Universal, he played a European count. His next with Mae Murray, *The Big Little Person,* was a costume drama again directed by Leonard for Universal. In this he was badly miscast as an Irishman and Mae was so caustic about his interpretation that he thought seriously of fleeing Hollywood and either returning to New York or going north to San Francisco.

Rodolpho's next offer was as an Apache dancer in *Rogue's Romance,* under the direction of James Young. Of course he would be the usual butt for the hero, Earle Williams, a Hairbreadth Harry type whose sideburns were short, bowtie austere and double-breasted coat cut from good Presbyterian cloth. But he considered the role because he had never worked at Vitagraph before—and he needed the money. His cooperation and willingness to work harder than required impressed Young, who recommended him to Victor Schertzinger for a part with Dorothy Dalton and Douglas MacLean in *The Homebreaker,* for Paramount. He was not especially unhappy when his villainy was cut to one brief scene, so Schertzinger, too, was impressed, because he had not behaved like an actor when most of his footage ended up on the cutting-room floor.

The Homebreaker was completed by the end of April and Rodolpho was out of work again. May became June, and June July, and he was so heavily in debt he again considered returning to New York or San Francisco. Had fate doomed him to spend his remaining years licking boots for small favors? He would be better off a barber. In despair, suddenly tearfully homesick for Italy, he wondered if it might not be better for him to go to Rome. With his Hollywood experience he might be able to break into Italian pictures, where the polish he had gained in the United States might permit him to be cast as a hero. But this only plunged him deeper into despair. Italian films were undistinguished and primarily *macchistas,* portrayals of ancient Roman and Greek mythology, which demanded a Hercules-Ursus-Samson-like hero, and he lacked the physique suitable to a loincloth. The bald truth was that Rodolpho Di Valentina was getting fat. Also, in his letters to his family he had somewhat exaggerated his success; to return to Italy would be to admit to failure, and this he was too proud to do.

So deeply in debt that he was publicly insulted by his creditors, he appealed to his friends and to everyone he had ever worked with to help him. Finally, Paul Powell, who had directed the pictures he had worked in with Carmel Myers, introduced him to the industry's outstanding director, D. W. Griffith, then casting *Out of Luck,* starring Dorothy Gish and Elmer Clifton. Griffith, who was not immune to typecasting, offered Rodolpho the part as the villain, and since it was an opportunity to work again, and under Griffith, he accepted.

Shortly after the picture was completed, he received a message from Griffith to report at the *maestro*'s office. Perhaps, at last, he was about to get his big break. Griffith's last completed picture, *The Greatest Thing in Life,* was soon to open at the Auditorium, and all the great director wanted was for him to dance with Carol Dempster on stage in an appropriate prologue to the main attraction. Yet a call from Griffith for any sort of performance was regarded by most actors as a sign of favor, and without a second thought (he had borrowed ten dollars for a new pair of pointed patent leather shoes to impress the director) he accepted, though the offer was only one hundred dollars for the week's run. After a short discussion, impatiently endured by Griffith, he went into rehearsals with Carol Dempster. He prayed this might be the break he had been waiting for, and went more deeply into debt for a custom-tailored suit.

The audience's enthusiastic reception of the dance prologue inspired Griffith to extend the engagement to a three-week run, and shortly thereafter he engaged the team to appear at the Grauman Theater, where they interpreted a stage prologue for his *Scarlet Days,* a picture in which Rodolpho had hoped to get the part played by Richard Barthelmess. Both had auditioned for the role of the Spanish dancer, but Barthelmess had a better, more restrained film technique. Rodolpho's gestures and expressions were bravura; the Barthelmess' quieter interpretation won him the part.

Rodolpho continued to drop around for the cocktail hour at the Alexandria, where casting directors, alas, remained unimpressed by his successes in the Griffith prologues. He had also begun to visit the lounge of the Los Angeles Athletic Club—a good place to masquerade as a successful man among people who did not frequent the Alexandria lobby. Charles Chaplin would nod and even pause for a pleasant word, but there was nothing Rodolpho could do in a Chaplin comedy, and he knew that to ask the famous comedian for a day's work as an extra would be the surest way to make Chaplin ignore him in the future.

One afternoon at the Alexandria, when he was feeling especially low, Norman Kerry introduced him to Harry Reichenbach, who had come out of the carnies and circuses to become the outstanding Hollywood publicity man. He was currently working for Jesse Lasky. Aware that Clara Kimball Young was looking for several young actors to play opposite her in *The Eyes of Youth*, a former stage success, Reichenbach recommended Rodolpho to Herbert Sanborn, Miss Young's manager.

He would at first appear as a straightforward young hero, but the final scenes would reveal him as a professional corespondent in the employ of Clara's husband, who sought a divorce. Rodolpho thought rapidly. Reichenbach was doing publicity for Jesse Lasky; he was in a position to know something about the future movies to be made by the Lasky organization. If he took the part, Reichenbach would remember him, and if he turned it down, Reichenbach might think him uncooperative and unappreciative. So he accepted, though once more he was to end up as a villain. But because of a physical defect with which he had been born, a slightly cauliflowered left ear, Herbert Sanborn turned him down until Reichenbach came to his rescue, explaining that this was a minor matter for a makeup man to remedy. Besides, why did Rodolpho's left profile have to be photographed at all; wouldn't the right do just as well?

Although he was unhappy with his role, *The Eyes of Youth* was to have a profound influence on his career, though it was not released until November, 1919. Meanwhile, he was once again at liberty. Desperate for any employment, he appealed to Reichenbach. Sincerely sorry for him, Reichenbach was unable to get him even a day's work as a crowd-scene Mexican bandit in a Poverty Row western, though he did employ him occasionally, between August and September, to distribute handbills and strike notices for Actors' Equity at ten dollars a day. Rodolpho took the occasional work, and wore a broad-brimmed hat to minimize the chances of his being recognized. He had been in Hollywood now for two years and even the most optimistic evaluation of his career showed he had gone steadily downhill. He was penniless, in debt to everyone, unable even to find work as a dancer. Desperation prompted him to write letters to Bonnie Glass and Joan Sawyer, in which he begged for their help, but neither replied.

Then he received a letter from his brother, Alberto, saying that their mother had died. He wept over the news and thought once more of returning home, but he lacked even the fare to New York. He felt that he had been a bad son. In her letters she had urged him repeatedly to give up acting, which she and all good people in Castellaneta considered a shameful profession. But he had ignored her advice, and now he wondered if she had thought of him with affection and love as she lay on her deathbed. Inconsolable, he would not eat, and Kerry and other friends became deeply concerned.

But gradually his sorrow abated and his thoughts returned to his career. He began to suspect that someone had cursed him with the evil eye. He had learned to ride, fence and swim, to play tennis, bridge and golf. He had read books to improve his English, and studied a manual of model letters for all occasions, of value only because it helped him stave off several unreasonable creditors. Although food was the only pleasure left him, he was once more a hungry man reduced to eating, if at all, in the cheapest of restaurants. In an attempt to look more Nordic, he had shortened his sideburns and even grown a British moustache, but he shaved it off because his friends said it made him look like a floorwalker.

He wondered who could have cursed him. There could be no other explanation. On his knees, he prayed for relief from the evil eye, from the curse that had dogged his career since Joan Sawyer had dismissed him three years before. He prayed long and hard—but his prayers were ignored. Terribly hungry, out of sorts with everything, envious of everyone, he felt there was nothing left for him to do. That night, unable to sleep, he thought of suicide. His religious training had taught him that this was a mortal sin, but so was the evil eye. He wondered if the person who had cursed and bewitched him was being punished.

Upon awakening the next morning, he felt strangely refreshed and unable to remember when last he had slept so soundly. After a breakfast of water, he dressed casually and went over to visit a garage on lower Sunset Boulevard where Italian mechanics specialized in the maintenance of expensive domestic and foreign cars. He had been surprised to discover he had some mechanical aptitude; in borrowed coveralls he often helped the mechanics with simple adjustments, for which they bought him a meal or gave him some silver at the end of the day. Although money and food were important, what he enjoyed most were the occasions when they let him borrow a tourer, and he could drive through Hollywood for all his fellow actors to see.

One late afternoon, as he was driving a borrowed car along Hollywood Boulevard, he heard his name called. He braked the Mercedes and turned to see Dagmar Godowsky waving at him.

During a happier time in New York he had met her, the beautiful daughter of the famous composer-conductor, and now he learned that she was a successful actress under contract to Metro. He swore he had not even known she was in Hollywood, and it was a joyous reunion. She insisted that he look in at a dinner celebration she was attending that evening at the Ship's Café in Santa Monica, to honor the completion of Nazimova's *Stronger than Death*.

He hesitated, because she had not invited him to the dinner, but she whispered dramatically that Maxwell Karger, the general manager of Metro, would be among the guests. Karger was a good man to encounter on an informal basis. She also mentioned that Jean Acker, one of Nazimova's closest friends, would be there. As he drove back to the garage, Rodolpho wondered if he should go. He still had some good clothes left and his friends at the garage would lend him the Mercedes and advance him enough gas for the fifty-mile round trip.

In her autobiography, *First Person Plural* (1958), Dagmar Godowsky has recorded what happened that evening.

> We must have been twenty at table—the studio bigwigs....
> It was all very gay, and Maxwell Karger . . . was toasting Nazimova when I saw a boy gliding across the dance floor toward me. He was dark and handsome. . . .
> He arrived at the table beaming with pleasure and I started to introduce him, but Nazimova lowered her head and froze. Her little frame was rigid and she looked as if she were having a divine fit. The whole table took its cue from her and one by one they too lowered their heads in this shocking form of grace. My voice trailed off and so did Guglielmi's.
> Nazimova broke the tableau and thundered, "How dare you bring that gigolo to my table? How dare you introduce that pimp to Nazimova?"

Stunned into silence, Dagmar watched as he turned and fled the restaurant. Immobilized, she endured Nazimova's tirade, that he "had come to California to avoid a nasty scandal in New York," and that Bianca De Saulles "had murdered her husband all for the love of this young man."

When the tears no longer blinded him, he felt like driving the car over the nearest cliff. He decided against returning to the restaurant and throttling the vicious bitch who had made it impossible for him ever to appear again publicly. Was it only gossip that this talented Russian actress, who comported herself as if she were Titania, Queen of Fairyland, maintained a court circle of young ladies, whose presence was forbidden to all men, including her husband—who was neither her husband nor her lover? The De Saulles divorce and murder were now more than two years behind him. Would he be haunted by these events for the rest of his life? But if he drove off a dock or the palisades overlooking the Pacific, the mechanics at the garage, his friends, would be liable for the loss of the car. At most his death would mean a day's headlines, a rehash of the De Saulles affair, and perhaps the introduction to local readers of his arrest in the apartment of Georgia Thym.

For three days after that disastrous evening he did not leave his room. He lay on his bed, stared at the wall and dreamed of revenge against everyone at the table, including Dagmar Godowsky. Why had she invited him? Why had she been so insistent? Had she conspired with his enemies in New York? For three days and three nights he lived and relived the scene in the restaurant, trying in his mind to make himself the hero. There were moments when he felt triumph, but reality would always intrude to mock him.

Then he had a caller. It was Douglas Gerrard, a director whom he had known when he worked at Universal. Gerrard apologized for dropping in without an invitation. Would he attend a party at Pauline Frederick's? She had heard, was indignant and wanted to apologize for everyone in the restaurant. She wanted him to know that Jean Acker, too, had been stunned by Nazimova's conduct. She had wept on the phone to Pauline, and told how she suffered for him. Even Mme Nazimova must have regretted her intemperance, because the dinner had ended within minutes of his flight. Gerrard urged Rodolpho to accept the invitation and prove he had the courage to ignore a stupid insult.

Pleased that he had been persuaded, he went to Pauline Frederick's and spent most of the evening talking with Jean Acker. At Metro, she admitted with laughter, her value to the company was purely decorative. How clever of Metro, Rodolpho said, as he admired the young actress's dark-brown hair, her hazel eyes, her petiteness. And her salary of two hundred dollars a week.

They talked of mutual ambitions, discussed common interests and spent the next several evenings together. He called for her at the Hollywood Hotel, where she lived—and how he envied her this elegant address! Two nights later they rented horses so they might ride in the moonlight. That night they talked more of ambitions and Jean agreed it might be a good idea for him to change his name from Rodolpho Di Valentina to Rudolph Valentino. It was less exotic, and would be less subject to snide comment.

Additional significant conversation occurred while they rode their horses through Beverly Hills. It was reported on November 6, 1919, by the Los Angeles *Examiner:*

"Isn't this romantic?" Jean Acker asked Rudolph.

"Yes, but wouldn't it be more so if we rode to Santa Ana and got married?" he suggested.

"You'd better not be serious about that or I'll take you up," she said.

And he said, "I am serious."

It was that sudden. By the time he returned Jean to the Hollywood Hotel, they had indeed decided to get married the next day. A license was secured and the Reverend James I. Myers agreed to perform the ceremony at the house of Joseph Engel, the treasurer of Metro. A hasty wedding buffet was planned; and among the small group of guests were Mr. and Mrs. Richard A. Rowland. Mr. Rowland was the president of Metro. Jean Acker was fairly well known to the local papers but Valentino was an unknown quantity. The *Examiner* referred to him throughout as Rudolph Balentino.

Later Hollywood historians, whose primary task is to enlarge and ennoble all occasions, placed the wedding at the Hollywood Hotel and made it one of the state social events of the Hollywood season. In truth, it was a small wedding, with a little supper thereafter, and some few small gifts to the bride and groom. Shortly before midnight the newlyweds left in Miss Acker's car. Joseph Engel's home was at Hollywood Boulevard and Mariposa Avenue, a ten-minute drive from the Hollywood Hotel. Jean suggested that it was unnecessary to trouble the desk clerk about a matter better explained the next morning. She permitted him to hold her hand as they walked toward her room, even allowed him to insert the key in the lock and smiled as he opened the door and bowed. Then, as he prepared to carry her across the threshold, she skipped nimbly into her room and slammed the door in his face.

He laughed and rapped on the door but Jean put the safety chain in position before she reopened the door and told him to go away, because their marriage had been a horrible mistake. Bewildered, he listened as she explained that she had married him out of pity, not love. She wanted to be his friend, not his wife; she had to be at the studio early in the morning and she was driving there herself. She didn't want him to telephone or be waiting for her when she returned; she had a lot of thinking to do and she would get in touch with him when she could think clearly enough to discuss calmly the mistake they had made. So would he please forgive her, because she was very tired, very upset. Please, would he get his fingers out of the way because she didn't want to hurt him when she shut the door again.

Now he realized there were other hells still left for him to endure. Why, he was worse off than any cuckold, for a cuckold at least could say he had consummated his marriage. Cursing himself, he pressed his forehead against the corridor wall and remembered that she had only permitted him to kiss her two or three times. She had never responded ardently—not even after she had accepted his proposal, not even tonight after the ceremony. She had preferred just to hold his hand. Was this some sort of American joke, a peculiar custom of some strange religious sect, a special test to which she was putting him to make them both more ardent?

He waited for more than an hour for Jean to open the door. Several times he heard footsteps and ran up the fire stairs. At last he realized that she did not intend to open the door and in a moment of rage he pounded his fists hard against it, then ran down the stairs and into the early Hollywood dawn, where in the shelter of a palm tree he threw up his wedding supper and wondered how he would ever be able to face people again. If a man was a villain, those who might hate him at least respected him. A man could be a fool and there would be some who pitied him. But a man who had been locked out of his bridal chamber on his wedding night could only be laughed at, a hilarious freak unworthy of even contempt.

ACT THREE: SCENE TWO

Jean refused to see him, would not even speak to him on the phone or answer his letters. But shortly afterward he was offered a small part in a picture called *An Adventuress*, which starred Julian Eltinge, a famous female impersonator. When Eltinge had appeared in *The Countess Charming* (1917), he had made so elegant an appearance in his evening dress and had so obviously stolen every scene that it became somewhat difficult to find players of either sex who were willing to compete with the ambi-sextrous star. As a man Eltinge was handsome, as a lady stunning, and whether the story demanded he play a man masquerading as a woman, or a woman impersonating a man, his unmasking always delighted audiences. But a job was a job, and Valentino gratefully accepted the small, undistinguished part. A full stomach helped ease the pain in his heart.

He felt better after he talked over his marital mess with Douglas Gerrard, who advised him not to be concerned about public reaction; at some later date Jean Acker might come to her senses and realize how shabbily she had treated him. He also suggested that Valentino take an apartment and continue his attempts to see his wife. But such advice was difficult to follow since Jean was always out to him. Nor was he allowed access to the apartment of Grace Darmond, an actress with whom Jean spent much of her time. Indeed, she refused even to take his phone messages. Gerrard then suggested that he attempt to establish communication by letter.

On November 22, 1919, Valentino wrote:

MY DEAR JEAN:

I am at a complete loss to understand your conduct towards me as I cannot receive any satisfactory explanation through telephoning or seeing you.

Since I cannot force my presence upon you, either at the hotel or at Grace's, where you spend most of your time, I guess I'd better give it up. I am always ready to furnish you a home and all the comfort to the best of my moderate means and ability, as well as all the love and care of a husband for his dear little wife.

Please, dear Jean, darling, come to your senses and give me an opportunity to prove my sincere love and eternal devotion to you.

Your unhappy loving husband,
RODOLPHO

She did not acknowledge this letter, but with the holiday season close at hand, Valentino continued his attempts to effect a reconciliation during Christmas week. But Jean had left for Lone Pine to film *The Roundup*, with Fatty Arbuckle, and on December 20, Rudolph received the following telegram.

I CANNOT PROMISE TO VISIT CHRISTMAS. HEARTBROKEN, BUT WORK BEFORE PLEASURE. BE A GOOD BOY. REMEMBER ME EVERY SECOND.

JEAN

In 1920 Valentino played the same part in several pictures all
produced in rapid succession: approximately fifty feet of villainy
in *The Cheater;* a bit as Norman Kerry's villainous brother in
Passion's Playground; and in *Once to Every Woman,* starring
Dorothy Phillips, his old, familiar role as the Italian count with
dark intentions, though at a salary of two hundred and fifty
dollars a week. Then—exactly as Douglas Gerrard had told him
it would happen—Maxwell Karger at Metro offered him work
in two features. He would still have to play heavies, but the
pictures would be shot in New York, and Metro was willing to
pay him three hundred dollars a week, plus transportation and
expenses.

The Four Horsemen of the Apocalypse, by Vicente Blasco-
Ibáñez, was published in America in 1918, translated from the
Spanish. Most of its scenes were laid in France although there
was also an Argentine interlude. Briefly, the novel told the story
of Marcelo Desnoyers, who in 1870, at the age of nineteen, left
France to escape military duty. In Argentina he prospered and
married a wealthy heiress, and shortly before 1914, Marcelo, his
wife and two children returned to France. When the war began
he regretted his evasion of military service in 1870 and in an
attempt to erase his former disloyalty, asked his son, Julio, a
dilettante who excelled only in idle amusements, to enlist. Julio
refused; he considered himself an Argentinian, and thought the
war was none of his business. But eventually Hun atrocities and
his innate nobility compelled him to enlist in the French army,
and he met a brave death on the battlefield. The four horsemen
of the title were, of course, War, Conquest, Famine and Death.
The novel was an instant success. Critics hailed it as a panoramic novel of impressive power. *Publishers' Weekly* observed
that the novel covered "fairly familiar ground," but that Ibáñez
had succeeded "in creating a series of war pictures unsurpassed
in the literature of the times." *The Review of Reviews* was

equally laudatory: "A lofty and impressive piece of action which critics acclaim as the best novel dealing with the events of the war since 1914."

Although the failure of its war pictures had created some considerable financial problems for Metro, Richard Rowland was impressed by the sales figures of *The Four Horsemen* and believed he was confronted by a unique entertainment paradox: America was making every effort to forget the war and anything related to it, which probably explained the failure of Metro's war pictures, yet the novel's sales figures continued to rise steadily week after week. When forty sizable printings of the book were still insufficient to satisfy the demand, he attempted to buy movie rights.

An enterprising opportunist managed to get into Rowland's New York office and offered to sell him *The Four Horsemen* for ten thousand dollars and 10 percent of the picture's gross, but Jack Meador, a Metro press agent, who knew Ibáñez's representative, later explained that no one but he could possibly deliver the book. So the opportunist was paid a thousand-dollar commission and Ibáñez's true representative was offered thirty thousand dollars. By this time Ibáñez was in the United States and thought thirty thousand dollars was not enough. Rowland then offered a contract calling for twenty thousand dollars against 10 percent of the picture's gross earnings, and Ibáñez agreed.

Now that he owned the book, Rowland wired the West Coast studio executives to read *The Four Horsemen*. A studio spokesman telegraphed back that no one was interested in the book because it was about the war. Rowland retorted rather huffily that he had bought *The Four Horsemen* and wanted it made into a picture. The studio replied it would withhold judgment until it saw a script.

June Mathis, one of the best writers Metro had ever employed, was in New York at this time, and Rowland assigned her the task of preparing a script. He liked what she did, and asked her if she could suggest a director. Without hesitation she recommended Rex Ingram as young, adventuresome and creative. Rowland agreed to assign Ingram to the picture. He then asked her if Carlyle Blackwell, a successful leading man in pictures since 1910, who had always delivered performances that pleased his audiences, would be suitable to interpret Julio Desnoyers. But Miss Mathis rejected Blackwell in favor of a comparative unknown whose last appearance of any consequence had been the year before, with Clara Kimball Young in the third vignette of *The Eyes of Youth*. His name was Rudolph Valentino.

It is presumptuous to assume, as later fan-magazine romancers did, that June Mathis, a plain and not too attractive woman, had fallen in love with the man she saw on the screen. There is no evidence to support this romantic confection; rather, as one of the truly competent and perceptive professionals in the film industry, June Mathis probably merely appreciated a good performance and saw him as ideal for the part. Rowland agreed. He hadn't actually read *The Four Horsemen* and had seen Valentino only at his wedding. To the president of Metro, he seemed an unfortunate young man dogged by hard luck, but he trusted June Mathis' know-how, and Valentino was offered the part at three hundred fifty a week.

After Valentino became famous, the fans were told how Rudy had read *The Four Horsemen* in Spanish, written Ibáñez to insist that only he be permitted to play Julio, and that as a condition of sale Ibáñez attempted to write him into his contract. Valentino had then returned to Los Angeles at his own expense to plead with Maxwell Karger for the role, only to have Karger brush him aside, saying he was neither right nor ready for the part. And only in the nick of time had June Mathis invaded Karger's office to tell him that no picture would be made with her script unless Valentino portrayed Julio, because *she* had recommended and negotiated the purchase of Ibáñez's novel for Metro only to create the greatest film star of all time.

Valentino actually was still working in New York, but arrangements were made to complete his scenes so he could return to Hollywood, where preproduction work under Rex Ingram had already begun. What he was not told was that Ingram was highly critical of Miss Mathis' choice.

Valentino had heard of June Mathis but never had met her, and that a stranger should have believed in his ability—with no thought of personal reward—stunned him. Never before had he heard of such generosity. With tears in his eyes, he almost kissed Mr. Rowland's hand. Mr. Rowland was so embarrassed by this display of Latin emotion he had to leave his office for the day.

To Valentino's delight he was treated as an important actor by everyone connected with the picture and he responded with overwhelming gratitude. He worked as hard after hours as he did on the set. Meeting June Mathis, he promised to do whatever she suggested, and she secured prints and showed him what had impressed her in his role opposite Clara Kimball Young. Prior to this he had used patently stock gestures and grimaces to register various emotions. In his role as Julio she wanted him to underplay still more, to show restraint, to feel with his eyes and employ only the slightest movement of his lips.

When he revealed he was self-conscious about his scar and cauliflower ear, she told him not to be. In her interpretation, Julio Desnoyers was an athletic dilettante who did not have to be picture-perfect. Any such physical defects would merely add to his character. Aware and appreciative of the opportunity granted him, he was the most cooperative of actors. Considerate of his leads and supporting players, he never once quarreled with Ingram, even when photographed behind gauze—a technique employed by the director to enhance the fragile beauty of Alice Terry. And as daily rushes were shown in the projection room, it became increasingly evident to Ingram, June Mathis and John Seitz, the cameraman who was responsible many years later for *Lost Weekend* and *Sunset Boulevard*, that the scenes with Julio Desnoyers, even when he wasn't garbed as a gaucho or dancing the tango, were remarkable. In a freakish turnabout, it was decided to rewrite the script to focus more on the character of Julio. Rex Ingram proved himself a superior director by permitting his fiancée's role to be subordinated to Valentino's.

From the set, word was flashed to the movie magazines that a new star was in the making. Stills of Valentino dressed as a gaucho and polo player were distributed by Metro's publicity men, who also began to supply Valentino with a romantic background and a past more suitable to destiny's child. *Motion Picture Classic* had the distinction of being the first to acknowledge the new star. In its June, 1920, issue was an article by C. Blythe Sherwood entitled "Enter Julio!" Sherwood wrote: "He resembles both Dick Barthelmess and Rod La Rocque. His accent is a composite of Leo Ditrichstein's, José Reuben's, and Pedro de Cordoba's." The article was still feeling its way and lamely commented on how out of character it was for an American leading man to be "so immaculately groomed."

> One never thinks of an artist or an appreciator of art, as being also an appreciator of cravats and imported eau de cologne. . . . Yet this phenomenal youth cannot relinquish his fidelity to Arthur Symons, D'Annunzio, Dante, Wilde, Fokine and Caruso. . . . Valentino, with all his complexities, and because of them, is normal. He has the indolence of Endymion who would dream; the reverence of Dante who would worship; the vitality of Don Juan who would woo; the extravagance of Don Quixote who would exaggerate; the courage of D'Artagnan who would dare; the restraint of Sordello who would court in deed; the desire of D'Annunzio who would achieve; the strength of Vulcan who would excel; and the philosophy of Omar whose "yesterday is dead and tomorrow never comes."

To conclude the article—for Valentino was not yet a star and so had to be presented in some other area of artistry—Sherwood told the world that "Nijinsky asked [Valentino] to give him a lesson in the tango—this from the primiere [*sic!*] danseur of the Bohm-Diaghileff Russian Ballet!" Since Nijinsky became mentally disturbed in 1917 and was institutionalized for the balance of his life in 1918, perhaps this failure to master the tango had been the true cause of his emotional collapse.

Valentino was delighted. He bought the magazine in quantity, looked up all the names that were strange to him, and memorized them; and he wondered how soon he would be able to afford a mansion with a library stocked with shelves of leather-bound books. The only thing about the article that disturbed him was the reference to his heavy accent. He began to listen intently to Rex Ingram, June Mathis and Alice Terry, and in privacy he attempted to duplicate their pronunciation.

Although *The Four Horsemen* was a contemporary picture, essentially it was a romance set in romantic locales and marked by spectacular scenes of symbolism. The Four Horsemen, galloping through the sky over battlefields and a world torn by emotional strife, were realistic enough to strike at the hearts of moviegoers—a technique developed with much success by D. W. Griffith. As an artistic composition, the completed film was a superb achievement, with individual scenes of striking beauty and arresting composition.

Ingram was a meticulous director and Marcus Loew, Metro's principal stockholder, was understandably disturbed at news that the picture would take twelve and possibly thirteen weeks to film and might cost as much as three-quarters of a million dollars. So depressing a communiqué demanded an immediate visit to the West Coast studio, where he was shown completed sequences of the film. Truly impressed by its artistry, Loew still wondered aloud whether audiences would understand the symbolism. There was also the failure of previous war pictures made by the company, and it is not impossible that if Loew's visit had come earlier the whole project might have been abandoned.

But the picture was in the final weeks of production and to scrap it would have meant a loss the company could ill afford.

After *The Four Horsemen* was completed but not yet released, Valentino began to receive feelers from other studios. Good sense made him direct such inquiries to June Mathis, who handled them diplomatically. Because he took her advice so gracefully, she suggested that he get another solid role or two under his belt. She agreed he was worth more money now, but if he felt gratitude toward Metro, Rowland, Karger, Ingram and herself, why not wait until the picture was released and then permit Metro to make a generous gesture? Valentino agreed and thanked her. But he was terribly in debt. Did Metro really intend to use him again? If so, how soon? Metro did indeed, and before he could contract new debts, he was hustled into a feature role in *Uncharted Seas*, in support of Alice Lake.

Although Rex Ingram and June Mathis were convinced their final version of *The Four Horsemen* would be a success and greatly enhance the box office of his next picture, the studio was still unwilling to accept Valentino as a type capable of finding favor among American women. Would Mary Pickford fall in love with a Latin? Of course not! Metro did not intend to dilute Valentino's romantic intensity, but most studio executives doubted that he would ever be a star.

But he was so overjoyed at being put to work on a new picture immediately upon the completion of *The Four Horsemen* that Valentino did not even ask for a raise—nor was one offered. *Uncharted Seas*, directed by Wesley Ruggles, was a trivial tale of a shipload of gold-seekers sailing north to Alaska. Valentino was pursuing Alice Lake, who was pledged to another. Immediately he suspected that he was being given another villainous role, but this time, after a thoroughly gentlemanly courtship, it was he who won Miss Lake.

Although he enjoyed working at Metro and delighted in the various attentions shown him by the publicity department, he was nervous and visibly embarrassed whenever he saw Jean Acker. During the filming of *The Four Horsemen* he had attempted to speak to her when they met once by chance, but she had hurried away and he could not help but notice that she was headed for Nazimova's dressing room. Occasionally he passed the great Russian actress and occasionally she granted him a regal nod, but mostly she looked directly through him. Yet he was working, paying off some of his more pressing debts and contracting some new ones, for the potential of *The Four Horsemen* had become apparent even to Hollywood merchants and automobile salesmen, who were dedicated to keeping the film colony insolvent.

With awe, Rudolph would contemplate what could happen if the pictures proved successful, though he probably doubted this would ever happen. Metro's barbers and masseurs had made him a splendid figure in athletic garb, casual clothing and evening dress, and many of the actresses and women about town invited him to spend an evening with them. But he was well aware of blackmail and was weary of casual liaisons. But perhaps most important, he had developed a feeling that he could never succeed with another woman because he had failed with his wife.

If his career was in the ascendant, Jean Acker's was not, which lent credence to the studio grapevine rumors that Nazimova was considering him to play opposite her in *Camille*. Accounts vary, but it is probable that Natacha Rambova, one of the young ladies closest to Nazimova, suggested him for the part of Armand. She was the set designer for the great actress—her sets for *Salome*, designed more than forty years ago, would be hailed today as highest camp—and probably thought that Valentino, whose fame was soon to be realized through *The Four Horsemen*, would be an asset to *Camille*. At any rate, Valentino was soon offered the part.

In a publicity release dated April 7, 1941, distributed during the remake of *Blood and Sand*, with Tyrone Power in the Valentino part and Nazimova playing the role of mother, Nazimova reminisced:

> "I was hunting for a young man to play Armand in 'Camille,' which I was making for Metro, when Rudolph Valentino sauntered into my office," recalled Madame Nazimova.
>
> "I had already interviewed scores of young men, but none seemed to match my idea of a romantic star. Even Valentino didn't. He was fat and far too swarthy. His bushy, black eyebrows were grotesque.
>
> "Yet I saw that if he could reduce and pluck his eye-brows, he would be the perfect Latin lover. He did just that. He was so good in 'Camille' that he went from that picture into 'The Four Horsemen of the Apocalypse' and 'Blood and Sand.'"

It had been sixteen years since Nazimova had made a picture in Hollywood. Her fall from stardom had been dramatic; she had lost her money and her power, and possibly, too, her ability to remember the proper sequence of events. *The Four Horsemen,* of course, had been completed long before *Camille* was even begun.

Although Ray C. Smallwood was the official director of *Camille* and Natacha Rambova—Nazimova's most talented protégée—merely the set designer, it soon became obvious that Miss Rambova, a narcissistic young woman of glacial beauty and hauteur, was the actual director of the film. Miss Rambova subordinated everything to her sets, and no detail of production was too small to escape her notice and criticism. When the picture was completed, the only ones at Metro who liked what they saw were Nazimova, who dominated the film to the exclusion of all others, and Miss Rambova. Although Valentino immersed himself in his role and wept tears of real grief during the takes of Nazimova's illness and eventual death, his slicked-down hair, popping eyeballs and elongated penciled eyebrows made him look unworthy of even the three hundred fifty a week he was receiving.

The opportunity to work in *Camille*, however, had provided him with a daily opportunity of observing Natacha Rambova, whom he considered blessed with incomparable bearing, beauty and brains. She seemed to him the most aristocratic woman in the world, and long before *Camille* was completed he was thoroughly smitten. He asked everyone about Natacha, but discovered that no one knew much about her save she had once been a ballerina and interpretive dancer. Some said that with a name like Rambova she might be a Romanoff; others unkindly suggested that Valentino ask Jean Acker about Natacha—or perhaps ask Nazimova herself.

It is futile to tell a man he has fallen in love with the wrong woman, and in Valentino's case no one bothered. His evident infatuation amused Nazimova, who had teased him on the set of *Camille* about making love to her rather than Natacha. And at Metro no one believed anything would come of it. Even the press agents, ever alert to convert a glance of recognition into a raging romance, ignored it. Who could love an iceberg? Let Valentino indicate interest in any young star, and Metro publicity would show the world how towering and Wagnerian a romance it could create. But Natacha? Unthinkable.

During the filming of *Camille*, Paul Ivano, a Russian cameraman, introduced a young French writer named Robert Florey to Nazimova. In turn she introduced both to Valentino. Florey and Ivano became two of Valentino's closest friends. With Douglas Gerrard and Mario Garillo, another friend of Valentino's, they boxed, rode horseback, played tennis and risked their necks in a succession of secondhand automobiles that broke down at the most inconvenient times—usually at great distances from Hollywood.

ACT THREE: SCENE THREE

During the Christmas week of 1920, Valentino had his first date with Natacha. She had been breathtaking in her flamenco dress and he handsome indeed in a gaucho costume borrowed from Metro's wardrobe department. In eveiyone's opinion they were one of the handsomest couples on the ballroom floor of the Ambassador Hotel, and photographers had jostled each other to take their picture. Although Natacha would not permit him to take her home, she later invited him to visit her studio bungalow, whose walls were covered with her sketches. Never had he seen such compositions, such color! Surely, he had told her, she had to be Italian.

On another evening she had shown him preliminary sketches for *Salome*, based on Oscar Wilde's play, and brushed aside his mention of a widely held Hollywood rumor that Mme Nazimova intended to employ only homosexuals for the picture. On New Year's Eve he telephoned her and wished her the best of coming years, and she wished him the same. Then he accompanied Douglas Gerrard to a party, where he flirted with the girls and clinked glasses with everyone. Yet promptly on the stroke of midnight he silently toasted Natacha.

During these weeks, he nervously anticipated the release of *The Four Horsemen* and wondered what to do about his relationship with Jean Acker. His peculiar marriage no longer distressed him, but it was an increasing inconvenience. The young blond actress was no longer at Metro. Discreet inquiries revealed that she was feeling poorly, and not working. But the thing that could really have proven embarrassing never occurred. Jean did not appear on the set of *Camille,* and some said she was no longer in Nazimova's favor. But on January 17, 1921, all public and private speculations about Jean Acker's feelings were revealed when Valentino was served notice of her suit against him for separate maintenance. She was charging that he deserted her, had refused to live with her and had never supported her. Hurt to the marrow, she demanded three hundred dollars a month maintenance and fifteen hundred dollars' attorney's fees.

There was no shooting on *Camille* that day because of Armand's monumental rage. Furiously he thought of Italy (and all other civilized Catholic countries), where no woman would have dared bring suit against her husband. If there was a God, why wasn't Jean Acker struck down for her falsehoods? Why, they had never even consummated their marriage! How could she lie and say he had deserted her, when he had pleaded with her to live with him?

In his dressing room, he raged and wept and pounded on the walls and then went to Maxwell Karger, who was too busy to see him. News of his distress reached several of his friends, who gathered at the studio to dissuade him from rushing off to confront Jean Acker. As spokesman for all, because he was the coolest of the lot, Douglas Gerrard explained that this would be the worst possible thing to do. He advised an attorney, and suggested W. I. Gilbert as knowledgeable and sympathetic.

A late-afternoon meeting was scheduled, and after Gilbert had made some sense out of the distraught actor's discourse, he questioned Valentino about meetings with his wife, and evaluated some of the letters and documents Valentino offered in evidence. Before the conference was concluded, Gilbert instructed Valentino to continue to swear he had never consummated the marriage, and return to work at the studio. It was of the greatest importance to leave the matter entirely in Gilbert's hands. Valentino was not to communicate with Miss Acker, nor see her friends, nor discuss the case with anyone. Reporters especially were to be referred to Mr. Gilbert, who intended to file a cross-complaint for divorce.

Although he was not a practicing Catholic, Valentino hesitated. The attorney pointed out the obvious: there had never been a marriage. True, Rudolph could file for an annulment, but this might impel the court to ask questions best avoided by a man whose career lay just ahead of him. But if Valentino disagreed, he was free to consult another attorney, and there would be no charge. The unhappy actor said that he liked Mr. Gilbert and felt they could get along, but he explained that he had only a week-to-week arrangement with Metro. Gilbert assured him that he could be paid in installments, and that his immediate legal strategy was to file a cross-complaint and have the case moved back for at least six months. That would give them adequate time to marshal their defense.

On March 6, 1921, *The Four Horsemen of the Apocalypse* opened at the Lyric Theater in New York. The picture was scheduled for an indefinite run and the opening-night audience, most of whom were in the theater by invitation, applauded wildly; it was more than a success, it was a triumph.

The New York Times review the following day said that the film had "genuine cinematographic qualities. . . . Mr. Ingram must have devoted much time and thought to composition and in a number of instances he has achieved something different and better than materials at the disposal of other directors. . . . He has given fluidity and unity to his [scenes]."

The review was most pleasing to Metro because it established Rex Ingram as a masterful director: "The photoplay has been cast with the clear eye for types and acting ability. The characters used primarily to give color to the picture—South American natives—Spanish, French and German specimens—are all strikingly individualized and those who have the more extensive roles not only look their parts but act them intelligibly, especially Rudolph Valentino as the young Julio . . . the central fact remains that [the picture] is an exceptionally done adaptation of a novel, and an extraordinary motion picture work to boot."

The next day there were long lines at the Lyric Theater and Richard Rowland's desk was covered with telegrams of congratulation and requests for immediate bookings. The telephone lines between New York and Hollywood hummed. Rex Ingram and June Mathis and Alice Terry were heroes at Metro. And Rudolph Valentino had suddenly become a star. It should have been his most triumphant hour, but it was not. He still earned a mere three hundred fifty dollars a week and was heavily in debt; he was lovesick over Natacha Rambova, and dreaded the eventual courtroom confrontation with Jean Acker.

As if to confirm its first appraisal of the film, *The New York Sunday Times Book Review and Magazine Section* for March 27 carried an essay by John Corbin entitled "An Epic of the Movies," illustrated by a still of the four horsemen spread across the entire page. The article compared the film with the grand panoramic tradition of the Elizabethan theater. Corbin pointed out that though the World War was still too recent to be seen in perspective, the novel and its eminently successful translation to the screen showed "that the real war was fought in the souls of the contending nations. . . . 'The Four Horsemen' has drawn its inspiration from a novel, the work of a vigorous and untrammeled spirit. Yet such a result could not have been attained if the technical resources of the picture stage had not also been vigorous and untrammeled."

By the end of March, 1921, Metro could claim to have produced the most successful film of the year. Only Douglas Fairbanks' *The Three Musketeers* could rival *The Four Horsemen*'s popularity, but it could not hope to compare as a work of art. Whenever it was shown, the film played to capacity audiences; wherever it was reviewed, nouns were overburdened with adjectives. Theaters fortunate enough to have booked the picture reported outstanding grosses.

European critics expressed mixed reactions, however. The French thought it magnificent, as did the Italians. But Sir William Jury, who had the British franchise to import American films, refused to book it because he thought it would prove to be repugnant to the British public. Metro rented a theater in London, showed the film to packed houses and proved Sir William wrong.

Throughout his later career, even after his quarrel with Rex Ingram, Valentino always spoke with unqualified gratitude about every technician and actor associated with the picture. On its completion, he distributed gifts far beyond his means to the technical crews and dressers. But the praise he showered on his peers was not reciprocated by Rex Ingram. When interviewed by Aline Mosby of United Press as late as 1949, Ingram was quoted as saying that he "could have done the same for anybody. . . . Valentino was just a good-looking, lucky guy who copped a sensational role and a good cameraman . . . it was a surefire role of a Spanish gigolo . . . it would have made anyone who was cast properly."

There was no more than a week's rest between Valentino's work in *Camille* and his next Metro assignment, opposite Alice

Terry in Balzac's *Eugénie Grandet*, a June Mathis script. The announcement to the press and movie magazines was the occasion for a happy luncheon and, disregarding June's advice, Valentino took this occasion to ask Ingram to intercede with Maxwell Karger about an increase in salary. He now needed more than three hundred fifty dollars a week to make ends meet; now that he was a star he was saddled with expenses he had never counted on. With a surprising lack of tact for so urbane a gentleman, Ingram curtly told Valentino that such problems were not in his province. Hurt and surprised, Valentino apologized, and telephoned Natacha. Could he visit her that evening and get the benefit of her advice?

After a cup of strong black coffee laced with brandy, Rudolph unburdened himself. He had made a sorry error, she explained; with a lesser reputation than Alice Terry, he was receiving all the publicity. Ingram was naturally jealous for his fiancée's sake. She advised him to speak firmly to Karger.

Karger was courteous, agreeable, sympathetic—but unwilling to raise his salary. He even pointed out that if Metro paid him more, Jean Acker's attorney would probably amend the complaint upward. Besides, only one of the important pictures he had made under Metro's banner had been released. To conclude the meeting on a pleasant note, Karger suggested he wait for the release of several more pictures. Should he find favor with the public in these . . . Karger's office door was always open.

This meeting irked Valentino, and reporting his failure to Natacha only added to his humiliation. But she was gentle with him, and consoled him with a good dinner. Afterward, she urged him to speak without hesitation about his problems and ambitions, and about his future. Valentino admitted he had no concrete plan of action. Natacha was at no such loss, however, and curled up at her feet, he listened in awe as she explained how to make himself important to any future pictures. Patiently she repeated the most important laws of cinema survival, until she was certain Valentino understood them thoroughly. The best friend an actor could have on a picture was not the director, she said, nor the cameraman. No, it was the lowly juicer—the man who worked with the master electrician to light the set. By controlling the lights, the juicer could ruin an actor's appearance. Ingram used gauze in front of the camera when photographing Alice Terry to complement her fragility and make her appear ethereal. An actress's face was photographed to round out and soften the contours. An actor, however, must be photographed starkly or he might not appear masculine. To give him a practical demonstration, she made herself up and arranged several gooseneck lamps to show how angles of light could sharpen or soften, lengthen or shorten her features.

Suppose, Valentino suddenly asked, Metro decided to punish him? Could they instruct makeup men or juicers to perform acts of insidious sabotage without his knowing? Natacha laughed and told him not to worry—she would look after him. For the remainder of the evening she made him up in a variety of ways and worked on his cauliflower ear until she had achieved an effect that made the ear appear normal. This accomplished, she instructed Rudolph about what to tell the makeup people the next morning, and how to instruct Ingram about lighting him.

It was a new Rudolph Valentino who arrived for the first day's shooting on *Eugénie Grandet*. The old Valentino had been cooperative and anxious to please; the new one was nervously belligerent as he told the makeup man what he wanted. Then he surprised the dresser by wondering if the lapels of the nineteenth-century coat might not be too wide. Previously he had been concerned only that they be pressed. And before he even appeared on the set, he made a circuit of the lights and shook hands with every one of the juicers. Several of them winked knowingly; someone had evidently given Valentino the first lesson in the mechanics of survival. That day also marked the beginnings of friction between Rex Ingram and his new star.

Suddenly to discover that his pliable, pliant, cooperative actor had become infected with temperament disturbed Ingram. He had often said that those who had achieved stardom were not welcome in his pictures if they insisted upon behaving like stars rather than actors. Now not a day passed without Valentino indulging himself in eruptions of temper. Once Ingram actually walked off the set, stormed into Maxwell Karger's office and demanded that the picture be begun again, with another actor replacing Valentino. Karger suggested the irate director leave the lot for an extended lunch while he had a disciplinary talk with "the stupid Italian."

Uncertain and apprehensive because he knew the studio still considered Rex Ingram the superior asset, Valentino presented himself at Karger's office where he attempted an explanation: he merely wanted to do his best and felt that he should be encouraged rather than hindered by his director. Karger made a cutting motion with his hand to interrupt and told Valentino that the studio had decided to reward him with a raise of fifty dollars a week. He expected Valentino to return to the set, apologize to Ingram, who would also apologize, and get on with the picture. Valentino agreed but the fifty-dollar raise had not made him wholly happy. This "throw the dog a bone" technique, for which all studios were famous, left his problems far from resolved.

Valentino lunched with June Mathis that day, and was gratified; she considered the fifty-dollar raise a cruel and callous insult. Having made him feel better by thus speaking her mind, she smiled and suggested he cheer up. The picture would be finished in another week or two, and meanwhile she would act as buffer between him and the director. But she assured him that Ingram was too fine an artist to light or photograph him at poor angles. If there had been errors, they were regrettable but not deliberate. She then advised him not to rely too completely on Natacha Rambova, who was an ambitious, iron-willed young woman, extremely bright but determined to claw her way to the top. It was quite obvious, she added, that Natacha saw him as a rising star who might further that ambition.

At the completion of *Eugénie Grandet,* which was retitled *The Conquering Power,* Ingram was asked if he would undertake another feature with Alice Terry and Valentino. He refused flatly. He had patched up his quarrel with Valentino but would not deny that he would have preferred to scrap the picture and begin again with a young actor named Ramon Samaniegas—soon to be introduced to the public as Ramon Navarro.

Meanwhile, *The Four Horsemen* was proving a bonanza to the studio. Reviewers were tripping over their superlatives to praise the work of Rex Ingram and Valentino. But the movie magazines were concentrating on the young Latin lover, for his performance had inspired clamoring thousands to write to the studio and to the fan magazines for more pictures and articles about Valentino. In its April, 1921, issue, *Motion Picture* Magazine featured a full-page photograph of the new star and congratulated Metro for "efficiently cast[ing] Rudolf Valentino in their screen version of 'The Four Horsemen of the Apocalypse.'" The June *Photoplay* also featured three pictures of Valentino: one as a gaucho, another as Armand Duval emoting over Camille, and the third as an elegant young gentleman in modern dress, complete with homburg.

The Conquering Power opened in July, 1921, and *The New York Times* applauded Valentino for his "finished performance as Charles Grandet. He is a pantomimist of marked ability." Most reviewers agreed that Ingram's photography and feeling for pictorial mood were remarkable and they generally congratulated him for not slighting Valentino in favor of Alice Terry. But by this time Valentino was no longer at Metro. He had signed a five-year contract with Jesse Lasky, who had combined his company with Adolph Zukor's organization at Paramount.

The Conquering Power had been finished since the end of March, although there was some added work in April for retakes and inserts, yet Valentino had been unable to persuade the studio to give him another starring role. Karger had offered a contract at four hundred dollars a week, but Valentino demanded four-fifty. The difference of fifty dollars a week might have been bridged, had not Karger believed he saw the finely manicured hand of Natacha Rambova in the demand. In any event, he refused to increase his offer. But what he did not know was that shortly after the release of *The Four Horsemen,* Jesse Lasky had written Valentino a congratulatory note.

He had not followed up this letter, but one spring day, to his happy surprise, his secretary announced a caller—Rudolph Valentino. Valentino had told her he merely wanted to thank Lasky personally for his kind letter. Lasky instructed his secretary he was out to everyone but Mr. Zukor, then offered an attentive ear. Valentino talked briefly about Metro's commercialism, its unsympathetic producers and directors, the company's unwillingness to cast him in stories of his choosing or to allow him to choose his set designers and directors. As Valentino talked, Lasky was impressed by the vitality of the actor, the expressiveness of his eyes, the nostrils flared with emotion, the animal grace with which he moved about the office. Lasky rocked in his chair, and nodded as Valentino continued his tirade. Finally, Valentino told Lasky that he had asked for four hundred fifty dollars a week and Metro had refused. Lasky expressed surprise, then anger.

Dramatically he summoned his secretary and ordered her to draw a five-year contract at five hundred dollars a week—the salary to commence immediately if Valentino signed before leaving his office. He explained certain options that could increase Valentino's salary regularly until he would be earning a thousand dollars a week and more.

Paramount's legal department established a record by producing a contract in less than an hour. Valentino signed, and walked out of Lasky's office with a full week's salary—a bonus—

in his pocket. Lasky also put a studio limousine at his disposal. Leaning back in the seat of the long black limousine, Valentino regally gave his destination to the uniformed chauffeur through the speaking tube.

Jubilantly, Valentino bounded into Natacha's bungalow, and waved the signed Paramount contract and check. She did her best to respond to his enthusiasm, but told him she regretted not having known that he had intended to see Lasky. He should have asked at least a thousand dollars a week. Finally she relented and they celebrated by having dinner at the Ship's Café in Santa Monica, the very place where Nazimova had cruelly insulted him. And to prove that she approved of his actions, even though he had not consulted her, Natacha permitted him, for the first time, to kiss her good night.

ACT THREE: SCENE FOUR

Meanwhile, Lasky deliberated how best to utilize his new star. To make another gaucho picture might be returning to the same well too soon. And Lasky had another problem: a recent company edict which placed a ten-thousand-dollar ceiling on the purchase of any new story properties. Yet how could he find a property as outstanding as Ibáñez's *Four Horsemen* that could be bought for ten thousand dollars? Suddenly he had an inspiration. The ideal property was already owned by Paramount; Valentino could be cast as Sheik Ahmed Ben Hassan in E. M. Hull's sensational novel *The Sheik*.

When it was first published in England, reviewers considered it a paltry tale without merit, but word of mouth had sold more copies of *The Sheik* than any favorable review could have. The discovery, by the British public, that the initials E. M. stood for Edith Maude had created a national sensation. That an English *maiden* lady had written a novel that for more than two-thirds of its torrid pages dealt with a miscegenetic love affair between an English noblewoman and a dusky Arabian rocketed sales until the book became an all-time best seller. Between the English edition by Small, Maynard and the American edition by A. L. Burt, *The Sheik* had sold over 1,200,000 copies.

As book sales of *The Sheik* continued to soar, English reviewers were begrudgingly compelled to grant some attention to a novel conservatively described as a *succèss de scandale,* and even as *le grande scandale de tout le monde.* French was used to describe this shocking book because it was deemed the fittest for pornography. True, no "words" had been used, but neither had they in *Fanny Hill.* What mattered was that a maiden lady of sound English schooling and background had written of illicit passion and its enthusiastic acceptance by another British lady. Furthermore, Miss Hull had described these in such fulsome detail that the British public felt compelled to buy *The Sheik* if only to keep it out of the bookshops, where it might fall into the hands of innocent youths and maidens. Once purchased, *The Sheik* was read behind closed doors in hundreds of thousands of British homes.

So great a success could not be overlooked. In March, 1921, the American edition appeared and proved that Americans were fully as immoral as their British cousins. The book was an immediate success. *The Book Review Digest* of 1921 synopsized the plot well enough:

> Diana Mayo is a young English girl, self-willed and fearless. When she plans a tour into the desert, unchaperoned, and with only natives in attendance, neither her friends nor her brother can dissuade her. So she starts, but very shortly is captured by the Sheik, an Arab chieftain with no standards of morality save those of a caveman. His caveman treatment of

her, however, wins her, for after a few months of agonizing
and despair, she suddenly finds herself desperately in love
with him, and only fearful lest she may have to leave him.
Incidents of her attempted escape and return, her capture by
a hostile tribe and her thrilling rescue, add to the lurid atmosphere of the story.

The Book Review Digest did not, of course, reveal that Sheik
Ahmed Ben Hassan was really Viscount Caryll, Earl of Glen-
caryll, and thus Lady Diana did not actually have to marry a
man of inferior national stock. How he had come to be a desert
sheik is explained only at the end of the novel, long after he has
abducted and raped Lady Diana. But because the French were
known to be much more liberal about racial attitudes, Miss Hull
set her story in the French Sahara.

American reviews were kinder than the British. The Boston
Transcript thought it ". . . entertaining in description and episode. It does not lack thrills." *The Literary Review* agreed that
". . . the story has undeniably vivid scenes of dramatic value,"
but asserted that "the central idea of it stands out, poisonously
salacious in conception. It is not prudery to stamp it as vicious."
The review compared the Lady Diana Mayo with Justine, the
evil heroine created by the Marquis de Sade. *The New York
Times* also had a mixed review, saying that ". . . outside the
shocker-appeal it must be admitted that the novel is written with
a high degree of literary skill in so far as the handling of incidents and suggestion of the reality of the characters involved is
accomplished," but that "such a story, viewed from a sane literary standpoint, is preposterous."

Overwhelming as it was, the novel's British success could not
compare with its bedazzling success in the United States. Despite a prim statement released by an official of the British Em-
bassy in Washington, who took an oath that no proper white lady
would have anything to do with a "wog," even an educated one,
the American presses were hard put to fill the flood of orders
placed by bookstores.

Walter Wanger claims to have "first proposed *The Sheik* to Paramount [and] they were shocked, as a love story between a white woman and an Arab was considered too radical." But although Paramount turned down his suggestion, Wanger had, in order to get a woman's reaction, given *The Sheik* to Jeane Cohen, who was Jesse Lasky's secretary. According to Lasky, the book "left her quivering," and she pleaded with him to read it immediately and buy it for the company. Reading was not a chore Mr. Lasky was willing to undertake, especially since Paramount employed readers at twenty-five dollars a week to compress dexterously the gist of a four-hundred-page novel into a two-page synopsis. He had always depended upon such capsule reports, but there were times when he was too busy even to read a few typewritten pages. So when Miss Cohen continued to press, Lasky instructed her to get one of the girls in the story department to tell it to him.

Miss Cohen arranged for one of the more skilled readers, Julia Herne, to prepare an oral outline. Miss Herne skimmed the volume, which is easy to do, and recounted the story to Mr. Lasky with dramatic verve. Her enthusiasm for the scenes of love, passion and conflict was unrestrained, and she, too, swore that a picture based on the book would captivate every woman in America. Most impressed, Lasky instructed Julia Herne to go out to the lot and tell the story to George Melford, one of the more prominent directors under contract to Paramount. Melford listened to the story and phoned Lasky to buy it.

The Sheik, a really hot book, would certainly have been grabbed up much earlier had it not featured a love affair between a white woman and a man whom Diana's brother, Sir Aubrey, had "indiscriminately class[ed] . . . as a 'damned nigger.' " Moreover, Miss Hull insisted that she be paid $12,500. But in spite of the new company edict, Lasky purchased the novel, though later he admitted that he hadn't known what to do with it. None of the Paramount stars could portray "a passionate desert savage. . . . Wallace Reid was too much the good-natured big-brother type, Rod La Rocque too suave and sophisticated, and Thomas Meighan seemed far too wholesome. Jack Holt was two-fisted and a good rider, but the role didn't suit him either—or anyone else we had under contract. We had to lay the story aside and I forgot about it in the press of things."

But now he wrote June Mathis, recently come over from Metro, a memo to whip up a script that could be put into immediate production by George Melford. Agnes Ayres was assigned the role of Diana Mayo, Adolphe Menjou was given the part of Vicomte Raoul de Saint Hubert, and Valentino, of course, would play the Sheik. Valentino was ordered to report to the studio for wardrobe fittings and instructed to polish up on his horsemanship. He was also told to prepare himself for hot weather in Buttercup Valley, a desert area near Yuma, Arizona, which could easily pass for the Sahara.

The new star was ecstatic. He had a five years' contract and the studio had immediately proved its good faith by giving him the title role in one of the best-selling novels of the year. Furthermore, he was delighted with the book, especially the scenes of derring-do, which had been marked up for him by a reader. An Arab chieftain, later revealed to be an English lord, was a real elevation of character.

Once more a studio limousine drove him to Natacha's bungalow, where her reactions upset him. Her delight over his being put to work so quickly was evident, yet she had read at the novel and considered it pure trash. She laughed disdainfully at the psychological motivations of Miss Hull's pathetic puppets, and predicted the picture would end Valentino's film career. He would be whistled at and hooted off the screen.

Every argument he offered was refuted by Natacha. She shook her head when he insisted that Paramount would not drop him if the picture was a failure because Mr. Lasky had spoken of future projects—among them *Blood and Sand*. This novel Natacha approved, and her parting words were that he should telephone Mr. Lasky in the morning and inform him of his willingness to appear only in *Blood and Sand*.

Shortly thereafter, an apprehensive Valentino left for location. But as the shooting progressed he wrote glowingly to Natacha about the scenario that had been turned in by Monte Katterjohn (June Mathis had begun work on *The Sheik*, had found the book not to her liking and asked to be relieved of the assignment) and how enthusiastic George Melford was over his daily performances. Natacha still offered no encouragement.

Interest in *The Sheik* continued to build and a studio press agent was assigned as a buffer between Valentino and the press. The completed picture pleased everyone at Paramount except Cecil B. De Mille, who was shown the film at Lasky's request. Later, in his *Autobiography* (1959), De Mille related how he had written Lasky, saying that *The Sheik* was "a very stupid, uninteresting picture, with not a moment of reality, and it bores one throughout. . . . There are some of the most beautiful shots of Arabs riding for so long that I would take little naps and wake to find them still riding." De Mille also "offered to bet Jesse $50 that the picture would be a failure."

Valentino was granted several weeks of rest after he completed *The Sheik*, a holiday he was unable to enjoy because of Jean Acker's impending lawsuit, for he had a southern Italian's native distrust of all law courts. Most evenings he spent with Natacha, who gave him considerable advice about how to handle himself during interviews. During the day he was seen often in restaurants, or on horseback or at the tennis courts with Douglas Gerrard, Robert Florey and Paul Ivano. At the studio he repeatedly begged to appear in *Blood and Sand*, but cleverly, Paramount held the Ibáñez novel out as bait. Meanwhile, they cast him in *Moran of the Lady Letty*, a novel written in 1898 by Frank Norris in the style of Jack London. In this seafaring story, Valentino played a young man about town who was shanghaied aboard the *Lady Letty,* where he promptly fell in love with Dorothy Dalton—Moran—the daughter of the kindly captain.

George Melford directed this saga of the sea, and went out of his way to assure the still nervous young star of the studio's enthusiasm for him. But Melford also offered some advice: Natacha Rambova, Melford suggested, was after all only human and therefore fallible. It was fine to talk of quality and artistry and poetic imagery, but if no one came to view the results, then what? An artistic flop was no credit to anyone. Melford knew how Valentino felt about Natacha, but facts were facts. He ended these paternal remarks by a reminder that the reviews of *Camille,* which had just been released, were something less than enthusiastic. Natacha's sets had received more notice than Valentino's performance.

If Melford's friendly advice had any effect on Valentino, it wasn't noticeable. Natacha's influence was very much in evidence in Valentino's daily comments on the sets, costumes, lighting, camera placement and just about every other phase of *Moran of the Lady Letty.* It was not an easy film to make. Nevertheless during this period Jesse Lasky voluntarily raised Rudolph Valentino's salary to seven hundred dollars a week.

But even this was not an unmixed blessing, for Jean Acker immediately increased her demands. The suit was scheduled for October 25—just a few days before the Los Angeles release of *The Sheik*—but Neil McCarthy, Jean's attorney, asked for a postponement because his client was ill and in the hospital. However, he did ask one hundred fifty dollars a week in alimony, retroactive to Jean's filing of her separation suit in January, and suggested that Valentino be responsible for his wife's hospital expenses.

Judge Thomas O. Toland ordered Valentino to pay his estranged wife for the period from January 17 to October 17, but advised Mr. McCarthy of his dissatisfaction with Miss Acker's conduct: "Do not consider any social function in your alimony request. There will be no allowance given for pajama parties. As for the amount listed as necessary for food, it's too high. It's extravagance." Taking his cue from Judge Toland's attitude, Valentino's lawyer charged Jean Acker with feigning an illness in order to engender sympathy. Judge Toland considered this speculation on Mr. Gilbert's part, then said he would appoint a reputable physician to visit her and report to the court. He set the next hearing for November 13, at which time a firm trial date would be set.

On Sunday, October 30, 1921, the Los Angeles *Examiner* and other local newspapers carried a striking ad in the theatrical section:

JESSE L. LASKY
presents
"THE SHEIK"
with
AGNES AYRES and RUDOLPH VALENTINO

Valentino was featured in Arab garb sweeping Agnes Ayres from her horse to his, and copy advised the public to "Shriek for the Sheik Will Seek You Too!!"

SEE
the auction of beautiful girls to
the lords of Algerian harems.

SEE
the barbaric gambling fete in the
glittering Casino at Biskra.

SEE
the heroine, disguised, invade the
Bedouins' secret slave rites.

SEE
Sheik Ahmed raid her caravan
and carry her off to his tent.

SEE

her captured by bandit tribesmen
and enslaved by their chief in his
stronghold.

SEE

the Sheik's vengeance, the storm
in the desert, a proud woman's
heart surrendered.

SEE

matchless scenes of gorgeous
color, and wild free life and love
in the year's supreme screen
thrill—3000 in the cast.

The *Examiner*'s review, by Doris Anderson, was headlined:
" 'SHEIK' FULL OF HIGH TENSION." Miss Anderson wrote: "It is
a courageous dramatist who sets his play of evanescent human
emotions and petty passions against the silent drama of desert
spaces. . . . George Melford dared that possibility. . . . He has
taken a drama of adventure and passion and made it seem consequential instead of absurd." The review praised "the vivid char-
acterizations of Rudolph Valentino as the Sheik. This young
actor, with his Latin subtlety and verve, blazes to sudden rage
with impressive conviction and as readily flashes white teeth in
nomadic frankness. His performance is vibrant and responsive to
every innuendo of his role." Miss Anderson, however, thought
Agnes Ayres' portrayal "drab and irritatingly unemotional
against this foil of Valentino's personality."

The film also inspired Tin Pan Alley, and the most successful
of the many songs published hard on the release of the picture
was "The Sheik of Araby," with lyrics by Harry B. Smith and
Francis Wheeler and music by Ted Snyder, a song that for the
rest of his life set Valentino's teeth on edge.

Libraries suddenly began to report record withdrawals of
books about Arabia and Arabs; police sought hundreds of run-

away girls whose destination was reported to be the Sahara; and women neglected their homes and flocked to the picture, even engaged in contests to determine who could see *The Sheik* most often. Women sighed, breathed heavily, gasped as Valentino swooped Agnes Ayres into his arms and kissed her, kissed her, kissed her, while his eyes burned with the pure flame of passion. How he scoffed at convention and disdainfully thrust a woman aside after he had used her! Sighing in their kitchens, parlors and bedrooms, American women longed for burning sands closer to home, demon lovers whose hot kisses seared their lips as strong fingers tore at their pretties.

Meanwhile, Jesse Lasky, Adolph Zukor and Charles Eyton, general manager of the West Coast studio, struggled with the problem of how best to manage their new star. The hero worship of movie fans was always appreciated by producing company, distributor and exhibitor. It was what made stars. But one of the unfortunate side effects seemed to be the emptying of the star's head of reason. It was decided, finally, that the dilemma could best be handled by the quiet introduction of more publicity people, who would be charged with control over all of Valentino's interviews, at least until his divorce trial was behind him. The studio executives in Hollywood assured their young star they wished him well in his ordeal and hoped he would receive justice in the courtroom. But New York executives telephoned him more concrete good wishes; they wanted to raise his salary to one thousand dollars a week for the remainder of the year if he would negotiate a new three-year contract. Overwhelmed by the continuing generosity of Famous Players-Lasky, Valentino agreed. The studio suggested he be represented by an established agent, so he employed the agency of Robertson and Webb to renegotiate a contract which would pay him $1,250 a week for 1922, $2,000 a week for 1923 and $3,000 a week for 1924. Everyone was delighted, especially Valentino, who immediately bought another used runabout from the mechanics who had first befriended him. He would take another off their hands within the next few weeks. Why shouldn't a star have three automobiles?

On Monday, November 14, 1921, the principals in Guglielmi *vs.* Guglielmi met again before Judge Toland in a preliminary hearing. Judge Toland set November 23 as the date for trial.

On November 23, a visually nervous Valentino appeared in court, convinced that his successful young career was about to be destroyed by certain portions of his wife's testimony. Jean Acker was sworn in first, and told the court how on January 10, 1920, after she had returned from film location at Lone Pine, she had gone directly to her apartment in Hollywood, which she rented from Mrs. Alice Johnson, actress Grace Darmond's mother. Under questioning by Neil McCarthy, her attorney, she introduced her first damaging accusation. "I was taking a bath," she told the jammed courtroom. "He came into my apartment and started hammering on the bathroom door, threatening to break it down unless I opened it. So I opened the door, we argued; he hit me with his fist and knocked me down."

The reporters and spectators reacted with such audible delight that Judge Toland had to use his gavel. He issued his first warning, and at a gesture from the bench, Miss Acker continued:

"After he knocked me down," she said, "he seemed sorry. My face was swelling from the blow. It was the first time anyone had struck me. I cried.

"He relented, begged for forgiveness, and I dressed and went down to the lobby of the apartment house with him.

"And then he told me he didn't want to be married to me any longer and intimated that he'd like to have me frame up divorce evidence. I refused. I was ill at the time. He said he'd always be my dear friend, but he didn't want to be my husband.

"In the heat of anger I told him I was going to Reno to get a divorce. He said that suited him fine. 'I have a future,' he said, 'and I don't want any woman hampering my career.'

"That was on January 10, 1920. I'd just returned from location, and so had he, although we'd been in different sections of the country."

Miss Acker appeared ill and distraught. She required several minutes to compose herself. Although Valentino had struck her brutally, she continued, the next day she had been compelled to go to him and ask for money because "I was not well and out of funds. He said he'd loan me money but wouldn't give me a penny." This had upset her so that a week later, on January 18, she had filed her suit for separate maintenance, asking three hundred dollars a month alimony and fifteen hundred dollars in attorney's fees. Under cross-examination by Mr. Gilbert, it was established that Miss Acker was twenty-five years old, had gone on the stage at the age of eighteen, and at the time she filed her suit was earning between one hundred fifty and two hundred dollars a week. When the proceedings were adjourned for the day, Valentino was visibly relieved.

The next day Grace Darmond appeared on the stand and corroborated Miss Acker's account of the assault. Miss Darmond, who occupied an apartment in the same building as Miss Acker, had heard the quarrel. The verbal commotion, she reported, was followed by the sound of someone hitting the floor. Mrs. Alice Johnson, following her daughter, told the court that Valentino had "called at the house, asked for his wife, and when I told him she was upstairs he pushed me aside and went upstairs. He was very angry. I heard them quarreling and said it must stop. I saw her red and swollen face subsequently." Miss Acker then returned to the stand and at the invitation of her attorney offered some philosophy on the subject of what a man owed a woman when he made her his wife.

"I did not marry him for money," she told the court, "I married him simply because I loved him. I thought when a man married he was in a position to take care of his wife. When I married my husband I did not know he was so broke and he was. . . . I wanted to make a man of him. I did not want him at my hotel, supporting him, until he received work. I wanted him to go to work. I gave him money, underwear and clothes. I was not going to take him into the [Hollywood] hotel to embarrass me, marrying a man like that. He was unknown then."

Although Valentino writhed and protested to his attorney that Jean had never lived with him or given him anything—certainly not money, underwear or clothes—Mr. Gilbert appeared to be quite pleased with Miss Acker's testimony. Mr. McCarthy, on the other hand, had now to undertake extensive courtroom engineering to get his client out of a quagmire of her own creation. Jean Acker had talked too much.

Cross-examining again, Mr. Gilbert asked the young actress a pointed question. "After you fed him up and curried him, you were willing to put him on exhibition?" The question was deemed irrelevant and Mr. Gilbert started another line of interrogation. Why had she not permitted her husband to visit her when she had been on location at Lone Pine? He established that Valentino had spent at least a hundred dollars on telegrams, pleading with her to see him, but that she had rejected his pleas. To prove that this was the case, Gilbert entered into exhibit two telegrams sent by Jean to her husband.

The first was dated December 29, 1919, and sent from Del Monte, California:

IMPOSSIBLE TO SPEND NEW YEAR'S WITH YOU. LEAVING TUESDAY AFTERNOON FOR VACATION. WILL WIRE ADDRESS WHEN ARRIVE. AWFULLY DISAPPOINTED. CAN'T BE HELPED. MY LOVE. PHONE ME AT 10 TONIGHT.

JEAN

The second was sent from Mojave, California, on January 16, 1920:

WIRE AND TELEPHONE CALLS VERY SWEET, BUT LETTERS EN-
TIRELY TOO SARCASTIC. MAKE YOUR OWN PLANS FOR EAST AND
ADVISE STRONGLY YOU DO NOT COME AS I AM WORKING MUCH
TOO HARD TO ENTERTAIN ANYONE, AND HOTEL ONLY HAS
ROOM FOR THE COMPANY.

JEAN

Mr. Gilbert then pointed out that Grace Darmond had been permitted to visit Valentino's wife at the Lone Pine Hotel. Miss Acker's explanation stirred laughter among the spectators: there were only two beds in the hotel room, she said, and moreover, it was an unwritten rule that husband and wife should not visit each other on location. Asked if she could furnish any evidence of this unwritten rule, Miss Acker could not. Valentino's attorney then asked her to tell the court specifically what support she had given her husband. Miss Acker replied that he had used too much of her expensive perfume.

A wise judge knows when he has heard enough. He would see the litigants the following day.

The next morning, Miss Acker's attorney introduced two surprise witnesses—Maxwell Karger, the Metro executive, and his wife. If Karger owed Valentino anything, the actor's leaving for Paramount had canceled the debt. But to Valentino's relief and Mr. Gilbert's satisfaction, it soon became evident that the testimony given by the Kargers was not going to help Jean Acker's case. Anna Karger testified that only six hours after the wedding ceremony, Miss Acker came to their home. "She came to me," said Mrs. Karger, "and said she was sorry they had married. Miss Acker told me she thought she had made a mistake. She threw herself on the bed and wept." Maxwell Karger added that a few weeks after the marriage, Miss Acker came to his office and told him she thought it best they separate.

Gilbert saw no reason to cross-examine either of the Kargers. After Maxwell Karger left the stand, excitement quickened in the crowded courtroom as a visibly embarrassed, profusely per-spiring Valentino took the witness stand. Clearing his throat frequently, he told the court how he had vainly pleaded with his wife to admit him to the bridal chamber and how, the morning after the wedding, he had pleaded with her once more. Letters he had written to Jean Acker were read aloud by Gilbert, and they proved to be the communications of a distraught husband bewildered and hurt by his wife's mercurial attitude. Valentino could not explain his wife's reactions to marriage. He had be-lieved her to be a normal woman; he had certainly not forced her to accompany him to the altar. He was completely unable to account for her behavior.

On cross-examination, Mr. McCarthy asked if his wife's earn-ings had not been his principal reason for marrying her. Valen-tino denied this angrily. "I didn't know for two years what salary my wife drew," he told the court, a reply somewhat less than the truth.

"Why didn't you ask her sooner?" Mr. McCarthy wanted to know.

"Oh, that wouldn't have been professional etiquette!" re-sponded Valentino.

Later, claiming severe provocation, Valentino admitted strik-ing his wife. On the rare occasions when he had been permitted to see her and plead for an explanation, her replies had been vague or she had answered by charging that he had married her only to further his career. On that one occasion he'd lost control of himself.

After Valentino left the stand he was followed by Douglas Gerrard, who proved to be his most effective witness. Gerrard described how his friend had grieved after his wife had locked him out of her hotel room. He also told of a chance meeting be-tween the Valentinos on December 5, 1919, when "Valentino kissed her and was so happy that he invited all of us to a hotel, where we celebrated the reunion." But the very next day Valentino had come to see Gerrard, more bewildered than ever before, and said, "Well, she's left me again."

Gerrard described Valentino's alternating despair and rage because he could not rationalize his wife's enigmatic conduct. "Every day for a week following I was with him," Gerrard told the court, "and every evening he would call her up but she always declined to meet him." When asked why Valentino was so persistent in his efforts to see his wife, Gerrard replied, "I met Mrs. Valentino for the first time December 5, 1919, and at once understood why her husband was so much in love with her."

Continuing his testimony, Gerrard then told the court how Jean Acker had moved in with Grace Darmond before she had gone on location to Lone Pine for the Arbuckle picture. When Valentino had written his wife for permission to visit her, she had sent him a telegram which he had never told Valentino about; however, he had shown it to John W. Taylor, a newspaper reporter and his neighbor.

Under oath Taylor identified the telegram. It read:

RUDOLPH THREATENS TO SEE ME. KEEP HIM AWAY. I DON'T WANT HIM UP HERE.

JEAN

On Monday afternoon, in an attempt to regain some lost ground, Jean Acker's attorney introduced into evidence an unusual photograph of Valentino wearing goatskin trousers and nude above the waist, as, curled up at Natacha Rambova's feet, he tootled on the pipes of Pan. Natacha appeared to be listening raptly. Valentino protested that the photograph was a still for a canceled movie entitled *The Faun Through the Ages*, but attorney McCarthy insisted the photograph was relevant, since it showed how Valentino had been carrying on while still married to Jean Acker. It also proved, McCarthy said, that instead of supporting his wife, Valentino was supporting Miss Natacha Rambova.

Judge Toland ordered the photograph sealed until properly introduced as relevant evidence of wrongdoing and sagely ruled "that the questions regarding the way in which Valentino spent his money would have to come later when the question of how much Miss Acker might be entitled to for separate maintenance was raised as an issue."

Although Gilbert did not think it a good idea, he acceded to Valentino's insistence and permitted the angry actor to take his place on the stand again. Handling himself with considerable composure, Valentino did not deny his friendship with Miss Rambova; he said they had been friends for a long time. She took care of his fan mail and—an admission he would have preferred not to make—he consulted Miss Rambova "regarding his scenarios and the art work on his pictures." At last the cat was out of the bag. What everyone from Rex Ingram to Jesse Lasky had suspected was true. Although this was a peripheral issue in the trial, the revelation, made under oath, was never forgotten in Hollywood.

Under further questioning, the actor recounted how, after he had been denied admission to Jean's room in the Hollywood Hotel, he had rented an apartment for thirty dollars a month which he hoped Jean would share with him. "I took her to be my wife for better or for worse, whether I be rich or whether I be poor."

To Valentino's dismay, Judge Toland then adjourned the case until December 16 to permit Dr. Frederick Spelk and Dr. J. E. Cowles to examine Jean Acker and report back on the state of her health and her ability to work. Throughout the proceedings she had been dosing herself with medicinal powders, which she took in full view of everyone.

During the trial, Paramount had bought Elinor Glyn's novel *Beyond the Rocks* (1906) and assigned Gloria Swanson to play the lead under the direction of Sam Wood. (*The New York*

Times in its review found that "The whole moral atmosphere of the book is of a decidedly unwholesome and vitiated character." Other reviewers had liked it even less.) They informed Valentino that they wished him to play opposite Miss Swanson. The story, a romantic triangle, was set in the Alps. Gloria Swanson would play the young wife of a rich but stupid fiftyish husband. Valentino would be the other man.

The author, Miss Glyn, an English import, was the acknowledged leader of the *new woman.* Her portentous pronouncements on life, love, sex and fashion were accepted as gospel by Hollywood and the Hearst press—but not by the British. That many of Miss Glyn's positions were in direct contradiction to one another did not seem to disconcert her, or her readers. Miss Glyn was also a classy spokeswoman for sex appeal, "It."

Paramount informed Valentino he would receive $1,250 a week as soon as he reported to work, and arranged for an interview with Don H. Eddy of the Los Angeles *Examiner.* From a prepared text, Valentino explained to Eddy his recipe for a happy marriage:

> "A mating of souls, then?"
> "A mating of souls! Not an attraction of face nor figure; not even common likes and dislikes, mutual characteristics! These things are dross.
> "The real gold of human companionship lies in the union of souls. The mating of souls in true matrimony.
> "Souls are not mated in three months, nor perhaps in three years. I have learned that lesson. Soul mates are rare, indeed.
> "Yet when I marry again—as I suppose some time I will if my divorce is granted—it will be only when I am sure the woman of my heart, of my dreams, is the mate of my soul.
> "And then my greatest ambition, greater than all the others of my heart, is to make that mate my wife, to have a home and children."

Mr. Eddy queried Valentino about rumors current in the industry that he intended to quit the screen because of the constant "pestering" of women fans. Valentino laughed. "Certainly I do not intend voluntarily to quit the screen," he said. "It would be foolish now, when I'm beginning to be known."

The article's conclusion was that the Sheik received at least nine hundred letters a week from smitten women.

When court reconvened on December 16, Dr. J. E. Cowles reported that Miss Acker's illness was caused by nervousness, but that proper rest would enable her to resume her theatrical career within a year. Valentino's salary came into question, therefore, and Mr. McCarthy compelled the actor to admit that since shooting had started on *Beyond the Rocks* he was receiving $1,250 a week. Jean Acker then took the stand to admit to a packed courtroom that the marriage had never been consummated, not even during the one night she had spent in her husband's apartment after their chance meeting and reconciliation on December 5, 1919. That ended the testimony. Judge Toland announced that he would render his verdict on January 10.

Outside the courtroom, Mr. Gilbert exuded great confidence. The evidence, he said, was certainly in Valentino's favor. Besides, Judge Toland himself had begun to refer to the local divorce court as "Alimony Alley" and did not take kindly to women who profited from alimony. Perhaps Mr. Gilbert also reminded Valentino that as yet he had made no move toward paying him. In any event, on December 24, 1921, Valentino sent his attorney the following letter:

W. I. GILBERT
TITLE INSURANCE BUILDING
LOS ANGELES, CALIFORNIA

DEAR SIR:

I hereby agree to waive our previous agreement on the financial remuneration for your professional services in the legal matter of Guglielmi vs. Guglielmi. I hereby pledge my-

self to pay you the sum of $1,000 for said services in separate
payments to be agreed upon at your convenience.

I hereby set my hand and seal this 24th day of December
in the year of our Lord 1921.

RUDOLPH VALENTINO

On January 10 the principals met in court again to hear Judge
Toland's verdict. The judge recapitulated the evidence at some
length, noted that the plaintiff, Miss Acker, had "twice stated
. . . there was never any cohabitation or living by her with the
defendant," then announced: "I have come to the fixed conclusion that there was desertion on [Jean Acker's part] and that
the defendant and cross-complainant is entitled to a divorce on
that ground."

Valentino's joy was visible all over the courtroom. "Well," he
exclaimed, "it's over at last. Thank heaven!"

Jean Acker, on the brink of tears, said, "How could he? Oh,
how could he?" Judge Toland had denied her request for attorney's fees but, since she was ill, had left open the matter of alimony or support until she could return to work.

Reporters clustered around Valentino to congratulate him on
his legal victory. The happy, ebullient actor embraced everyone
theatrically. "Are you going to get married again?" a reporter
asked, now that his infatuation for Miss Rambova was no longer
a secret.

"Not just now." Valentino winked wisely. "Give me time
to think it over."

Jean Acker's reactions to the verdict also interested the reporters, so they sought her out at Miss Darmond's apartment,
where she had taken refuge. Miss Darmond answered the door
and told the reporters that only one of them might come in.
After a reporter from the *Examiner* was chosen to represent
the press, Miss Darmond called in to the interior of the house,
"Do you feel able to see him, dear?"

"I—I suppose so," came a muffled half-whisper. A moment
later Miss Acker appeared. She dabbed at her eyes with a

lavender silk handkerchief and invited the reporter to follow her into the living room, where she sank into a sofa and continued to sob noisily. "I—I lost. Oh, how could the judge decide that way? The doctors told him I wouldn't be able to work for a year. Everyone knows I'm absolutely destitute, that I—I haven't a cent to live on. And now—now what am I going to do?

"I'm going on!" she said suddenly, in reply to her rhetorical question. "That is, I think I am. I don't know for certain just yet. They tell me I can fight it right up to the higher courts, and I think now that I will. But I haven't decided for sure."

Although the Volstead Act forbade the drinking of intoxicating beverages, Valentino threw a small champagne party, which came to a sudden end when Jesse Lasky sent for the happy actor. He, too, wished to congratulate Valentino—and give him some very good news. He had been finally assigned to play Juan Gallardo in *Blood and Sand*.

Valentino cried with joy. This was the film he wanted more than any other. But despite his delight, there were still some practical questions. Did Paramount intend to make *Blood and Sand* in Spain; and would he be permitted to choose the director? He had recently met George Fitzmaurice and had been impressed by him.

Lasky nodded amiably. "All things are possible," he said, "between people who get along with one another." He added that he was giving a feature story to all the papers about Paramount's elaborate plans for 1922 and Rudolph Valentino. Lasky then suggested that he see his attorney about arranging some sort of settlement with Jean Acker. The matter of alimony had been left open and if Jean was ill she would not hesitate to appeal Judge Toland's verdict. Public sympathy might influence a new decision; if Valentino's attorney could arrange a quitclaim at a reasonable figure, Lasky advised him to do so.

Gilbert thought Lasky's suggestion a wise one, and promised to pursue the matter.

ACT THREE: SCENE FIVE

On January 13, the *Examiner* carried a lead story about Lasky's production plans:

> "The signing of Rudolph Valentino as a Paramount star for three years insures the exhibitors who book Paramount pictures the drawing power of one of the strongest box office personalities in the profession today," says Mr. Lasky.
>
> "Mr. Valentino's first appearance under his new contract will be as the toreador in Blasco Ibáñez's stirring novel and play, 'Blood and Sand.' It is a colorful story of Spanish life, centering around Spain's most picturesque institution, the bullfight.
>
> "To insure the proper translation to the screen of Ibáñez's atmosphere we have engaged June Mathis, whose adaptation of 'The Four Horsemen' was one of the finest pieces of screen writing I have ever seen.

"In the production of 'Blood and Sand' we plan to give Mr. Valentino one of the greatest supporting casts ever assembled. Bebe Daniels, who I believe is ideally suited for the role, will probably be seen as the Spanish vamp, and May McAvoy will be seen as the wife.

"Who will direct this production has not yet been decided upon, but we are considering several of the best known directors in the profession, and it is probable that a man who knows Valentino's great capabilities will be selected."

The announcement pleased Valentino even more than the full-color cover painting of him, by Flohri, that decorated *Motion Picture* magazine's issue of February, 1922.

The New York Times review of *Moran of the Lady Letty* reaffirmed his conviction that costume parts were best for his career. *The Times* observed:

Rudolph Valentino, as the hero, of course, is not so well-suited to the sea. He fits better into the romantic and melodramatic excesses of the story. Of course, he's supposed to be a wealthy young blood who has been shanghaied and falls in love with the sure-footed Moran of the Lady Letty, so you do not expect him to be salty, but even if you make this allowance for him, he is too slick. He doesn't impress one as the kind of youth who would be attracted by Moran, except momentarily, or attractive to her. In some of his scenes he is persuasive, but in others it seems a pity that he ever left the ballroom. And it is through his character, too, that the story becomes just movie stuff, so he naturally is not as acceptable as the others.

Valentino was hurt by the review; Paramount was undisturbed. When he completed *Beyond the Rocks*, on January 25, the studio sent him to San Francisco for several days of personal appearances. Other unfavorable reviews of *Moran* followed, but Lasky assured him that every actor had to try a variety of roles until he found those best suited for his personality. *The Four Horsemen* was still playing profitably, *The Sheik* was in enormous demand, and *Blood and Sand* would give him another exotic costume role that would lift his career to new heights.

It was during these talks that the first note of discord appeared in conversations between Paramount officials and Valentino. Although he was under contract to agents Robertson and Webb, he rarely let them speak for him, because he disdained intermediaries. Therefore they were not present when he told Lasky and Zukor that he had clearly understood their intention was to make *Blood and Sand* in Spain, where he had planned to take instruction in bullfighting from the best matadors. He had also specifically asked that George Fitzmaurice direct the picture. Gratitude to the studio assured them of his cooperation, but gratitude also made him concerned and critical. How could the studio hope to duplicate Spain on its local sets? Authenticity of locale would add to the picture's budget, but shooting in Spain would give the picture an air of realism impossible to attain in Hollywood.

This opinion disturbed several Paramount executives, but especially Charles Eyton, who had been a fight promoter and theater manager in Los Angeles before his association with the Paramount organization. Eyton felt that to prefer any place to Hollywood for picturemaking clearly showed disloyalty to the industry. Eyton also detected coaching in Valentino's protests and wondered aloud why he was paying an agency for professional advice but listening only to Miss Rambova? The studio was always open to suggestions, had not they replaced Bebe Daniels with the sultrier Nita Naldi? They were at all times sympathetic to an actor's problems, but Miss Rambova's compulsive need for authority would not be permitted to interfere with operations at Paramount.

When shooting got under way with Fred Niblo directing, Valentino continued to waste his time in prolonged bullfighting lessons and research into Spanish dress and costumes. As company spokesman, Eyton suggested that his time would be better spent in holding more interviews with the movie magazines, which, despite the star's growing aloofness, were willing to devote unlimited space to him. Valentino protested that Eyton was a domineering blusterer who believed in "bullying first" and rejected reason even when no other avenue of negotiation was open to him. No matter what suggestion he made, Valentino charged, it was never received gracefully; indeed, Eyton constantly threatened him with suspension and took out his dislike in petty ways. There was, for example, the matter of dressing rooms. Those normally assigned to the stars were larger and had private bathrooms; his was a small, uncomfortable cubicle. Certainly his status entitled him to a star's dressing room, but Eyton insisted that none was available, though after a personal survey he had discovered at least a dozen vacant ones. Eyton replied that so long as he said all the stars' dressing rooms were occupied, Valentino would have to accept it.

To punish Valentino, Eyton even refused his next request—that at least he be assigned two small, adjacent dressing rooms—one to rest in and the other to change his clothes in. Eyton also complained that Valentino left the lights on when he was not in his dressing room and used far too many towels. He even instructed the switchboard operators not to take his messages and told the studio police to refuse admission to Valentino's friends.

As Eyton became more arbitrary, Valentino countered by refusing to appear on any set if Eyton was present. He challenged Eyton, whenever they met, to put on the gloves with him at any place of his choosing. Indeed, the situation grew so serious that Fred Niblo advised Lasky to keep Eyton away from the sets because they were working with real swords, *picas* and *banderillas*. But to maintain the studio's authority, Lasky backed Eyton, who promptly increased his harassment in every way possible.

Progress on *Blood and Sand*, meanwhile, was slow, mainly because of these constant clashes of authority. Lasky became aware that on the days Miss Rambova appeared on the set, work went better, so he encouraged her presence, though Fred Niblo increasingly resented Natacha's interference and finally threatened to walk off the picture. Valentino responded with a like threat. The more he steeped himself in Juan Gallardo's arrogant character, the more cutting became his public statements, especially about fan magazines and some of their more prominent writers. It was not altogether surprising, therefore, that Dick Dorgan produced a leaden lampoon of *The Sheik* in April's *Photoplay*.

> . . . Back in the Sheik's canvas bungalow, Diana sat up all night long with St. Hubert, beside the Sheik's bed. The Saint tells her that the Sheik is a bum Arab, that he is really an Englishman whose mother was a *wop* or something like that, to help him make the story end well. . . .

Valentino stormed from office to office, pounded desk after desk, demanded that he be protected from all outside reporters, and that Dick Dorgan never again be allowed on the Paramount lot. Fully sharing Valentino's outrage, Lasky telephoned editor James Quirk in New York to tell him that no apology, no matter how profuse, could undo what Dorgan had done. The insult had been cruelly stupid, and if Valentino decided to sue *Photoplay*, the studio would stand behind him. Adolph Zukor shared Lasky's annoyance and also called Quirk, who promised to reprimand Dorgan and to compensate by reproducing in succeeding issues a series of full-page photographs of Valentino, with captions designed to please even the most captious star.

Somewhat mollified, Valentino returned to work. *Blood and Sand* was finally completed and he was informed that he would soon star in another costume film, as yet undetermined. Because of its rigorous physical demands, and his feud with Eyton, *Blood and Sand* had been difficult. He looked forward to the month of May, when he could take a long rest and, most important, fulfill his greatest desire by marrying Natacha. During the preceding weeks their friendship had deepened. She had been pleasant to his small circle of friends; evenings alone with her delighted him; he shared her pleasure in pets and she was tolerant of his enthusiasm for startling shirts and ties, and for large foreign cars in need of major overhaul.

Natacha agreed to be his wife, but under the court decision, Valentino would have to wait until March, 1923, before his divorce became final. But if they married in Mexico they could certainly not be accused of violating any California law. Other impatient actors and actors had remarried in Mexico and no action had been taken against them.

The settlement with Jean Acker was still in negotiation and Valentino urged Gilbert to speed the matter. On May 1, 1922, an agreement was signed by Valentino and Jean Acker in which he contracted to pay his former wife $12,100 in installments, and she in turn promised to release him from all future claims for alimony or attorney's fees. He borrowed five thousand dollars from the studio to make the first payment.

ACT THREE: SCENE SIX

By May 10, 1922, even *The New York Times* decided its readers should be told that Rudolph Valentino would soon marry Natacha Rambova. To the public at large Miss Rambova was now revealed as Winifred Hudnut, stepdaughter of Richard Hudnut, the millionaire cosmetics manufacturer, and the dark, dashing Valentino and the beautiful, aloof and the suddenly rich Rambova seemed like the prince and princess in a fairy story. Every effort was made to sharpen this impression. Valentino was suddenly endowed with a degree, Doctor of Agriculture. His deceased father was even elevated from village veterinary to head of an excellent old Italian family.

Richard Hudnut, en route to Europe from New York, told dockside reporters what he thought of the match:

I am greatly pleased to confirm the announcement of the engagement of my daughter to Mr. Rudolph Valentino. Both Mrs. Hudnut and I respect and admire him, and the fact that they are to be married makes us very happy. He is a man of great personal charm and comes from an excellent Italian family, and has shown conspicuous ability in making his way to success in this, a foreign country, where, at the start, he was absolutely unknown.

The Hudnuts were returning to their château on the Riviera and hoped to get the house and grounds ready by the spring of 1923, when they would be joined by the newlyweds. The actual wedding date had not yet been set.

Reporters flocked to the Paramount Studios. The mystery of Natacha Rambova had always intrigued them, and the revelation that she was the authentic and beloved stepdaughter of a multi-millionaire was real news. Not even Valentino had known who she really was; he had first learned of Natacha's exalted background from the newspapers. Nevertheless, he was overjoyed and believed himself the most blessed of men. He was going to marry a beautiful and brilliant woman whom he admired and adored, and since he was now earning more than fifty thousand dollars a year, he didn't need her money. He had done even better than Bonnie Glass.

Adela Rogers St. Johns, in an interview, asked Valentino why and how he had fallen in love with Natacha. She quoted his reply in full:

"I held Natacha in my arms and that was life itself," Rudy said to me. "Only one woman makes a man whole. No other woman ever made me touch ecstasy, all the rest were stuffed with sawdust. Why? If you know why—how—. . ."

" 'If thou must love me, let it be for nought except for love's sake only,' " I quoted Sonnets from the Portuguese. " 'Do not say, I love her for her smile, her look . . . for a trick of thought that falls in well with mine . . . but love me for love's sake—' "

"She knew," Rudy said quietly of Elizabeth Barrett Browning.

A somewhat less inspired reason was given by Natacha to a reporter for *Movie Weekly*. She confided that she had decided to marry Rudy "not for romance but for congeniality."

On May 12, accompanied by Douglas Gerrard, Paul Ivano and Nazimova, the engaged couple left for Palm Springs. The next morning the wedding party drove south to Mexicali, just across the border, where Natacha and Valentino were married in the home of Mayor Otto Moller. The Mayor was pleased that Americans, especially such prominent ones, were no longer afraid to visit his community. The previous November a band of more than four hundred rebels had attacked the outlying villages and fought a pitched battle with government troops and their Yaqui Indian reinforcements. Thirteen rebels were killed and four more had been captured and summarily executed.

The Mayor would have preferred more time to arrange a proper fete for the young couple, but he was able to muster a military band, which played a Spanish wedding march before the ceremony and triumphal music afterward. News of the ceremony had been broadcast throughout the Mexican city, and a crowd of several thousand people gathered to cheer the couple when they appeared. The occasion demanded a speech of appreciation and Valentino obliged. He told the assembled crowd, in Italian which was translated into Spanish, that he was "happy to know that Mexico extends such a generous and hospitable greeting to Americans when they come to this country especially to be married."

Rudolph and Natacha intended to honeymoon for a month in Palm Springs and San Diego before returning to Los Angeles, but on May 15 there appeared the first tiny cloud in Valentino's seemingly sunny future. Judge John W. Summerfield of Los Angeles offered reporters a dramatic opinion: Valentino's marriage, solemnized at Mexicali the past Saturday, was not valid in California. In his opinion, Summerfield added, Valentino had subjected himself to criminal process since "the entry of an interlocutory decree of divorce was nothing more than an order of the court that, nothing interfering, the parties would be entitled to a divorce after a year had elapsed. If they attempted another marriage within that year the result was bigamy."

No one at Paramount's Hollywood offices could be reached for comment.

Judge Toland, who had granted Valentino's divorce, declined to discuss the case. But Mr. Neil McCarthy, Jean Acker's attorney, was more than willing to say something to the press: "In my opinion such a marriage as Mr. Valentino's most recent one is of a bigamous nature, but it is not Miss Acker's duty to ask that such a complaint be issued. It is a matter for the state authorities."

The seriousness of the situation was communicated by telephone to the Valentinos in Palm Springs by Jesse Lasky himself. A flustered, apprehensive bridegroom informed Lasky that he and his bride were leaving for New York, where they would remain until technicalities connected with the divorce were cleared up. Sternly, Lasky ordered Valentino to stay where he was unless he wished to be considered a fugitive from justice as well as a bigamist. Lasky also informed Rudolph that Will Hays, the recently appointed "czar" of the industry, was very angry and had suggested privately that for the health of the industry it might be necessary to blacklist Valentino.

When Valentino hung up he sat paralyzed. Lasky had really frightened him, and even Natacha was momentarily uncertain about what to do. The Los Angeles newspapers added to their uneasiness by reporting the district attorney's interest in the Mexicali marriage; he had already summoned Jean Acker to his office for a discussion. Thoroughly unnerved, Valentino appealed to his friends for relief from this persecution. American attitudes and customs were insane and contradictory, he said, and deliberately legislated to make his life miserable. He was half ready to accept Natacha's suggestion that they not remain in the United States, where provincialism reigned over democracy, but go abroad and make movies there.

Before he made any such decision, however, he decided to speak to Jesse Lasky again. Lasky assured the distraught actor that he was not angry with him, but that he would have to listen to reason. Flight would not save Valentino; to run away would be an admission of guilt. He must return at once to Los Angeles. That act alone would do much to deflate the scandal-mongering newspapers and publicity-seeking public officials who were harassing him. In a sense perhaps he had unintentionally committed bigamy, but he was willing to bet most people were unable to understand an interlocutory decree. A divorce was a divorce. That a technicality had been overlooked by an irrepressible and romantically inclined young man whom all the world worshiped as a lover might well be forgiven by the American public—if only he did not flee the country. Finally, Lasky pointed out that although Valentino had been in the United States since 1913, he had never taken steps toward citizenship. If he went abroad, charges of moral turpitude (bigamy) might forever prevent his returning.

What Lasky said made sense to Valentino. He calmed down a little and explained that his first thoughts of flight had been motivated by fear for Natacha. Could they arrest her, too? When he was assured that this could not happen, he agreed to return to Los Angeles. Unobtrusively as possible, the unhappy young couple and their wedding guests returned. A short meeting was held at a private home near the studio, where attorneys for Paramount and W. I. Gilbert, for the Valentinos, agreed that Natacha should leave immediately for New York, her trunks to be packed and sent on later.

Natacha alone objected. She was afraid to leave Valentino to the mercy of men like Los Angeles District Attorney Thomas Lee Woolwine, who had sworn to subject her husband to immediate arrest and prosecution as soon as he entered Los Angeles County. Lasky and his attorneys assured Natacha that she was not Valentino's only friend. They had done some investigating and happily discovered that Woolwine was having troubles of his own: he was being charged with certain indiscretions by a Miss Ida Wright Jones, a recently discharged employee. Miss Jones was willing to make an affidavit declaring that she had been intimate with him over a period of years. Woolwine was not likely to cause too much trouble.

Finally convinced that their marriage could be saved only if she left California, Natacha and her Pekingese puppy, Rudy, boarded a train for New York. Her luggage consisted of one small hatbox.

Despite Lasky's revelations about Woolwine's personal difficulties, that intrepid public servant did not ignore the Valentino marriage. He went personally to Mexicali, and there, in the sweltering heat, he verified the marriage and took the names of the witnesses. He then returned to filmland, ready to do what the taxpayers had elected him to do. There were other storm warnings, such as the announced intention of the federal Department of Justice to investigate the marriage for a possible violation of the Mann Act.

On Sunday morning, May 21, 1922, Valentino, accompanied by W. I. Gilbert, went to the district attorney's office, where he surrendered himself and pleaded guilty to a charge of bigamy before a justice of the peace. Bail was set at ten thousand dollars. Only half following the proceedings, Valentino prepared to leave—and was stopped. His bail was ten thousand dollars. But it was Sunday, the banks were closed, and he did not carry such sums on his person. Nor did Mr. Gilbert have the money at hand. Paramount officials could not or would not provide the bail in cash—as was required.

Valentino was clapped into a cell.

In durance vile, surrounded by belligerent and bedraggled weekend drunks, and hailed by an assortment of vagrants, petty criminals and gamblers, Valentino beat against the bars, shouting imprecations in English and Italian about the persecutions inflicted upon him merely because he was a movie actor and famous. He refused to drink the coffee brought him in a tin cup and swore he would have his revenge on the district attorney. He would take his case to the American public. They would understand.

Why Paramount permitted Valentino to languish for even one hour in a cell is incomprehensible. Perhaps the studio executives felt that it would serve as a warning to him not to do anything important in the future without first clearing it with them. It seems only barely possible that the studio officials could not raise the ten thousand dollars in cash even on a Sunday. But the beginning of Valentino's disaffection with Paramount can accurately be traced to those hours in jail. Soon enough other people came forward, among them Joseph Schenck, who offered to post any bond up to two hundred thousand dollars. The actual bond was put up in part by his old friend and booster June Mathis, George Melford, and Thomas Meighan, an actor who knew Valentino only slightly but whose sympathies for what he considered unreasonable persecution had been aroused.

Valentino was hurried from the jail past an army of reporters. Gilbert advised him to say nothing but Valentino ignored this advice and told the reporters a confused story about marriages being performed in New Jersey shortly after divorces were granted in New York, and that he supposed the same condition existed in California. No matter what the outcome of this difficulty, he added, he knew he would be exonerated. He would, as always, "adhere strictly to the law. It is needless to say that this year's delay will not in any way lessen our love."

Finally, he read a hastily prepared statement by his attorney:

> I, of course, regret deeply that I should have done anything that would lower me in the estimation of the American people, who have been so kind to me and have accepted me at every turn for more than I conceive to be my real worth, and who have graciously called me "the lover of the screen." I will say that the love that made me do what I have done was prompted by the noblest intention that a man could have. I loved deeply, but in loving I may have erred.

Meanwhile, as Natacha continued her journey, reporters boarded the train at every station but failed to get any statement until she reached Chicago. There she was told of Rudolph's brave surrender to the police and his imprisonment until bail could be arranged. At this startling news, she tried desperately to maintain her composure. "The little people in the Los Angeles district attorney's office make me weary," she said. Suddenly she burst into tears and charged that "most of her troubles were due to a personal enemy who stirs things up." She would not, however, name the "enemy." Instead, she pledged her love to Rudolph, swore she would always be at his side, and vowed that after consultation with attorneys in New York she would return to Los Angeles.

A layover of several hours in Chicago enabled her to send nine telegrams and a special-delivery letter to her beleaguered husband—and to receive twelve in return, all replete with phrases dear to the hearts of movie fans: "Bushels of love." "Don't worry. Everything will be all right." "Love you so much." "God take care of you." And "Your darling sweetheart."

When Natacha grew weary of the reporters, she concealed herself in a baggage car. Discovered there by the hounds of the press, she refused to read the newspaper accounts of her husband's arrest. "I'm not interested," she insisted, brushing the papers aside. "Some people just envy me and are trying to make trouble."

The reporters did not take kindly to Natacha's lack of cooperation and were no doubt irritated by her haughty manner. Therefore, the intriguing question of her identity and background was a matter they could turn to with enthusiasm, and turn to it they did. They had a field day over Natacha Rambova Shaughnessy Hudnut Valentino's true story—a delicious revelation to readers from coast to coast. She was actually only the stepdaughter of Richard Hudnut, whom she called Uncle Dickie. She was of a good family and her mother, before her marriage to Mr. Hudnut, had been a prominent member of society's lorgnette level in San Francisco and New York. But in 1915, at the age of sixteen, Natacha—Winifred then—had disappeared from her private school in England, and two American senators, the Russian ambassador and scores of public and private detectives had been unable to find her. For almost four years her mother had continued to employ private detective agencies in the United States and Europe but Winifred had always remained one step ahead of them. From England she had gone to France, and from France had traveled to Russia, where she studied ballet with Theodore Kosloff. In 1916 the war made it perilous to remain in Russia, so Kosloff and his troupe—which now included Natacha Rambova—went to the United States on a national tour. Private detectives caught up with Kosloff in Chicago and, disregarding danger, perched on ledges outside his hotel window to spy on the *maestro*. Kosloff was properly outraged and the private detectives abandoned their perches. But they were replaced by federal agents, who also stationed themselves on the roof of another Chicago hotel where Natacha had taken a room. What they hoped to discover from this vantage point has never been explained, but Kosloff was summoned to the Chicago office of the United States Department of Justice, where, after answering questions, the inquiry was dropped.

By this time Mrs. Hudnut had arrived in Chicago and been reunited with her daughter, but had been unable to persuade her to give up her career as a dancer. Natacha rejoined Kosloff's company in Omaha, and to people who knew her intimately she would acknowledge that her name was Winifred Shaughnessy Hudnut, though she preferred to be known as Natacha Rambova. Some time later the company disbanded in Los Angeles, where Kosloff found work in the film colony as a character actor and dancer. At this point, Natacha joined the circle of talented women around Nazimova.

At one point, she was erroneously identified as Vera Fredova, who had also been a member of Kosloff's company, but a reporter for the Los Angeles *Examiner* interviewed Kosloff, and he introduced him to the real, authentic Vera Fredova. Miss Fredova breathlessly related that she had already been studying with Mr. Kosloff when Natacha had been accepted as a pupil; no, they could not possibly be the same person. And Miss Fredova added wistfully, "Assuredly I am not married to Rudolph Valentino."

It was impossible to make a goat of the Valentinos without the district attorney's office risking a charge of persecution of the movie colony, so Woolwine also charged with bigamy twenty other couples who had remarried before their interlocutory decrees had become final. In the best traditions of the law, Woolwine and his staff scurried about for witnesses and photographs to strengthen their case against Valentino, who was receiving much public support except from the local Ku Klux Klan.

Then on June 1, Ida Wright Jones asked the Civil Service Board for an open hearing of her charges against Woolwine. In evidence she offered the names and dates of motels where she had registered with Mr. Woolwine in San Diego. Miss Jones also furnished the board copies of solicitous letters and telegrams sent to her by Mr. Woolwine and denied that she had ever threatened to sell the communications to the district attorney's enemies. Valentino, clearly, was not the only one having his troubles.

The bigamy case against Valentino was heard before Justice of the Peace J. Walter Hanby, and Valentino's defense soon became clear. Dr. Floretta M. White, who had chaperoned the wedding party before and after the ceremony; Mrs. J. Hicks, owner of the bungalow where the Valentinos were the guests of Dr. White; Marie Nugent, identified as a neighbor of Dr. White; and Carol Lynch, a real estate broker, all were brought from Palm Springs to testify. Each, in turn, swore that at no time, either day or night, had Natacha and Rudolph been alone. They had not, in short, consummated their marriage: therefore, no marriage in fact existed.

A Mrs. Romaldo Lugo, the maid who had taken care of the Valentino bungalow, was also called. Bravely, as if she were reconstructing the position of armies and weapons on a battlefield, Mrs. Lugo used a chart to identify the location of various pieces of furniture in the bungalow, paying special attention to the position of twin beds, a double bed and a couch. Next Paul Ivano swore, under oath, that Valentino had slept on a couch in the front room of the cottage on the first night of its occupancy and on a porch couch during the second. And although he was subjected to intensive drilling and much sarcasm by Deputy District Attorney James Costello, he did not change his story. To the best of his knowledge Valentino and his bride had occupied separate beds during their stay in the bungalow and had never slept in the same room.

Interest in the proceedings livened considerably when two dainty silk suits, one white, one purple, were produced and represented as belonging to Valentino and his bride. Judicial wis-

dom was called upon to determine what the garments really
were, for the prosecution charged they were pajamas, while the
attorneys for Valentino insisted they were Chinese silk suits.
Palm Springs witnesses, however, swore under oath that these
unusual garments had actually been worn during public daytime
appearances by the star and his bride. And finally Douglas
Gerrard testified that throughout the stay of the wedding party
in Palm Springs, he had shared a room with Valentino. When
asked why Valentino hadn't shared the room with his wife, he
replied that she had been ill.

The next witness to be heard was Nazimova, who had been
difficult to find and serve with a summons. She had been discovered, heavily veiled, at the railroad terminal, about to embark for New York. Still veiled, and accompanied by her attorney, she made a belated entrance into a courtroom jammed with
Shebas, flappers and young schoolgirls. Nazimova also took an
oath that to the best of her knowledge the couple had not
shared the same bedroom. She was followed by Dr. White, who
testified that Mrs. Valentino had complained to her about being
ill and she had advised that the bride sleep alone until she was
fully recovered. To make this possible, Dr. White had suggested
that the men permit Valentino to share their bedroom.

In summation, Deputy District Attorney Costello charged
that Paramount Pictures had been instrumental in blocking justice by placing certain important material witnesses outside the
jurisdiction of the state. Frank James, the Paramount attorney,
countered with the assertion that the district attorney's office
was more interested in publicity than justice, and seemed determined to send Valentino to the penitentiary.

"The only interest that the Lasky Company has in this matter
is to see that this young man is not railroaded to San Quentin,"
declared Attorney James. "There is no doubt in my mind that
the district attorney of Los Angeles has taken up the hue and
cry in this case merely for the sake of publicity. That he is a

past master in getting his name on the front pages of the daily papers is a well-known fact. With crime rampant in Los Angeles he has gone out of his jurisdiction to investigate some alleged crime in Riverside County."

On June 5, Justice Hanby ruled that there was insufficient evidence to support the complaint against Valentino and freed the actor of the bigamy charge. The justice stated "that while the charge of bigamy was a serious one, that had an important bearing upon the social fabric, he felt that evidence of cohabitation could not be sufficiently shown to bring in a verdict of guilty from a jury, and that in view of this he did not think the county should be put to the heavy expense of a trial." Although Woolwine was not barred from asking for grand jury action, everyone believed he would let the matter drop. A whimsical touch was added when Valentino invited Woolwine and Costello to a second wedding—which he planned with Natacha a year hence. Both prosecutors accepted.

Freed from the shadow of San Quentin, Valentino was grateful enough to follow instructions and read a statement prepared for him by Gilbert and James. He thanked Justice Hanby for his careful and impartial consideration of the case, and even thanked the district attorney's office for its diligence. He was a law-abiding citizen who "would not, under any condition, assume marital relations with my present Mrs. Valentino until time fixed by the law shall have expired, upon which we will be married here in Los Angeles. I am happy to feel there are no hard feelings from the district attorney's office as Mr. Costello very graciously accepted the invitation I proffered to him and Mr. Woolwine to be guests at my wedding a year hence.

"For the present," he told the court, "I know that Winifred plans to spend a month with her parents in the Adirondacks. I am glad she has decided to do this because she needs the rest."

Then he departed from the prepared text to tell the reporters how difficult the separation would be for him because Natacha had been of such great assistance to him. "She is sketching the settings now for my next picture, *The Young Rajah*," he said, "and is sending these sketches on to California."

This last revelation hardly overjoyed the studio officials at Paramount.

Valentino's ordeal had been worth a million dollars in publicity, and the studio was anxious to start work immediately on his next picture. But despite his prepared statement of delight about *The Young Rajah*, Valentino was actually furious with Jesse Lasky. Letters and telegrams from Natacha complained of the insufferable snubs, humiliations and cruelties she had suffered at the hands of Paramount's minions in New York. Valentino also demanded an explanation of why his studio had refused to post his bail. And while his attorney, good Mr. Gilbert, had agreed to an adjustment of his fee because his services had not been as extended as anticipated, Famous Players-Lasky insisted upon Valentino's sharing an expensive bill for James's legal services. He failed to see why the studio should charge one of its own for his defense. Unwilling to wait for an answer, Valentino left the studio and said that he would return to discuss pictures only after he had completed his negotiations for a lot on Whitley Heights, overlooking Hollywood, where he was planning to build a suitable house for his bride.

While Lasky and the Paramount brass fumed, Valentino threw himself into his projected dream house. He wanted, he told the architect, a showplace suitable to his wife's position—a classic Mediterranean structure set into the hillside, with most of the house below street level. It was to include a small indoor swimming pool; a barbecue pit in one of the patios in order to facilitate the open-fire cooking techniques of the Arabs—whose way of life he had so authentically depicted in *The Sheik*—and there were to be rooms on half levels, as well as a master bedroom with two baths.

Valentino explained to the architect that although he had fullest confidence in his professional ability, whatever Natacha might suggest was to be incorporated without debate. The architect agreed, and from New York Natacha dispatched memos about the furnishings, which, Valentino thought, showed a "magic touch." There were to be floors of black tile, scattered black rugs throughout the house, and black velvet couches.

Only after the lot was purchased and the architect had begun his preliminary work was Paramount able to get Valentino to a high-level conference. Lasky, in no humor for nonsense, told him bluntly that Natacha was not to return to Hollywood, and if she did, the studio intended to ignore her suggestions, which they considered unwelcome interference. Lasky then brought up Valentino's recent legal difficulties. Put on the defensive by the whole tone of the meeting, Valentino described himself as an unfortunate victim of envy and circumstance, but Lasky would have none of this. He warned Valentino against the slightest indiscretion, and when he discovered that Valentino had recently secured a license to carry a gun, he expressed deep disapproval. Valentino replied that his friends Douglas Gerrard and Paul Ivano had also secured licenses and, once building began on Whitley Heights, they had planned to guard the property against vandals.

Lasky threw up his hands in disgust, but recovered quickly. Voice bland but eyes snapping, he asked if it were true, as reported, that without consulting the studio Valentino had chosen the story for his next picture? Valentino crossed the room and stood with his back against the wall. Yes, he admitted, he had chosen the story for his next movie and announced it publicly, and with a certain belligerence he added that he had no intention of changing his mind. He would either make *The Young Rajah,* or Paramount could cancel his contract.

Lasky offered several alternatives, but Valentino remained steadfast. Finally, making no effort to hide his displeasure, Lasky capitulated. With a bite in his voice, he expressed the hope that at least Valentino would cooperate with June Mathis, who had written the script, and Philip Rosen, who would direct *The Young Rajah*. Lasky then asked Valentino to thank Natacha for agreeing with him on the script—that it was of little consequence or entertainment: he doubted this would ever happen again.

Finally, Lasky read Valentino a statement the district attorney had given the press:

> The public should be warned that the decision in the case of *People vs. Rudolph Valentino* does not constitute a final adjudication of the questions involved in that case. It is the opinion of the District Attorney's office that the facts in the Valentino case would justify a conviction for bigamy assuming that Valentino and his alleged wife lived together as man and wife at any place in the State of California, and the decision of Justice Hanby sitting as the justice of the peace and a committing magistrate only is not the decision of a court of record and can in no way be construed as a final determination of any question involved before him. This is said with all due respect to Justice Hanby, who exercised his lawful discretion in this matter.

Valentino, grateful that the ordeal was over, stalked out. He continued to call Natacha almost every night for advice, which he attempted to follow.

Philip Rosen did the best he could for Paramount with *The Young Rajah*, a thin story about an Indian youth whose throne has been usurped, but everyone wondered if Valentino, wearing outlandish bangles and beads and reclining on Hindu swan-boat barges, could possibly escape the guffaws of the audience. When it opened, however, although the reviews were devastating, Valentino fans turned out to view him as a Hindu in sufficient numbers to reap a small profit.

But a continuing source of despair to Paramount was Valentino's behavior off the lot. It was not that he indulged in women or drink. Perhaps he considered such vices beneath him or even, with Natacha in New York, much too dangerous. Rather, he seemed bent upon an even more devastating form of dissipation —vast expenditures of money. In July he was sued by an automobile dealer for $2,262.08, which represented several years of repairs on his various automobiles. The studio had advanced Valentino $12,100 to pay Jean Acker, and later almost $40,000 to get the Whitley Heights house into construction. A lesser man might have been unnerved by being at least $60,000 in debt, but Valentino seemed inspired by such figures. Current chits for haberdashery and jewelry were forwarded to his agents—who had not as yet been paid one dollar of their commission—and quite naturally the agency forwarded them on to Lasky's office. However, any attempt on his part to reason with Valentino merely elicited an angry demand to see a profit sheet on *The Sheik*. His salary was pittance, Valentino said; the studio had made millions. They were going to make millions more on *Blood and Sand;* and they could have made more millions if they had not insisted on refusing to allow Natacha to rejoin him in California.

Furthermore, Valentino declared, the studio had not barred Dick Dorgan of *Photoplay* from the lot, and one day he stormed into Lasky's office and threw the July issue of the magazine on the executive's desk, opened to page 26. In a boxed article entitled "A Song of Hate," illustrated by two offensive caricatures of a "he-vamp," Dick Dorgan wrote:

> I hate Valentino! All men hate Valentino. I hate his oriental optics; I hate his classic nose; I hate his Roman face; I hate his smile; I hate his glistening teeth; I hate his patent leather hair; I hate his Svengali glare; I hate him because he dances too well; I hate him because he's a slicker; I hate him because he's the great lover of the screen; I hate him because he's an embezzler of hearts; I hate him because he's too apt in the art of osculation; I hate him because he's leading man for Gloria Swanson; I hate him because he's too good-looking.

Ever since he came galloping in with the "Four Horse-men" he has been the cause of more home cooked battle royals than they can print in the papers. The women are all dizzy over him. The men have formed a secret order (of which I am running for president and chief executioner as you may notice) to loathe, hate and despise him for obvious reasons.

What! Me jealous?—Oh, no—I just hate him.

Valentino paced furiously back and forth across Lasky's office, swearing to kill Dorgan on sight. In a black rage he pointed to the telephone and demanded that Lasky call James Quirk immediately. If not, he would neither set foot in Paramount's offices in New York nor attend the August 6 Broadway opening of *Blood and Sand*. The gift of a cane with a silver handle calmed Valentino somewhat, and Lasky eventually promised to telephone Quirk. Emotionally drained and so hoarse he had to have his throat sprayed, Valentino at last agreed to go to New York.

But no matter how much Lasky pleaded, he refused to attend opening night at the Rivoli. Pointing a dramatic warning finger at Lasky, he told the harried executive about a recent discussion by telephone with Natacha. He agreed that it was a disgrace for the studio to make him a target for screaming, stupid girls and women who only wished to tear off his clothes. He was willing to leave on August 10, after the picture would have begun its run at the Rivoli, and he would then be willing to make personal appearances if they were in good taste, but only if Lasky made the telephone call to James Quirk.

Lasky finally capitulated and telephoned Quirk to tell him of Paramount's displeasure over Dick Dorgan. He was calling over Valentino's protests, he said, for the actor modestly wished no issue made of the matter. Indeed, Lasky told Quirk, Valentino was so modest he would not even appear for the opening at the Rivoli.

The New York Times, in its review of August 17, 1922, liked
Blood and Sand:

> Rudolph Valentino acts his part of the bullfighter. Mr. Valen-
> tino has not been doing much acting of late. He's been slicking
> his hair and posing for the most part. But here he becomes
> an actor again. He makes one know Juan Gallardo as a real
> person, with thoughts and feelings as well as mannerisms
> and a fine physique. ·

The golf clubs presented to him by the studio just before he
left seemed to appease Valentino, but by the time he arrived in
Chicago he again seethed with anger over Paramount's treatment
of Natacha. He decided that this justified him in his decision
not to keep his promise to Jesse Lasky to help sell *Blood and
Sand,* though some exhibitors were coming from as far west as
Indiana to meet him. Rather, he put on a pair of enormous dark
glasses and further disguised himself by a small beard, which he
fastened to his chin with spirit gum, but when he debarked at
Grand Central Station he was immediately recognized by the
reporters. He refused to answer questions and insisted, as would
a later star, that he wished to be alone.

The reporters were not the only ones to recognize him. Within
moments, hundreds of squealing women surrounded him, and he
barely managed to escape to the train for Albany. There he
changed into a tweed golf suit, rented two cars (one to carry
his luggage) and was whisked off to Foxlair Camp in the Adirondacks, the retreat owned by the Hudnuts, where, at long last,
he would be reunited with Natacha.

Valentino's arrival and departure from New York had not
gone unnoticed by Paramount. Foxlair was immediately subjected to a bombardment of telephone pleas that he return to
New York. Many interviews had been scheduled and James
Quirk wished to see him.

Valentino was unimpressed.

ACT THREE: SCENE SEVEN

For five days Valentino relaxed at luxurious Foxlair and acclimated himself to the ducal life. He fished, rode a horse over the woodland trails and became better acquainted with the Hudnuts, who warmed to him without reservation. The family seemed to be genuinely pleased with Natacha's choice of a husband, and Mrs. Hudnut was heard to remark that his accented English was most distinguished. But at last Mr. Hudnut drew Rudy aside and suggested that his son-in-law *did* have a contractual obligation to his studio, that business ethics dictated his return to New York and full cooperation with Paramount. Some days later he and Mrs. Hudnut would follow Valentino with Natacha. There they would all spend several "gay evenings" before the three of them left for Europe with Natacha. It was their intention to remain until March, 1923, when the interlocutory degree became final. The advice seemed sound, so on August 20, Valentino departed Foxlair for New York.

But at North Creek Station he was told by the conductor, who had recognized him, that a suspicious man had got on the train at the same time and seated himself in the next car. The stranger had identified himself as a reporter, but the conductor had become suspicious of the way he had questioned him. If his opinion was of any value to Mr. Valentino, he would say the stranger was a private detective. Valentino thanked the conductor, and got off at the next station. The man in the next car also left the train. Casually, for he had thrown himself quickly into the role of an intelligence agent trailed by an enemy spy, Valentino walked toward the man, who quickly turned and ran off. The train had already departed but Valentino was able to hire someone to drive him to New York. When he arrived at the Waldorf, the desk clerk informed him that an operative of the Flynn Detective Agency had been making inquiries about him. The description tallied with that of the man on the train, and amused by the thickening plot, Valentino rather regretted that he had left his false beard at Foxlair. The detective, of course, had to be the bright idea of someone at Paramount. In time this rather rankled, and Valentino returned to Foxlair the next morning without ever having contacted Paramount.

At Albany he telephoned Natacha for permission to invite Douglas Gerrard, who was between pictures, to come East and join them. To his delight, she approved, for of all his friends she liked him best; she considered him a gentleman. About five days later Gerrard arrived at Foxlair, whose twelve hundred acres of mountain land were, as Mrs. Hudnut later described it in a letter of reminiscence, "an ideal place for a happy vacation . . . its large lake, fishing pond, private golf links and deer hunting gave the children plenty of opportunity for good sport. They practically lived in their bathing suits, swimming, boating and golfing the whole day long, never thinking of dressing until time for dinner. I used to sit up in my boudoir and hear those three screaming and laughing as if no cloud had ever come to shadow their happiness. . . . They were no longer the fretful, anxious children of a few weeks before."

Valentino, Natacha and Douglas Gerrard spent an apparently idyllic holiday until Sunday, August 27, 1922, when a violent storm struck the region and later settled into a slow, steady rain. That day a maid noticed a small Ford coupé parked down the road from the lodge but made no mention of it to Mrs. Hudnut, who had taken to her bed with a headache. Mr. Hudnut was in New York for several days on business.

After dinner that night Natacha, Valentino and Douglas Gerrard decided to play three-handed bridge in front of the living-room fireplace, where a crackling fire made a warm and cheerful backdrop. Shortly before midnight Natacha whispered that a prowler was on the veranda; Valentino whispered back that it was only the wind. But Natacha insisted, though she continued to play her cards, that she had seen the shadow of a man. Uncle Dickie's revolver was in the top drawer of his bureau, why not have Douglas go upstairs and get it while she and Rudy pretended to play out the hand?

Gerrard agreed, stretched, and in a casual voice said he was going to make fresh drinks. Once he had the revolver, he made his way down the back stairs, circled around to the veranda and spotted the prowler. He shouted to surrender or he would shoot, but the stranger turned, grappled with him and shoved him over the railing. The twelve-foot fall temporarily stunned him, but when he recovered, he fired three shots after the fleeing stranger. He heard a scream. One of the bullets had apparently found its target.

Meanwhile, Valentino had run upstairs for a shotgun. As he was about to go to the aid of his friend, Natacha blocked his way and screamed, "Don't do it! You may be killed or disfigured for life! Remember you belong to the screen—the public!"

But Valentino insisted and found "Gerry soaked to the skin and so covered with mud that only the whites of his eyes and his white teeth shone through."

The next morning revealed footprints all around the house, and farther down the road tire tracks. After breakfast the Valentinos and Gerrard drove to the North Creek Station to inquire if any stranger had left by the early train. The stationmaster nodded. A Ford with two men in it had driven up to the station. One of them had hobbled out painfully; his foot was heavily bandaged. The other had purchased a ticket for New York City, assisted his companion onto the train and then driven off in the Ford.

When Mr. Hudnut returned to the lodge, he advised Valentino's immediate departure for New York.

In Hollywood, where the skies were sunny and blue, Jesse Lasky informed the Paramount office in New York to post gale warnings; he had been unable to get word to or from Valentino, and on September 2 the storm broke, when all metropolitan New York newspapers carried reports that Valentino was dissatisfied with Paramount and intended to sever relations with the company. To prove this no idle threat, he had engaged Arthur Butler Graham, of New York, as his attorney. Paramount reacted to this unfriendliness by calling in the formidable law firm of Guggenheimer, Untermeyer and Marshall, and sent a letter to Will H. Hays to announce the film company's intent to bring a law suit against Valentino, should such action be necessary to compel him to honor their contract.

In his attorney's office, an irate Valentino called a press conference. Nattily dressed, with rings of beaten silver on each of his little fingers, he discussed his grievances. As an innocent, he said, he had signed with Famous Players-Lasky at a minute salary on which no star could exist because he had been promised extraordinary publicity. *The Sheik* had already netted

Paramount more than a million dollars in profit and *Blood and Sand* would easily double that. When a reporter observed that they might also have lost a million or two, Valentino answered that money was not the real issue. Choice of properties, rather than salary, was the crux of his complaint, and he was convinced that Paramount had breached their contract by failing to provide him with publicity commensurate with stardom.

"I will not return to Hollywood at the present time," he added. "The reports that I will desert America to return to Italy are ridiculous. I have made my success in America and shall remain here. If I return to Italy it will be only for the purpose of visiting my parents whom I have not seen in a long time."

Reporters picked him up immediately on the last statement. Weren't his parents dead? A flustered Valentino explained that he meant his brother and sister, though naturally he also intended to visit his parents' graves.

"I have been dissatisfied with the photography, management and direction—the handling of my films," Valentino went on. "They do not live up to my artistic ambitions."

Suddenly Valentino leaped up from his chair and in a startling exhibition of temper began to berate the studio and its executives, then just as suddenly his mercurial rage turned to cold anger. And as the reporters clustered around him with pencils ready, he revealed one of the most carefully kept of all filmdom's secret practices. Deliberately turning his back on Graham and ignoring all attempts at interruption, Valentino said that it was time that the public was informed of how Paramount and all the other studios did business. His studio, for example, produced about eighty-two pictures a year, and any exhibitor who wanted to show any *one* of these would be contractually bound to show all eighty-two. Even if an exhibitor refused to show an individual film, he would still have to pay for it. Paramount and all other major studios enforced this "block-booking system," and an exhibitor "was helpless, for he had neither the time nor strength of resources to buck the studio 'trust.' "

Calming himself after this major revelation (which no newspaper printed), Valentino said, "I have given instructions to the Famous Players-Lasky Corporation not to pay me further salary, and I have given instructions to my bank not to accept any checks."

Mr. Graham thought it wisest to conclude the interview, but Valentino hadn't finished. At great length he explained to the reporters that although Mrs. Valentino was in New York, she was staying with her parents at the Biltmore. They had no intention of breaching their pledge to the State of California.

The New York offices of every major studio soon buzzed with the news that Valentino had told reporters about the block-booking system. What strings had been pulled to keep it out of the newspapers was the source of much conjecture, but motion picture executives were in total agreement about one thing. Valentino, for whom the movies had done so much, wasn't a gaucho, a sheik, or a bullfighter—he was just a lousy, double-crossing Italian black-hander.

At Paramount everyone was dismayed and bewildered by such apostasy. Never before in the history of the movies had a studio done so much for a star. Now industry-wide principles were involved and despite conciliatory feelers from Graham, Paramount refused to consider any compromise. Outraged by such betrayal, they intended to prosecute vigorously. If Valentino wished to abide by his contract, the studio would cooperate with him; if he sought to breach it, the studio would take every legal step necessary to keep him off the screen.

When the news of Paramount's obduracy was relayed to Natacha, she canceled her passage on the *Olympic*. Although she was forbidden to live with her husband, she would comfort him in spirit and advise him in his legal battle with the philistines.

Bidding her mother and Uncle Dickie bon voyage, Natacha returned to the Biltmore. For the next two weeks the handsome couple would make no further statements to the press. They were seen at the better restaurants and at all the plays, but always chaperoned by Natacha's aunt, Mrs. Theresa Werner.

Negotiations between the attorneys for the contesting parties continued, but neither would now give in on any point, and on September 14, 1922, the Famous Players-Lasky Corporation filed for an injunction in the State Supreme Court. The court promptly restrained Valentino "from making a contract to appear for any person or corporation during the life of the present contract"—which did not terminate until February 7, 1924—"either in pictures or on the speaking stage." The following day, papers for the suit were filed with Justice Isidore Wasservogel. Included was Adolph Zukor's affidavit that Valentino's present salary was $1,250 a week and that on September 1 the star had been notified of the company's intention to exercise its option for another year at an increase in salary. Furthermore, over and above his salary, the corporation had advanced him substantial sums and guaranteed certain contracts entered into by the actor —a euphemistic way of saying that Valentino owed them a lot of money and they expected him to pay it. Zukor also stated that *The Spanish Cavalier*, which had been scheduled to go into production on September 4, had already sustained a loss of thirty thousand dollars, and the amount was growing daily.

On September 18 the principals met in the courtroom and presented their arguments to the bench. Louis Marshall, one of the attorneys retained by Famous Players-Lasky, argued that Valentino "was a college man and knew what he was doing when he signed the contract he was now accused of trying to break." Valentino stated in rebuttal that fan-magazine articles tended to exaggerate his education, but that even college men could become confused by the legalistic language and cumbersome locutions of long and involved contracts. His attorney, Arthur

Butler Graham, then stated that "misrepresentations were made to the actor as to the contract he had signed, and that he was told it was the same as that signed by Thomas Meighan." He also contended that Famous Players-Lasky Corporation "broke the contract first by featuring two women in *Blood and Sand* as costars when they were not stars, which had damaged [Valentino's] standing." The judge then suggested that Valentino's attorney prepare a brief which the court would submit to Famous Players-Lasky for refutation, and that Famous Players Lasky execute a similar brief for Valentino to answer.

Such briefs were prepared, and shortly after the death of Valentino the file of the entire case disappeared from New York City's Hall of Records. However, since various journals published sections it can be reconstructed. It charged, among other things, that Valentino had been shadowed by the Flynn Detective Agency and the only reason he could suggest for such surveillance was Paramount's hope of finding him living with his wife in violation of California law, so it could blackmail him into submission. He also complained that he had been assured his contract would provide for his making at least one picture a year in New York with all his expenses paid, and no such clause was in his contract. Other beefs concerned the cost of answering his fan mail, which Paramount refused to share, improper billing and inadequate dressing-room facilities.

After citing examples of the studio's mistreatment of Natacha, it ended with the statement: "I cannot work for this motion picture corporation. I cannot endure the tyranny, the broken promises, the arrogance or the system of production. I cannot forgive the cruelty of the company to Mrs. Valentino. I cannot look forward to a sure eclipse of what promises to be a lasting career of great success, provided that I am permitted to make productions consistent with my drawing power."

Judge Wasservogel promised a speedy verdict.

While awaiting the outcome, Natacha and her aunt, Mrs.

Werner, took an apartment on West Sixty-seventh Street just off Central Park, and Valentino moved into the Hotel des Artistes on the same block.

It was during this period of legal thrust and riposte that the Valentinos became interested in psychic phenomena. It all began, as Natacha later explained, when a dear friend of hers lost her mother; several weeks later the dear friend telephoned in great excitement to say that her mother had sent Rudy a message. The Valentinos hurried over and were introduced to the medium who was in communication not only with the friend's mother but with Rudy's as well.

Interested but fearful, excited and a little frightened, Natacha and Valentino began to attend seances. Other souls departed from Castellaneta and now in residence in heaven began to send messages, but the ones that always gave Valentino the greatest delight were those relayed by his mother. Through the medium, the Valentinos soon learned how to communicate without benefit of intermediaries. They established congenial relationships with Meselope, an Egyptian born before Christ, and Black Feather, an Indian guide who thought the law against fire water, and its open flouting, proved that the white man talked with a forked tongue. Neither the medium nor the spirits, however, warned Valentino that at the end of September Justice Wasservogel would grant Famous Players-Lasky an injunction which would compel him either to honor his contract or to forgo movie-making.

An immediate appeal to the Appellate Court was filed by Mr. Graham. But he urged Valentino to try to negotiate his differences with Famous Players-Lasky and Paramount, who now seemed ready to be reasonable. Although he pointed out that his services were costing Valentino about twenty-five hundred dollars a week, Valentino rejected any attempt at arbitration. He was determined to stand firm until the Paramount organization agreed to give him absolute control over his films.

Despite Valentino's official obduracy, inactivity was beginning to chafe. Without Natacha's initial approval or knowledge, informal conversations did take place, and the difficulties might have been resolved had *The Young Rajah* turned out to be a good film. But the reviews had been poor and at the meeting, which Valentino himself attended, the contending parties went at each other again, hammer and tongs. The studio's lawyer pointed out how Lasky had pleaded with Rudy not to make *The Young Rajah*, and did this not prove that neither his critical nor his emotional judgment could be trusted? Nevertheless, Paramount was willing to forget the past and make a lavish concession; they would renegotiate his salary up to seven thousand dollars a week, but they insisted on retaining full control.

Seven thousand dollars a week. Valentino had scarcely permitted himself to dream of such a sum. He was sorely tempted, but he stalled and said he would have to discuss it with Natacha first. She simply shook her pretty head. The conditions were ungallant, unthinkable. Unwilling as always to disobey her, Valentino told the studio officials the next morning that he would prefer to wait until the Appellate Court ruled on his appeal.

The die cast, Valentino grew increasingly moody and difficult and people began to avoid him. And it didn't help when he learned that Jean Acker had petitioned the Superior Court in Los Angeles for the right to change her name from Jean Acker Guglielmi to Jean Acker Valentino. He immediately telephoned W. I. Gilbert who, the following week, filed an objection stating "that his true name was Rodolpho Guglielmi and that Rudolph Valentino was his stage name . . . and Miss Acker was attempting to make the change so that she might 'advertise herself.' "

The weather grew colder and Valentino's resources slimmer. On December 2, a hearing was held in the Appellate Court before presiding Justice John Proctor Clarke, with Frank C. Loughlin representing Valentino and Louis Marshall appearing again for Famous Players.

"This man," said Mr. Marshall in presenting his case, "may enjoy a larger income under this contract than do nine Supreme Court justices. He is now receiving a weekly salary of $1,250 or $65,000 a year, almost as much as the President of the United States receives. After February 13 he is to receive $2,000 weekly and after February 1, 1925, if a renewal option is exercised, $3,000 weekly."

The judge agreed that these were considerable sums but asked if it were not true that Valentino had recently been offered seven thousand dollars a week? Mr. Marshall acknowledged this but added that Valentino's willful stubbornness had compelled the company to withdraw the offer.

Judge Clarke forbore comment.

"It is to be borne in mind," said Mr. Loughlin in rebuttal, "that the defendant is a young man who was unable to speak English when he arrived here. And, according to his affidavit, which on these points is uncontroverted, was wholly unfamiliar with business affairs or the salaries paid to motion picture actors. He was lulled into security and reliance upon the promises and representations of the officers of that plaintiff, who by professions of friendship and interest won his confidence."

Judge Clarke reserved decision.

ACT THREE: SCENE EIGHT

Beginning early in October, Herbert Howe had made numerous attempts to establish communications with Valentino in order to prepare his autobiography. Howe, who was employed by *Photoplay*, was born in Dakota—whether North or South was never revealed—and was reported to have "graduated from the State University." His uncle was a motion picture exhibitor and through this connection he began to write publicity, and later one- and two-reel shorts. He also contributed pieces to movie magazines, where his facility soon attracted the attention of James Quirk. Within a short time he became one of the two most important staff writers for *Photoplay*, the other being Adela Rogers St. Johns. Quirk was prepared to devote three consecutive issues to the autobiography, and Valentino's differences with Paramount would not influence the content, but the plan would

215

have to be abandoned unless Valentino was willing to devote a full week to working with Herbert Howe.

After his appearance in Appellate Court, Natacha advised her husband to cooperate. Valentino did, but only on condition that Natacha would permit them to work in her apartment. Natacha agreed, and Mrs. Werner offered to provide every motherly comfort while the two young men engaged in their literary labors. The first meeting was over lunch, where James Quirk introduced Howe to the Valentinos and the details of a work schedule were worked out. To the delight of the Valentinos, Howe proved to be an engaging young man and most sympathetic to Valentino's difficulties.

The next morning Howe presented himself at Natacha's apartment, and Valentino became increasingly enthusiastic. For six days Howe listened attentively to Valentino, and admired the star's appreciation of fictional embroidery. What gratitude he showed when with a click of the typewriter keys Howe conferred nobility on him. Valentino was delighted with the family tree Howe constructed, and only occasionally wondered if the readers might not check the facts, but Howe assured him the chances were one in several million. He should not concern himself with such trivial matters; if a fan challenged the accuracy of any detail, what magazine would allot him space to publish his findings?

Valentino's enchantment over the project grew with each meeting. Even when Howe had gathered enough material to complete the autobiography, he seemed reluctant to end the daily sessions. Diffidently he asked if he might not occasionally review the work in progress, and Howe generously gave this right to the author. Valentino repeatedly called for Howe's reassurance that only his own name would really appear on the autobiography, and Howe promised. He kept that word, for only after Valentino's death, in several articles of reminiscence, did Howe admit that he had actually ghost-written the series.

In the courts, meanwhile, where facts are facts and artistic temperament without legal standing, things were going badly for Valentino. Letters from his attorney in Hollywood advised him to drop his objections to Jean Acker's use of his name, since what little advantage she might get from calling herself Valentino could only make her friendly in the future; furthermore, prolonged legal representation might prove expensive. Into this communication Valentino read a suggestion that Mr. Gilbert would be pleased to receive some payment for past services rendered, and after Valentino lost his appeal in the Appellate Court, Mr. Graham once again pleaded for arbitration, and also mentioned in passing that his office had extended considerable credit.

Valentino wept and ranted but refused to capitulate. He still believed that the first installment of his autobiography, which would begin in the February issue of *Photoplay*, would arouse such a public clamor against the movie magnates that they would offer unconditional surrender to all of his terms. Inspired by this dream—so right for the screen—he telephoned James Quirk and asked if the editor would be interested in publishing some sort of statement of principle that he and Herbert Howe might whip up for the January issue. Would it not make readers anticipate the first installment of his autobiography? Quirk thought it a good idea and once again the collaborators met to create a literary manifesto. Valentino then telephoned Mr. Graham's office and in tones of lofty hauteur instructed his attorney to continue negotiations with Zukor and Lasky—and to be generous when they surrendered.

Although so deeply in debt that his creditors had to support him if ever they hoped to be paid, Valentino abandoned himself to a holiday shopping spree and ran up a telephone bill of several hundred dollars because he insisted upon speaking daily with the men at work on the house on Whitley Heights. They, too, were at a point of no return: unless they completed the house, they could never hope to be paid.

On December 22, in connection with the American Radio

Exposition at Grand Central Palace in New York, Valentino broadcast a manifesto called "The Truth About Myself." The title was a misnomer, for his talk was actually devoted to yet another attack on the motion picture industry, which he charged was one gigantic trust. "Seventy-five percent of the pictures released today," he told his radio audience, "are a brazen insult to the public's intelligence." The trust was responsible for this intellectual poverty, although stars such as Douglas Fairbanks, Mary Pickford and Charles Chaplin, and directors of the caliber of D. W. Griffith, were joined with him in his crusade to make the movie an authentic art form.

After the broadcast, he was asked by a reporter if he did not think Rex Ingram was an artist? Valentino's eyes narrowed and became so icy cold that the reporter quickly put himself beyond the actor's reach.

After heads cleared and Christmas decorations were taken down, movie executives agreed that they were witnessing a rare historical phenomenon: a young man whose profile was worth millions was cutting his own throat in full view of the nation. How else could rational businessmen explain his open letter to the American public in the January, 1923, issue of *Photoplay*, in which Valentino claimed to be neither temperamental nor grasping, nor even considered himself a great actor, though he wanted to become one, because within him was "a deep feeling for the art of the motion picture, gratitude to the public and an overwhelming, almost terrifying feeling of my responsibility to continue to appear in good pictures and to continue to be worthy of the praise heaped upon me."

The Young Rajah, he went on, had disappointed him—but the producers had compelled him to make the picture. Therefore, when the producers had "offered $7,000 a week . . . if he would go back to work on the cut-and-dry program picture basis," he had refused. However, he had offered to arbitrate all other differences if he would be permitted to share artistic control with a director and writer whom he approved. This reasonable offer had been rejected by the company, and because art could not be measured in dollars, he would not return to work.

Valentino's signature to this "declaration of principle" was bold and uncompromising, and *Photoplay* editorialized that when he appeared on the street he stopped traffic. The magazine's readers were then assured that "his life story, written by himself —not by any press agent, for he hasn't any—will begin in the next issue. . . . In all fiction there is not a more thrilling tale."

The solid reaction of support to this open letter thrilled Valentino, and he was further delighted when James Quirk invited Lasky and Zukor to visit *Photoplay*'s offices and view the ever-increasing fan mail. Indeed, Quirk hoped Famous Players-Lasky would remove the overflowing baskets of letters and reply to them, since he had neither the space nor the staff to answer even the smallest portion. This failing, Quirk offered himself as a peacemaker between actor and studio. Zukor rejected the offer because he now demanded an absolute capitulation on the part of Valentino. True, the Appellate Court had modified its injunction against Valentino, which had originally restrained him from engaging in "any other business of any kind or class whatsoever," but he was still prohibited from accepting any employment as an actor. What, Zukor asked, could Valentino do to make a living? Go back to washing dishes—or—gigoloing?

Quirk replied that Valentino had already received offers of six thousand dollars a week for dance engagements and five thousand dollars plus royalties to make recordings. Neither Zukor nor his attorney was impressed. The injunction forbade Valentino to work as an actor. Dancing professionally, making phonograph records—such activities would be construed as "acting" and the injunction expressly forbade such employment. If the foolish young man persisted in his stubbornness and remained off the screen until the end of 1923, he would be just another name. That might eventually be true, Quirk reflected, but at the present time he was still big news, and when he returned to his office he ordered the print order for the February issue of *Photoplay* increased.

Photoplay's readers cherished the stunning photograph of Valentino in the February, 1923, issue and thought its caption— "The Screen Idol of America"—a modest statement of fact. The first installment of "My Life Story" was subtitled "Under Italian Skies," and in it was formally introduced to his public Signor Rodolpho Alfonzo Raffaelo Pierre Filibert Guglielmi di Valentina d'Antonguolla. The actor explained that the Rodolpho Alfonzo Raffaelo belonged to his father's house and the Pierre Filibert to his mother's. "The di Valentina was a papal title; the d'Antonguolla indicate[d] an obscure right to certain royal property which [was] entirely forgotten now because one of [his] ancestors [had] fought a duel."

Whatever the reason or explanation, the readers of *Photoplay* were denied full knowledge of the truly grand background of Valentino; this revelation had to wait for more than four decades before it was broadcast to the world. It is entirely possible that Valentino was too modest, too retiring; or, he may have had doubts if the world of movie fans were really ready for the full knowledge of his distinguished genealogy.

Thus it was not until 1965—forty-two years later—that the Occidental world was offered *The Voice of Valentino*, a book by Lynn Russell; she had received oral messages from Valentino through the mediumship of Mr. Leslie Flint; Miss Russell had taped the messages so that they would not perish from the earth.

As a matter of record Miss Russell had asked Valentino, after he had been contacted in the Beyond, if she "could omit certain revelations which he had given [her]. To which he invariably replied, 'I do not like half-truths. If we are going to offer half-truths . . . why should we expect the reader to accept any other part of this book as the whole truth which we know it is?' "

Credo stated, Valentino told the medium and Miss Russell that he had visited this earth many many times but he was only interested in discussing his "recent incarnations, let us say those within the last four thousand years!"

Now that limits had been defined, Valentino was willing to reveal that he had been a contemporary of Cesare Borgia, which explained why he had been so anxious to play Cesare in a film; this was somewhat strange, considering that "Our families were not exactly enemies but we were certainly not on friendly terms." But the Borgias were recent history: "most of my films have had incarnation throwbacks. In one incarnation I lived in India [the film *The Young Rajah*], in another in the desert [two films] and in another in ancient Egypt." Queried as to whether he—Valentino had been in "ancient Egypt," and who he had been, the Ascended One replied—"Ramses."

Moving forward several millenia, Valentino revealed that during the course of his eighteen *recent* incarnations he had also been a man of the desert and a Moor; this was why he had been so interested in depicting a gallant Moor in his unproduced film, *The Hooded Falcon*. Valentino also confided that he had never been a Muscovite, so *The Eagle* was truly play-acting, but—there were more dramatic revelations to follow—after Miss Russell had established through Mr. Flint a true friendship with Valentino, his astral voice told her of his residence in ancient Judea, at the time of Christ; and in this incarnation Miss Russell and he had been "just ordinary humble Jews. We were very impressed with the teachings of Christ but, like so many others, we did not put them into practice. But we lived at the time of the Nazarene . . . it was dangerous to take part in something that was against all known religions. He was an outcast, and we were too afraid to come out into the open like some did."

Miss Russell and he had not been nameless, Valentino said; at that dramatic time in history his "name was Josephus and yours was Miriam . . . they were common names and we were just peasants working on the land . . . brother and sister."

So Valentino was Jewish too. In 1923, in the United States, such a revelation might not have been propitious. But now it can be told.

The father of this young scion of ancient nobility was presented as a cavalry captain who had voluntarily resigned his commission to return to his ancestral estate at Castellaneta, where he devoted himself to the reading of military philosophy, the practice of veterinary medicine, and scientific correspondence with the Pasteur Institute concerning rare diseases in cattle. His father's dedication to the eradication of malaria, which was endemic to men and beasts of the region, caused him to contract that fatal illness, and on his deathbed, he had ordered his sons to his side to say, "My boys, love your mother, and above all love your country."

Young Valentino had been a harum-scarum as full of mischief as Peck's Bad Boy. He was in and out of the olive trees and into everyone's barn, was expelled from school, fell in love with little girls named Teolinda, and was soon known as the family remittance man. To finance a holiday he had taken the ancestral heirlooms to Paris, where he "played among the smiles and jewels of her boulevards" and kicked up his heels while he pursued *amour*. In Monte Carlo he had lost his fortune, and a few weeks later, at the ripe old age of eighteen, enacted that perennial tragedy "The Return of the Prodigal." His escapades had not won him "the title of Pride of the Family," and at a family conclave it was decided to give him four thousand dollars and exile him to America.

The autobiography read so well that Rudolph wished he had really written it. He also wished that it were really the truth, especially the part about his Parisian adventures.

ACT THREE: SCENE NINE

In his quiet business office, a public relations man named S. George Ullman read with interest the first installment of Valentino's autobiography. Later he took a walk from newsstand to newsstand and found that this issue of *Photoplay* was selling like hot cakes. Several telephone calls to friends in the entertainment industry informed Ullman that Zukor and Paramount intended to capitalize on this literary effort by rebooking all his films. Ullman also remembered a six-thousand-dollar-a-week offer from the Keith Circuit which Valentino had been unable to accept because of the court injunction. But suppose, he thought, one of his own clients were to employ the Valentinos to advertise their product? They could dance for the public, who would be most grateful for such a free performance, and if Valentino then gave a little talk plugging the sponsor's product . . . ? A call to a friend at the Keith office verified that the Valentinos really had been offered six thousand dollars a week. His client then would have to offer seven thousand dollars. For several weeks Ullman brooded over the idea.

Finally he decided that the most likely sponsor would be the Mineralava Beauty Clay Company, which manufactured a product greatly favored by the ladies. But would women come to see Valentino perform with his wife? Wouldn't this erase some of the glamour from the Sheik? Ullman did not think so—women with whom he talked did not think of Valentino as a possible husband. Rather, he personified high emotional adventure with the one man to whom they could never be bound in permanent union. He held a preliminary conference with the Mineralava Company, and they listened with interest. They asked if Ullman could deliver the Valentinos at seven thousand dollars a week; he replied that he thought he could when they were ready to make a firm commitment.

Meanwhile, the March installment of Valentino's autobiography, "Broadway Nights," appeared, which was devoted mostly to proving that Valentino had not been a draft dodger. Indeed, he had actually made valiant efforts to enlist in Italy's armed forces as an aviator. That Italy had no air force in World War I was not, however, the reason given for his rejection; he had, it seemed, a visual defect in his left eye. Later he had made application to the American office of the British Royal Flying Corps and once more was rejected. After this second frustration, suffered in San Francisco, he had accepted Al Jolson's invitation to travel with his company to Los Angeles.

And so, once again, I was in a new place, starting on a new career, without money. If I had known, while waiting outside the studio gates of Hollywood, the obstacles that lay ahead of me, I would never have had the courage to batter my way in. Fortunately, there is a destiny which drops a

curtain over the future. . . . What I found behind that curtain
I will tell you in my next chapter.

Toward the end of February Ullman received from the Mineralava Company the firm commitment he had been waiting for.
Offer in pocket, he entrained for Chicago, where the couple were
planning to remarry as soon as the divorce decree became final.
Three years later, after the star's death, Ullman described this
first meeting:

> Naturally, I was familiar with his pictures and thought of him
> as a handsome boy. I had no idea of his magnetism nor of the
> fine quality of his manhood. To say that I was enveloped by
> his personality with the first clasp of his sinewy hand and my
> first glance into his inscrutable eyes, is to state it mildly. I
> was literally engulfed, swept off my feet, which is unusual be-
> tween two men. Had he been a beautiful woman and I a
> bachelor, it would not have been so surprising. I am not an
> emotional man. I have, in fact, often been referred to as
> coolheaded; but, in this instance, meeting a real he-man, I
> found myself moved by the most powerful personality I had
> ever encountered in man or woman.

Upon arrival, Ullman discovered that a fiasco had occurred.
At nine that morning, the Valentinos and their wedding party
had assembled at the Blackstone Hotel. Douglas Gerrard had
come on from Hollywood to be best man and Mrs. Werner,
Natacha's aunt, represented the Hudnuts. They awaited only
official word from Los Angeles, but shortly after nine, an attorney arrived, called the Valentinos aside and shared with them
the unhappy news that they had confused their dates. The interlocutory decree had been signed on March 19, 1922; they were
not free to marry for another two weeks. The judge who was to
officiate at the ceremony regretted the delay, patted the young
man's shoulder and left for his court.

The Los Angeles *Times* tied its coverage of this tragedy with a notice that Jean Acker Valentino was appearing with her act in Chicago; then the paper suggested she "must have grinned sardonically." And to make it even worse, the Chicago *Tribune* suddenly decided to set Valentino up as a target. The editorial published in that sturdy sheet dedicated to xenophobia probably upset him more than any other single newspaper item since 1916, for it derided Valentino and called him a sissy. Proof of this charge? Why, he wore a wristwatch. . . .

To Valentino the editorial could mean only one thing: the *Tribune* was referring obliquely to a similar charge made against him back in 1916, when Manhattan Assistant District Attorney James E. Smith had also made much of this. At first he considered offering the newspaper a bribe to let him alone; instead he stormed into the city room and without preliminaries challenged every reporter in sight to immediate combat, with fists or any other weapon of their choice. No one accepted, so after a long, contemptuous glare around the room, pausing only to flick a necktie or two, he strode out again.

A few days later Ullman managed to present his proposition. Valentino was immediately interested, but asked that Natacha be included in the discussion. When she arrived, Ullman managed to convince her, after much persuasive argument, that such a tour would be a dignified endeavor—after all, her stepfather was a cosmetics manufacturer. Most persuasive, however, was the seven thousand dollars a week and all expenses paid. It would enable Valentino to repay the more pressing of his many debts and afford him a magnificent opportunity to meet the millions of people who sided with him—and his wife—in their gallant stand against Paramount. Though Natacha had some misgivings, they signed a contract with Ullman calling for a seventeen-week tour to begin immediately after their remarriage. A substantial check served as a binder, and Valentino insisted that Ullman was good luck, for shortly news arrived from California that the interlocutory year had begun on the day the divorce had been granted, not when it had been entered in the records. As one reporter noted in a splendidly mixed metaphor: "The chuck-hole in the Sheik's matrimonial road was filled and he could toss the ship of matrimony into high and step on the accelerator without further fear of broken springs."

Actually, the reporter had guessed wrong, for it now developed that the Illinois marriage license had been issued in error. True, Illinois recognized the validity of a California divorce, but Illinois required a year to elapse after the granting of the *final* decree before a remarriage would be permitted within its boundaries. Appealed to for help, Ullman suggested that they find a nearby state which would allow them to marry immediately. And so on March 14, 1923, with Ullman and Mrs. Werner as witnesses, the Valentinos were remarried in a quiet ceremony in Crown Point, Indiana.

At long last the young couple could live under one roof, without society's condemnation or fear of violating California law. However, two weeks later, on March 29, Mrs. Edward Franklin White, Deputy Attorney General of Indiana, expressed an informal opinion that the marriage at Crown Point was probably illegal; strictly interpreted, Indiana law required a female applicant for a marriage license to be a resident of the county in which she made application. The world thus informed, the state authorities, in a burst of judicial generosity, announced that they contemplated no punitive action.

Back in Chicago, Ullman conducted the young married couple to the private railroad car he had engaged for their tour. It was sumptuous enough for an Indian potentate and Valentino's enthusiasm on seeing it was irrepressible. The car contained three staterooms, each with a full bath, oriental rugs, gilt mirrors, oil paintings and a huge walnut desk. There was even a dining saloon, a galley and sleeping quarters for a chef and a steward. They had been hounded unmercifully by reporters determined to incite him to verbal indiscretions, and plagued by bill collectors who seemed unaware of the obvious—that they were addressing a gentleman and his lady. Now there was peace at last.

All their expenses were being paid on this tour, Valentino told Natacha, and if they were careful and restrained any impulses to buy needlessly, they could pay off everything they owed, and still have almost twenty thousand dollars. The tour would also prove to Zukor and Lasky that the Valentinos could survive without them, and many thousands in the audiences might write Zukor and Lasky and demand the return of Valentino. Natacha listened, and reserved judgment.

Valentino left her then to discuss the itinerary with George Ullman and establish what should be said in praise of Mineralava Beauty Clay. The sales pitch troubled him; he pleaded that their presentations be dignified and as brief as possible. Ullman agreed. In only one instance did Ullman refuse to cooperate: the Mineralava Company would not pay Robert Florey to handle Valentino's personal publicity or to make a film record of the nationwide tour.

Their first stop was Omaha. An unseasonable snowstorm held the city in the grip of winter, and by nightfall it had blown itself into a blizzard. All streets were deep in drifts, with public transportation at a standstill. At the large auditorium, Ullman wondered how many people would leave their comfortable homes to come and see the Valentinos dance. But he need not have worried, for by eight the house was overflowing. Normally, so large an audience would not have been permitted, but all had braved the harsh weather to see the Sheik, and safety regulations were ignored. The crowd, moreover, seemed in good humor and applauded when Ullman asked their permission to delay the curtain for a half hour. Presently the orchestra played the overture, and the curtain rose. With Valentino in gaucho costume and Natacha in Spanish attire, they glided gracefully across the stage in an exotic tango.

The applause subsided only after Valentino begged for silence and told everyone how delighted he was to be in Omaha, where warm civic hearts defied the cold, and how grateful he was to the Mineralava Company for making his appearance possible. He hoped his good friends would try the company's product. Mrs. Valentino—his lovely wife and dancing partner—used it, he concluded, and with a courtly gesture he introduced Natacha, who managed to smile graciously and say several nice things about Mineralava's beauty clay.

After the performance, a tired Valentino signed hundreds of autographs. Although both he and Natacha were exhausted, they had enjoyed themselves and she had surprised him by offering her autograph, too. Ullman too was delighted, for he felt that the dancing Valentinos had contributed handsomely to the Mineralava Company image.

What especially pleased Valentino was the reception he received throughout the Midwest Bible Belt, the second most important bastion of the Ku Klux Klan. Men and women outdid themselves everywhere to show their friendliness, and the occasional heckler was roughly handled by the other spectators. Wherever they appeared, people lined the railroad tracks. Valentino enjoyed standing on the platform with Ullman to wave at the crowds, and occasionally Natacha could be persuaded to join them. And in Wichita, where a daytime performance had been scheduled, the public schools were closed down to enable children to attend.

Financially the tour was successful beyond Ullman's most optimistic projection. The only unpleasantness, aside from the discomforts of travel, was Natacha's continuing insistence that Valentino be given greater authority in the management of the tour. At first this embarrassed Valentino, but soon he began, as always, to side with her. Things came to a head between Ullman and Natacha in Salt Lake City. The auditorium was filled by eight o'clock, but the Valentinos insisted they were too fatigued to perform. Both Ullman and the manager of the auditorium pleaded that the crowd was becoming unruly, and by ten-thirty the manager was ready to call for the police. The audience threatened to tear the building apart, and only then, when the situation had become truly dangerous, did the Valentinos finally appear. Valentino calmed the crowd with a statement about the traffic, and as if ashamed of the anguish he had caused Ullman, he performed brilliantly. For the rest of the tour Valentino saw to it that he and Natacha were punctual and cooperative.

Meanwhile, magazines and newspapers continued to devote many pages to the dancing Valentinos, who were attracting some of the largest audiences in history. To refute newspaper stories about his hospitalization at Johns Hopkins Hospital in Baltimore for nervous and mental exhaustion, Valentino performed a variety of calisthenics on stage, and concluded by suggesting that the neurotic executives of Paramount were the insane ones if they believed he or his public would be influenced by the stupid stories circulated by their publicity hacks. They were attempting to depict him, said Valentino, "as a wan, pale and beardless youth, leisurely reclining on down sofas, supported by silken pillows and wickedly smoking sheikishly perfumed cigarettes." The audiences always responded with delight. They even purchased hundreds of thousands of copies of *Day Dreams*, purportedly written by Rudolph Valentino, and recently published by Macfadden Publications.

The preface to this remarkable volume, indited on May 29, 1923, speaks for itself:

To you, my gentle reader, I wish to say a foreword of warning before you peruse the contents of this book. I am not a poet nor a scholar, therefore you shall find neither poems nor prose. Just dreams—*Day Dreams*—a bit of romance, a bit of sentimentalism, a bit of philosophy, not studied, but acquired by constant observation of the greatest of masters! . . . *Nature!*

While lying idle, not through choice, but because forcibly

kept from my preferred and actual field of activity, I took
to dreams to forget the tediousness of worldly strife and the
boredom of jurisprudence's pedantic etiquette.

Happily indeed I shall be if my *Day Dreams* will bring you
as much enjoyment as they brought to me in the writing.

Fans loved the book, they loved Valentino's sturdy pledge to
continue his combat against the studio magnates no matter how
long it might take. So overwhelming were sales that Valentino
hastened to New York, where at autographing parties he reaped
the spiritual rewards for his aesthetic labors by being photographed with Bernarr Macfadden, his wife and his five daugh-
ters. Then Mr. Macfadden would congratulate him for this book
of verse which "uncover[ed] his very soul—his loves, his hates,
his sorrows, his joys, his thrills, his triumphs."

Some examples of these soul-baring poems are perhaps in
order:

A BABY'S SKIN

Texture of a butterfly's wing,
Colored like a dawned rose,
Whose perfume is the breath of God.
Such is the web wherein is held
The treasure of the treasure chest,
The priceless gift—the Child of Love.

DUST TO DUST

I take a bone—I gaze at it in wonder. You,
O bit of strength that was. In you to-day I
see the white sepulcher of nothingness—but
you were the shaft that held together the
vehicle of Man until God called and the Soul
answered.

YOU

You are the History of Love and its Justification.
The Symbol of Devotion.
The Blessedness of Womanhood.
The Incentive of Chivalry.
The Reality of Ideals.

The Verity of Joy.
Idolatry's Defense.
The Proof of Goodness.
The Power of Gentleness.
Beauty's Acknowledgement.
Vanity's Excuse.
The Promise of Truth.
The Melody of Life.
The Caress of Romance.
The Dreams of Desire.
The Sympathy of Understanding.
My Heart's Home.
The Proof of Faith.
Sanctuary of my Soul.
My Belief of Heaven.
Eternity of all Happiness.
My Prayers.
You.

Sales of the book continued to soar, and it was bought by thousands of citizens who normally correlated poetry with effeminacy. For the rest of the tour Valentino visited bookstores everywhere and with becoming modesty introduced himself to clerks and customers, behaving like any other author. After the Great Lover's death, Natacha revealed the significance of the initials below the titles of most of the poems. They identified, she said, the actual authors, whose *psychic* communications proved they had neither abandoned the muse nor grown slothful in heaven. It was really a miscellany with heavenly contributions by Robert and Elizabeth Browning, George Sand, Walt Whitman and James Whitcomb Riley.

Photoplay had concluded Valentino's autobiography with an installment appropriately titled "Hollywood." In it was described "how I fought the fight that everyone must wage who wants to break into pictures." Valentino brought his narrative to an end by telling his readers:

As I write this I am involved in more lawsuits that I ever thought could come upon one man. My side of the controversy has not been presented fairly. The sincerity of my motive has been ridiculed. It seems impossible for some people to believe that a player would stand out for good productions. They intimate that I am simply using that demand as a pretext for getting an increase in salary. . . . Eventually they will realize that I have been speaking the truth when I say that I will never come back until I can have something to say about the quality of the pictures that feature my name. Already the opposition is crumbling. I am now permitted to earn a living—off-screen. But I intend to fight to the finish and justify my stand. I believe I can soon tell you the outcome.

It was great satisfaction to Valentino, who followed the movie news closely, to know that in the Hollywood *Weltanschauung*, with its focus on the pubic triangle, Ramon Navarro, John Gilbert, Rod La Rocque, Antonio Moreno, Edmund Lowe, and Ivor Novello had been unable to replace him with the ladies. But satisfaction that he was still America's most popular heart-throb could not overcome his fears for the future: the tour was drawing to a close and that meant unemployment, therefore, Valentino's longing to settle his differences with his producers became increasingly apparent. He began to buy popular novels and often discussed with Ullman his interpretations of the leading characters. With increasing frequency he cloaked himself in some fictional personality, and after reading Rafael Sabatini's *The Sea-Hawk*, the normally fastidious actor threw himself so enthusiastically into the lead role, and became so rough and gross at table, that Natacha actually refused to eat with him.

Then, on June 20, 1923, Arthur Butler Graham, with whom Valentino had severed relations because he had continued to stress the wisdom and financial benefits of arbitration, initiated steps against the actor to collect $48,295 for legal services and cash disbursements made in Valentino's behalf. A deputy sheriff delivered a copy of Mr. Graham's attachment to a branch of the

National City Bank in New York, where, it was believed, about fifty thousand dollars was on deposit, although it was not known whether the money belonged to Valentino or his wife. A second copy was served on the Mineralava Company, and Ullman's ear was almost burned off by a telephone call from the home office, and he demanded an immediate conference with Valentino and his wife.

Valentino apologized profusely, ordered Natacha to remain silent, and suddenly begged George Ullman to take over the management of his affairs. They were in a terrible mess, and his career had suffered for it. He had made enemies and embarrassed his friends. He was heavily in debt, and his debts seemed to multiply as his difficulties increased.

Surprised, but sympathetic, Ullman asked for a reasonable time to think it over. However, without preamble, he made it quite clear that if he accepted he would insist upon absolute, unconditional control over Valentino's business affairs and over what he thought best for the actor's career. And if he accepted, he would have to be business manager in fact as well as title, which meant Natacha would be excluded from business conferences and certainly would not be permitted to veto any of his decisions. Because he had a sublime faith in any new situation, Valentino agreed. Ullman must later have had reservations when the Valentinos told him, with all the fervor of converts to some primitive faith, that they had communicated with their good friends Meselope and Black Feather of the spirit world for approval before agreeing to dance their way into the nation's heart.

As soon as the tour was completed, Ullman returned to New York, and hired Max D. Steuer as Valentino's lawyer. The bill for legal services presented by Arthur Butler Graham was settled, and eleven thousand dollars was repaid Joseph Schenck, the studio and production head of United Artists, who had advanced Valentino money to live on before the tour began. Almost all debts were similarly discharged, and the Valentinos moved into Rudolph's old apartment at the Hotel des Artistes. With the Valentinos kept carefully in the background, Steuer's office began new discussions with Zukor, Lasky and J. D. Williams, president of Ritz-Carlton Pictures, Inc., a new motion picture company.

On July 18, an agreement was announced at a dinner by Williams. Under the terms of the settlement, Valentino would make two more pictures for the Paramount organization at their New York studios, at seventy-five hundred dollars a week. He would be given sufficient control over the stories, stars, writers and directors, and Mrs. Valentino would contribute to the technical aspects of each film. Once the two pictures were completed, Valentino would be free to join the Ritz-Carlton Company. Valentino wished to begin work immediately, but the Paramount organization had no roles for him until fall. Ullman, however, insisted that his client's salary begin immediately and the company capitulated. The victory was complete.

Ullman then suggested that the Valentinos go abroad for a holiday.

Before they left, Natacha insisted upon a quick trip to California to note the progress on the Whitley Heights house and order some of its appointments. Almost everything proved to her satisfaction, and she returned in time to accompany her husband to an Italian restaurant in New York City's Little Italy for a farewell party. For a year and a half Valentino had been a frequent patron and never been recognized; but this night police reserves had to be called to disperse the crowd of five thousand that massed around the restaurant.

The following day, July 23, the Valentinos and Mrs. Werner, Natacha's favorite aunt, fought their way through crowds of uninhibited women who tried to rush the gangplank of the *Aquitania* in their determination to gaze upon the Sheik at close range. Mr. and Mrs. George Arliss were also on the passenger list. They had no trouble boarding the vessel.

For Valentino, the voyage was a triumph. Ten years before, he had come to the United States in the steerage; now he trod the first-class deck in a magnificent belted greatcoat with a fur collar and cuffs, and in the hold were fifteen trunks and other assorted pieces of luggage. He was treated with honors by the captain, at whose table he sat at dinner and whose bridge he also visited. Every day he received a thick bundle of radiograms, many of them from Europe, with invitations from people whose names he would not have dared breathe had he remained in Castellaneta. Valentino saw himself as a modern Maecenas returning in triumph, but always his greatest joy was Natacha, whose regal beauty won the admiration of everyone in the first class. Her poise, manner, diction and style brought a hush to every room she entered. Valentino gloried in this and the trip was a happy one. Not once did Natacha find fault with him.

Although they arrived in London at midnight, Valentino was ready at nine the next morning for press interviews, and handled them gracefully. Most of the reporters asked questions about women and his ideals of beauty and whether he thought American women were superior to the British or Italian. Generalities sufficed and Valentino hurried off to Bond Street for a flurry of custom fittings. His objective was the purchase of a complete British wardrobe for every possible occasion that might arise in the life of a gentleman.

During their London stay, Richard Guinness, the director of Guinness, invited them to dine at his town house on Great Cumberland Place, and over lunch they met Lord and Lady Birkenhead and Artur Rubinstein. They visited the London theater in the evening and were interviewed by the press during the day. Their sole disappointment was their failure to meet the Prince of Wales. Natacha also bought three Pekingese dogs.

They flew from London to Paris, and neither Natacha, her Pekingese dogs, nor Valentino experienced any airsickness, and without incident the plane landed at Le Bourget, where four hundred people were on hand to greet them. Several cabs were required to carry their baggage to the Hotel Plaza Athénée and a suite filled with bouquets, messages of welcome and formal invitations from people of importance. The press was out in force to welcome them, and reporters were delighted with Natacha's elegance and wrote that she comported herself with the élan vital of a great lady.

Shopping was as necessary as breathing for both Valentinos. Dressmakers and couturiers vied for Natacha's patronage but she chose Poiret, and the gowns and ensembles designed for her were later featured in *Photoplay*. And among Rudolph's more exotic purchases was a Voisin racing tourer, which he ordered upholstered in vermilion morocco. Because the car could not be completed during their short stay in Paris, the company lent Valentino another car for his use while in Europe. Was he not the best advertisement the company could ever hope for?

Jacques Herbertot, owner of the Théâtre Champs Élysées, invited them to Deauville for the Grand Prix, an event which was ruined by harsh, wet weather. At the casino Valentino gambled only modestly because Natacha did not approve of the tables. Back in Paris, they found the Folies Bergère a disappointment, and within hearing of French reporters Valentino undiplomatically observed that French chorus girls could not begin to compete with their American sisters. Besides, Ziegfeld's productions were far grander.

Montmartre did not impress the Valentinos, either, and Ciro's was filled with tourists. However, the stay in Paris was not an absolute failure because Valentino had been able to purchase three dozen silk shirts, tailored to order, several dozen pairs of pajamas, twelve lounging robes and as many quilted smoking jackets. He also found time to be measured for fine silk underwear. Also M. Herbertot gave him a Doberman pinscher named Kabar. So with four·dogs and considerably more luggage, they left Paris in the borrowed Voisin tourer for the Hudnut château.

During the run from Paris to the Riviera the Valentinos had their first serious quarrel. Valentino had insisted upon traveling over the Alps by way of Grenoble and Dijon, instead of taking the easier route through Lyons, and every cart, bicycle or car seemed a challenge. Every straightaway had to be entered at full throttle, every curve taken at maximum speed. As the road twisted into the mountains he took one curve too fast and as Natacha screamed in terror, he just managed to brake before the car could go over the precipice. Trembling, eyes closed and hands still gripping the wheel, he at last was able to whisper hoarsely: Had Natacha noticed that Black Feather, their Indian spirit guide, had leaned over at the very last moment to "help him give the wheel the wrench that saved us"? Natacha had seen nothing but was willing to believe some guardian angel had saved them, and said so. For the rest of the trip, Valentino drove slowly and with great care.

When the Hudnuts had purchased their villa of more than twenty rooms, with servants' quarters and formal gardens, from a Russian prince, its architecture had been vaguely Moorish. But Mrs. Hudnut had declared this unsuitable and after much study decided it should be Louis XVI. The château had been undergoing renovations and alterations for more than a year, and there were still several rooms to be done. Happily, the suite of rooms reserved for the young couple had been completed and was pleasant and comfortable. Valentino informed them that he could enjoy living here for some part of every year, and the Hudnuts listened tolerantly to his talk of kennels and stables, and agreed to his suggestions about a boathouse and small theater. During the visit they gave several small but lavish parties to introduce their daughter and famous son-in-law.

Ten days passed before Valentino felt strong enough to abandon the dogs and proceed to Milan, where his sister lived. In a burst of affection he invited Mrs. Werner to accompany them and promised that he would drive more carefully. He did, for about an hour, but it was obvious to his wife and her aunt that he was not happy about it. Suddenly a wagon appeared ahead of them and with a sudden burst of speed the tourer overtook the startled farmer; Valentino then continued to accelerate until they were flying down the road, a rising cloud of dust behind them. As they swooped around curves or passed other vehicles, Valentino shouted with joy, but Natacha screamed steadily and embraced her aunt, who sat with eyes closed and lips moving in prayer. Reveling in the power of the car, Valentino seemed totally unaware of his terrified passengers.

At midnight, with a roar of power, they entered Genoa. At their hotel Natacha wept herself to sleep, and the next morning said she was suffering from "a nervous breakdown," and flatly refused to continue their journey unless Valentino swore on his honor as a gentleman not to speed again. If he had no consideration for her, couldn't he at least have some for her aunt? Again Valentino promised and on the drive to Bologna kept his word every kilometer of the way. Then, just as they arrived in Bologna at sundown, he ran into a telephone pole. What irked him was that he had been driving slowly, and paying careful attention to the comfort of his wife and her aunt. But the telephone pole was painted gray and in the changing light he had been unable to see it. One fender was slightly dented and while it was being straightened they visited the piazza and leaning towers. After dinner they continued to Milan, where they found a telegram from Maria awaiting them at their hotel. Maria had gone to Genoa to meet them, and was now on her way back.

The next morning Valentino and his sister met after eleven years. They wept in each other's arms. To Natacha the girl seemed incredibly dowdy, and Maria looked suspiciously upon Natacha's powder and lip rouge. Why, she even used perfume in broad daylight! As Natacha recalled later: "She was frightfully concerned over her brother's reputation, and could not refrain from the suggestion that I at least should not wear a glove over my wedding ring." Valentino, too, appeared disturbed at his sister's provinciality and prevailed upon Maria to permit Natacha to choose a more becoming wardrobe for her. Maria agreed. After this had been accomplished, Natacha permitted her to guide them through the more famous Milanese churches.

Valentino arranged with an official of the Unione Cinematografica to show *The Four Horsemen* for Maria. A print of the movie had been loaned to him before he left Paris. Maria delighted in seeing her brother on the screen, marveled at his importance and could not understand his complaint that the print had been badly edited.

Five days were spent in Milan, and then they left for the south with Maria. As they motored toward Siena, they ran into a cart driven by an old crone. Valentino claimed he had to hit the cart to avoid smashing into another automobile, but when they arrived in Florence late that night with their thirteen pieces of luggage, Natacha insisted once more that she could not continue. Why, just getting in and out of the Voisin was a problem: there were two automobile trunks strapped to the fenders on each side; six valises were secured to the roof; and two hatboxes, a huge leather steamer trunk, three cameras and boxes of automobile tools shared the back seat with Mrs. Werner. Hotel porters sometimes seemed surprised to discover two women behind all that luggage.

At every hotel Mrs. Werner endeared herself to the staff, but Rudolph and Natacha were never satisfied with the service and complained loudly about the dust, the outmoded furniture and telephones that never seemed to work. Valentino was determined to continue his automobile journey at least to Rome, and Mrs. Werner was able to restrain Natacha from abandoning the tour at every stop. She felt confident, she told Natacha, that once they reached Rome, whatever further travel was necessary could be done by rail. A hired driver could return the Voisin to Paris.

In Siena they stopped at an old antique shop and found a painting of Anne of Cleves, signed by Holbein, which they bought for a small sum. That night they stayed at a small inn between Siena and Florence, and after dinner Rudolph and Natacha locked the door of their chamber and prepared themselves for one of their regular sessions. Natacha later wrote that there were no chairs in the room, only a wobbly little stool, and that they had to use the bed to communicate with the spirits. Among those who visited them that night were Rudolph's mother, and departed friends and relations, and of course their two faithful guides, Black Feather and Meselope. The spirits admired the painting and agreed that the wormholes were genuine, though they were of the unanimous opinion that though the painting was good and talented in composition, it was not really a Holbein. Strangely, no effort was made to communicate with Holbein.

Another disappointment was the discovery that Valentino was almost unknown in Italy because American films were rarely shown there until they were at least five years old. Valentino observed in a letter to a friend: "Ten years from now I will be popular in Italy, *perhaps*. BUT *they don't know me now*. That much is certain. From the chance wayfarer along the road, to the first and second run picture houses, I was as I had been when I left Italy, as unknown to films as films were unknown and unexpected to me."

Without further incident the Voisin entered Rome. That evening the Valentinos dined with two important members of the Italian film industry, who were delighted to learn that an Italian, in truth, had done so well in American films. Over wine they told Valentino how everyone had doubted the stories of his career when they had first heard about them.

Nulla e difficile a chi vuole. Chi non semine non raccoglie.
La fine corona l'opera.

Baron Fassini invited the Valentinos to visit the set of *Quo*
Vadis, which was then being filmed in Rome with Emil Jannings,
and promised that he would attempt to arrange a meeting with
Benito Mussolini, for the Premier occupied an apartment above
Fassini's in the Palazzo Titoni. Unfortunately, Il Duce was too
busy. The Valentinos spent several days on the set, where Mrs.
Jannings acted as interpreter, for her husband spoke no English.
As more people discovered that Valentino really was an important star in the United States, a variety of studio tours were
arranged for him. Now evenings were filled with dinners and
parties and Valentino was delighted to be seated at table above
many members of the Italian nobility.

For a week telegrams had been arriving from Ullman, urging
that Valentino advise about his plans for returning to New
York. Natacha was anxious to leave but Rudolph insisted
he would first have to visit his brother, Alberto, and Castellaneta.
At this Natacha balked; she refused to go one kilometer farther
south even if Valentino traveled by automobile and she by rail.
She had no desire to see the poverty in southern Italy or to
risk malaria, which was the major cause of death there.

On September 11, Natacha left for Paris and Maria, Mrs.
Werner and Valentino continued south toward Campo Bazzo in
the province of Abruzzi, where Alberto lived. They arrived in
the early evening and were warmly welcomed by Alberto, his
wife and their nine-year-old son, Jean. After a week's visit,
Valentino insisted on continuing on to Castellaneta, and all attempts to dissuade him failed. Alberto refused to make the
journey, insisting there was nothing to see and that Rudolph
was subjecting Mrs. Werner and Maria to unnecessary hard-
ship, since the roads were poor. Maria decided to remain with
Alberto but Valentino was adamant; he had come this far and

intended to return to the town of his birth. Bravely, Mrs. Werner agreed to accompany him. They suffered three flat tires along the way as they drove doggedly through a sad land of primitive villages and silent farms long abandoned because nothing grew there but dust, rocks and despair.

It was difficult but Mrs. Werner managed to feign impatience to see the house in which Rudolph had been born. Valentino was truly excited and sang and laughed more loudly as he began to recognize old landmarks. On his entire European journey he had looked forward most to this return to his boyhood home and he honked the horn joyously when he came to the first clusters of houses on the outskirts. But as he braked to a screeching halt in the town square and the dust settled they were surrounded by the silence of poverty, distrust and suspicion. Valentino raised his driving goggles, saw the dark eyes of strangers peering at him from shadowy doorways and realized he should never have returned. Slowly, as if about to attack from all sides, the crowd moved toward the car. Mrs. Werner shuddered as she saw their dark faces and slack mouths filled with broken teeth. Most depressing was their resigned shuffle, and when they came close enough to the car to touch it, their broken fingers and filthy nails.

His cousins were suspicious and became hostile, rude and threatening when he refused their requests for money. Neighbors whom he had known as a boy had died; those who were still alive lost interest in him when he rejected their appeal for huge sums that would enable them to escape to the north. But even when they threatened or cursed him, they did so with eyes to the ground. Mrs. Werner was anxious to leave, and told Valentino that the townspeople resented his camera. Ignorant and superstitious, they believed he was attempting to capture their souls with his black box.

In desperation Valentino visited the priest and asked that holy and learned man to be his intermediary, to explain the camera to his parishioners. But the priest preferred to speak of a large donation of money to restore his crumbling church. Given a hundred lire, he stuffed the banknote into his rusty cassock, made a perfunctory sign of blessing and left Valentino standing on the doorstep of the church.

Suddenly a man whom Valentino did not remember approached and, as a crowd gathered, challenged him with a tattered copy of the February *Photoplay*. Valentino attempted to break through but the crowd moved to block his escape, and as the man began to read in a loud voice, translating the article into Italian as he went along, eyes came alive, lips turned up in smiles. Suddenly someone began to chuckle and black mouths opened wide in laughter as the speaker recited the nonsense about Valentino's grand name, his nobility, and how he had been sent to the United States with four thousand American dollars! A bit of dry dung hit Valentino in the face, and with a curse he struck out and ran with Mrs. Werner for the car. His left arm raised to shield his face, he got her into the car and sped through the streets of Castellaneta. Until they reached the last houses, they had to run a gauntlet of rotting vegetables, garbage and stones.

At Taranto, Valentino secluded himself in his hotel room. Later Mrs. Werner assured her unhappy nephew by marriage that she would never tell anyone what had happened. But he could never forget. Forever after he hated Castellaneta and the entire south of Italy.

THERE'S A NEW STAR IN HEAVEN TO-NIGHT

(RUDOLPH VALENTINO)

by
J. Keirn Brennan
writer of "A Little Bit Of Heaven" etc.
Irving Mills
and
Jimmy McHugh

JACK MILLS INC.
Music Publishers
Jack Mills Building
148-150 W. 46 St. New York

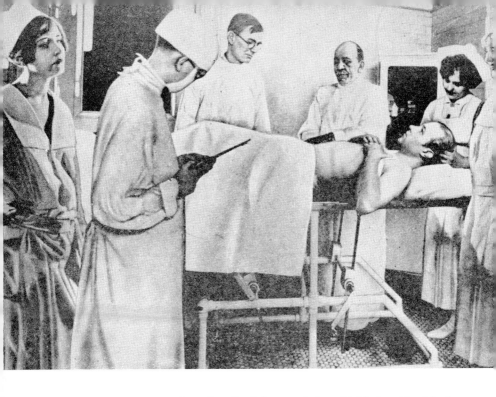

THE GRAPHIC, *that short-lived but spritely tabloid, brashly faked a variety of Valentino pictures—above, the operation from which he never recovered and, below, Valentino's arrival in the great beyond....*

Valentino was an enthusiastic horseman, a talent he found useful in THE FOUR HORSEMEN, *the movie that started him on his way to stardom....*

Natacha thought THE SHEIK *utter trash and predicted it would end his career; instead it made Rudy the lover American women of all ages had secretly been longing for. . . .*

THE YOUNG RAJAH, *which the studio made under protest, was perhaps the least successful movie Valentino ever made. . . .*

The public demanded all the accouterments of stardom, but some-how Rudy seemed to need more—a number of foreign motor cars and a dazzling wardrobe, preferably tailored on Bond Street. . . .

One of the advantages of becoming famous was the company one kept—Douglas Fairbanks, right, Rudy, left, and Jackie Coogan, front and center. . . .

MONSIEUR BEAUCAIRE *grossed well in New York but bombed in the boondocks, where audiences were offended by the heart-shaped beauty mark alongside Rudy's nose. . . .*

After making THE FOUR HORSEMEN, *Valentino wanted to appear in another Ibáñez novel,* BLOOD AND SAND, *but the studio kept putting him off. When finally it was filmed he gave the best performance, perhaps, of any in his career. . . .*

Critics called THE SON OF THE SHEIK *a tasteless hodgepodge, almost a parody of* THE SHEIK, *but Rudy's fans loved it and applauded wildly whether he portrayed the old sheik or his young son. . . .*

Though dusky of skin, the son of the sheik, as had his father before him, turns out actually to be a well-bred Englishman. . . .

When Valentino and Natacha glided across the stage in a sensual tango audiences went wild—the Mineralava tour was an unqualified success, breaking attendance records everywhere. . . .

Deeply troubled by marital problems, Rudy lost himself in THE EAGLE, *from a Pushkin novel, in which he played a sort of Russian Robin Hood. Clarence Brown, the director, is the other man on the ladder.*

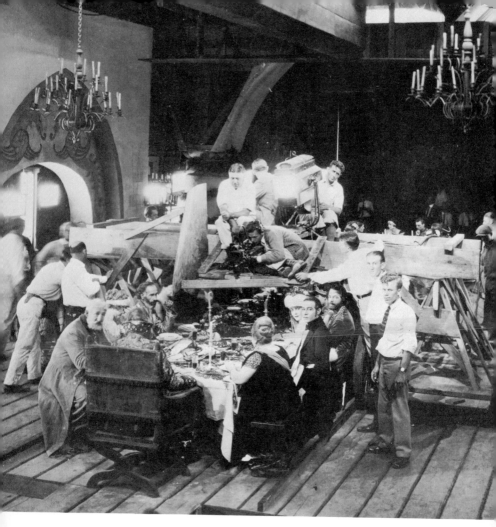

Natacha disapproved heartily of THE EAGLE, *but by now Rudy's contract barred her from even appearing on the set. This was the beginning of the end; shortly after this they separated. . . .*

After playing a South American cowboy in THE FOUR HORSEMEN, *Rudy always felt an affinity for the North American counterpart. . . .*

Fan magazines clamored endlessly for publicity shots of the star. One of the more unusual, perhaps inspired by Rudy's spirit contact, Black Feather. . . .

ooo

ACT THREE: SCENE TEN

ooooooooooooooooooooooooooooooooooooooooooooooooo

A chastened Rudolph, withdrawn and so nervous he reacted violently to any raised voice, rejoined his wife at Nice. To the cool queries of Natacha, and the friendly questions of her parents about his trip to Castellaneta, he made the proper replies. The homecoming had been a success; everyone had been overjoyed to see him; the town had offered him every conceivable honor; Alberto and Maria had regretted their decision not to accompany him. But inwardly Valentino seethed. The whole Italian trip had been a failure: Mussolini had not granted him an audience; his pictures were unknown to Italian theatergoers; and people would forever laugh at him in Castellaneta.

At the château he rested and in time recovered some of his old ebullience. Although the mild autumn weather and luxury of the surroundings were balm to his battered spirit, he was genuinely delighted when Natacha agreed that their return to Hollywood, because of new picture commitments, was inevitable. Passage was booked on the *Belgenland*, from Southampton, and the very next day Valentino got a cablegram from J. D. Williams. A matter of utmost importance, it said, demanded that he and Natacha board the *Leviathan* at Cherbourg, where Williams would meet them. To comply with the cablegram necessitated furiously rapid packing because the *Leviathan* was due to dock at Cherbourg on October 6. The Valentinos wired ahead for new reservations, which were confirmed, but when they arrived at the pier, the customs guards insisted upon opening and searching every valise and trunk in their mountain of luggage. By the time the inspection was completed and their trunks repacked, the *Leviathan* had sailed and they had to hire a tug to give chase.

Despite several attempts to board, huge waves made it impossible. When the captain of the tug finally refused to put his craft in further jeopardy, they returned to Cherbourg, soaked to the bone and shaken by their experience. Some of their baggage had been washed overboard and the rest was drenched. The frustrated travelers checked in at the Hotel de France in Cherbourg and made plans to continue on to London to meet Williams as soon as possible.

"Why did you want us to come aboard the *Leviathan* at Cherbourg?" Valentino asked when they met.

"Oh," Williams explained. "Oh, yes. Why, we had a nice party arranged for you. We wanted you to have a good time. We had a band all ready."

On October 15 the *Belgenland* sailed for New York and the Valentinos were aboard. After a relaxing crossing, the travelers registered at the Ritz Carlton Hotel on the twenty-first. There, they conferred with Ullman and Max Steuer to discuss several projects Famous Players-Lasky was willing to put into immediate production. Valentino preferred *Captain Blood* by Rafael Sabatini, but Natacha thought it better for him to return to the screen in Tarkington's *Monsieur Beaucaire*. As usual, her choice prevailed.

The Astoria, New York, studio of Famous Players was told to prepare for the production and—most important—to accord Mrs. Valentino every courtesy. Still, there were journalistic irritants to mar these avowals of harmony and good fellowship. The November issue of *Film Classics* carried an article by Valentino called "When I Come Back," which had actually been ghosted before the European trip. Generally critical of the motion picture industry, it was illustrated by a full-length photograph of Rudy in loincloth, Indian headdress and bow and arrow. Russell Ball, the photographer, had posed him with his right hand raised to shield his eyes as he peered toward a distant mountain of fan mail. This camera study pleased neither Natacha nor Famous Players-Lasky, although it was well received by the fans. In the article Valentino promised them that when he returned, he intended to "be again the romantic lover. It is what I can do best and it is what most people want . . . romance and drama are what most lives lack and I shall try to supply it."

Monsieur Beaucaire was rewritten to provide some beef-cake scenes in a supersetting for a "romantic lover." This anatomical overhaul of Booth Tarkington's novel gave the Valentinos a chance to enjoy their return to New York. But the script for *Beaucaire*, which was being written by Forrest Halsey, did not please Natacha and—miraculously—Lasky for once agreed with her criticism. In addition to the rewriting, there were some technical problems, so it was decided to hold over production until 1924. The Valentinos decided to spend the intervening time in Nice with the Hudnuts, and on December 9 they sailed again on the *Aquitania*. Reporters who saw them off were most intrigued by a spiked platinum bracelet that Valentino wore on his right wrist. He would only say that it was a "family secret." In a confidential mood, he also told reporters of a gold bracelet that he wore to bed. Who had given him the bracelets? Were they really slave bracelets? What exactly was their significance? Valentino only smiled mysteriously.

A real American Christmas celebration had been planned by the Hudnuts, whose château was generously decorated with mistletoe and holly. A huge Christmas tree, adorned with colored balls, gifts and artificial snowflakes, was set up in the library. Hundreds of small colored candles were attached to the tree, but the Hudnuts preferred not to light them. Valentino, however, was enchanted and insisted that they be lighted, and the enthusiasm of her handsome son-in-law was so infectious that Mrs. Hudnut overcame her reservations and agreed. The candles were carefully ignited and their glow warmed the room. Then Valentino noticed one unlit candle far back in the branches. He reached in with a taper, and in a moment the great tree was ablaze.

Mrs. Hudnut screamed for everyone to save her Gobelin tapestries and Saint Ceré needlepoint chairs. Buckets of water and a small garden hose that Valentino dragged into the library finally extinguished the fire, but the spirit of Christmas was extinguished with it, and the day after New Year's, Mrs. Hudnut noted in a letter, the "children" departed for America.

Valentino's absence from the screen had not caused him to lose popularity with his fans; he was still the undisputed masculine sex menace of American society. Because he made no films in 1923, moviegoers went to see his earlier films again and again and the magic grew, for with each viewing women seemed to read more into them than had ever been intended. He was the lover of their dreams and hearts, the violent, exciting, secret lover who never pleaded for a lady's favors but took them without scruple. "Lie still," he had said to Agnes Ayres in *The Sheik*. "Lie still, you little fool!"

Passion was more important than civilization. All conventions were ignored when his smoldering eyes fastened upon the lady of his desire. He was the mysterious lover who rode into every woman's humdrum town to capture and carry her off to a primitive desert, an untouched strand or a grim castle high upon a crag. No American worthy of his Christian heritage would dare kidnap or ravish a woman; this was foreign and disloyal and certainly anathema to the sturdy platitudes that comprised the platform of the Republican party. But this perhaps made it attractive to all women, especially since at the proper time they would be rescued by their American husbands and sweethearts—for, in reality, they were only at the movies.

As soon as it was announced that *Monsieur Beaucaire* would shortly begin production in Astoria, all vacant apartments in Long Island City were snapped up and real estate agents noted a brisk increase in the purchase of private homes in the area. Studio telephones could not handle the thousands of calls from women who pleaded for the opportunity to appear as extras or work as waitresses in the commissary or take any jobs that would permit them even a momentary glimpse of Valentino. They would gladly work without pay.

The thousands of letters received by the studio and addressed to Valentino required two secretaries and a mail clerk to process. A good many of them included photographs and two censors had to be employed by the studios to remove those that might embarrass the secretaries, for many of the posers were completely nude. There were letters that pleaded for intimate garments once worn by Valentino; there were effusions beseeching him for one hour of his love. Even that small boon would suffice for a lifetime.

The adulation bewildered Valentino; his growing scores of imitators alternately amused and annoyed him. But the sum total of the unpleasant aspects of fame caused him to speak increasingly of his desire to do no more than two pictures a year—six months' work at most—and spend the remaining six months of each year at the Hudnut château in Nice. At first, the affection with which he had been greeted at the studio had pleased him. But petty annoyances and the constant pilferage of souvenirs from his dressing room became intolerable nuisances. Once the picture actually got under way he insisted that at all times the studio station a guard at his dressing-room door.

The new scenario for *Monsieur Beaucaire* pleased Valentino; so did the studio's choice of Bebe Daniels to play opposite him. But director Sidney Olcott protested frequently to Lasky and Zukor that no matter how trivial the decision, the traditional authority wielded by a director was denied him by Mrs. Valentino's constant interference. He should, he insisted, be removed from the film because he served no function. Studio officials begged him to be patient; the daily rushes were far beyond their most optimistic expectations, and advance interest in the film was already greater than in any competing picture in production. Lasky pleaded with everyone to be as patient and self-sacrificing as Mr. Zukor and himself.

To keep potential audience interest high, Paramount's publicity staff outdid itself. Valentino had become a greater lover during his absence from the screen, one story ran, by spending his time poring over arcane love tomes unavailable to the general public. From these secret volumes he had discovered the ten ways of infinite delight indefinitely prolonged into eternity. . . .

Although Valentino found this publicity amusing, Natacha failed to find anything humorous about it. What was there to laugh about in the presentation of her husband as a rake and an adulterer? Valentino vainly tried to persuade her that it was all part of the movie business, and they quarreled. The spats were private as well as public, for the presence of interested onlookers never tempered Natacha's denunciations of her husband's stupidity. But to berate a man for stupidity was less exciting than to charge him with infidelity, so many of the gossip columnists and fan-magazine writers hinted to their readers that Natacha fought with her husband because of the amorous attentions he paid his leading ladies.

In an effort to smooth the abrasive presence of Natacha, Lasky assigned Harry Reichenbach to handle Rudolph's personal publicity. Reichenbach, pleased with the assignment, hurried to the Astoria studio to see the man for whom he had got the part that had begun his career. But when Reichenbach arrived at the studio, Valentino's dressing-room door was locked. He knocked and a valet appeared.

"What do you want?" the valet asked.

"Tell Mr. Valentino that Harry Reichenbach wants to see him."

"Does Mr. Valentino know you?"

"I think so." Reichenbach was becoming irritated. "He used to borrow two or three dollars at a time from me."

The valet locked the dressing-room door behind him and as Harry waited he regretted his petulant outburst and planned to make a joke about it when he saw Valentino. But in less than a minute the valet opened the door again, though he did not invite Reichenbach to enter.

"Mr. Valentino is resting just now," he announced. "He's very tired. He suggested that you see Mrs. Valentino, since she handles all his publicity matters."

Reichenbach pondered for only a moment and boiled over. "I see. Well, you tell him that if *Mrs.* Valentino handles these matters, then let her call Mrs. Reichenbach."

Within the hour Reichenbach returned to Lasky's office and told everyone he "would have nothing to do with Mrs. Valentino." Although the company sympathized with him, Lasky explained that one of the stipulations in the reconciliation between the company and Valentino provided for Natacha's approval of all publicity. For the sake of peace, Reichenbach agreed to see Natacha and present her with some of his publicity ideas and the advertising copy he had prepared for the picture.

Their first meeting was not a happy one. Natacha vetoed everything he proposed and quite coldly informed him that only she had the right to prepare copy.

Each day Reichenbach asked to be relieved of his assignment; each day the Paramount officials begged him to try to work with Natacha. In the end, the only way to get anything done was to demand that she supply ideas rather than vetoes. If her suggestions were of any value, Harry incorporated them in his copy; if not, he listened to her and did as he pleased. Reichenbach's work on *Monsieur Beaucaire* could be used as a textbook on how interest is generated and maintained during a film production. In the Sunday *Times* of March 2, Reichenbach managed to get a full column on the problems of translating *Beaucaire* to the screen. He also kept peace with *Photoplay*, which insisted upon featuring some photographs of Bebe Daniels, and did what he could to have Adela Rogers St. Johns handle Valentino with care. He did not wholly succeed. In her article in the April issue—"What Kind of Men Attract Women Most?" —Miss St. Johns called Wallace Reid "the epitome of charm," Richard Dix "manly, brave and daring," Ramon Navarro "romantic" and Antonio Moreno "the gay and poetic wooer." Valentino was merely "passion personified." In further elaboration Miss St. Johns wrote: "Beyond question, Reid and Valentino stand as the two great matinee idols of this generation. Probably they are the two greatest matinee idols the world has ever known."

But she really let the Sheik have it in succeeding paragraphs:

> . . . Valentino, with his small eyes, his flat nose and large mouth, fails to measure up to the standards of male beauty usually accepted in this country. . . . The majority of women will swear that they prefer respect to love. If they do, why do they choose a Rudolph Valentino as their idol? . . . The lure of Valentino is wholly, entirely, obviously the lure of the flesh. . . . The men of America have resented Rudolph's popu-

larity. . . . They resent it because they believe he appeals to
the worst side of women, because they claim his is the same
attraction for women that a vampire has for men. . . . Strangely
enough . . . he is an ordinary young man, with atrocious
taste in clothes, whose attributes render him devoid of physical
charm . . . all the women who knew him well in a professional way and the women who knew him before he became
famous, feel about him exactly as I do. They are amazed and
a little amused by the power and pull of his sex attraction on
the screen. They like him, find him pleasant enough, but as far
as I can discover not one of them has ever fallen in love with
him. Yet every one of them will admit he stirs them on the
screen.

For the most part, however, magazine and newspaper comments on Valentino and *Monsieur Beaucaire* were favorable.
Most important, day by day new ones, equally favorable, appeared.

George Ullman's attempts to reason with Natacha and to explain
to her that she was embarrassing everyone by her injudicious
exercise of prerogatives failed utterly. In private conversations
with Valentino, he reminded the actor of his sworn promises to
make his own decisions. But Valentino insisted that Natacha
had more taste and ability than anyone associated with the production, so Ullman gave up.

Once again Valentino was wildly throwing money around—
buying everything in sight, lavishing thousands of dollars on
clothing and jewelry on his wife. He had also commenced the
prodigal purchases of expensive antiques for the Wedgewood
Place house on Whitley Heights, and he bought indiscriminately.
The New York Times reported his acquisition at auction of an
eighteenth-century Moorish *drap d'or* crimson scarf with ends
woven in varied gold, blue, green and crimson stripes. The
scarf was more than thirteen feet long and about nineteen
inches wide. What he would do with it, Ullman did not know.
Another purchase was a seventeenth-century Albanian gold-em-

broidered crimson velvet coat, with front panels of gold scrollings and an hourglass back with chevroned stripes of silver bordered in gold.

Most evenings Valentino could be found at some major auction house and scarcely a night passed when he did not spend at least a thousand dollars. From the Tolentino Collection of Italian art and furniture, auctioned off at the American Art Galleries, he made several purchases, among them a fifteenth-century French Gothic carved walnut chest, the entire front a facade of cathedral windows with pointed arches and elaborate Gothic tracery in bas-relief. Another evening he paid $640 for two decidedly mediocre Spanish paintings. Everything was crated and dispatched to Hollywood, the bills sent to Ullman, and by the middle of April the worried manager had to report that Valentino was once again in debt to Paramount.

An unconcerned Valentino continued to buy books, illuminated manuscripts, rugs, chests, exotic costumes, Turkish and Arabic furniture, throne chairs, bad portraits, dinner services, linens, inkwells and miscellaneous pieces of armor that every antique dealer in New York had despaired of ever selling. With growing expansiveness, he considered a yacht, a racing stable and a private airplane, but Ullman at least managed to veto these financial conceits.

For Valentino's return to the screen Paramount utilized the services of two assistant directors to work with Olcott; two assistant cameramen to work with Harry Fischbeck; three assistants for Natacha, who was art director; a scenic artist and two assistants; a costume director and four wardrobe women; an art selector, an interior decorator and an assistant; an expert draper, a company of musicians, a caterer's crew—besides those normally associated with production. Then a supervisor of makeup was added to the staff, as well as a director of etiquette, an expert on period carriages, a gardener and a specialist in tapestries. Under the firm supervision of Natacha, sixty elaborate costumes were designed by George Barbier, a French illustrator. These were completed in Paris after two French period experts had spent a month of research to ensure their authenticity. There was a fencing master and a dancing master, a reader of poetry to Valentino and a private fiddler, a tobacconist, and two assistants to his valet. Also a physiotherapist and a calisthenist, a man to duplicate Valentino's signature on autographs and a librarian hired to catalogue his miscellaneous purchases. There was even a masseur. Nevertheless, the picture was completed only a few days over schedule and Valentino planned to rest for several weeks before he undertook another major period of romantic history in Astoria.

Throughout the entire production of *Beaucaire*, George Ullman had been frustrated in his consistent attempts to curb Valentino's expenditures, and even to prevent him from ignoring old bills. But Valentino disregarded all advice, then acted as if he had been unfairly injured when, on July 9, 1924, an action was brought against him in New York City by his former agents, Robertson and Webb, who hoped to recover commissions due them since 1921. Robertson and Webb claimed they had renegotiated the Famous Players-Lasky contract and that after paying them $2,833, Valentino had neglected, then refused, to pay further commissions. They claimed a balance due the agency of $16,625. Outraged, Valentino demanded to know why Ullman had not attended to this matter.

Ullman pointed out that time and time again he had called Valentino's attention to letters received from Robertson and Webb and that Valentino had always insisted he had orally discharged the agency. Ullman suggested a settlement with the agency, but this was rejected. The matter did not come to trial until June, 1926, when Clifford Robertson and Eugene Webb,

Jr., were awarded $1,667, $550 of which was deducted from the award because Valentino had advanced Robertson that amount as a loan.

Monsieur Beaucaire opened at the Mark Strand during the week of August 10. *Weekly Variety* called it a "money" picture and reported long lines outside the Strand all Sunday afternoon and evening. Although hot and humid weather made the theater's interior well-nigh unbearable, packed audiences guaranteed a long holdover. What surprised *Variety* was "the wholesale relegating of practically the entire cast to the background, so that this feature amounts to nothing less than 100 minutes of Valentino." But this did not seem to displease metropolitan movie fans, who, though impressed by the settings and costumes, reserved their applause for Valentino alone. *Variety*'s reviewer concluded that *Beaucaire* was "as choice a bit of picking as could have been done in the selecting of a piece for Valentino's screen return. The women will 'go' for this one by the thousands."

The New York Times opened its review with a paragraph that made the Paramount executives dance in their offices:

> Clad in embroidered satin and costly laces, his glossy dark hair covered by a white wig, Rudolph Valentino, after an absence of two years, has returned to the screen and is to be seen this week at the Mark Strand in the title role of the picturization of Booth Tarkington's exquisite story, "Monsieur Beaucaire." Gorgeous is a word we invariably dodge, but this pictorial effort is thoroughly deserving of such an adjective, as never have such wondrous settings or beautiful costumes been seen in a photoplay.

The review was favorable throughout and found little fault with Valentino except to call attention to his tendency to speak out of one side of his mouth. Otherwise, the reviewer found him to be a good-looking and athletic Beaucaire, "agile in the fighting scenes and exceptionally affectionate in the love sequences."

Mordaunt Hall did a Sunday feature for *The New York Times* on *Beaucaire* in which he wrote that he preferred Tarkington's novel to its screen adaptation by Forrest Halsey. He was also critical of Valentino's performance, and deemed him to be no more than a screen actor with "an attractive physiognomy and the ability to appear as an impetuous and ardent lover with an omnipresent underlying consciousness of his own popularity." Nevertheless, honest objectivity compelled Hall to conclude with a paragraph of approval:

> There is too much of Valentino in Beaucaire and not enough of the aristocratic Frenchman. However, it does not alter the fact that with all the digression from the narrative this is a beautiful and a most interesting production. It is unfortunate that the producers decided to make it a glorious box-office movie instead of an artistic motion picture, which in the end might have appealed to audiences just as much as and perhaps more than does this pictorial effort.

There is no intent here to compare *The New York Times* with movie magazines, but the latter were of far greater importance to moviegoers—and their reviewers were disappointed. How well these magazines could judge average audience reaction was revealed in the film's ultimate gross. *Monsieur Beaucaire* proved a failure, and in small-town theaters audiences jeered Valentino's performance, dandified appearance and heart-shaped beauty mark aside his nose—or stayed away in droves.

The September issue of *Photoplay* carried James R. Quirk's opinion:

> Something has happened to the Valentino of "The Sheik" and "Blood and Sand." I am afraid the dyed-in-the-wool Valentino fans will be a little disappointed in their idol in "Monsieur Beaucaire." Rudy is trying to be an actor at the expense of the personality that made him a sensation. The production is lavish and beautiful, but throughout the entire

picture every personality, including Bebe Daniels, Lois Wilson and Doris Kenyon, is thrown out of focus.

Rudy plays the part of a prince of France, and, except for one or two situations in which he puts over rattling good sword fights, the old spark disappears. He doesn't look a bit dangerous to women.

The fact of the matter is that they like their Rudy a little wicked. He had what is known in pictures as "menace" to a higher degree than any actor on the screen. In "Beaucaire" he has about as much of this quality as Charlie Chaplin.

The entire picture was made inside the studio and that detracts somewhat from the convincing quality of the production. Mrs. Valentino supervised the entire production and while her artistic ability has resulted in beautiful sets and costumes, the picture gives you the impression of a terrific striving for something that was not quite attained. It is beautiful but self-conscious.

Paramount pondered Quirk's negative editorial. The sultry style of Valentino's lovemaking had endeared him to millions of women. *Beaucaire,* with its choppy scenes and its absurdly elaborate costumes suggesting effeminacy, had not met with public enthusiasm. The Paramount organization had only two choices: it could release Valentino from his contract or immediately star him in one more picture. The second course of action seemed more profitable.

Of the properties submitted to Rudolph Valentino for this last film under his contract with Paramount, Natacha approved Rex Beach's story "Rope's End," and ordered the assignment of Forrest Halsey as scenarist. Although Natacha was aware of Paramount's intention to complete its contractual obligation as economically as possible, she insisted that this tale of adventure in South America be mounted handsomely and that there be no skimping on costs. With Valentino at her side, she began to reply to criticism of the actor—and of her influence over him—by barring interviews and press releases to anyone she personally found offensive. All casting had also to be submitted to her.

She approved Nita Naldi (who had not replaced Bebe Daniels in *Beaucaire*) as Carlotta—the other woman—and the film was retitled *A Sainted Devil*. The role of the bride was awarded by Natacha to Helene D'Algy, and that of a third woman—a vamp named Donna Florencia—was allotted to Jetta Goudal, a French actress under contract to Paramount. A beautiful and striking woman, well schooled in the uses of publicity, Miss Goudal made no effort to deny her personal interest in investigating the menace that was Valentino. When she arrived in New York, her ease with reporters did not please Natacha, and neither did her expressions of disappointment in Mrs. Valentino as a fashion designer. The two were separated before anything inflammatory could be said, and then the facts of life were explained to Jeta.

An uneasy peace prevailed for a time as Natacha prepared her sketches of Miss Goudal's costumes. Then came the first fitting. Miss Goudal looked at the sketches and shook her head, then began to make faces. Suddenly she inhaled and screamed operatically that Mrs. Valentino's only talent had been in marrying her famous husband and in designing costumes for men who were not men, and under no circumstances would she even look at, much less wear, such monstrous clothes. Witnesses to this battle agreed that Miss Goudal won the shouting match, but she lost her part in *A Sainted Devil*, for Paramount officials almost immediately issued a communiqué that "Miss Goudal had withdrawn from the cast."

An immediate replacement, more docile and cooperative, had to be found and when Natacha was able to speak again, she approved Dagmar Godowsky who was just completing two pictures at the same time in Hollywood. Dagmar was ordered to rush through them and report to Astoria for an interview, where her dark hair and green eyes pleased Natacha; more important, Dagmar's well-known equanimity and patience under stress made it simple for her to work with Valentino's mentor. With a tact that endeared her to Paramount, Dagmar gave rave interviews about the gowns designed for her, told everyone she "adored" working with Valentino, and even acted as an ambassador between Natacha and Joseph Henaberry, the director of the film. To facilitate shooting, the sets were closed to visitors, a quarantine which kept Miss Godowsky's admirers at a distance but pleased Natacha mightily.

The New York Times devoted a long article—"Argentine in Astoria"—to describe the elaborate ranch-house courtyard, the fine blooded animals, the musicians who played mood music, and the skilled camera crew that worked smoothly under Henaberry's direction, and concluded with what was of most interest to readers—a description of Valentino as the sainted devil.

> Over at the side of the set sat a man in sparkling bolero, knickerbockers and silk stockings. This glistening person was none other than Valentino, the star of the production, who at a sign received a cigarette from his valet. Mr. Valentino takes his film work with due seriousness. He came over to us and outlined the story of "The Sainted Devil," regarding which he was most enthusiastic. He referred to the hard and tedious work of making pictures. He knew that he had been sitting and waiting for more than an hour and that the director was then not nearly ready to call upon him. Mr. Valentino was cleverly made up, so that he appeared far more natural than many of the other players.

Particularly pleasing to Rudolph was the opportunity his role gave him to play a drunkard, rather than the usual slick hero he had come to despise. Whenever a scene called for him to appear as hopelessly despondent and unable to find solace in his cups, he acted with conviction; and whenever he escaped

Natacha's surveillance he approached Henaberry to ask if other scenes of despair and emotional turmoil could not be written into the film. To the enormous relief of everyone at Paramount, the picture was finished without unusual incident and was scheduled for late November release.

Hands were shaken all around, cups of friendship drunk, good wishes extended, and Valentino promised to assist Paramount in publicizing this last picture under its banner. The gross of *Beaucaire* had proved a disappointment to him and he told Jesse Lasky privately that if it were possible to do the picture over again, it would be a more virile production in keeping with the spirit of the novel. Paramount officials were equally friendly and wished Valentino every success. Their doors were always open, they assured him, if ever he wished to visit or ask their advice. But no sooner was he out of earshot than Paramount executives congratulated each other on finally being rid of "a double hernia."

When Lasky returned to California, he immediately undertook a search for someone to replace Valentino. The Latin appearance and grace of another dancer caught Lasky's eye and he invited the young man to visit him at Paramount. Jack Crane, formerly Jacob Krantz, was willing to be a movie actor and agreed to change his name to any that suited the studio. Mr. Lasky got Ricardo from the box of cigars on his desk, then ran down the alphabet for suitable surnames. The letter *C* yielded Cortez.

ACT THREE: SCENE ELEVEN

If, when all was said and done, Valentino had certain misgivings about leaving Paramount, Natacha certainly did not. Under the pseudonym of Justice Layne, she had been writing an original screen story called *The Scarlet Power*, which J. D. Williams, to her delight, had approved. It would be set in medieval Spain, and Valentino would play a noble Moor who led his countrymen back and forth across the Spanish peninsula in conquests of war and love. The part would require Valentino to darken his skin, and he might even wear an attractive beard.

The story had been discussed with June Mathis, who felt that, properly developed and mounted, *The Scarlet Power* could be as impressive as *The Four Horsemen* and fully as popular as *The Sheik*. She agreed to work on the script, once Natacha completed the development of this superspectacle. Would J. D. Williams permit the picture to be filmed in Spain, she asked, and was he prepared to spend more than a million dollars? Natacha considered these minor problems. Every conversation with Williams had been pleasant and already he had authorized her to spend forty thousand dollars on research. The Valentinos quickly departed for Europe and dutifully spent a few days at the Hudnut château, but they were anxious to get to Spain and delve into Moorish history.

The excitement of the projected jaunt appealed to Mrs. Hudnut, who asked if she might accompany the children. Permission granted, she hastily persuaded Valentino to travel by train. In Madrid the three of them visited galleries and museums, and industriously noted the costumes and architecture of the period. Every important antique shop and book dealer in the Spanish capital was visited by the Valentinos, and they managed to purchase an average of almost two thousand dollars' worth of "research" materials each day.

Although there would be no bullfighting in Natacha's Moorish epic, Valentino could not resist purchasing some antique toreador costumes and several modern "suits of lights." Natacha bought dresses and expensive mantillas. The merchants of Madrid were truly sorry to see the Valentinos depart for Seville, where their shopping spree continued, including additional trunks to store books and artifacts too precious to be sent by express. The Valentinos also visited the Seville bullfight, but the blood upset the ladies, who left early. They thereafter devoted themselves to the study of ancient Moorish architectural monuments, along with quantity purchases of more books, colored plates, etchings, tapestries, antique arms and suitable costumes. All bills were sent to J. D. Williams, President, Ritz-Carlton Productions, who honored them even after the forty thousand dollars originally agreed on had been exhausted. In toto, the Valentinos spent one hundred thousand dollars on Spanish artifacts alone. Exhausted at last by history and shopping, they filled half a baggage car with their trunks and returned with Mrs. Hudnut to Nice.

A few days later, Natacha and Valentino left for a short trip to Paris, where Natacha planned to sketch at the Louvre and continue her research into fourteenth-century Moorish dress. Valentino, meanwhile, took delivery on the Voisin he had ordered the year before. Delighted with the new car, he drove it to Nice, with a new Doberman pinscher at his side. Natacha sat in the back, where she kept order among the five Pekingeses she had purchased to add to her menagerie at home. In the trunk was a print of *Monsieur Beaucaire* and following them, ensconced on a truck, was a large film projector which Valentino had borrowed in Paris that he might show *Beaucaire* to the Hudnuts and selected guests.

After dinner on the night of the premiere, the assembled family and guests moved to the library, but no sooner had seats been taken and the film begun, than every fuse in the château blew. By candlelight, amid much milling confusion, the guests were dispatched and the Hudnuts and their unhappy son-in-law stumbled up to their chambers. During each of the next four days, electricians drove to the château, replaced fuses and left. And each night, as promptly, the projector blew them. On the fifth, the electricians installed the new, heavy-duty wiring the projector required. Finally *Beaucaire* was shown, and hailed by its somewhat prejudiced audience as a remarkable movie.

It was during this visit that Valentino, who had a sincere enthusiasm for all types of machinery, became intrigued by the Hudnuts' new electric piano. To learn more about its mysterious workings and complicated innards, he took it apart one afternoon and examined every coil and gear before neatly labeling each and placing it in proper sequence on a scatter rug put there for this purpose. But the five Pekingeses and the Doberman chose that moment to become playful, and before they could be stopped, scrambled the parts hopelessly. Valentino was unable to reassemble the piano but Uncle Dickie made no issue of the matter, merely waited until the "children" departed, then wired London to dispatch a mechanic to put the piano back together.

After serious dialogue with herself, Natacha decided to rename her Moorish epic *The Hooded Falcon*. This trenchant decision made, she concentrated on her study of voluminous cloaks and masks of the fourteenth century, while Valentino improvised acrobatic scenes that would make Douglas Fairbanks spin with envy. Nita Naldi arrived in Paris and Natacha invited her to accompany them on a trip through the northern provinces of France to visit old châteaus and medieval cities. Nita agreed, was most enthusiastic about *The Hooded Falcon*, and offered to play any starring part assigned her. During this junket, cablegrams from J. D. Williams in New York greeted the travelers at every stop. Their tone grew more and more impatient until finally they could no longer be ignored. At October's end, Natacha, Valentino and Nita boarded the *Leviathan*.

Meanwhile, Paramount was preparing for the release of *A Sainted Devil* and turned once more to Harry Reichenbach to conjure up some sensational publicity device. The problem was simple, he assured them. If Paramount could persuade Valentino to grow a beard, they would be guaranteed the kind of publicity money couldn't buy. A Paramount representative communicated the request to Valentino, who was delighted. Natacha wanted him to grow a beard for *The Hooded Falcon* anyway, and he had started on it during the trip through the château country. When the Valentinos landed in New York on November 11, 1924, his new look got all the newspaper coverage Reichenbach had predicted, and he himself took the occasion to explain that the goatee would be worn in *The Hooded Falcon*, his next movie, which was going to "center on the romantic days of the Moors at Granada and their encounters with the Spanish knights who sought to drive them from their stronghold." He had visited

Seville, Madrid, Granada and Cordova, he said, and had found them very interesting. Rudolph also told friends and reporters how he had actually found and visited the house of Juan Gallardo, the hero of *Blood and Sand*. The hovel was even poorer than the house he had occupied in Castellaneta—the mere mention of which now made him shudder—but he had felt the spirit of the dead bullfighter and the vibrations he had received from the hovel were happy ones, for Juan had approved of Rudolph's portrayal of him on the screen.

This business completed, Reichenbach got in touch with the Master Barbers Association of America, then in convention at the Hotel Sherman in Chicago, and sounded a warning: Valentino had tremendous influence on style and fashion. If he wore a beard, American youth would be certain to follow. And then what would happen to the noble profession of barbering? Under the heading of emergency business, Valentino's beard was debated in open session and by voice acclamation the barbers approved a resolution that if Valentino failed to shave it off, all barbers, their families and friends would boycott his pictures, for "such a fashion would not only work harmful injury to barbers, but would so utterly deface America as to make American citizens difficult to distinguish from Russians."

The meeting with Mr. Williams was hardly a happy occasion. Williams was clearly more than a little miffed by the hundred thousand dollars they had spent on "research materials" and stated that he did not believe it could be absorbed by the utilization of the articles in the picture. He was also convinced, he said, that the West Coast was the proper base of operations for planning *The Hooded Falcon*, and that he intended to move the entire company to Hollywood. Although Williams agreed that Spain was the most suitable place to shoot the Moorish epic, he was unwilling actually to *guarantee* that the picture would be made there. Furthermore, he was reluctant to budget more than half a million dollars for the production, and doubted it could be done for so little in Spain. To speed preliminary production, he had asked June Mathis to transcribe *The Hooded Falcon*, as conceived by Natacha, into a shooting script, but individual scenes of grandeur required connection to some logical plot line if they were to result in a story, and June was having difficulties. But when they got to the West Coast the Valentinos could read what June had thus far completed.

And even before Valentino and Natacha could absorb all this, Williams added that inasmuch as they lacked a completed script for *The Hooded Falcon*, he wanted to put Valentino into a different picture immediately and had taken it upon himself to purchase the film rights to *Cobra*, a successful stage play by Martin Brown. *Cobra*, with Judith Anderson and Louis Calhern in the lead roles, had run on Broadway for almost a year, and with luck, it could be made into a picture in about two months, just sufficient time to finish the preliminaries on *The Hooded Falcon*. As the Valentinos listened in silent disappointment, Williams added quickly that he had hired Joseph Henaberry, who had directed *A Sainted Devil*, to direct *Cobra*. There were prizefight scenes in the picture, he pointed out, which would enable Valentino to show his handsome physique and reveal his skills as a boxer.

There was nothing for Rudolph and Natacha to do but accept and hurry through *Cobra*. On their journey to California they read June Mathis' script and realized that a lot of work would be required to reduce the scope of *The Hooded Falcon* to fit it into a half-million-dollar budget. There was also much to be done if the script was to have any semblance of a story, and here Natacha and Valentino first discovered that they no longer saw eye to eye. Their junket was filled with dissension.

Shortly afterward, in an effort to placate her, Williams offered Natacha the opportunity to design *Cobra* but she turned him down. As she later wrote: "It was a modern story and modern stories have always bored me to tears—I neither cared nor understood anything about them, unless by chance they were fantastical or symbolical, which was rarely the case."

A Sainted Devil opened at the Mark Strand, and although *The New York Times* thought the picture somewhat slow in parts, with subtitles covering action that should have been included as scenes, the reviewer's salute to Valentino was unqualified:

> Mr. Valentino is, however, a far better actor in this film than in "Monsieur Beaucaire." The atmosphere evidently suits him. Toward the end of the film he flings aside all thoughts of good looks and soft smiles, and gives a splendid portrayal of a man seeing red. His rage in this sequence is most impressive, as it comes as a marked contrast to his calm bearing throughout most of the other stretches.

Throughout its two-week engagement, the strength of the review and the usual feminine interest in Valentino helped the picture play to standing-room-only crowds. But the Mark Strand was not the only theater in the United States, nor were the grosses at first-run houses a true measure of profit. The review in *Weekly Variety* had less style, but it presaged what was to come:

> Since Valentino's "Monsieur Beaucaire" is said to have done a flop outside of the big towns there is some speculation over "A Sainted Devil," which isn't as good a proposition as the first film upon the Mineralava ballyhoo's return to the screen. "Beaucaire" had the advantage in that it was the artistic type of production to draw good notices from the dailies, but unless Rudy makes a swing over the country and feeds the newspaper boys and girls like he did in New York it doesn't look like he'll get much of a newspaper break. The women reviewers in New York—and they predominate— always give him a break here, be the film good or bad. . . .

The picture is not notably produced, although it is evident a flock of money has been spent. The Henaberry direction is undistinguished and featured principally by the number of soft focus closeups which he gives the star, closeups which give full face, profile, ear, eye, nose and throat views of Rudy, which may be what the women want. The combination, too, of the two exotics, Nita Naldi and Dagmar Godowsky, may help the film, but of the two, Nita is the only one who shows any knowledge of acting. Dagmar is just a subtraction mark when it comes to acting, so to make up the "diff" she wears some weird-looking vamp property costumes.

The executives at Paramount were beginning to regret not having released the two pictures sooner: Valentino's appeal was assuming increasing aspects of worship, but as in many religions, the people who believe do not always support their church by attendance. J. D. Williams, also disturbed by the reviews of *A Sainted Devil*, began to work closely with Henaberry and his production people to keep costs to a minimum. Occasionally he was heard to wonder aloud if the Paramount organization, with whom he had contracted to distribute his films, would really make every effort to put his company's offerings across.

Valentino good-naturedly submitted to the shaving of his beard by Ellis G. Bond, a barber who had worked on many a famous chin. The operation concluded, Harry Reichenbach announced that the famous soup-catcher was purchased by a great western museum whose name he was not at liberty to divulge. Soon after this ceremonial shaving Valentino's hair began to thin at the temples and on the top of his head. After he was convinced that he had not been cursed by the Master Barbers Association, he entrusted himself to toupee engineers, whose small camouflages caused him little personal discomfort. But he began to carry amulets.

It had been more than two years since Natacha had actually

seen the Whitley Heights house, and she inspected everything critically on her return. Most of the special features of the house had, of course, been her own suggestions. The master bathroom had a shower stall with five heads. The second bathroom had a scalloped toilet seat in bright yellow, which did not, however, compare with its awesome counterpart. There, overwhelmingly, was a carved, gold-trimmed *chaise percée;* its thronelike appearance frequently sent guests in search of another bathroom. But Valentino enjoyed this touch of aristocratic elegance because similar thrones had been favored by the nobility of southern Italy. Outside, the pleasant garden was filled with statuary and several areas were shaded by canopies of red velvet.

The tons of furniture purchased over the two-year period were moved into the house—and for the most part immediately dispatched to storage; little of what had been bought fitted or complemented the severity of design Natacha now favored. One of the more fascinating items of furniture in her dressing room was a vanity with a frosted-glass perfume burner that, by means of an electrically operated blower underneath the tabletop, wafted scented vapor throughout the room. But with its black floors and gray walls, the Whitley Heights house was restrained when compared to other Hollywood palaces. Nearby, Gloria Swanson laved in a golden bathtub set into a room of black marble; movie cowboy Tom Mix had a dining room with a fountain that sprayed a full spectrum of colored waters; Lilyan Tashman received guests in an all-white drawing room with an all-white piano festooned with blue satin ribbon; and John Barrymore inhabited a hilltop establishment that he chose to call "the Chinese tenement." It was a warren with an English taproom, three swimming pools, a bowling green and a skeet range, among other modest necessities. And of course there was always the simple ninety-room Georgian bungalow occupied by Marion Davies on the Santa Monica oceanfront.

After the Valentinos got their house in order, it was incumbent upon them to give a dinner party, and they chose the ballroom of the Ambassador Hotel to entertain their several hundred guests. It had been two years since Valentino had left for the East, and he now wished to settle down and become a part of the Hollywood community. Among those invited were Charles Chaplin, Tom Mix and his wife, Richard Barthelmess, John Barrymore, Mary Pickford and Douglas Fairbanks, Mr. and Mrs. Thomas Meighan, Harold Lloyd, Marion Davies, Mae Murray and John Gilbert.

At nine-thirty, when Natacha had been assured that most of the notables had arrived, she adjusted her jeweled turban and permitted Valentino to escort her into the ballroom. Like a queen she walked beside him on a long velvet carpet, pausing occasionally to bestow a word or two upon a guest. Others, less favored, had to be content with a half smile or nod. By ten-thirty most of the assembly began to feel pangs of hunger and Valentino whispered that some movement should be made toward the tables. But Natacha vetoed this; even after several guests left, she was not yet in the mood to dine. One of the early departers was Adela Rogers St. Johns, who later described Valentino's telephone call the next morning.

"Natacha is very angry," Rudolph began. "When it was time to sit down, where were you?"

"Tucked in my little bed," Miss St. Johns replied. "I'm a peasant. Did you want me to stay there and starve to death?"

"I'm on the pan," Rudolph replied. "I asked you to be at my table, so there was one empty chair. My good wife says fine kind of friends you have. No manners, these reporters."

"You want me to write and apologize?" Miss St. Johns asked.

"Please," Rudy whispered.

Miss St. Johns added that she did write the note of apology, but "I never got an answer and she never spoke to me again."

Despite the tension of the party, Valentino was pleased to be home and anxious to get under way with another picture. George Ullman continued to scold him for his extravagances, but Valentino paid little attention. Instead, he told Ullman of Natacha's plans for future films, and of her desire for another house, since the Whitley Heights place was already too small. It was during this period that Natacha arranged to have Federico Beltran y Masses, the Spanish court painter who had recently received a commission to paint Marion Davies, agree to do one, or possibly two portraits of Valentino.

Although Valentino had enjoyed living in New York and visiting the great cities of Europe, he had looked forward to his return. He had also anticipated spending time with his closest friends—Douglas Gerrard, Paul Ivano, Manuel Reachi, Robert Florey and the other members of the bachelor group he had sorely missed. He envisioned expansive evenings of good fellowship in the house on Whitley Heights, but to his surprise and disappointment Natacha did not make them welcome. To spare them embarrassment, he met these companions of his prestar days at restaurants, tennis courts and riding stables, though he wished that Natacha could have been kinder, especially to Gerrard and Florey.

Since Natacha now wished a grander house in a more fashionable area, Valentino instructed George Ullman to find them one large enough for Natacha to decorate to her taste. For himself he demanded a large stable, kennels and dog runs, or sufficient grounds to build them. Because he hastened to honor Natacha's every whim, Valentino believed he might make his wife happy by permitting himself to be quoted in an interview as saying: "A man may admire a woman without desiring her. He may respect the brilliance of her mind, the nobility of her character, yes, even the beauty of her face and body, yet she may not move him emotionally." Natacha read the interview and instead of liking it, slapped his face; was he attempting to lend credence to the gossip about her being a lesbian? Evenings at home became tests to determine how much he could stand without losing his temper.

Natacha fought with him constantly, insisting that Hollywood was a hotbed of malice populated by parasites and human leeches. She laughed over his defense of his friends, named everyone who had ever borrowed money or clothes from him, and even speculated on how much money he had loaned them to play the stock market. The failure of his recent pictures was not her fault; the sets and costumes she had planned for him had always enhanced his brilliance as an actor, his magnificence as a lover. The problem, Natacha insisted, lay in the poor scripts in which he had permitted himself to be cast. Natacha's model for him became "Douglas Fairbanks, whose great business ability and commercial sense, together with his artistic appreciation and fearlessness, formed a combination difficult to equal." She could not understand "why, with his ability, romance, magnetism and proved drawing power, he should not have the best—why he should continually be thrust into small, trifling, cheap, commercial pictures, while other artists of far less ability and popularity were given big stories and big productions."

The quarrels usually ended with a recital of all the things his "friends" had said about her and how malicious columnists and other Hollywoodites whom she loathed and despised would never make her surrender her artistic integrity. No matter how they tried, they could never get her to enjoy their insipid picnics, stupid dinners and even stupider formal parties.

Meanwhile, Rudolph prepared himself for *Cobra* and continued to sit for his portraits. He enjoyed the company of Beltran y Masses, for the painter had a Continental wit and a fund of anecdotes that kept the sittings free from boredom. They also gave him the opportunity to brush up on his French and Spanish. Beltran y Masses, however, was in Hollywood for whatever commissions he could pick up, and without the permission of Valentino or Natacha took it upon himself to extend invitations to actors, actresses and Hollywood columnists to visit the Whitley Heights house and view the work in progress. Fortunately, Natacha spent little time at home, for she had recently learned to drive and had begun to take long spins into the country and along the seashore.

Valentino's one encounter with Louella Parsons terrified him, for the influence of Hearst's Hollywood columnist was prodigious. Miss Parsons had come to view the painting, and when Beltran y Masses left her alone with Valentino, she told him she considered the Spaniard a pompous and arrogant nobody, and to her mind far from a great painter.

When she asked where he intended to hang the finished work, Valentino shook his head. He did not know, he answered. He was reluctant to contradict Louella, though he thought the painting rather good, and it seemed unfair to prejudge an unfinished likeness. Miss Parsons turned up her lip in a parody of amiability and suggested that one of the numerous toilets might be appropriate. Then, still smiling like an executioner whetting an ax, she asked if he would mind her quoting him as saying it?

Rudolph begged her not to, and during his lifetime she never did. But in *The Gay Illiterate* (1944), Louella attributed such a comment to Valentino, and said of the Beltran y Masses portrait of Marion Davies: "All I can say, as an amateur art critic, is that it took a caricaturist to distort Marion's beauty—but this boy did it!"

While Valentino was still making *Cobra,* Ullman undertook negotiations to purchase for the Valentinos a house that had been built in 1923 by George E. Read, a Beverly Hills realtor. The Mediterranean-style structure stood on a hilltop, and contained thirteen rooms, plus stables, garages and a six room servants' quarters—all surrounded by eight acres of land. The houses of several screen notables, including John Gilbert, were within hailing distance, and after Valentino persuaded Natacha to view it with him, she agreed it might be suitable for habitation. But Mr. Read was not anxious to sell, and had informed Ullman that his price of $150,000, plus $25,000 for the undeveloped acreage, was firm. Throughout the negotiations Read parried every offer that did not meet this and even refused to take Valentino's note. He wanted the $175,000 in hand before he turned over the deed, and not until Joseph Schenck, of United Artists, agreed to stand behind the purchase did the Reads actually move out.

Valentino named the property Falcon Lair and invited Natacha to make any alterations she desired—to do anything, in fact, that she wished so long as he had a masculine den and business office. But Natacha seemed to have lost her enthusiasm for decoration—at least for houses, this chore was turned over to George Ullman, who had also recently been appointed production manager on *Cobra*, Natacha evidently being content with final approval of whatever was done. She was still devoting her main energies to *The Hooded Falcon*, the picture through which she would prove that, given the proper vehicle and production backgrounds, her husband could surpass Douglas Fairbanks.

Cobra was not moving along as it should have. The chief cameraman had quit after a few weeks, and the second cameraman was having trouble adapting himself to the artistic style of his predecessor. Also depressing were the gossip columns filled with little paragraphs about the quarrels that were carried from Whitley Heights to the studio and how, through it all, Valentino insisted upon wearing the slave bracelet that tended to blind him to reality and imprison his mind and judgment. In public Valentino never failed to defend his wife, though this loyalty alienated many of his friends. *Cobra* was finished in gloom and pessimism at the end of February, for the rough cut of the picture proved it to be deadly. Disgusted with everything about it, Valentino asked Natacha to join him in Palm Springs, where they could rest before they began *The Hooded Falcon*. Once they were reconciled to their disappointment over *Cobra*, he intended to take her up into the mountains to see the great stands of fir and pine, but their stay was cut short by a frantic telephone call from George Ullman.

They had to return at once because J. D. Williams had said publicly what everyone knew in private: *Cobra* was awful because of Natacha, who had ordered so many alterations in the story that in the end it became no story. Despairing of his star's ability to be as manly in his private life as he was on the screen, Williams intended to break his contract by abandoning *The Hooded Falcon*. Preproduction costs of the film would be written off as a loss and no arbitration was possible because he was dissolving his company.

ACT THREE: SCENE TWELVE

The return of Valentino and Natacha to Hollywood was effected in a smoldering silence. The conference in Ullman's office that afternoon was certainly anything but tranquil, and for once the distraught business manager, whose goodwill was just about exhausted, insisted upon speaking bluntly: *The Hooded Falcon* had been abandoned because Williams was no longer willing to honor his original contract which had granted the Valentinos *absolute* supervision of their pictures.

Natacha attempted to speak, but Ullman cut her off sharply. This was no time for oratorical harangues about art and philistines; they were in serious trouble and considerable debt. The public's adulation of Valentino was not being reflected at the box office, and Ullman strongly advised that in his negotiations with Joseph Schenck at United Artists he alone be permitted to represent Valentino. Schenck wanted the Great Lover, had always wanted him, and appeared willing to improve on Williams' contract. He was offering ten thousand dollars a week and up to 50 percent of the net profits of each picture. Schenck had never forgotten that *The Four Horsemen* had returned to Metro a net profit of four and a half million dollars. The new contract—Ullman spoke slowly and distinctly—could earn Valentino a million dollars a year. . . .

Though Natacha was furious at Williams' breach of contract, she could not help but be impressed by the financial prospects offered by Schenck. But why, she asked, couldn't Mr. Schenck guarantee the million dollars a year *and* the quality of production which her husband should have? Again Ullman cut her short. Unless he alone was permitted to represent Rudolph Valentino in the negotiations, he wished to resign immediately. There was no moving him from this fixed position, and finally the Valentinos capitulated.

On March 9 Ullman returned with the contract. Valentino was to receive $520,000 a year in salary, and a minimum of 42 percent of the profits on three pictures a year. Ullman insisted that Valentino read the contract carefully, especially one clause. Valentino did so, scowled and went to Joseph Schenck himself. Schenck smiled amiably and agreed that the clause was exactly as Valentino interpreted it: his wife was to have *no* voice in the selection of material, cast, design, staging or the employment of technicians. So long as Valentino would be under contract to United Artists, Natacha would be allowed no official connection with any of his pictures.

Furious and close to tears, Valentino ran from Schenck's office. Back at Whitley Heights he told Natacha angrily that he had refused to sign the contract and why. Her cold ingratitude to this loyalty stunned him, for with neither sympathy nor compassion she launched into a tirade of abuse, accusing him of lacking backbone. He was not half the man Douglas Fairbanks was.

When Ullman arrived, he begged Valentino to sign the contract. Natacha laughed. Rudy, she said, was not man enough. The taunt brought Valentino to his feet. This was too much, he shouted. He was the butt of hundreds of bad jokes, a laughingstock because of her arrogance. His debts were astronomical. He had lost his friends because of her. But he had married her because he loved her and wanted a wife, a home and eventually children. He would no longer permit Natacha to have any other career except that of wife, homemaker and mother. For the first and only time in their marriage he had the final word.

Hands trembling, he signed the contracts, while Ullman turned the pages and blotted his signatures. When the manager left, an ominous silence settled over the house on Whitley Heights, broken only by telephone calls or congratulatory telegrams from Mary Pickford, Norma Talmadge, Charles Chaplin and Douglas Fairbanks—the big four of United Artists.

To give an illusion of domestic harmony, Natacha was quoted in the press as saying: "Heretofore I have done what I could to protect Mr. Valentino in his contracts but with Mr. Schenck there will no longer be any need for that, for Mr. Schenck is a wonderful man."

She denied the existence of any clause which forbade her to set foot within the United Artists Studios when her husband was working. "That is perfectly ridiculous," she said. "My husband would not work under any such contract. We have always worked together and we always will. There have been a lot of rumors, I know, but that is because women are not generally liked in the motion picture industry. People just can't believe my husband and I are happy."

She then told the reporters that she and Rudolph were returning soon to Palm Springs, where they planned to buy a weekend house.

Valentino celebrated his thirtieth birthday by donning overalls and working for a full eight hours under one of his many auto-mobiles. That evening, Mr. and Mrs. Ullman were the only guests at a birthday dinner at Whitley Heights, where Valentino seemed visibly affected by the many telegrams and cablegrams of goodwill addressed to him from all over the world. Happy for his client, Ullman noted that Valentino and Natacha were pleasant to each other rather than formally polite. When he said good night at the end of the evening, Valentino told him not to worry. Everything would be all right as soon as he and Natacha moved into Falcon Lair.

A week later Rudolph was informed that on June 6 he would begin a screen version of Alexander Pushkin's *Dubrovsky*. Natacha was unimpressed by the novel, disapproved of his being cast as a Russian Robin Hood, and thought *The Eagle*—the suggested title for the film—as silly a name as *Dubrovsky*. Rather spitefully, perhaps, he replied that United Artists had secured Vilma Banky to play opposite him, believing her blond beauty would emphasize his dark masculinity, and in addition had provided him a luxurious bungalow containing a large living room, complete with fireplace, and a corner for dining. It would have impressed her and it was a pity she could not visit him there. There was even a small kitchen presided over by a cook, and a valet to assist him in dressing. Autographed photographs from his many friends in the industry lined the walls and all of them wished him well. Would Natacha like to have her photo-graph hung? He was sure space could be found.

The next morning, he regretted this rudeness, and made every effort to rectify what was to him a breach of good manners. Humble and diffident, he asked Ullman if there was any possi-bility that Joseph Schenck would permit Natacha to visit the set so that she could see how well the picture was going. Ullman said no but as an alternative suggested that Natacha be per-mitted to produce a picture of her own. She could be responsible for the entire production, even with Nita Naldi in the cast, the picture could probably be budgeted at twenty-five thousand dollars—well within the reach of a man who would earn a million dollars that year.

Natacha was enchanted with the idea and immediately devised a satirical story about woman's eternal quest for beauty. Studio space was secured, and despite an attempt by a New York producer, who sought to halt production because its title, *What Price Beauty?*, was too similar to *What Price Glory?*, Natacha went ahead with the project. In time she ran into both script problems and unforeseen expenses, but Valentino ordered Ullman to make available whatever additional sums she required. Peace, at any price, was a bargain.

Though they were no longer in conflict, separate careers failed to bridge their differences. Rather, Natacha resented her husband's enthusiasm for *The Eagle* and considered his failure to bring home a script for her to read an insufferable affront and discourtesy. Nor was she amused at a story, given out to the press by Vilma Banky, that filming had to be stopped daily while heavily breathing ladies were routed from places of concealment on the set. In time she forbade her house to anyone associated with United Artists and would permit no mention of *The Eagle* in her presence. More and more, when he returned from the studio, the butler would announce that Mrs. Valentino would not be at dinner.

A little of Natacha's disdain for her husband's friends and professional associates rubbed off and some important people began to cross Mrs. Valentino from their guest lists. Increasingly isolated after he left the studio at the end of the day, Valentino spent his time puttering in his garden, tinkering with his cars, doing calisthenics or talking by telephone to his dwindling circle of friends. His loneliness became a matter of concern to George Ullman, who often called together the small group of men still close to Valentino and practically ordered them to keep him company. Only when he visited Falcon Lair and jested with the laborers as they worked on the house, did he seem relaxed and able to smile.

By the first of August, Falcon Lair was ready, but Natacha not only refused to move; her spleen kept her from even approaching the premises. Her temper was especially short because she had completed *What Price Beauty?* but was unable to find a distributor for it. Actually, it was no worse than many a picture being shown, but most men in the industry understandably hesitated to do business with its producer. Natacha's stubborn refusal to move to Falcon Lair prevented Ullman from putting the Whitley Heights house on the market at a time when it would have been easy to sell, if only because it had belonged to Valentino. Instead, she announced her intentions of going East to arrange for the release of her picture, and expected Ullman to come along and act as her business spokesman. Before Ullman left, Valentino visited him and was photographed with his children, whom he loved. Later that day, he instructed his business manager to offer Natacha every assistance.

Valentino saw his wife off on August 13. They were photographed at the railroad station before she entered her drawing room, and husband and wife seemed solemn and ill at ease. In New York, Natacha moved into an apartment at 270 Park Avenue with her aunt, Mrs. Werner. Perhaps even earlier than Valentino, Ullman suspected that she had no intention of returning to Hollywood or to her husband, and in New York he asked her this point blank. As Ullman later recalled the meeting, she was wearing a white negligee embroidered in gold, her hair hung in two loose braids, and her eyes were ringed as if she had not slept for several nights. Without preliminary niceties, he asked if she still loved Rudy.

"I—I don't know!"

"Do you want to get a divorce and lose Rudy forever?"

Natacha wrung her hands. "I don't know! I don't know!"

Ullman telephoned his client that things were not going well in New York, which was no surprise since Valentino had already received several letters and telegrams of recrimination from Natacha. But what hurt and shocked him most were cablegrams from Mrs. Hudnut accusing him of wickedness and mental cruelty. He wanted to go East to confront her with her mother's cablegrams but there was still work to be done on *The Eagle*. Shortly after this he read in the papers that Natacha was taking "a sort of marital vacation."

"I'm sure this marital holiday will be a good thing for us both," she had told reporters. "When a husband and wife both are working and both are the possessors of temperaments, I think they should have a vacation from each other. Since I've begun making my own pictures we have been drawn more or less apart, and I can't find the time to devote to the home that I used to. My husband is a great lover of home life."

Frantic and desperate, Valentino attempted to reach Natacha, but the phone was not answered in her apartment. He telephoned Ullman at the Ambassador Hotel who would say only that everything would probably work out for the best. At the studio everyone commiserated with Valentino and assured him that Natacha did love and cherish him.

One morning Vilma Banky approached him and through an interpreter, for her English was poor, told him of a wonderful seer—Dareos—who lived in Santa Monica. He had told the fortunes of many important people in movies; even Norma Talmadge and Joseph Schenck had visited him. Might not a visit to Dareos tell Rudy what the future held for his marriage? Rudolph deliberated and agreed to go. Later that week, Vilma and Valentino slipped into a Santa Monica apartment to seat themselves around a table upon which a crystal ball was centered. Dareos shut his eyes, crinkled his forehead, opened his eyes again, and stared at the crystal while Valentino told him of his undying devotion and love for Natacha.

The seer listened, still staring at the crystal, and his sigh was audible as he told Valentino that his wife and he would never be reconciled, for she preferred a career to a home and children. "You were born to have many romances," Dareos told the actor. "You should never have got married."

Valentino raged that the crystal ball was in error, but Dareos insisted it told only the truth; Valentino would have to be a man and accept his fate. The actor paid for his peep into the future and left hurriedly, with Miss Banky trailing after him. On the way back Valentino insisted that Dareos was wrong, and he felt compelled to telephone Ullman again and beg for good news about Natacha. Ullman had none to offer.

News of the separation delighted almost all of Hollywood. The correspondent for *The New York Times* was given a guarded and diplomatic statement by Valentino, which United Artists, his friends and his attorney had all helped draft:

> Mrs. Valentino and I have agreed on a marital vacation. A dispatch from New York quoting our business manager, S. George Ullman, as asserting Mrs. Valentino would sue me for divorce is incorrect. I talked to Mr. Ullman this morning by long distance telephone and he told me he had not made the statement.
>
> Mrs. Valentino and I are the best of friends. Owing to a difference in temperament we decided to separate for a short time. It is impossible for me to tell what the future will bring forth.
>
> For Mrs. Valentino I have the greatest respect and admiration. We have been happy together and may be again. I am sorry that this had to happen, but we cannot always order our lives the way we would like to have them.

For hours on end Rudolph vainly attempted to reach Natacha by telephone. Mrs. Werner, more and more distressed, tried to get her niece to take his calls, but Natacha would not. All the while the daily papers tortured the actor with stories, some outright falsifications and others, unfortunately, true. One, identified by the Los Angeles *Times* as an "EXCLUSIVE DISPATCH," was an account of a press conference at Natacha's apartment. Dressed all in white from turban to toes, she had revealed she was going to join her parents in Nice by the end of the month. However, she said, she was writing her husband regularly and they had often spoken on the telephone.

" 'With butlers and super-butlers, maids and the rest,' " the EXCLUSIVE DISPATCH continued, " 'what work is there for a housewife? I won't be a parasite. I won't sit and twiddle my fingers, waiting for a husband who goes on the lot at 5:00 A.M., and gets home at midnight and receives mail from girls in Oshkosh and Kalamazoo.' "

Valentino was having trouble sleeping. He also began to drive recklessly and received a ticket for speeding in Santa Monica. A week later he crashed his car into a tree. Increasingly disoriented and suicidal, he refused to use a double in a scene from *The Eagle* in which Vilma Banky's coach was being dragged off by runaway horses and he was supposed to pursue the coach and stop it. Such heroics are usually performed by stunt men, but disregarding all advice, and specifically the orders of Clarence Brown, he ordered Nicky Caruso out of the saddle, as if this was the only way left to demonstrate his manhood. But when he grabbed for the lead horse, he was yanked from the saddle and dragged along the ground for almost a hundred feet.

He suffered severe cuts, bruises, abrasions and considerable pain, but he did not permit these to interfere with work on the picture. At the conclusion of that day's shooting, in response to queries from reporters, he stoutly maintained that neither Ullman nor he knew anything about private detectives shadowing Natacha, and demanded that whoever had hired detectives call them off. Angry at continued questions, he stomped from his bungalow and left the floor to Ullman, who at last confessed that he had hired them on his own initiative.

On September 24, 1925, Natacha and her mother snappishly received reporters at the Hotel Plaza Athénée in Paris. Natacha told them she planned to return to New York in November because Valentino had not come to Paris as he had promised. Becoming impatient, she dismissed the press when a reporter attempted to question her. "I won't be interviewed," she said, "but my husband has no intention of divorcing me." Mrs. Hudnut was equally nettled and termed reports of an impending divorce "ridiculous."

In Hollywood, Valentino was distraught with grief and confusion, and his attorney advised him to stop reading the papers because Natacha's statements were wild and contradictory, and often seemed invented by the wayward gentlemen of the press. But Valentino felt it necessary to call a press conference, and at it he was most emphatic. "Mrs. Valentino cannot have a career and be my wife at the same time," he said. "If she wants her freedom, or wants to star in pictures, all right. She understood this before she left here. She can't be my wife at the same time."

On November 3 he left for New York for the opening of *The Eagle*. At the railroad station in Pasadena, obviously nervous and tense, he made his plans quite clear; from New York he was sailing to London, and while in New York he was not going to see his wife, although she would probably have arrived there from Paris.

"You know that I am just beginning to feel that I was as well off single as I was married. I love and appreciate beauty. I realize now that it is my nature," he said as he put on and removed his gloves. "This quality may have given Mrs. Valentino cause for jealousy and I may have been a very poor husband in that respect. She wanted to isolate me as much as possible. That was her nature. I don't know definitely whether we will be reconciled or divorced. But of one thing I am certain. She cannot come back as my wife as long as she is seeking a career in pictures."

On his arrival in New York on November 7, his statement to the press was extremely brief: "I do not know what Mrs. Valentino wishes to do. But all I wish to do is oblige her. I shall await developments and try to keep my sense of humor."

Natacha was on the high seas but due to dock in three days. Meanwhile, Valentino busied himself with plans for a European tour. Everyone who asked was assured that he was managing quite well and reconciled to the loss of Natacha. Joseph Schenck telephoned him at the Ritz Carlton, and advised him to be extremely careful about whom he saw or entertained. The reasons were obvious, and Valentino agreed. Then they discussed briefly his appearance next day at the Mark Strand.

Tired, emotionally on edge, Valentino refused to see anyone that Saturday evening except Beulah Livingstone, who worked in the New York publicity office of United Artists. Miss Livingstone had met him when she had gone to Los Angeles to see the filming of *The Eagle.* Her diplomatic avoidance of any reference to Natacha had so impressed Valentino that he invited her now to go to the New Amsterdam Theater to see Marilyn Miller in *Sunny.* After the musical he intended to take her on a round of the city's better clubs.

They had been seated in the theater no longer than ten minutes when people began to turn in their direction, then leave their seats for the aisle to get a better look. He asked them politely to permit him to see the performance, but his pleas were ignored and after a half hour of signing autographs, while the curtain was held, he requested an usher to help him and Miss Livingstone leave the theater. The theater manager telephoned for a police escort but the crowd was so thick and unruly around his limousine that the policemen were swept aside by the fans who demanded his autograph. One ingenious young woman even removed a pair of small scissors from her purse and snipped a button off his coat. A second later, a hundred yammering women were tearing at his clothes.

Before he and Miss Livingstone were rescued and helped into the limousine, Valentino's bowtie was gone, his collar smudged, more buttons had been removed from his coat, and his handkerchiefs and scarf had disappeared, along with several of his studs and one glove. In addition, both sleeves of his evening coat were split under the arms. Miss Livingstone fared little better; she had lost every hairpin, her evening gown had been torn, and pieces of fur had been plucked from the fox collar of her evening wrap.

Although they were now safely in the limousine, the chauffeur could not move the car because people were so tightly packed around it. Then Valentino remembered the two baskets of bright metal souvenir coins that had been minted for the opening of *The Eagle*. Rolling down the window, he and Miss Livingstone threw handfuls of them into the street, and as people began to scramble for them, the car managed to escape. Miss Livingstone begged Valentino not to take her to any nightclub because the experience had really frightened her, but he insisted that she change to ordinary street dress and at least have late supper with him in a quiet east side restaurant.

On Sunday afternoon, dozens of policemen were on hand to keep order outside the Mark Strand Theater. Inside, the audience, in gay mood, applauded the playing of Tchaikovsky's "1812 Overture," then stamped and cheered at Valentino's first appearance as a Cossack officer. The applause at the conclusion of the picture was thunderous and Valentino's appearance on the stage received a standing ovation that misted his eyes. After some measure of order was restored, he thanked the audience for their friendliness, for liking the picture and for all their many kindnesses to him. In conclusion he pledged himself to work hard and make pictures that would keep him their friend.

The next morning's review of *The Eagle* in *The New York Times* said: "In this production, which might suit several male screen celebrities, including the agile Douglas Fairbanks, Mr. Valentino acquits himself with distinction." The reviewer concluded that Valentino's "distinction" had been made possible by Clarence Brown's direction and Hans Kraely's clever scenario.

On the whole, Valentino was pleased, but it depressed him that such overall teamwork might have been possible in all his recent pictures if—only Natacha had been different. And the review that appeared in *Weekly Variety* a few days later confirmed this:

> . . . Rudolph Valentino as a Russian Robin Hood of more modern times. In "The Eagle" the sheik, who says he is tired of being dubbed as strictly a ladies' man, really goes out and does some "he-man" stuff and rides in a manner that is going to make Tom Mix and a couple of the riding boys look to their laurels. . . .
>
> But Rudy is doing considerable of a comeback with this picture and if Joe Schenck can follow it with another as good, the chances are that he will have this star right on the real road to popularity.

On November 10, 1925, Valentino appeared at the Federal Building to make application for his first citizenship papers. Wearing a gray suit, a gray cravat, a gray hat and tan shoes, he stood by the side of his sponsor, William J. Burns, the former chief of the United States Secret Service, and answered the usual questions. Valentino told the clerk he was five feet eleven and a half inches tall and weighed 164 pounds. He gave the date and place of his birth, said he had sailed to this country from Genoa, and gave his present place of residence as 270 Park Avenue. He also swore that his wife had been born in Salt Lake City.

Elsewhere in Manhattan, on that same day, Natacha arrived from Europe on the *Leviathan*. With rare friendliness, she granted a long interview and revealed her plans to star in a picture aptly titled *When Love Grows Cold*, which would go into production almost immediately. Asked about Valentino's statement that he wished to do the picturemaking for the family, she continued to smile, then said: "I will let him do the talking. I do not care to discuss my private affairs with the public. It is all very well to have and rear children, but no woman should embark on this phase of life until she is prepared to give up everything for the children. This I will not do yet."

"Do you consider a sheik an ideal husband?" a reporter asked.

"I can't say," Natacha replied. "I have never been married to a sheik."

"What kind of a man do you consider an ideal husband?"

"What a question! I am not sure there is such an animal."

"Did you know," the brash reporter persisted, to his colleagues' delight, "that he gave an interview in Chicago saying that if you want to make up you'll have to give up your dogs?"

"How interesting!" Natacha sniffed. "He hasn't much room to talk. He has a dozen dogs of his own—airedales, bulldogs, collies and what not."

Told that her husband was at the Ritz Carlton, Natacha replied that she was going to her newly rented apartment at 9 West Eighty-first Street. If Valentino wanted to see her, he would have to make the first move.

Now United Artists was satisfied by two events: at the box office *The Eagle* continued to be a resounding success; and Valentino not only refused to go to his wife, whose statements had denigrated his dignity, but for the very first time began to wonder if Natacha was as bright as he always had thought. The press, of course, could not be kept out of the Ritz Carlton, and hounded though he was by foolish questions, he still managed a remarkable semblance of composure and consistency. Repeatedly he interpreted his wife's trip to Europe as nothing more than a visit to her mother, refused to acknowledge the possibility of divorce, and referred to their separation as "a marital vacation." But illusion was no longer possible when he learned that Benjamin H. Connor, an attorney from Quebec, had just returned from Paris, where, at the request of Natacha, he had filed a suit for divorce.

Until he felt absolutely in control of himself, Valentino refused to see anyone. He then told reporters that if Natacha had filed for a French divorce, he intended "to defer to her wishes in this matter," and would not contest it.

This said, he waived aside a reporter's question about Natacha's charge that it had taken him three years "to develop his lack of appreciation for her ambition to become a motion picture star." He would say only that if his wife was "fed up" with Hollywood, he was willing to maintain a home in the East or in Europe, and would limit his stay in the motion picture capital to meet shooting schedules. Every reporter present, even those dedicated to sensationalism and the exploitation of psychological misery, felt sorry for him. They wished him well, and said so.

On November 14, Valentino boarded the *Leviathan* once more. Surrounded by reporters and photographers, he laughed as they itemized his apparel: a green-and-gray-striped suit over which he wore a gray suede topcoat with Australian opossum collar and cuffs. On his person was a quantity of antique gold and diamond jewelry, but reporters admired most his platinum cigarette case and lighter crested with a coiled cobra. Thanking one reporter for calling him a glass of fashion, the actor acknowledged his fondness for unusual, striking clothes, but remarked that Oxford bags, with their thirty-six-inch bottoms, were best worn by college boys. He preferred narrow trousers and a longer coat; they made him look taller. However, he rejected the charge that he was a clothes horse and said that "clothes should not be of importance in the life of any man."

Asked if he intended to see *Cobra*, which was to open the following month, he replied that blindness never eliminated error and that refusing to recognize trouble neither altered nor delayed it. He would see the picture and perhaps learn some cruel lessons from it.

"Do you still love Mrs. Valentino?" he was asked.

He shook his head. "That is all past now. Yes, all past now. What has happened has happened."

"But do you still love your wife?"

"It is no longer a question of love. It is a matter of pride."

"What is your general view on women?" another reporter asked.

"To generalize on women is dangerous," Valentino replied. "To specialize on them is infinitely worse. No, I shall not discuss Mrs. Valentino or any other woman." The narrowing of his eyes froze a reporter's smile. "There is nothing in our case that would invite satire or cynicism. Mrs. Valentino seeks the divorce. She has stated her grounds and I yield to those grounds. That is all there is to it. I now intend to go through life alone."

The reporters scribbled busily and paused only when one of them asked if he was interested in Mae Murray.

"I usually dine with an attractive woman," he replied. "But no woman is the object of my deeper affection. There is none. This was to have been a trip of pleasure for me and now it is filled with sadness."

To conclude the interview, Valentino told reporters that he looked forward to a visit with his brother, Alberto, whose lovely wife and fine son stirred his pride. After the ship sounded the signal for all visitors to go ashore, Valentino walked to the gangplank with a reporter from *The New York Times* and asked him to convey his regards to Mordaunt Hall, whom he considered an excellent critic and reporter.

Next day the *Times* noted: "On previous departures Mr. Valentino has always been merry and bright and quoted poetry to the reporters from his own book of poems published for circulation among his friends. This time he was sad."

ACT THREE: SCENE THIRTEEN

As the *Leviathan* steamed majestically off toward Europe, reporters hurried from the pier to the Pec-Art Studio at 318 East Forty-eighth Street for a press conference with a piqued Natacha, whose husband had made no effort to see her before his departure. His placid acceptance of her divorce proceedings was not quite what she had expected. However, the wheels were in motion and it was best to offer a brave face to the world.

"All is over between Mr. Valentino and myself," she said dramatically. "I instituted divorce proceedings while I was in Paris this fall. I have done my duty. It's up to Valentino to go ahead and do the rest. He knew what I was when I married him. I have been working since I was seventeen. Homes and babies are all very nice, but you can't have them and a career as well. I intended, and intend, to have a career and Valentino knew it. If he wants a housewife he'll have to look again."

Aboard ship, Valentino arranged to take his meals in his cabin and seldom appeared on deck before nightfall. The passengers soon realized that the actor's suffering was genuine and left him pretty much alone. He occupied himself with calisthenics, sent dozens of cablegrams and read a carton of books sent aboard by United Artists. Although plans for his next picture were pretty well advanced, Joseph Schenck wanted him to read the latest costume novels as inspiration. United Artists thought well of his suggestion that he portray Cesare Borgia, Leonardo da Vinci or Benvenuto Cellini, but these would require foreign productions and Schenck wanted to make a few more pictures at home before taking a company abroad.

Privacy afforded Rudolph time to think and to reconcile himself to a future without Natacha and to plan what to do after he left London. His first order of business in Paris would be to comply with the French divorce laws, which stipulated that both parties had to be domiciled in France before the divorce could be granted. This unpleasantness behind him, he hoped to spend Christmas week and New Year's Day in Rome with his sister and his brother's family, to all of whom he sent daily cablegrams. Then he would travel on to Spain to visit Blasco-Ibáñez and Rafael Sabatini, whom he hoped to persuade to write novels expressly for him.

The *Leviathan* docked at Southampton on November 21, a cold and gloomy day that must have suited Valentino's somber mood. Before the ship was even in its slip, the English representatives of United Artists, who had come aboard from a chartered tug, held their first conference with Valentino. They were delighted to see him looking so well, though they were rather unhappy at the unrestrained candor with which he had discussed with the press his impending divorce. The English, they explained to him, were far more reticent and reserved about their private lives and they feared that *The Eagle* might turn out to be a lame duck at the box office. But Valentino told them not to worry; box-office receipts in New York had skyrocketed after Natacha had announced she was divorcing him.

In a formal press interview held later at dockside, he swore to the English and Continental reporters that he had never hated his wife's Pekingese dogs. How could such friendly little animals have anything to do with his marital problems? Rather, he had hoped and prayed, even until the last moment before sailing, for some word from his estranged wife. No, he was not professionally jealous of Mrs. Valentino, merely "old fashioned enough to believe if I can supply her with everything, that is enough without a career on her side of the family." Then firmly, in a voice edged with anger, he denied rumors of affairs and declared that Natacha had the right to expect fidelity from him and he had never violated that obligation. But, he added, she had no right to "alienate me from my men friends. . . . I woke up from my dream of love, finally, to find myself lost to my friends."

This statement was made with candor, and impressed the gentlemen of the London press, who proceeded to treat Valentino with sympathy in all their stories.

The next evening, at his appearance at the London premiere of *The Eagle* at the Marble Arch Pavilion Cinema, thousands of screaming women and girls massed, and a hundred bobbies had to clear a path for him into the theater. Despite this, a dozen women managed to form a sort of flying wedge that broke through the police escort, and tackled the actor, who lost his poise as well as his footing, and stripped him of his hat, gloves, scarf and breath. At no time during his London stay was he free from hysterical feminine admirers. Whenever he ventured from his hotel room, United Artists' representatives protected him with the zealousness of Swiss guards—against females, homosexuals and certain American members of the press whose questions were neither pertinent nor civilized.

Valentino utilized his London stay to visit Bond Street and the Burlington Arcade, spending many of his mornings and afternoons in the silver vaults, where he bought almost four thousand pounds worth of assorted hallmark silver. He longed for some word from Natacha, but none came. By the end of November, after a day of seclusion in his hotel suite during which he wrote her letter after letter, none of which he ever mailed, he was finally willing to admit that their marriage was beyond salvage. On December 12, he boarded the boat train for Paris.

Instead of proceeding directly to the Plaza Athénée, he was driven in a limousine to a château near Fountainebleau, where he was the guest of United Artists' French representatives. He rested at the château and slipped into Paris at night for discreet visits to Montmartre and the business offices of film executives and legal advisers. At these nocturnal meetings he became increasingly frustrated when his Paris attorneys failed to provide him with any news of significance. But as it turned out, there was none. Painstaking searches by his attorneys (and reporters) of the court records at the Palace of Justice had failed to turn up any petition for divorce. That strangers should dare search legal records of no concern to them outraged him as much as this obvious maneuver by Natacha's attorneys to compel *him* to file the divorce action. Was there, he roared, no limits to French duplicity?

At the Gare du Nord, more than two thousand Frenchwomen waited for hours in the bitter December cold for Valentino's "official" arrival in Paris. No gendarmes were at the station to maintain order because the Paris prefect of police had believed Frenchwomen more sensible than their English or American sisters but the prefect was in error. As Valentino descended from the train, the women on the platform ran amok; they bowled over the gentlemen with him and kicked harder than the men who sought to rescue him. Clothing torn, face scratched, Valentino managed to fight his way to a waiting limousine just as the gendarmes arrived in force. Lovesick ladies embraced the wheels, clung to the roof and clawed at the windows. Others attempted to tear off the doors.

Once safely ensconced in the Plaza Athénée, he learned that Mrs. Richard Hudnut had come to Paris to meet her daughter; and also that in Rome young Fascists had held public meetings to advocate a boycott of his films. Then they had marched in strength on two theaters where *The Eagle* was playing, only to be confronted by strong detachments of Fascist militia. After the administration of some physical censures to the backs and backsides of the ringleaders, they were turned back. A sudden depression overwhelmed Valentino that Italians should react so violently to his seeking American citizenship.

Reporters cabled their papers that though Valentino was seen with Jean Nash, the Dolly sisters and several French actresses, they could discover no scandal. The reason is not too difficult to understand. The United Artists' representatives in Paris had warned Valentino against all the women with whom it was unsafe for him to be seen, and whenever he disregarded their warnings he would find himself suddenly in the company of private detectives eager to escort him back to the Plaza Athénée. Besides, he realized how vulnerable he now was to blackmail.

But more important, probably, was that women had deified him, had granted him the omnipotence of a god, and if he were to fail a woman in bed, then what? He had been laughed at too hard, too long, and he was well aware that he was a man bound by physical and psychological limitations. The domination he had submitted to in both his marriages had quite possibly made him all but impotent, and in terms of his image there was never any need to enter into any physical liaison. There were more than enough women willing to claim that they had slept with him and found him, as all the world knew, the most magnificent, subtle and doughty of lovers. Such rumors inspired envy, aroused tempers, incited feuds but also enhanced his reputation. Mornings, when he was greeted by reporters and asked how he had spent the previous evening, he needed to do no more than smile cryptically.

Despite this, Valentino was able to cable Ullman of the good times he was having with Prince Habile-Lotfallah, an Egyptian of enormous wealth who wanted him to make the story of Antony and Cleopatra in Cairo, with the entire resources of the Egyptian Government at his disposal. Another evening Valentino cabled Ullman about a magnificent party given for him, at which there had been at least two hundred guests. The orchestras had played through breakfast and never in his entire life, Valentino wrote, had he been so honored.

But a few weeks later, enormous bills for the party began to pile up on Ullman's desk. Others followed, for equally lavish entertainments. Frightened by their size and number, Ullman cabled Valentino. He replied by cable collect that he had read all the reviews of *Cobra*, which had opened in New York on December 6 and been soundly rapped. Evidently pleased, he instructed Ullman to mail all the reviews to Natacha and underline the portion of Mordaunt Hall's review that read: "Of course, the redoubtable Valentino could not permit Nita Naldi, who figures in the title role, to run away with the picture, so the cobra's fangs were pulled out, and in the operation this twisted the yarn from a good drama into an incredibly ludicrous affair."

Even more ludicrous than *Cobra* was Valentino's comic-opera encounter with a Baron Imre Lukatz, a Hungarian millionaire, who before the war had fallen in love with Vilma Banky. The Baron had gone off to military service and Vilma had emigrated to Berlin, where she had become a successful German star and was eventually signed by Samuel Goldwyn. In Europe, Vilma's pictures were popular with everyone but Lukatz, who raged at the sight of her making love on the screen. And no actor made Lukatz as jealous as Valentino, for no actor had ever made love to her as he had in *The Eagle*.

That evening, as Valentino was leaving the Plaza Athénée, he was confronted by the Baron, who introduced himself to the astonished actor as the man who was going to marry Vilma Banky. Valentino congratulated him on his good fortune but at the top of his lungs the Baron began to revile Rudolph. Astonished and confused by this unreasonable verbal barrage, Valentino attempted to placate Lukatz but only succeeded in infuriating him further. At last he called Valentino a seducer and a pimp, and the actor promptly punched him in the nose, knocking him backward into a potted palm, then challenged him to a duel. The challenge was accepted, seconds were appointed and the men arranged to meet the next morning at dawn in a nearby *bois* with swords.

In the weak light of morning, as the vapors rose from the cold ground of the glade where the duelists met, the seconds conferred, and to everyone's relief Baron Lukatz offered his apologies and both men shook hands.

Valentino suffered the only casualty—a cold in the nose—and later that day, as he sat with his feet in a pan of hot water, and sipped a glass of warm lemonade and whiskey, he disputed Christopher Marlowe's references to Helen of Troy: "I don't believe the most beautiful woman in the world is worth even a cold in the head."

ACT THREE: SCENE FOURTEEN

By December 18, Valentino had completed his required residence in France. Pressed for a statement about his marital future, he would say only that what his estranged wife intended to do was a mystery that even time might never solve. Meanwhile, he planned a short visit to Germany before returning to London for Christmas. Dour of aspect, even after he discovered that Mae Murray was on his train to Berlin, he joined her in a stern denial of any romance. "We met quite by accident at the station in London and found we were going to Berlin on the same train," Rudolph declared.

With coyness appropriate to her famous smile, Miss Murray said she had known Rudy for just years and years and they were really just very good, very old friends. "It is very complimentary to me to be accused of being in a romance with him—only, unfortunately, it is not true." She fluttered her eyelashes nicely for the photographers. "He is still married, you know. And besides, it would not be fair to take him away from his feminine admirers all over the world, would it?"

At the Berlin *Banhof* a group of untidy National Socialists protested the arrival of Valentino. With Prussian thoroughness they cursed him in cadence for his role in *The Four Horsemen,* in which German officers had been portrayed as brutal and cowardly rather than brutal and brave, until police batons drummed good manners into their heads. At the Aldon, a jewel of a hotel, Valentino and Miss Murray were welcomed with splendid cordiality, then publicly escorted to their respective suites on different floors.

Before the Sheik dismissed everyone, he tipped liberally and complimented the reporters on the good manners of German fräuleins, so much better behaved and disciplined than their French cousins. But despite his approval of everything German, including *Kinder, Kirche* and *Küche,* he refused to discuss his domestic problems and parried all questions with unyielding firmness. He had come, he said, to gain some privacy and get a firsthand look at German methods of film production and distribution.

From Berlin, after he had kissed Mae Murray's hand in farewell, Valentino went directly to Nice to meet Natacha, who was by then in France. A legend persisted after his death that when Natacha had left Hollywood for New York in August he never saw her again. Actually, they met, discussed movies and property settlement, and if they could not be husband and wife, it seemed they at least could be friends. For several days afterward, he and Natacha lunched and dined, visited the casino at Monte Carlo and were seen frequently in each other's company. Observers remarked over their gaiety and wondered whether these meetings presaged a reconciliation.

Suddenly, at the insistence of his attorney, Valentino left

Nice, for his legal adviser had expressed distress over the actor's conduct. How could he fail to consider the French legal attitude? Although its courts were liberal in matters of divorce, French jurists did not approve of continued friendship between two principals in a divorce action, especially since they had filed suit for legal separation. Propriety was still expected of them.

A week later, the initial phase of the newsworthy divorce action was heard before the Tribunal of the Seine. In keeping with the code of a gentleman, Valentino was not present at court and was discreetly referred to as M. Guglielmi. Natacha's attorney identified her as Mme Winifred Hudnut, who swore that she, the complainant, was a resident of Indiana, a state that permitted divorce on the grounds of desertion, but also maintained a legal domicile in Paris.

Once it was established that an effort at reconciliation had failed, the judges heard evidence that for the past two years M. Guglielmi had failed to provide support for his wife, Mme Hudnut. The three judges nodded regretfully when no denial was made of this charge but seemed relieved when Natacha's attorney explained that actually the lovely lady had adequate resources of her own. She merely preferred to live her own life and share none of it with M. Guglielmi.

After some short deliberation, to prove that each French divorce was discussed by the jurists, the court ordered the decree granted. On January 18, 1926, the attorneys in the case were notified that legal documents would be forthcoming within a matter of weeks. Thus ended for Valentino his marriage to the one woman he had adored above all others.

In Cherbourg, reporters announced the news to Valentino before he had even received it from his attorneys. Trapped on the deck of the *Leviathan,* he permitted himself to be questioned by all reporters and posed patiently for photographs, and in rare tribute to a rather nice guy, reporters included in their dispatches expressions of admiration for Valentino's self-control.

"I was expecting a telegram, but you are ahead. You are the first to bring the news," he said to the reporters after he affectionately introduced his brother, sister-in-law and young nephew, who had met him some days before and were accompanying him to Hollywood.

He smiled before offering his profile for photographers to record his newly grown stiletto sideburns, which were long, thin and tended to curl down his cheeks. Modestly, for he was not Beau Brummell, he refused to say whether these would become popular with American sheiks and their Shebas, but he wholeheartedly approved the high Russian boots worn by Sophie Tucker, who was also aboard the *Leviathan,* and thought they would make sound footwear for the streets of many wintry cities in the United States.

Across the sea, when Natacha was interviewed by a *Times* reporter, she was far less generous: "She was interested in her career and not in Mr. Valentino . . . she said she had no intention of marrying again."

When the *Leviathan* docked on January 27, Valentino told the New York reporters who were there to welcome him that he enjoyed his "restoration to bachelorhood." This said, he dismissed as unqualified piffle the romantic rumors that had linked him with Mae Murray. After going through customs, he announced his plans: He intended to clean up some minor business matters in New York City, then take his brother's family to Hollywood.

To Alberto, his wife and their son, the Hotel Marguery seemed a residence of true magnificence where, because they were related to a famous star, they, too, were treated as royalty. Alberto was delighted with luxury, but the wild prodigality of his younger brother frightened him and he felt called upon to protest Rudolph's purchase of an Irish wolfhound from Mrs.

Glenn Stuart of eastern Maryland for five thousand dollars. Rudolph explained that he wanted the wolfhound—a remarkable dog that was nearly four feet tall at the shoulder and weighed more than two hundred pounds—as a companion for Kabar, his Doberman, but Alberto was appalled. The dog had to be lodged in special quarters at the hotel. Mrs. Stuart, who had agreed to sell Centaur Pendragon only after nine months of negotiation, during which she had thoroughly investigated the actor's references, had also drawn up a contract providing that Valentino stand the expenses of a veterinary to accompany the dog from Maryland. During the journey, the contract further stipulated, the dog would travel in comfort, under the constant care of an attendant, and only by day. The dog was certainly treated better than anyone Alberto had ever known in Castellaneta.

If Alberto was concerned with his brother's prodigality, Valentino's immediate concern was focused on *The New York Times Index* for October-December, 1925, which for some umbrageous reason had decided to list him as "GUGLIELMI, Rudolph, see VALENTINO, R." He construed this as the first step in a full-scale raking up of his dead past; the last time he had been listed as "Guglielmi" by the *Index* was ten years before, when the matter of his arrest had been documented and indexed for easy reference. In the past the occasional references to this arrest and the attempts of seedy adventurers to profit by it had been handled successfully, without publicity, and small expense. Now, he pointed out to everyone in authority at United Artists, he had become a millionaire—at least he had the income of a millionaire—and what purpose other than embarrassment to him, could the *Times* have for listing him under this old name? Was the *Times* determined that his brother find out about this black episode in his past? Why, he demanded of Schenck, hadn't his police file been expunged? What was United Artists going to do about the *Index?* Assured that diplomatic representation would be made to the *Times* to restore the listing he preferred in the *Index,* the actor, his brother, sister-in-law and nine-year-old nephew were escorted aboard the Broadway Limited.

At Chicago, where he told reporters he liked his stiletto sideburns, Valentino was advised that Natacha was going to open at the Palace in a vaudeville sketch, "The Purple Vial." He wished her good fortune and publicly dictated a telegram to this effect. Then, in rare good humor, he laughed aside all questions of the heart and refused to discuss a rumor that the new Polish star, Pola Negri, through spokesmen, had expressed an affectionate interest in Valentino but had not as yet, she announced, decided to accept his proposal of marriage when he made it. The word "marriage" compelled the actor to react with displeasure. He hardly knew the passionate Polish star, who had come to be identified with slumberous, tigerous, gypsy passion. She was merely a casual friend, a fellow professional.

ACT THREE: SCENE FIFTEEN

After the dissolution of his second marriage, Valentino seemed to undergo a deep alteration of character. For three years he had suppressed his own wishes. Whatever he had purchased, whatever courses of action he had pursued, had been directed by Natacha. Now, as if determined to prove the steel and strength of his ego, he was determined to do and buy what pleased him. No cavalier rake or regency blood could have been more contemptuous than Valentino on his return as he brushed aside the increasing number of bills that covered the top of Ullman's desk.

He also told his harried business manager of his determination to refurbish Falcon Lair. Ullman was to sell or get rid of everything in the house that could be associated in any way with Natacha. Refusing to listen to any account of his debts, Valentino decreed sweeping changes in the main house and stables. He ordered new kennels built to accommodate Kabar, the Doberman, and Centaur Pendragon, the wolfhound, who, it developed, did not like one another.

For Ullman, the only saving feature of "the new Valentino" was his acceptance of Edith M. Hull's new book *The Sons of the Sheik*. As a businessman he knew that almost all problems can be resolved by money and he saw in this sequel to *The Sheik* a way for Valentino to pay all his bills and achieve again some semblance of solvency, even perhaps accumulate a cash balance at the bank. *The Sheik* had shown a profit of almost three million dollars for Paramount; there was no reason to believe its sequel could not do equally well. Although the Boston *Transcript* thought " 'The Sons of the Sheik' . . . a pale sequel to a sensational story," the *Literary Review* and the New York *Herald Tribune* both found the novel enjoyable, eloquent and even intelligent.

To simplify the plot for the film, one of the twin sons would be eliminated, and the composite would of course be played by Valentino. With a touch of inspiration, Valentino asked why he could not do something quite original—play Sheik Ahmed and also his son and namesake? He visualized several scenes on a split screen that would delight his audiences, confound his critics and discomfit his detractors and pale imitators.

Ullman was so astonished at this sudden cooperation by his star, that in silence he handed Rudolph the January 16, 1926, issue of *Collier's*, which featured an interview Valentino had had with John R. Winkler before he had gone to Europe in November. The article—"I'm Tired of Being a Sheik"—was a declaration of emancipation from any desert roles whatsoever:

> "Heaven knows, I'm no sheik"—Rudolph Valentino tamped a slug of tobacco into the broad bowl of his brier, borrowed a match and puffed away like DeWolf Hopper at a ball game. . . .
> "I had to pose as a sheik for five years!" exclaimed Valentino. "A lot of the perfumed ballyhooing was my own fault.

I wanted to make a lot of money, and so I let them play me up as a lounge lizard, a soft, handsome devil whose only sin in life was to sit around and be admired by women.

"And all the time I was a farmer at heart, and I still am. When I am working I go to bed at nine-thirty and get up at five. Honest, I really believe I was happier when I slept on a bench in Central Park than during all the years of that 'perfect-lover' stuff.

"Right now, if I were home, on my little five-acre patch in California, you'd never find me breakfasting in the afternoon.

"No, I am through with sheiking. No more posing-Apollo stuff for me. If any producer comes to me with a sheik part I am going to murder him! I am going to show I am a real actor if I have to play Hamlet in a waiter's tuxedo. I am sure I shall be able to live down the past. Look at this—" He picked up a sheet upon which there were typed figures.

"This is an analysis of 5,100 letters that have come in this week—letters from the knockers and the boosters and the autograph hunters. More than half of them *are from men.* Most of them say they like my work *as an actor,* in legitimate romantic comedy. . . ."

It was "The Sheik" that thrust Valentino into world-wide fame. And it was the mantle placed upon him then that is most irksome now.

"The newspapers picked up the term," he said bitterly, "and soon I was looked upon by silly people as the most ardent lover since Elinor Glyn's 'Three Weeks.' I was so sweet I'd melt a chocolate in its wrapper. . . .

"Nope—no more sheiking for me," ended Valentino as he shook the ashes out of his pipe, stretched himself to his full height and strode into the next room to superintend the packing of seventeen trunks.

Valentino was amused, and even laughed off a reference Winkler had made to his thinning hair.

Even the most sanguine reader could make little more of the scenario for *The Son of the Sheik*—which had been written by Frances Marion and Mme Fred de Gresac—than that it was a frothy fribble of desert storms, dancing girls, fights against overwhelming odds and picturesque unbelievability. Yet it was bound to please all women, from the youngest to those who had long passed through their climacteric. And because the picture was certain to make him a million dollars, Valentino threw himself into the spirit of the endeavor with enthusiasm. Happily, he was working with Vilma Banky, who would play Yasmin, the dancing girl, and director George Fitzmaurice, a man whose ability he had always admired and respected.

In anticipation of the fabulous financial returns from the picture, Valentino decided to be the best-dressed sheik in all of Araby. The splendor of his raiment so awed reporters throughout the world that numerous publications, even of sober editorial judgment, itemized his full wardrobe and its cost:

Sapphire ring set in platinum	$3,000
Antique silver bracelet (imported)	150
Wristwatch	150
Cigarette case (jeweled)	300
Patent lighter (jeweled)	150
Revolver	35
Belt and knife (antique)	550
Sword	4,000
Spurs (silver)	50
Turban	25
Two Arabian burnooses	450
Two silk headdresses	70
Two lamb's wool shirts	100
Two embroidered vests	300
Embroidered outer garment	350
Sash	20
Gold-embroidered cloak	500
Two jewel-studded belts	600
Embroidered revolver holster	25
Arabian trousers	175
Breeches with braided trimming	75
Two pair imported boots	155
Slippers	30
	$11,260

Thus accoutered, Valentino departed for Yuma, Arizona, where the desert scenes were to be shot, and threw himself into the innocence of the script with such fervor that he inspired everyone to give more than their contracts demanded. The final result was an opera that moved so swiftly it could never be tripped up by plot, and the problem it presented film editors was unique in film history—every scene dropped was fully as good as what remained. Although some of the actors objected to Rudy's enthusiastic use, whenever possible, of the giant wind machines, they realized that this picture presented a special psychological challenge. He hated his role and his reidentification as the Sheik, but was determined to prove he could make a genuine hero out of even this distressing stereotype.

By the time the company returned to the studio, Rudolph gave every evidence of having adjusted to bachelorhood. Of more importance to his friends was the restoration of his tolerance and humor, for with remarkable good nature he accepted the role assigned to him by Pola Negri, who told everyone how she loved Valentino and how ardently he wooed her every moment of the day and night. It was good publicity, he felt, for him as well as Pola, and he played along with the fiction by appearing at the proper parties with Miss Negri, and was a frequent visitor at the home of her friend Marion Davies, whose hospitality he enjoyed.

In the meantime, frantically determined to keep busy, he consulted daily with George Ullman about his screen future, and made dozens of long-range plans for his career. As he supervised changes at Falcon Lair, which he was determined to make into one of the most masculine homes in southern California, he decided that after his present contract was completed, he would make but two pictures a year. At the end of five years the salary and profits derived from these would make him wealthy enough to be completely independent. Then he would begin a new career, as a director. Several months of each year would be spent in England, where he would maintain two houses, and two or three months would probably be allotted to France or Spain. The remaining six would be for Hollywood and New York and work.

But he was becoming increasingly irritated by his fans, who demanded that he engage in romance even while off the screen. At the moment, Pola Negri was the lady of their choice. In an attempt to thwart them, he would occasionally escort other actresses in public, but neither his fans nor the social arbiters of Hollywood approved. And Miss Negri, a lady of rhetorical vigor and steely determination, soon managed to have him exclusively at all parties, balls and fetes of consequence. Miss Negri seemed always to be stalking him. If he resented questions about marriage, she did not. In private moments he referred to himself as Sinbad.

Only occasionally did he manage to free himself. Then he would lock himself behind the gates of Falcon Lair with Douglas Gerrard, Paul Ivano, Manuel Reachi and Beltran y Masses, whom he entertained with burlesques of his roles, his leading ladies and the more prominent of the simpering sob sisters who infested the studios. He considered them all quite obviously insane, but less so than the industry that indulged their madness.

He began to have trouble sleeping again and needed the fatigue induced by rigorous exercise and long rides. His life was changed, but his problem was still the same—Natacha. He tried, he swore, he determined that he would get over her, but, aware that he had failed, he plunged into more frequent and increasingly deeper depressions. Beltran y Masses claims that one day he came upon Valentino in his den with a revolver at his temple. On tiptoe the painter crossed the room to knock the gun aside, and as it fell to the carpet Valentino turned on him in a rage, then collapsed in tears. He pledged his friend to silence and only after the actor's death did the Spanish painter reveal this sad anecdote.

His reckless driving soon became so notorious that only strangers would ride with him. The closest brush with death came on February 28, 1926, when Valentino was returning from San Francisco in his Isotta Fraschini limousine. By swearing on their long friendship that he would permit his chauffeur, Ralph Rogers, to drive all the way, he had persuaded Douglas Gerrard to accompany him. The trip north had been uneventful. A valet had been engaged and Valentino had bought another dog, a basset hound, but shortly after they left Palo Alto, he persuaded Gerrard to release him from his promise. Would it not be a lark to have the valet, the chauffeur and the dog ride in the luxurious interior of the limousine while he drove and Gerrard played the role of footman? Against his better judgment, Gerrard agreed.

And once he had been given his way, Rudolph insisted they drive straight through; there would be less traffic and they could sing songs and enjoy the clear winter skies. By four in the morning, fog had begun to shroud the roads; still Valentino drove with one hand on the horn and a heavy foot on the gas. An hour later he sped through Santa Margarita, eleven miles north of San Luis Obispo. Just south of the town he roared into an unbanked curve at better than eighty miles an hour and tires screamed in protest as the big limousine began to skid across the damp highway. The car leaped a ditch, bounced over the Southern Pacific railroad tracks, wrecked a crossing signal and crashed to a stop against a telegraph pole.

At that moment, a Southern Pacific locomotive loomed out of the night. As the headlights caught the catapulting car, the engineer slammed on his brakes. The rails screamed as the wheels locked, and the train ground to a halt only a few feet from the wrecked car. Valentino had been thrown clear of the automobile, as had Gerrard, but the chauffeur, the valet and the dog were badly bruised and cut by flying glass.

After the police arrived, the four injured men were rushed to a hospital and a cordon of officers was placed around the car to keep it from being dismantled by the hundreds of souvenir hunters who quickly gathered in the meadow and along the tracks. The shock to Alberto and his family was no greater than that of Ullman and Schenck, who made immediate plans to sell every one of Valentino's automobiles. It did not require a psychologist to realize that he was deliberately courting a dramatic, romantic and quick end.

Newspapers did not take kindly to this accident. In headlines bold they disapproved of his reckless driving, which might cause injury and death to innocent people, and the Los Angeles *Examiner*, a paper much given to moral rectitude, emphasized its editorial displeasure on March 10:

"END THIS RECKLESS SORT OF CAREER!"
"Put a beggar on horseback and he will ride to the devil," is the old saying.
This modernized version is, "Give a swell-headed upstart an automobile and he will break his own neck or somebody else's in short order."
Mr. Rudolph Valentino is a case in point. His latest exploit was to wrap his automobile around a post at San Luis Obispo while going at a mad speed. This reckless, irresponsible person is always driving his automobile at dangerously high speed and is frequently in automobile accidents. His dangerous career should be rudely interrupted by the strong hand of the law.

What the strong hand of the law, newspaper editorials, his family, George Ullman and Pola Negri could not accomplish, Joseph Schenck did. Without any ceremony, he pointed out that Valentino's recklessness had been a matter of gossip, which he had chosen to ignore, but now he had to face it: his rash disregard of mechanics or roads could have killed everyone in the car. Suppose Valentino alone had survived? Schenck doubted that audiences would have been willing to tolerate him on the screen again. As surely as Arbuckle's career had been terminated by scandal, and Mary Miles Minter's and Mabel Normand's, too, so could Valentino's.

He then forbade Valentino ever to make long automobile trips or at any time to drive above fifty miles an hour. Schenck embraced him and pleaded with Valentino to stop brooding and to enjoy his popularity, his income, the long, rich and fruitful life which Schenck could envision if only he would behave.

Valentino promised and Ullman was pleased. He then asked if the studio executive could also advise them how to deal with Pola Negri, who managed to be quoted at least once a day in some major-circulation media about her romance with Valentino. As a case in point Ullman showed Schenck a solemn interview in *The New York Times* of March 6:

"The supreme test will come when I leave shortly for Germany to make a moving picture abroad."

"And what about Mr. Valentino?"

"Rudy will stay in Hollywood. If I feel as I do now upon my return and Rudy also feels the same, there is nothing to prevent our marriage. I love him deeply, very deeply indeed. I am not ashamed to confess that."

"For what qualities?"

"I think he is the supreme man. He is perfection. But, although many things have been said, I take marriage very seriously. If I am ever married I expect nothing to break the link. It shall be for all time. But first I want to prove my love. I will be gone for four months shortly. Rudy will be working here. True love ought to outlive this separation."

"Then you are engaged?" the reporter had asked carefully.

Miss Negri laughed. "Engaged?" she trilled. "I do not like the word. It sounds too much like a prison or a business engagement. I know Rudy very well, very well indeed. And I say he is the supreme man. Believe me, I have had enough experience with men. Really, I am a connoisseur of men. But this is a great love affair, I can tell you that. I am so eager to be tested by separation."

Schenck read the interview and remarked that it was rude, indiscreet and foolhardy for one man to advise another in an affair of the heart. But personally he believed a vacation from marriage would be of extravagant benefit to the actor and his public.

Rudolph pondered this.

If Valentino eventually came to regard Pola Negri as an act of God, sometimes amusing, often a nuisance, but always invaluable publicity for his own pictures, he solaced himself with the knowledge that she had only seized public possession of him. His private life, by God, was still his own. But wherever screen notables gathered, Miss Negri was Valentino's constant companion. A photograph of a birthday party given for Richard Barthelmess on May 9, 1926, at the Santa Monica home of Constance Talmadge included Valentino and Miss Negri. Valentino was now welcomed in the most rarefied of Hollywood social circles, but the lumpen snobbery that excluded his close friends, who were not the industry's exalted, was a convention he refused to accept. At Falcon Lair the old friends of his lean years were his only welcome guests.

ACT THREE: SCENE SIXTEEN

The Son of the Sheik had premiered in Los Angeles at Grauman's Million Dollar Theater, and for this state occasion a grim, close-mouthed Valentino escorted Miss Negri, who wore a close-fitting silver sheath gown, with a diamond tiara and a pearl necklace. The audience's reaction was enthusiastic; it was well paced and well performed, certain to be appreciated by the fans, and would make money and strengthen Valentino's reputation at the box office. With one or two more such pictures behind him, George Fitzmaurice told the dispirited Sheik, audiences would pay merely to see his name flashed on the screen. Without question he would next portray Cellini, Borgia, Machiavelli or some dashing hero of the Crusades. Why not Marco Polo, Fitzmaurice suggested, and Valentino was gratefully delighted.

In rare spirits, he departed with George Ullman for San

Francisco, where Mayor James R. Rolph was host at a luncheon at the Fairmont Hotel. From San Francisco Rudolph telephoned Alberto and asked him to meet him in New York City, and Alberto agreed, for although the Guglielmis had enjoyed their visit, they were anxious to return to Italy. A heat wave was gripping the country, and on the train to Chicago Valentino lounged in silk pajamas, read and continued to make plans for a European production. He still persisted in the belief that *The Hooded Falcon* was a germinal idea that contained all the elements for a successful picture. Joseph Schenck had rejected *Falcon* because its hero was a Moor, but minor alterations could turn him into a crusading Christian knight recently returned from the Holy Land to rescue Spain from the infidel. Pleased with this notion, Rudolph began to elaborate on it in a notebook, and when he and Ullman arrived in Chicago three days later, he was ebullient.

The Chicago premiere was as successful as the one in Los Angeles, and the newspaper reporters and crowds at the Blackstone Hotel, where the actor and his manager intended to spend several hours between trains, were even larger than those in San Francisco. But the weather was hot, and once again Valentino's good spirits were dashed by his old bête noire, the Chicago *Tribune,* a paper determined to prove the truth of one of *Time*'s observations (August 2, 1926), that "the masculinity of U.S. newspapers [was] as proverbial as the femininity of the U.S. magazines." Thus, a *Tribune* reporter's hackles rose when he came upon a sign above a machine in the *men's* lounge of a Chicago dance hall; the sign invited young sheiks and cake-eaters to "Insert coin. Hold personal puff beneath the tube. Then pull the lever." Pink face powder and powder puffs for—males?—was too epicene for a real man to tolerate; and the reporter prepared an editorial that blasted Valentino as a corrupting influence who should have been "quietly drown[ed] . . . years ago [.]" *Time* reported: "Over a hotel breakfast a closely muscled man, whose sombre skin was clouded with talcum and whose thick wrists tinkled with a perpetual arpeggio of fine gold bangles, read the effusion with rapidly mounting fury." In what was almost a repetition of his earlier brush with the Fourth Estate Valentino issued a public challenge to the anonymous writer but again it was not accepted though this time he went out of his way to flush out his tormentor.

When he arrived in New York City on July 20, he held another interview at the offices of United Artists, where he reaffirmed his desire to fight the editorial writer. He had no grievance, he repeated, against the Chicago *Tribune* and generously assumed "that the editorial had got into the paper unnoticed by the directing head."

"Do you intend to sue the *Tribune?*" a reporter asked.

Valentino shook his head. "I am not suing the paper. But if the man who wrote the editorial doesn't answer me or accept my challenge I'm going to write the *Tribune* management and demand a retraction and apology. I am now waiting for that individual to make himself known. I am ready to go through with it. This is not publicity. The man overstepped all bounds of decency and right thinking."

No one who heard Valentino that day could doubt his sincerity; unfortunately, he was naive. While he waited for an acknowledgment of his challenge, he saw Alberto and his family off to Europe and charged Gloria Swanson, also sailing for France with her husband the Marquis, with looking after them. But it is doubtful whether the Marquis or his consort were concerned with anything but their own problem: the Marquis's six-month permit to visit the democratic United States had expired, and he had been ordered by the immigration authorities to return to his own republic and make application for a new one.

Several nights later, Valentino made every gossip column when he appeared at Texas Guinan's speakeasy with Jean Acker, but he refused comment. And in Hollywood Estelle Taylor, at that time married to Jack Dempsey, breathlessly announced her joy at being chosen as Valentino's next leading lady in a yet untitled movie. With so many ladies competing for the attentions of Valentino, Miss Pola Negri deemed it necessary to confide in Louella Parsons that "I am glad to work hard because with Rudy in New York I would be so lonesome."

But Valentino was more concerned with the critical reception of *The Son of the Sheik* by *The New York Times*, the paper he feared and honored most. Ullman and Schenck insisted his fears were groundless, and to everyone's delight they were proved correct. Valentino's latest libretto of film love was enjoyed by the reviewer for the *Times*, who noted that the New York opening was a smash. The critic was also impressed by the huge crowd that milled around the Mark Strand Theater in the hope of seeing Valentino, who was to make a personal appearance after the first showing, and incorporated into his review a report on how bravely the police had worked to clear a side entrance into the theater, for "the sands of the desert weren't any hotter than the crowd which stood in the sun . . . to see if '*The Son of the Sheik*' was as good as his old man in running away with maidens who wandered carelessly into the desert. . . ." And although the major part of the review spoofed the picture, the reviewer concluded that "In its setting of desert sands . . . this latest offering of Valentino makes a very good romantic picture." The reviewer added that he, personally, enjoyed the picture hugely.

This delighted Valentino until, in a reappraisal several weeks later, the *Times* critic observed that the sequel, although entertaining, gave "Valentino an opportunity to exhibit his only two expressions, a smile and a haughty immobility." But he went on to say:

He has an arm like a blacksmith, and his approach to a horse is as likely to be through the air as by the stirrup. He shows no more hesitancy in hurling himself off a horse and dragging another man from his mount than he would in driving into the deeply cushioned bed in his desert tent. He drops from a balcony during a fight in a headlong way which scatters a small army of opponents, and shows an utter disregard for furniture.

But aside from the fighting thrills which make a rousing ending to the picture, it also contains some remarkable doubling by Valentino. He plays not only the son of the sheik, but the sheik himself, and is actually better as an elderly sheik with a beard and a hot temper than as the more romantic son traveling in father's footsteps.

Photoplay hailed the picture as one of the best of the month and exhorted every fan in the country to revere it as "Rudy's best." The tabloids, although they depended in greatest part for their circulation on murders and movie scandal, recommended the picture to their fans, though they could not resist lampooning it. Dorothy Herzog in the *Daily Mirror* called it "Asbestos, preposterous hocum. Rudy and the other principals dress in a way to shadow any musical comedy . . . the story is one of those things. Those going to see this picture will expect exactly what they get."

But the proof of any picture's success is at the box office, and *The Son of the Sheik* was packed at every performance. United Artists pleaded with Valentino to spend another week in New York and make more appearances at the theater. But Rudy was off to Chicago, where he informed reporters there was no significance in his having dined with Jean Acker; of significance was that he had taken a day out of a busy schedule to come to Chicago for an answer to his challenge.

"I must return to New York tomorrow," he told reporters. "My business there is not completed. But I challenged that man to fight and that's my business in Chicago now."

Valentino waited twenty-eight hours, but the craven remained hidden in a recess of the Tribune Tower. Fully vindicated and victorious for a second time over the *Tribune,* Valentino then distributed another statement, which was given prominent space by all Chicago papers—with the logical exception of the *Tribune.*

> It is evident you cannot make a coward fight any more than you can draw blood out of a turnip. The heroic silence of the writer who chose to attack me without any provocation in the Chicago *Tribune* leaves no doubt as to the total absence of manliness in his whole make-up.
>
> I feel I have been vindicated because I consider his silence as a tacit retraction and an admission which I am forced to accept, even though it is not entirely to my liking.
>
> The newspaper men and women whom it has been my privilege to know briefly or for a longer time have been so absolutely fair and so loyal to their profession and their publications that I need hardly say how conspicuous is this exception to the newspaper profession.

The star's next film was not scheduled to go into production before October, and United Artists told Valentino that another European jaunt might be good business. At the same time United Artists planned, if necessary, to move diplomatic mountains to arrange a cordial meeting between Valentino and Mussolini. The continued hostility of Fascists rankled the actor and he wished an end put to their harassment. Plans were made for Valentino to leave no later than the end of August, and the actor immediately ordered a new set of matching wardrobe trunks and luggage to house the dozen new suits a famous New York custom tailor was running up.

As he prepared for his departure, Valentino asked Ullman if it might not be wise to see Adolph Zukor and patch up his past quarrels with Paramount. Ullman agreed, and in his autobiography, *The Public Is Never Wrong* (1953), Zukor told of his meeting with Valentino at the Colony, where "every woman in the place having the slightest acquaintance with me felt an irresistible urge to rush to my table with greetings. Though overwhelmed, I remained in sufficient command of my senses to observe the amenities by introducing each to Valentino."

"I only wanted to tell you," Valentino said after things had quieted down, "that I'm sorry about the trouble I made—my strike against the studio and all that. I was wrong and I now want to get it off my conscience by saying so."

Zukor accepted the apology and listened with interest as Valentino told of his ambition to direct pictures when he could no longer play young romantic roles. Zukor had the feeling "that here was a young man to whom fame—and of a rather odd sort —had come too rapidly upon the heels of lean years and he hadn't known the best way to deal with it." But what he told Valentino that night was, "It's water over the dam. In this business if we can't disagree, sometimes violently, and then forget about it, we'll never get anywhere. You're young. Many good years are ahead of you."

ACT THREE: SCENE SEVENTEEN

But ten days later, on Monday, August 16, 1926, every important newspaper in the United States carried a front-page story that Valentino was so seriously stricken that he had required two emergency operations. Newspapers reported that Valentino and his valet had been alone in his suite in the Ambassador Hotel when the actor had suddenly gasped, clutched his stomach and fallen in a faint. The valet had immediately summoned Mr. and Mrs. Ullman from their nearby suite and then telephoned Barclay Warburton, Jr., a broker and friend of Valentino's, who had hurried to the Ambassador from his apartment on Park Avenue. He suggested to the Ullmans that Dr. Paul E. Durham be called immediately.

This advice was acted upon and Dr. Durham, after examining the semiconscious Valentino, had called in Dr. Harold D. Meeker for a consultation. The doctors began treating Valentino at noon, and four hours later agreed he should be transferred to the Polyclinic Hospital by ambulance because his condition demanded immediate surgery. It was a hot and stifling Sunday and most of the medical staff had left the city to escape the unusual heat, so he was not operated on until seven o'clock that evening, though he had been diagnosed as suffering from an acute gastric ulcer and a ruptured appendix.

Dr. Meeker performed the operation and he was assisted by Dr. Durham and Dr. Golden Rhind Battey, senior house physician at the Polyclinic. The ulcer was sewn up and Valentino's appendix removed. A private room had been made ready and strictest orders were given to the nurses and other attendants that no visitors, however prominent or insistent, were to see the patient, nor was any information to be given by anyone on the staff to reporters or other persons. All such requests were to be referred to George Ullman, whose only statement to the assembled reporters was, "It will be three or four days before we know anything about how he is going to come out of this."

The dissatisfied reporters demanded more information. Ullman then told them that Drs. Meeker and Durham had called in a third physician, G. R. Manning, who would assist in the treatment of Valentino because peritonitis, a dangerous complication, had set in. The physicians believed it had been checked but until a crisis occurred, in about forty-eight hours, they would be unable to tell whether the condition had been localized or would begin to spread. Shortly before midnight, Valentino's condition was described as "fair."

As news of the actor's illness spread over the country by radio, the switchboard at the Polyclinic Hospital was clogged with calls demanding detailed information. From Los Angeles came dramatic reports of sorrow and shock in the film colony, especially accounts of Pola Negri's overwhelming grief. Bound by the schedule of her picture from any immediate departure for his bedside, Pola assured all the scribes that news of Rudy's illness had stunned her beyond any linguistic description. "It was so sudden. I had no inkling that he was so sick. I would like to rush to him now, but business will delay me. In about ten days, however, I feel that I can make arrangements to get away and no train will be fast enough to carry me East." But because any medical details were meager, most papers merely fleshed out their articles with biographical sketches of the Sheik, and a recital of his recent feud with the Chicago *Tribune.*

Late Monday afternoon there appeared to be good news: Valentino's condition had improved from "fair" to "favorable." Nevertheless Drs. Durham, Meeker and Manning issued a cautious statement: "The condition of Mr. Valentino is still serious. At present he is doing as well as can be expected and he is resting quietly. Temperature is 103, pulse 100, respiration 26." And in the early evening an unofficial statement was given reporters by George Ullman, who told them his friend felt better and was able to smile.

More than a thousand telegrams had been sent to the hospital and hundreds of others had been addressed to Valentino at the Hotel Ambassador. Many of the waiting rooms at the hospital were filled with floral tributes, baskets of fruit and boxes of candy for the actor, and it was announced that Valentino had directed George Ullman to distribute these to less fortunate patients throughout the hospital.

During the afternoon, Valentino was able to thank his nurses personally for their care, the reporters were told by the staff physician now doubling as information officer. And they were also informed that he had directed his manager to send his solicitudes to Pola Negri in Los Angeles and cables of assurance to his brother, Alberto, in Paris and to his sister, Maria, in Rome. From his sickbed, he had also expressed regret that he would have to postpone his visit to Philadelphia, where he was to have toured the Sesquicentennial Exposition with Mayor W. Freeland Kendrick.

But reporters were far less interested in such civic inspections than in ascertaining if Jean Acker had telephoned to inquire about the actor's condition. Mr. Ullman replied that she had not, and remarked in bitter tones that Natacha, who was in Paris, hadn't dispatched so much as a single word, either. However, he assured the press that Valentino occupied "the most expensive suite in the hospital, consisting of two rooms and bath. It has been called the 'lucky' suite, for it was there that Mary Pickford, in 1912, recovered from a serious illness; nevertheless, it would be at least 48 to 72 hours before any firm statement of improvement could be made by the physicians."

Valentino was conscious of and interested in his surroundings, and was able to read messages from his close friends. One of the calls that cheered him most was from Jack Dempsey and it amused him that the switchboard was so tied up by calls that the hospital had been compelled to order the installation of another. During his stay some two thousand calls an hour were received. On Wednesday morning Valentino's illness was still considered sufficiently important by *The New York Times* to be covered by a long first-page story. The *Herald Tribune*, of a similar editorial opinion (the tabloids carried cartoon biographies), reprinted the official hospital bulletin issued at seven o'clock the previous evening, which was signed by Drs. Durham, Meeker and Manning: "There is no change in Mr. Valentino's condition. His temperature is 103, respiration 26, and pulse 108."

Despite the bulletin's evidence of continuing grave illness, Ullman was cheerful as he told reporters that when Valentino had awakened from a strengthening sleep he had told the nurses at his bed how "marvelous" he felt. Also, Mayor James J. Walker had telephoned for information about the actor, and a message of concern had finally been received from Jean Acker.

Although she planned to leave for Europe on Friday, before sailing she would try her best to see her former husband. Charles Chaplin had sent a telegram from Los Angeles, and Mary Pickford and Douglas Fairbanks, both in Paris, had sent their wishes for recovery by cablegram. Joseph Schenck and Norma Talmadge had come to the hospital, only to be told that they could not see the actor. Visitors, no matter how well-meaning, were still not allowed.

Every orderly and attendant who could be reached by the hospital was ordered to return to work, and Ullman telephoned the Burns Agency for a private detective to patrol the corridor before Valentino's suite on the eighth floor. That afternoon a wild-eyed young man had been found wandering the floor, though when collared by two orderlies, the distracted one confessed nothing more than a desire "to kneel by the bedside of the movie actor and pray for his recovery."

Other strangers were routed from the hospital but one resolute young lady, who identified herself as a poetess, insisted that she be permitted to present her most recent inspiration to Valentino, for its sentiments would surely help speed his recovery. Refused the opportunity, she became hysterical and had to be placed under observation. As she was led off, she uttered loud lamentation for the safety of her "beloved," then burst into tears and could not be comforted despite the offer of several chocolates from one of the boxes Valentino had sent the telephone operators. She was promised that her rhymed offering would be shown to her idol, and whether this pledge was kept is unknown. But the *Daily Mirror* believed aesthetes among its readers would appreciate reading the poem, called "A Dreamer's Thought":

> *I knew a young man,*
> *He's a dreamer it is true,*
> *He dreamed of fame and Broadway lights—*
> *Well, yes, that dream came true.*

He wanted someone to love him,
This Broadway butterfly.
But the dream didn't come true,
So far apart they went by.

A second love he went to find.
Not long before he knew
His Dreams were never true.
Then he longed for a baby
To hold it close in his arms.
A queer way, we say
————Try and get it,
And so again his dream went by.

Another of the most individual would-be visitors was a winsome and petite blonde who appeared with a personable monkey dressed as a Zouave. The little creature was on a leash and identified as Pepy, and the blonde sought admission to Valentino's room because "Rudy used to come to the Brooklyn cabaret where I work and he used to laugh and laugh at Pepy, so I thought maybe if I brought the monkey over he might cheer Rudy up." The hospital authorities, stodgy types, were unimpressed. The dancer and her pert pet were immediately escorted from the hospital.

Scores of photographers gathered outside the hospital, where they worked energetically to photograph the scores of little girls, adolescent misses, young ladies and matrons who brought flowers, cakes and bottles of spirits concealed in floral boxes. Many of them were attractive and posed willingly for the photographers. In their search for auguries, one of the more optimistic tokens treasured by many of the young ladies was a photograph published by the Hearst press of Valentino in athletic shorts, sleeveless shirt and boxing gloves. The photograph called attention to the "perfect biceps" and "broad chest" of the actor, and pointed out that he had "no superfluous flesh. This rugged constitution, coupled with his keen urge to live, is responsible for the gallant fight he is making," the caption said.

Valentino's sudden illness had about it many mysterious elements demanding plain explanations. One was that he had attended a party on Saturday evening, August 14, at the apartment of Barclay Warburton. Before he disappeared for a much-needed rest behind the walls of the Harbor Sanatorium, Warburton had denied that there had ever been such a party, but Harry Richman told reporters there had indeed been one, and that Valentino had attended it with Marian Benda, a Ziegfeld beauty, recently reported engaged to Zeppo Marx.

"We had some drinks, music and dancing," Richman reported, "until about one thirty, when Rudy was taken violently ill and was rushed to his apartment at the Ambassador."

Another report was that Valentino had been found in the gutter and removed to Bellevue Hospital before he had been recognized and returned to the Ambassador. There is no substantiation for this version, but James Thurber in *The Years with Ross* (1959) reported:

> That great matinee idol, incidentally, was to collapse outside a New York cabaret in 1926 with an agony in his stomach that turned out to be a fatal perforating ulcer. When he fell, his opera hat rolled into the street, and was rescued by one of those who rushed to his aid, none other than Harold Ross, the young editor of *The New Yorker*. . . . Ross kept his opera hat, intending to return it to him when he left the hospital, which he never did alive. The hat was accidentally thrown out when Ross and his first wife moved from their house on West 47th Street in 1928. "I thought it was an old hat of Aleck's," Jane Grant, Ross's first wife, told me. Alexander Woollcott had shared the cooperative in the West Forties.

The summer's heat helped such rumors to spread, and most versions of Valentino's illness were given more credence than any official explanation. One much in favor was that Valentino had been shot by a jealous husband whose wife, although she had never met the actor, was in love with him. Another account had it that friends of Jack De Saulles, who still insisted that Valentino had been responsible for the murder of their friend, had at last found an opportunity for revenge. And a third, one of the more startling, was attributed to a Hollywood film figure who knew Valentino well. He claimed that there had been an affair between the mistress of a multimillionaire dabbler in films, and that when the millionaire discovered that Valentino had been swiving his sweetheart, he had followed the unsuspecting actor East and gunned Valentino down. But Valentino had only been wounded, and was removed to a small private hospital on Long Island that specialized in the treatment of alcoholics, dope addicts, women inconvenienced by pregnancy and embarrassing gunshot wounds. He had been returned too quickly to New York from the little hospital—and now was very ill.

Whatever the plausibility of such rumors, one strange fact stands out. Before Valentino had left for New York he had been examined by his personal physician in Hollywood,.Dr. Frank B. Browning, who had pronounced him fit as a fiddle.

∴ Thirty years later, Sidney Skolsky in his *This Was Hollywood* (1955), an annual devoted to "the loves, glamour, and tragedies of filmdom's Golden Age," averred that Valentino died "of septicemia brought on by years of malnutrition."

At seven that evening the three physicians issued a bulletin that could be interpreted as optimistic, if all the hedges were discounted: "Mr. Valentino's condition remains favorable. Unless unforeseen complications develop, recovery is considered probable. His temperature is 100.8, respiration 20 and pulse 86."

Reporters were told of the pain suffered by the star during the day and how he had breakfasted on chicken broth. Later, peptonized milk and vichy water had been added to his diet. Fighting for his life, Valentino was unaware that his illness had inspired thousands of New Yorkers to congregate around the hospital, and that their presence made it increasingly difficult for the Polyclinic staff to maintain a normal hospital regimen. Nine nurses had been engaged in three shifts to keep the actor under constant observation. Additional private detectives had also been employed. Several hundred Bibles were sent from well wishers and, from Chicago, a copy of *Snowshoe Al's Bedtime Stories for Grown-Up Guys*. There were copies of prayers, holy pictures, rosaries and beads, and numerous medical suggestions, such as the use of leeches. An anonymous donor sent a sandalwood box purported to contain sacred oil; the contents were sent to the laboratory for analysis.

Of encouragement to the physicians, Schenck and Ullman was the fact that during that day Valentino had overcome some of his lethargy: he had been able to understand what was said to him and even made a few rational responses. For example, he had been pleased over a cablegram from Natacha and Mrs. Werner, and had thanked United Artists for the "resolution of sympathy" sent by the corporation's directors. Tammany Young, the noted gate crasher, had also communicated with the hospital, and Valentino had smiled over his message: "Dear Pal, God always takes care of regular fellows. He'll take care of you." He even had acknowledged Pola Negri's telephone call and Jean Acker's plan to visit the hospital before she sailed. But most heartening of all, the physicians agreed, was Valentino's increasing restlessness over the length of his hospital stay.

Wednesday, August 19, has journalistic interest because on this day Bernarr Macfadden's *Evening Graphic* by the boldest of journalistic coups established a proprietary interest in the stricken star. In an historic determination to capture every reader whose intellectual penumbra and taste was zero, the New York *Evening Graphic* had made its first appearance on September 19, 1924. Although it was also a tabloid newspaper with pictures, in imitation of its two older competitors, the *News* and *Mirror*, neither noted for offering their readers healthy cerebral food, the antic disposition of the *Graphic*, its bizarre concept of what was news and newsworthy, and what the publisher and its staff would do to create news was so unorthodox and idiosyncratic, that by comparison the older tabloids appeared to be nineteenth-century bastions of American Victorian conservatism, edited in the tradition of Louisa May Alcott and the shyest of her little women.

Two years later the *Graphic* still was unable to get any respectable advertisement in its pages, for the attitude of the city's department stores, automobile agencies and manufacturers of national products was that the minds of the *Graphic*'s readers were uncluttered by intelligence and their pockets held little cash to purchase anything of value. What the *Graphic* could not earn through advertising it had to compensate by circulation, and as soon as the *Graphic*'s editor, Emile H. Gauvreau, was convinced that Valentino's illness was not a publicity hoax he had ordered, for the paper's readers, the creation of a large composograph of Valentino on the operating table at the Polyclinic Hospital. The star, serious of mien, was nude above the waist, for which a good torso shot of a gymnosophist was used, and he was attended by three gowned physicians, equally solemn, although the surgeon with the forceps looked as if he had studied the healing art at Serutan University. Three nurses were in the shot, one grim, one smiling and one enamored of Valentino, whose sleek, shining hairpiece she touched with gentle fingers. Following this composition, which took almost a dozen photos to create, a message from Bernarr Macfadden reminded his March hare reporters and editors that Macfadden Publications had published several of Valentino's books, the paper had featured a photograph of Valentino with the publisher and his family, and had recently contracted with the Sheik to publish his "diary" and other revelations of interest to readers of the youngest of the city's tabloids. Gauvreau assigned every available reporter and photographer to the Polyclinic Hospital and told them to write news: what had not occurred could be manufactured and if the day's events were less than newsworthy, inspiration and exaggeration were to be employed without regard for fact.

Thus New York City was startled Wednesday noon when its leather-lunged newsboys began to hawk an extra addition of the *Graphic* which bore the startling headline "RUDY DEAD!" and in much smaller type "Cry Startles Film World as Sheik Rallies." The story to accompany the headlines told of a rumor of death that had swept Broadway because telephone calls to the Polyclinic Hospital had revealed that the actor's condition had worsened from "fair" to "critical."

The *Graphic*'s headline and story were responsible for the swamping of the switchboard at the hospital where hundreds of calls were answered merely by the operator shouting into the mouthpiece—"he's alive!" Naturally, the *Graphic* sold thousands of copies of this afternoon edition and other papers, if they were able to restrain their reporters who suggested similar stunts, knew they had to maintain around-the-clock staffs at the hospital in case anything did happen to the sick actor.

Then, as reported by the Los Angeles *Examiner*, George Ullman changed his first account of Valentino's illness. Now he admitted that his client had been "first stricken Saturday night while in the Park Avenue apartment of Barclay Warburton. . . . Rudy and Warburton and several others had been to a show. It had been suggested that they go afterward to a party in the apartment of Lenore Ulric, the actress. But Rudy demurred, saying that he was not feeling well. So *we* [italics added] went to Warburton's apartment. Rudy was sitting on a divan talking to the others when he collapsed."

Although the star suffered some heartburn Wednesday night, when he awakened Thursday morning the physicians were so pleased with his progress that they disregarded professional caution and made their first truly optimistic pronouncement. Valentino, they announced, was on the road to recovery and they intended to issue no more bulletins "unless unexpected developments occur."

The doctors told Valentino of their optimism, and he was cheered by it; with George Ullman at his bedside, he began to make plans. Together they discussed a suitable site for his convalescence. Valentino agreed that a stay at the summer home of Hiram Abrams, the president of United Artists, might be wise. Abrams' home was at Poland Springs, Maine, and Valentino wondered if there was good fishing and sailing nearby.

He even composed a statement, which was given to the press:

> I have been deeply touched by the many telegrams, cables, and letters that have come to my bedside. It is wonderful to know that I have so many friends and well-wishers, both among those it has been my privilege to meet and among the loyal unknown thousands who have seen me on the screen and whom I have never seen at all.
>
> Some of the tributes that have affected me the most have come from my "fan" friends—men, women and little children. God bless them. Indeed, I feel that my recovery has been greatly advanced by the encouragement given me by every one.

During the afternoon Valentino began to read *The Prisoner of Chance* by Bernard Grasett, which had been suggested as a possible film by Gloria Swanson and later he diverted himself by looking at some of the many bouquets sent him. He suggested that the red roses from Pola Negri be sent to the charity ward. Because all newspapers had been kept from him, he had not realized how grave his condition was.

By Friday, he was chafing at his inability to sit up, and spoke, when permitted, of nothing but leaving the hospital. He still took pride in the piles of letters and telegrams that continued to arrive, and often thanked his nurses for their kindness. He also apologized for the behavior of his fans, many of whom had been too energetic in their solicitude.

On Saturday, alas, Valentino was not the cheerful patient of the day before. He wanted to smoke, and to sit up, but both requests were denied. The staff of Polyclinic was concerned because a morning examination revealed the spread of pleurisy to Valentino's upper left trunk, and Drs. Meeker and Durham felt called upon to issue a bulletin at one-ten in the afternoon. "There is a slight spread of the infection in the abdominal wall causing considerable discomfort. There is nothing about the condition to cause undue anxiety at the present time. His temperature is 101, pulse 90, respiration 22."

By four in the afternoon, Valentino's temperature had risen to a dangerous 104.2 and the two physicians believed the young star's situation so grave they began to think of blood transfusions. They consulted with Dr. Manning, who believed a transfusion was neither warranted nor of any medical value. Valentino's condition continued grave through the afternoon and the doctors were especially concerned because his temperature refused to drop and the pain had become almost unbearable. To relieve this, a hypodermic was administered, which made Valentino so lethargic and listless that he no longer seemed to care about anything.

Later that afternoon the three anxious doctors were joined by Dr. William Bryant Rawles, the house physician at the Polyclinic. By seven in the evening the three left the hospital, but not before they issued a second bulletin: "Mr. Valentino has developed pleurisy in the left chest; has had a very restless day. Temperature 103.2, pulse 120, respiration 26."

The hospital steps were crowded with pallid, tear-stained young women who prayed for the recovery of the Great Lover, but the reporters clustered around Frances "Peaches" Browning when she appeared in a limousine to bubble prettily about her concern. Greater interest was displayed by the press and bystanders when, late that afternoon, another limousine parked at the curb and a maid who identified herself as in the employ of Jean Acker delivered a package to a hospital attendant. The reporters were present when the package was opened and its contents were revealed as a white counterpane with lace ruffles and the name "Rudy" nicely embroidered in blue on the four corners, and a pillowcase to match.

Late that night, Father Edward F. Leonard, pastor of St. Malachy's chapel, arrived at the hospital to hear Valentino's confession and grant him absolution.

ACT THREE: SCENE EIGHTEEN

On his popular Sunday-night program over radio station WEAF, Major Edward Bowes, manager and impresario of the Capitol Theater and an energetic prospector for amateur talent, broadcast a ringing religious plea to his many radio listeners. Fervently, in brotherhood, they were to pray for the full and speedy recovery of the stricken actor. Hundreds of thousands of the Major's listeners harkened and prayed.

Within the hospital, Dr. Meeker had been informed of the appeal made by Major Bowes and appreciated the request for a miracle. At about three-thirty on Monday morning, August 23, 1926, Valentino roused from a fitful slumber and the doctor examined him. Aware that he was at the bedside, Valentino smiled weakly, cleared his throat with some difficulty and thanked the nurse as she wiped his forehead and lips. Then, in a faint whisper, he told the doctor he looked forward to going fishing with him, but the doctor would have to supply the tackle. Dr. Meeker attempted a smile as he made some light comment, then shook his head as Valentino closed his eyes. It was apparent to him that the actor's condition was worsening rapidly, and he called for his medical colleagues, Drs. Manning and Durham.

Shortly before six, when true daylight had come to the city, Valentino began to babble in Italian, and a nurse hurried to awaken Edward Day, a hospital technician whose blood type was the same as Valentino's. But a few minutes later he was told to return to his room. Valentino's heart was too weak to withstand the strain of a transfusion.

At six, Joseph Schenck arrived and attempted to comfort George Ullman, who had spent most of the night outside Valentino's door. He then dictated cables to Maria and Albert Guglielmi. Some hours later, a cablegram from Alberto was received by Mr. Schenck: Valentino's brother intended to book passage for New York on the first available liner. No acknowledgment was ever received from Maria.

Reconciled to the worst, but still hoping for the best, Schenck entered the sickroom and spoke softly. Valentino merely babbled deliriously in Italian. Schenck joined Ullman in a private waiting room, and at eight o'clock Valentino lapsed into a coma. Shortly after ten the Reverend Joseph H. Congedo, of the Church of the Sacred Hearts of Jesus and Mary, entered the hospital through an inconspicuous side door to administer extreme unction. Father Congedo was said to have come from Castellaneta and been long acquainted with Valentino.

Around noon Father Congedo was joined by Father Leonard, who had been at the hospital earlier the night before. To the actor's lips Father Leonard pressed a crucifix that was reputed to contain a relic from the true Cross. Valentino did not respond. The team of physicians prepared for death and, to make their task less painful, they asked Mrs. Ullman to suggest that her husband return to the Ambassador Hotel and get some rest. Assured by Joseph Schenck that he would be called, that nothing important would be done without his knowledge, Ullman dictated a statement, then left the hospital before it was given to the press:

> Mr. Valentino was greatly cheered during his last days by the thousands of messages sent him by his friends and motion picture admirers, and while he was too weak to read all of them, it was a great comfort to him to know that so many friends were kind and sympathetic. I know he would want me to express the gratitude he felt. Personally, I want to thank the physicians and nurses and hospital attaches who worked so hard and conscientiously.

On Monday, August 23, 1926, in New York City, at ten minutes past high noon, Rudolph Valentino died. At that moment the world lost a man and gained a new god of Love and Romance.

ACT FOUR
LIFE
IN THE HEREAFTER

IN MEMORIAM
By Margaret Sangster

His feet had carried him so very swiftly,
  Into the lands of wonder and romance;
And yet, although they travelled far, they never
  Forgot to dance.

His lips had learned to speak a stranger language,
  His smile had warmed the wistful, lonely earth—
Yet fame had never taken, from his spirit,
  The gift of mirth!

Although his eyes glimpsed bitterness and sadness,
  They saw a dream that few folk ever see—
God grant the dream may tinge, with lovely color,
  Death's Mystery!

Photoplay, October, 1926

ACT FOUR: SCENE ONE

Frank Campbell had enjoyed his stay in Los Angeles. Expansively he praised the climate, palm trees and regional grief merchants, and he told the local hagiographers assigned to cover the Valentino rites that he hoped to return again. Campbell estimated, with considerable pride and satisfaction, that from the last hospital expense to the final disposition of the body, a similar funeral, if it hoped for a like success, could not be undertaken for less than a hundred thousand dollars, which included the cost of cross-country ceremonies. He estimated that at least a million people had seen some part of the rites, and as a happy result United Artists had been deluged with letters from all over the world demanding the immediate booking of Valentino films in their local theaters.

Paramount, meanwhile, was delighted to learn that within a

day or two, Pola Negri intended to return to work on her interrupted picture.

"My picture, it must be finished," she announced bravely. "These people have been kind to me, and I cannot let my grief make their penalty too heavy. There are still thirty scenes to be taken. Many of these are close-ups of me. The picture must be finished this week. I realize I am in terrible condition; I can hardly stand. But I will summon up my strength to help me."

Dr. Louis Folger, Pola's physician, believed it would take more than several days; Pola was still given to swoons and tears at the mention of Valentino's name, though she found much solace in the company of Alberto, in residence at a nearby bungalow at the Ambassador. Pola had promised herself a vacation after she had completed *Hotel Imperial,* but instead she chose not to leave Los Angeles until she had enshrined Alberto's gift—the painting of Valentino as a Spanish gentleman by Beltran y Masses.

The painting could not be hallowed immediately; she would have to wait until the estate had been probated and distributed in accordance with Valentino's last will, a surprising document—so much so that most newspapers, including those in New York, had published it in full. It divided the actor's estate into equal thirds—among his brother, Alberto Valentino-Guglielmi; his sister, Maria Guglielmi; and Mrs. Theresa Werner, of Salt Lake City, Utah, Natacha's aunt.

Mrs. Werner was in Paris, but upon notification of her legacy the good lady made immediate plans to return to the United States. The will had revealed the "actor's tender regard for his wife's aunt and the fact that she had endeavored to make his home life comfortable for him after Natacha Rambova left for Paris to get her divorce." Mrs. Werner had had no previous inkling of Valentino's depth of feeling and gratitude, but she expressed the greatest surprise at the third specific paragraph in the will, which stipulated: "I give, devise and bequeath to my wife, Natacha Rambova, also known as Natacha Guglielmi, the sum of one dollar, it being my intention, desire and will that she receive this sum and no more." Jean Acker was not mentioned at all.

"Never for one moment did I expect to be mentioned in Rudy's will," declared Miss Acker to New York reporters before she announced her intention of returning to the silver screen as soon as she had recuperated from her grief. "Money was not a factor in our relations. So far as contesting the will is concerned I don't know what my rights are and I don't care. I am not interested. It was the lasting, beautiful love which I had for him that counted."

S. George Ullman was named executor and manager of the estate, and with Mr. Gilbert, Valentino's California attorney, he filed the will. Because of the bequest to Mrs. Werner, both men prepared themselves for a rough and stormy voyage through the courts, inasmuch as Alberto had already issued his first challenges. He objected to the provision that named Ullman executor. In an effort at conciliation, Ullman listened sympathetically to all of Alberto's observations and promised to consult him at all times. But as the man most closely involved and fully aware of the various ramifications of Valentino's financial affairs, he felt that if any money was to accrue to the estate it was best that he remain executor. Otherwise, he pointed out, provisions like those directing the executor to "pay all of my just debts and funeral expenses as soon as may be practicable after my death" might become worrisome. The wisest course of action, he suggested, was to compile an inventory and evaluation of Valentino's possessions as quickly as possible.

George Ullman had already begun his own appraisals. Valentino's percentages in *The Eagle* and *The Son of the Sheik* might, if the present interest continued, amount to a million dollars. Falcon Lair and its surrounding acreage might be worth between $140,000 and $175,000. Ullman valued Valentino's house and grounds on Whitley Heights at $65,000 and his collection of Italian and Spanish armor and weapons and books at between $50,000 and $70,000. The art collection, with its two full-length portraits of Valentino—one of which was reported promised to Pola Negri—should bring between $50,000 and $70,000. Valentino's yacht *Phoenix*—$8,000; fourteen thoroughbred dogs of various breeds—$10,000; five thoroughbred riding horses— $10,000; three Isotta Fraschini automobiles—$35,000; three other cars—$7,500. Unimproved real estate—$25,000; jewelry —$50,000; his costumes, furniture and antiques—$15,000; his interest in past films—$10,000. If good auction prices were realized the estate might realize an additional half million dollars. These evaluations appeared to be conservative and sound. In addition, a quick inventory of the actor's wardrobe revealed that he had owned fifty suits of clothing, all purchased since January, 1926, fifty pairs of shoes, three fur coats, twenty hats, three hundred ties, a thousand pairs of hose and several hundred silk shirts. There was also the possibility that Valentino had carried a personal life insurance policy for $50,000.

But Alberto did not change his mind. He believed that the provisions of the "surprising" will demanded consultation with an attorney other than Mr. Gilbert, even if the advice given him might result in a prolonged and expensive courtroom battle. In a matter of hours, Milton Cohen, another Los Angeles attorney, announced that he had been retained by Alberto, who also represented Maria, and that the will might indeed be contested. He described the document as a "vague instrument which leaves many points to be clarified. Tomorrow I will examine the original in the office of W. I. Gilbert, Valentino's attorney. If it's a fair will I shall not contest it. If it turns out to be unfair, I will. If the document is the same as published, I think it is a vague instrument."

Elaborating on this thesis, Mr. Cohen directed attention to

the paragraph in which Valentino had ordered the trust income to be received and dispersed by George Ullman. The point at issue was the line which provided for Ullman "to finally distribute the said trust estate according to my wish and will, as I have this day instructed him." What were these oral charges that had not been disclosed in the will? Mr. Cohen demanded to be told.

Ullman replied that this was not the time to divulge them. He would tell them to a judge only under court order. Ullman also pointed out that Valentino had exempted him from bond because "that's the way we did business when he was alive." Undaunted by threats of brewing legal storms, Ullman continued to act as executor, for claims against the estate were already pouring in. After a few weeks they amounted to almost $150,000 for "expenses connected with the funeral, his personal debts, and mortgages against the two homes." Valentino's estate seemed in grave danger of foundering.

Determined to raise money wherever possible, Ullman hoped to arrange with Joseph Schenck for the domestic release of Natacha's film *What Price Beauty?* The picture had opened in England, where neither the critics nor the public had been enthusiastic. It was obviously a financial failure, yet eighty thousand dollars in production costs had still to be paid and the Valentino estate would probably be liable. Ullman hoped to discharge these through the American box office, and Joseph Schenck saw the logic of this and agreed to distribute the film. At this point he warned the principals that their falling out within two days of Valentino's burial in Hollywood Cemetery did not sit well with the public, and might seriously impair the future value of Valentino's pictures.

There was too much good common sense in this opinion to dispute, so a conference was scheduled in the office of W. I. Gilbert between the disputants and their attorneys. Points at issue were conciliated and a formal statement of concord was issued. First, Alberto Guglielmi, through his attorneys, Milton

Cohen and R. D. Knickerbocker, approved the terms of the will. Second, George Ullman revealed the nature of the oral instructions he had received from Valentino: Ullman would (1) administer the estate, (2) guard its assets until a settlement of all debts had been made and there were assets to distribute, and (3) divide these assets among the three beneficiaries. Ullman had had a telegram from Mrs. Werner which empowered him to act in her behalf, and all the principals were made aware that the State of California gave heirs a year in which to file a complaint, so this agreement to promote harmony was not restrictive. Only as an afterthought did attorneys for both sides note that if the will was broken it could stir up another hornet's nest: it might validate an earlier will, which named Natacha Rambova as Valentino's sole heir.

Meanwhile, Ullman undertook the sale of Valentino's houses and other properties. He decided that an auction would be the best way to dispose of the thousands of items in the estate. Whatever had not been sold by the end of October would be offered through an impressive auction catalogue, which itself would sell for two dollars. Ullman was also approached by Macy-Masius, New York publishers, who urged him to prepare an "official" biography of Valentino, to be published quickly so that it might capitalize on the public's overwhelming interest.

The publishers and Ullman were aware that a Valentino biography had already been published privately in Hollywood by Ben Newman, who used the literary pseudonym Ben-Allah. His volume, *Rudolph Valentino, His Romantic Life and Death*, was dedicated to "The discoverer of Rudolph Valentino" and its contents were a compilation of Valentino's romantic life as movie fans had wanted it to be:

It may be that in his heart when he passed to the Great Beyond was the memory of an early love, forgotten of name, but remembered with the lightness of wisteria in the air. . . . Within his soul there was never the desire to be a Don Juan. Though in individual cases he may have manifested a high ardor, though his enacting of fiery scenes must in some measure have been founded on a knowledge, still WITH VALENTINO LOVE RESTED AS AN ORDERLY EMOTION OF THE SOUL. . . . Along the avenues of Hollywood, where he stepped from obscurity to fame, he is missed. Though not an ever-present figure on the leafy lanes of picturedom he was nonetheless the cynosure in a city of actors that boasts itself "blasely" along. . . . The pain of death mercifully leaves him and he finds himself rising from the snow-white bed where he rests and assumes a standing position. He is led away by influences which he sees not. He suddenly finds himself dressed in his old Vaquero garb. Again he is Julio riding the range with The Centaur. . . . There is a touch on his shoulder and he is told to arise and follow. It is the angel of the darker drink bearing a cup of his own brew for the Great Lover.

Macy-Masius saw nothing in Ben-Allah's paper-covered book to alter its decision that a biography, properly bound, illustrated with appropriate photographs and with a foreword by O. O. McIntyre, the popular Hearst columnist, would have a profitable sale throughout the land. The astral events of the Ben-Allah biography, a slender volume padded with statements of grief by famous Hollywood personalities, would certainly not be covered by Ullman, who would after all receive the assistance of professional editors.

Ullman's biography, *Valentino as I Knew Him*, was published on October 24, 1926, which is evidence of a remarkable ability to write quickly. Early event by early event, Mr. Ullman rehashed Valentino's career as first published in the *Photoplay* autobiography, but a goodly section was devoted to Valentino's illness, and this tragic section was original. It was impossible for the author to ignore Pola Negri and her nuptial claims, so he diplomatically settled that area of speculation by writing:

"He never told me so, and I never asked him." However, Ullman did mention Valentino's oath to him never to remarry until he had retired from the screen.

Ullman's biography was well reviewed by the Boston *Transcript* and the New York *World*. *The New York Times Sunday Book Section* of November 14 acknowledged the book but offered no critical comment; instead it told its readers: "The author has gathered his material, he says, for this last tribute to his friend 'from stories he told me here and there, some related in the great bay window of his Hollywood home, some on horseback riding over the desert at Palm Springs, some on our long railway journeys between California and the East.'" The review also offered Mr. Ullman's conviction that Valentino's "life may have been shortened because of his anger and mental suffering over a reference to him in an editorial in a Chicago paper not long before his final illness." The book's reception pleased Ullman and his associates; a good domestic sale was the inspiration for an English edition published early the following year, bearing a new title: *The Real Valentino*.

Some exception to the book was taken by Natacha Rambova, because she had not been portrayed as an ideal wife, but her criticisms were ignored, and to present her view of Rudy's life, their marriage and his communications to her *after* death, Natacha published *Rudy: An Intimate Portrait of Rudolph Valentino by His Wife*. The book was completed in New York by December, 1926, and the English edition, published by Hutchinson and Company, was 224 pages in length and included sixteen photographs. An abridged American edition of 128 pages was copyrighted in 1927 and published in 1928 by Jacobsen-Hodgkinson under the title *Rudolph Valentino, Recollections, Intimate and Interesting Reminiscences of the Life of the Late World Famous Star by Natacha Rambova His Wife*. Natacha's biography of her famous husband is so unique that it can be fully discussed only later in context with other events related to the psychic phenomena associated with Valentino.

In France the most interesting of the quick, derivative biographies was written by Edouard Ramond, whose *La Vie Amoureuse de Rudolph Valentino* was published by Librairie Saudiniere in 1927. Written in *le drugstore* French, the tale is told in the device of a frame story and flashback. After a hard-day's work at the studio, Rudy greeted *la pauvre* pet of *"poor little Mary Pickford"* and exchanged *"un hand-shake* with Douglas Fairbanks, who was accompanied by his famous dog Zorro. While Rudy was driven home he commented upon some of the fabulous mansions of the stars and he was stirred by the home of Thomas Ince, for it was a faithful replica of *"la maison du glorieux Washington."*

Once Rudy arrived at Falcon Lair he played with his two favorite dogs and commanded them in the language of *"Dante et Mussolini."* Relaxed, in reverie, Rudy reflected upon his early life, as invented by Herbert Howe for *Photoplay*, but Gallic innovations made his past into a French souffle, for much was made of a romance with Bettina, a Castellanetan beauty beneath him in family and social rank. The romance was frustrated when Bettina's cruel father took her to America. When Rudy was exiled to the United States he made the voyage a merry one by organizing and performing with a musical group. After he cleared Ellis Island he took rooms at the Ritz and awaited the return of a countryman from *"des Grand Lacs et de la capitale du Corned Beef,"* for this businessman was to introduce Rudy to people of consequence and wealth.

Photoplay continued to be followed but the biographer made a radical alteration when he introduced Norman Kerry as a great *actress. "Elle est une star de moyenne grandeur, une etoile entre tant d'autre au firmament de l'ecran. Seduisante d'ailleurs . . . Pour Rudolph, elle est une femme entre les femmes. . . ."*

When Rudy quarreled with Paramount, the French biographer explained why The Sheik could not make ends meet on $1,250 a week; every week he had to pay $250 to his secretary, $250 for legal expenses, $250 to repay old debts, $250 to Jean Acker and $250 to his family—so what was left for him? *"Et nous savons que de ses douze cent cinquante dollars par semaine, il ne lui reste rien pour vivre!"* Therefore, in due time, he died.

ACT FOUR: SCENE TWO

In his workmanlike Hollywood office, Ullman continued to labor to make Valentino's estate into something of value. Although he would have preferred to concentrate on the administration of the will, he had to spend an inordinate amount of time on the increasing volume of mail from Valentino fans. Each letter demanded a reply. Such mail appeared in bagfuls, addressed to United Artists; to Pola Negri; to Joseph Schenck; to Norma and Constance Talmadge; to several railroads; to Frank E. Campbell's; to the Hollywood Cemetery; to the mayor of Los Angeles and the governor of California; to all the Hollywood studios; to Alberto, and even to Rudolph himself—for there were many fans who believed in the Great Beyond. The letters necessitated kindly acknowledgment because each represented one or more tickets at the box office, and every admission meant something of value for the three principals mentioned in the will.

With the letters came requests for Valentino photographs, so arrangements were made to reproduce and distribute favorite stills of the star to people considerate enough to include a small sum to cover mailing costs. Added staff had to be employed and larger quarters leased to handle the unusual volume of correspondence. The mail did not abate for more than ten years.

If Ullman was busy with administrative chores and the processing of mail, Alberto spent just as much time in conferences with his attorneys. Too soon it became evident that the peace parley held in the middle of September had engendered nothing more than an uneasy truce. On October 4, prior to the probating of the will, Alberto's attorneys delivered a stern ultimatum to Ullman and his legal staff: the terms of surrender offered were quite unconditional; Alberto and his sister would not contest the will provided Alberto was named coexecutor. Ullman consulted with his attorney and decided to withhold comment until confronted by his adversaries in the courtroom.

The first hearing, before Superior Court Judge Henry M. Willis, took place early in October. Judge Willis harkened to the Guglielmi petitions, took them under advisement for a week, and on October 11 rendered a decision that pleased neither the Guglielmis nor their attorneys. Judge Willis continued Ullman as the sole executor but, in direct contravention of the will, ordered him to secure a hundred-thousand-dollar bond.

As soon as Judge Willis made this decision, R. D. Knickerbocker announced that he and his colleagues in the Guglielmi cadre of barristers had been instructed by Alberto to make every effort to break the will. "The effort to break the will," he explained, "will center on the clause leaving the entire estate in trust to Ullman for the benefit of the two Guglielmis and Mrs. Theresa Werner, aunt of Valentino's divorced wife, Natacha Rambova."

Battle lines were drawn, redoubts strengthened, new positions fortified. Legal maneuvers to repel punitive thrusts consumed all

his time, but Ullman stretched his days to sponsor an architectural competition for a memorial mausoleum, not to cost
more than ten thousand dollars. The first plans were too like a
cathedral, even for the new god of Romance, and *Photoplay* sadly
informed the Valentino Memorial Committee that its offices were
unequipped to handle the multitude of contributions it was receiving—most of them one dollar—so wherever possible, they
were returned to the senders with letters of thanks.

While Ullman conferred with his attorneys, with film executives and with an expert appraiser, the estate, reputed to be
worth millions, lacked the cash to lift a federal income tax lien
of $6,490.95 filed in the United States District Court of Los
Angeles by the District Director of Internal Revenue.

The principals named in Valentino's will were of little concern to the film studios, who were engaged in a much larger
problem—who was to replace the Sheik? Who could be found
to project from the screen an intimate but courtly sexuality that
would ecstasize females and stimulate them to wholesome erotic
fantasy?

Barclay Warburton, Jr., host of the mysterious party at which
Valentino had become ill, made publicists aware of his interest
in a Hollywood career, and Louella Parsons fluttered that Lloyd
Pantages, ambitious son of a theatrical father, had on his courageous own presented himself to the Fox Company to make a
series of screen tests. William Fox—a remarkable bootstrap
executive who had recently coined the bon mot "once an actor,
always a horse's ass"—saw the tests in his eastern office and
commented on the lad's marked resemblance to Valentino. Although Lloyd was somewhat shorter, he was dark, olive-skinned
and slender, the best physiological characteristics for any male
determined upon a sheikish role. In Hollywood offices and at
restaurant tables, where the most reliable rumors were spawned,
many egopinionated oracles nominated Ricardo Cortez, though

the success of *Ben Hur*, a four-million-dollar epic released in 1926, made Ramon Navarro a prominent contender. Trains, buses, autos—and shanks' mare—brought thousands of hopefuls to Hollywood, many of whom claimed to be Rudolph's actual reincarnation. But Valentino's brother Alberto was courted most vigorously of all.

There was some disparity in height, but camera angles and ramps could overcome this, and, most important, there was a family resemblance. Virtually every studio sent secret couriers and diplomatic envoys to Alberto to extend sympathies and invite him to tour their sets. But reports were generally disappointing. Alberto did not have Rudolph's magnificent profile. No matter how he was photographed, his bulbous nose could never inspire tender feelings among the females who had been addicted to his brother.

The magic of Hollywood, the full cornucopia of riches it could provide, the fame it might bring did not escape Alberto, who, as the *Literary Digest* related, was "loathe to lose the spell of fame the handsome young screen idol had cast. . . . Eagerly [Valentino's family] reached out to clutch some of the glory in the hope of keeping it alive. The most determined in this endeavor was Albert[o] Guglielmi, Rudolph's elder brother." In private conversations with Sylvano Balboni, the young director who had married June Mathis, Alberto listened to his friend's sympathetic analysis of the situation:

"The public idolizes your brother. It would receive you with open arms in pictures. You look like him, all but your nose"—Balboni paused.

"So what must be done?" demanded Guglielmi. "I have my nose. I have no other. Perhaps you could tell me how to change it."

"There are ways," said Balboni. "Jack Dempsey had a nose the camera did not like. It was remedied."

"But how?" urged Guglielmi.

"Plastic surgery," whispered Balboni. He gave the whisper the importance of sesame for Guglielmi's entrance into the motion-picture financial pastures.

"Plastic surgery?" echoed Guglielmi. "You mean cut the nose to fit?"

"Exactly," said Balboni.

The *Literary Digest* continued: "The Modern *Cyrano* did not hesitate, but followed his nose into an establishment for the reparation, mitigation, and renovation of human features."

The pressures of the approaching auction took so much of Ullman's time that he had to instruct his attorneys to request a continuance, until the following year, of any legal action that might challenge his position as executor. No matter the opposition of the Guglielmis, the auction had to be successful or the estate would not have sufficient funds to meet the federal income tax lien, pay the fees of five attorneys and discharge the other mounting bills, let alone make any bequests meaningful. The auction, to begin on December 10 and to be held afternoons and evenings so long as there were items to sell and bidders to buy, was well advertised and the interest was further stimulated by the sale of an elaborate catalogue, slightly smaller than quarto, entitled *The Estate of Rudolph Valentino*. Under the title appeared a something less than authentic coat of arms with the dog-Latin motto *Et Avula Flores*. S. George Ullman was listed as administrator, A. H. Weil as auctioneer. The end papers were transparent and stamped with a design of interlacing spider webs, and as a frontispiece a handsome photograph of Valentino. The foreword to the catalogue, written in part by Ullman, told of his "heart-felt regret that I find the unfeeling course of law necessitates the disposal of the intimate belongings which Rudolph Valentino assembled with such discrimination. Although I dislike the necessity of putting up for public sale things which Mr. Valentino loved with such boyish enthusiasm, still my aversion to such a sale is lessened when I realize that it will give those who loved him the opportunity of possessing a cherished memento of one of the most honored personalities of this age."

The catalogue was also illustrated profusely with photographs of Falcon Lair, the house on Whitley Heights, one of the several Isotta Fraschini limousines, Valentino standing before his Avion Voisin tourer, shots of his horses—Firefly, Yaqui, Ramadan and Haroun—and of his yacht, *Phoenix*. It also included the portrait Alberto had purportedly promised to Pola Negri. All in all, the catalogue listed some 2,036 items.

On December 10, item No. 1, Falcon Lair, was offered for sale and purchased by Jules Howard of New York City, who telegraphed the high bid of $145,000, and an unimproved tract of not quite seven acres adjacent to the house was sold for $21,000. But to the dismay of Ullman and the auctioneer, an Isotta Fraschini limousine went for only $7,900, to Alexander Davison, an oil man from Amarillo, and the Avion Voisin, two other automobiles and a Ford truck brought only $4,600. Firefly, the horse ridden by Valentino in *The Son of the Sheik* and valued at more than ten thousand dollars, was bid in at $1,225, and the other three horses as a lot for only $2,025. The actor's Franklin coupé, Ullman later learned, had been sold for $2,100 to Alberto, who had posted his bid through an agent. Although the first day's sale was disappointing—for with the exception of Falcon Lair, everything else had failed to elicit even middling bids—Mr. Weil still hoped the auction would realize a million dollars.

When the Whitley Heights house—a "temple of love"—was put up for sale on December 11, the auctioneer reminded everyone that it had been the home in which the late screen idol had lived with his second wife, Natacha Rambova. The "temple" was rich in idolatry and had substantial value in its construction; with its four adjacent lots, it would make a fine residence for any of the motion picture stars in attendance at the auction. The property carried a thirty-thousand-dollar mortgage but was valued at double that. When, after several hours of exhortation, the best bid was ten thousand dollars, it was rejected and the house withdrawn from sale by Mr. Weil, who intended to offer it again at some future date.

The auction attracted many of the first lords and ladies of filmdom and their anticipated attendance attracted thousands of tourists, who arrived early and fought to enter that they might see how Hollywood royalty comported itself and how lavishly it would bid for Valentino's effects. They also eagerly awaited the grand arrival of Pola Negri to rescue item No. 268 before it could be touched by the auctioneer's hammer. But seldom did any bid made by a star come close to either the value of the article or what Valentino had paid for it; $2,200 worth of stock in the *Hollywood Music Box Review* brought $500; an Italian player piano for which Valentino had paid $11,000 was purchased for $2,100. The crowd was polite, whispering regrets to one another that such riches commanded poorer prices than could have been realized in an auction parlor on the Atlantic City boardwalk, and waited hopefully for Pola Negri to make her majestic entrance.

Adolph Menjou bought a Tuscany oak cabinet and a carved Spanish screen; Maurice De Mond a French throne chair; and a marble replica of the hand of the late screen star, carved by Fred Troubetzskoy, was purchased by Mrs. A. I. Cowan for $150. Bebe Daniels bid in six antique firearms for slightly more than a thousand dollars. Tourists, local citizens of low degree and penny-pinchers purchased Valentino's shoes, handkerchiefs, collars, Japanese silk pajamas (these inspired spirited twenty-five-cent increases in the bidding) and other personal items of clothing for modest sums. Many bought individual books from Valentino's library for between three and ten dollars apiece, and looked immediately for the bookplate—*"Ex Libris,* Rudolph Valentino"—then sighed with satisfaction when it was there.

By the fifth day, attendance had dropped from an SRO of

four thousand to fifty bidders, and not even 40 percent of the furnishings offered had been sold. Still, there was no acute reason for pessimism. But few persons of prominence were in evidence on the sixth day, and bidding was desultory and dispirited. No special enthusiasm was engendered even when the auctioneer offered the original costumes designed by Adrian for *The Hooded Falcon,* Natacha's unfilmed epic—a project whose planning could be likened to building a house around a keyhole. Most of the costumes had been made in Europe at a cost of almost twenty thousand dollars, but the prices realized barely covered the cost of thread. Adrian appeared to purchase one costume, which he took home with him.

Attendance continued sparse until Mrs. Werner arrived and expressed a desire to attend at least one session. Mr. Weil, the auctioneer, asked her if there were any particular items she wished put up for sale, and the elderly lady expressed a desire to bid on No. 269, a portrait of Valentino as a Persian warlord. In private she had expressed the opinion that she would have preferred to bid on No. 268, for Valentino as a gaucho was a more contemporary subject and more representative of his character. However, she would not bid because she had read of its being promised to Miss Negri for her shrine.

The night Nos. 268 and 269 were put up, most of the seats were taken, for people still eagerly awaited the climactic appearance of Pola Negri or someone who could readily be identified as her proxy. Mr. Weil spoke enthusiastically of the merits of No. 269, and told the audience something of Beltran y Masses' reputation. He was a member of the Royal Academy, a painter to the court of Spain, and recognized as one of Europe's foremost portraitists. The audience listened politely, nodded their agreement that the painting was valued conservatively at six thousand dollars, but sat tight-lipped throughout the bidding. Mrs. Werner bought "Dawn le Faucon Noir" for four hundred dollars. Whether the audience by remaining silent cooperated with Mrs. Werner can be neither proved nor disproved, but Natacha's aunt seemed delighted with her purchase and shed a tear that it had cost so little when she'd have been willing to spend far more. Then No. 268 was brought to the stand. The auctioneer could no longer delay putting it on the block, and several dealers bid for it. The painting was finally sold to an anonymous matron, represented by proxy, for $1,550.

At the studios, on December 24, the Christmas office parties started early, and many lachrymal toasts were drunk to the memory of Valentino. Story after story was told of his naïveté; his impulsive generosity; how lavish he had been with money; how easy he had been to approach for a loan; how seldom he had demanded repayment; how he really had preferred a good spaghetti dinner to any woman; and how—despite his eminent position—he was at heart a simple, shy and insecure man, who was more often used by women than loved by them. Songs sad, jolly and *gemütlich* were sung, for the recent, untimely death of Valentino made eschatological philosophers of everyone—and throughout the industry people left early to decorate trees and hide the last Christmas gifts they had purchased for friends and loved ones.

On December 24 even Pola Negri was busy wrapping last-minute gifts and addressing little cards of the season, but her secretary, Florence Hein, was at the Probate Court to file an action against the Valentino estate for fifteen thousand dollars. Jolly news, it managed to steal most of the headlines from Santa Claus. Miss Hein explained that Miss Negri had loaned Valentino the fifteen thousand dollars about a year before and that "it was a business proposition from one person to another. The money was advanced to meet a payment on Beverly Hills property on which Mr. Valentino had contracted to build a pretentious home. This happened about the beginning of the year 1926, and at the time the loan was extended it was apparently very much needed."

For the first time in Hollywood's history the silence on its screens was duplicated by the silence in its homes. And everyone agreed that George Ullman had told the truth about the romance and engagement between Pola and Rudy: "He never told me so, and I never asked him."

Once again Pola had stolen the show.

ACT FOUR: SCENE THREE

Superior Court Judge Charles C. Crail, on February 9, 1927, substantiated Pola Negri's claim against the estate. Her note was to have run for six months and bear interest at 7 percent, so Ullman agreed this note would have to be paid. He also approved another, for $21,300, which Valentino had assigned to United Artists Corporation as a loan against advance salary. A spate of other claims, most of them for federal taxes, were then filed against the estate, which prompted George Ullman to enter his own, for forty-nine thousand and five hundred four dollars, a sum advanced out of his own reserves for the production of *What Price Beauty?* All were allowed by Judge Crail and added to the estate's accounts payable.

Meanwhile, Rudolph's sister, Maria, now married to Eugenio Strada, an Italian architect, had arrived in Los Angeles on January 30, moved into the Hollywood Plaza Hotel, and immediately engaged two attorneys to represent her interests in her brother's will. This swelled the number of attorneys involved to seven, which proved to delighted spectators at the brewing battle the truth of Cadmus Blackstone's Law: Attorneys are not born; they are created full-bodied by enthusiastic and/or sharp-toothed litigants.

Ullman found it impossible to have any prolonged conversations with Mrs. Strada, for he had to leave the next morning for San Francisco to set up a new auction at the Curtis Studios. On the first evening, eight thousand dollars' worth of articles were sold, but the amount realized for the entire auction was disappointing. At the end of April, when Ullman reported total sales to the probate court, he revealed that exclusive of the real estate sold during the auction, all of Valentino's other personal effects had netted just $96,654. This sum, added to the real estate, brought the total to somewhat less than a quarter of the million dollars Ullman and the auctioneer had hoped for.

In September, 1926, Pola Negri had wept to reporters that "the world does not know my grief." In June, 1927, she married Prince Serge Mdivani, and became related by marriage to Mae Murray.

"Red roses for passion!" Pola called gaily to the French journalists who gathered around to congratulate her when she returned to Paris, but no good wishes were offered by *Photoplay*. James Quirk in his July, 1927, "Close-Ups and Long-Shots" asked: "Isn't it about time someone called Pola Negri's attention to the possibility of living her emotional life in private instead of a show window? . . . We make no charge of insincerity, nor have we any right to criticize Pola's personal temperament, but it is no wonder that the public, judging all screen stars by the emotional outbursts of a few, are quite ready to believe they are all temperamental freaks."

To further prove its displeasure with Miss Negri, *Photoplay* retained "a noted Slavonic genealogist to investigate the claims of the [Mdivani] brothers to their titles of nobility," and the genealogist's report revealed what everyone had known all along: any handsome male who came from Georgia—a Russian province on the Black Sea—and owned a chicken that laid at least one egg a day called himself a prince. Yet *Photoplay* still remembered Valentino with affection, and never stripped him of the noble lineage conferred upon him by that magazine in 1923.

ACT FOUR: SCENE FOUR

Shortly after he had appeared at the solemn ceremonies that marked the first anniversary of his brother's death, Alberto prepared to undergo plastic surgery at the hands of Dr. William Balsinger, who had remodeled dozens of Hollywood faces. Soon after the operation, when the bandages were removed, the Hearst papers published before and after photos of Alberto, whose nose, formerly pudgy about the nostrils and "dipped at the tip," was now of classic proportions. But movie moguls found the nose not quite right and suggested additional surgery.

The growing coolness between Ullman and the Guglielmis came to a head in the next round of courtroom confrontations, in October of 1927, when Alberto and Maria announced that they were going to challenge the provision in the will which awarded one-third of Valentino's estate to Mrs. Theresa Werner. Judge Willis cautioned them that filing such an action might jeopardize their own position and asked that they consider the matter for a week before returning to his courtroom. W. I. Gilbert said again that the will as drawn was incontestable, but the Guglielmi attorneys scoffed and insisted they would return in a week to file not only that action but also one to make Alberto coexecutor of the estate.

Throughout all of this it was quite evident that Ullman wanted only to complete Valentino's posthumous affairs and go on to other matters. He could not devote his entire career to the affairs of a dead man, no matter how close they had been in life. And since the will provided that anyone filing an unsustained challenge could be cut off with a dollar, Ullman warned the Guglielmis that they were jeopardizing their own positions severely, and that if they persisted the entire estate might ultimately go to Mrs. Werner. Alberto and Maria were neither dismayed nor intimidated; they told their attorneys to proceed.

Meanwhile, a Mrs. B. E. Woodford presented a bill to the estate for $160,000. Valentino, she contended, had purchased 111 acres of farmland from her, and had never paid for it. There seemed to be some justice in Mrs. Woodford's claim, and when she refused to accept the return of the land, the probate court stood ready to allow her $100,000. According to an accounting filed with Judge Walter J. Desmond by Ullman, the estate now contained a balance of $287,462. Original assets, which had been appraised at $677,555, had been reduced seriously by the payment of liabilities. If Mrs. Woodford's claim was allowed, this would further reduce the cash balance, and Ullman was unprepared to assume the responsibility for liquidation of so large a parcel of farm acreage. And to confuse the issue further, a letter from a gentleman from Wisconsin to the Los Angeles County Clerk, L. E. Lampton, claimed that he was the only legitimate heir of Rudolph Valentino.

The claimant lived in an isolated community, never went to the movies, and most of the year was too busy to listen to the radio. But news of Valentino's death had finally filtered down to Rhinelander and he wrote that "it looks to me like this is my estate. This Valentino is an old cattle buyer and my mother's first cousin. I knew he went West somewhere. I ask the court to bar all bills because it is my estate." Lampton assumed that George Ullman would be interested in this hitherto unpublished revelation about Valentino's past—if he actually had worked as a cowboy, it explained his good portrayal on the screen of an Argentine gaucho—and forwarded the letter on to the harried executor.

Hard on this, the Guglielmis, flanked by their attorneys, appeared in the courts to file an objection to Ullman's first annual accounting of the estate. Alberto took issue with no less than sixty-five items in the list offered for probate by Ullman and demanded a further accounting. In addition he asked the court to set aside Ullman's claim of $49,504, previously allowed the executor. The complaint continued that Ullman had dispersed large sums in behalf of Valentino; had in his own name or in the name of some corporation he controlled taken title to parcels of Valentino's estate; had failed to furnish a completely detailed inventory; had not declared $23,948 that he had withdrawn from the bank; had failed to show sums received in a compromise settlement with Feature Productions; and had not included in his annual accounting a rebate received from the Cinema Finance Corporation.

Continuances alternated with courtroom skirmishes, and still hundreds of letters continued to pour in to poor Ullman. Many of them contained suggestions that one or more mountains, rivers, plains, colleges or even cities should be renamed to honor the Sheik; most of the senders were enthusiasts willing to begin work if only some small retainer was sent them. Portrait painters, sculptors, tapestry weavers all sought commissions, and a manufacturer of a Home Valentino Shrine, complete with photograph, candles, crucifix and incense burner, only wanted its endorsement as the "official" shrine. The rejection of this offer was responsible for a barrage of letters from satisfied purchasers, who numbered in the thousands, and all were addressed to Ullman.

It was now June, 1928, and time to plan for the second anniversary of Valentino's death. Although Ullman urged a private observance, Joseph Schenck thought otherwise; he decreed public ceremonies so that thousands could participate in the services at the Hollywood Cemetery. It was quite evident that Valentino societies and cults were already strongly entrenched in the national folkways, and were of major economic importance if Valentino's films were to be exhibited and bring benefit to his estate.

Many women had enshrined photographs of the Sheik in their homes. At chapter meetings, the ladies intoned poems to Valentino, and a devotional chant with antiphonal responses was also part of their liturgy. British newspapers reported that a great memorial service had been held in London, and that women came from all over England to attend. There were even authenticated cases of women making walking pilgrimages to London—the most pious in their bare feet. And it was not uncommon, in Hollywood, for mausoleum attendants to find women prostrate on the marble floor before Valentino's crypt, and knowledgeable attendants began to carry aromatic spirits to revive the reclining ladies. Women who should have known better had to be ordered out of the mausoleum when its doors were shut for the night.

George Ullman's office received letters so depressing, clinical and insane they made his flesh creep. Some of the communications were on good note stationery and penned by elegant hands; others were on the cheapest paper and filled with misspellings.

But each asked the same question: "How can we go on in this life when you are in the hereafter?"

"My life is empty, a void, send me a sign that you want me in heaven and I will join you there."

"I have been wicked! And I shall never go to heaven unless you pray for me. Pray for me, Rudolph dear, Rudolph dear saint, for you and I know there was no love like ours, and when my husband takes me, in silence I cry your name. It is your heart beating against my full breasts that I feel, not his."

"It gives me a little relief to write to you. It seems to bring you back for a moment."

"While love exists, Valentino will not be forgotten. He taught the world what passionate love was. He alone has brought me to climax."

Many such letters were sent by Englishwomen, but they also came from all over the world. Ullman's office received pleading letters that offered to buy a pair of socks, a handkerchief, any intimate belonging of the dead Sheik. There was certainly evidence of a movement toward folk canonization. But talking pictures were now the only ones movie audiences would pay to see, and despite this international adoration, the Valentino estate did not prosper.

Several days before the second anniversary of Valentino's death, the Guglielmis and Ullman and their attorneys met. A settlement of the conflicting claims was worked out, and the Guglielmis' action in Superior Court was removed from the calendar. All the principals shook hands, and promised to meet again at the second annual memorial rites.

The ceremony, with Father Joseph A. Sullivan presiding, took place at the mausoleum. A huge cross had been erected on its steps; a heart in its center bore the inscription: "We never forget." Alberto was one of several speakers to address the delegates. Thousands of spectators had been expected but only some hundreds came. (Simultaneous ceremonies took place in the gardens of the Italian Hospital in Queen's Square, London, where the fences around the garden bore likenesses of Valentino framed by laurel.)

James Quirk in the October, 1928, *Photoplay* conceded that talkies were "here to stick" and "the only actor of any note who graced the scene [of Valentino's memorial service in Hollywood] was H. B. Warner, who spoke feelingly of the dead star. The other notables of the lots were conspicuous by their absence. . . . New gods glitter on the Hollywood Olympus. . . . Perhaps it is as well that Valentino was spared the heartbreak of change and decay."

Reporters, however, were entertained by the fainting women, and especially by one dowager in a magnificent pink feather boa, who read an ode of her own composition so erotic in its imagery that she was peremptorily ordered from the cemetery grounds by the ceremony's officials.

On December 31, Los Angeles papers reported the filing of another tax lien in the United States District Courts; the federal government demanded payment of $3,644.67 for estate taxes. And the New Year brought a suit filed by Alessandro Gabelleri, a Hollywood marble importer, naming Alberto Guglielmi and George Ullman as defendants. Gabelleri demanded $950 for plans he had drawn for a Valentino mausoleum and for expenses he had incurred in journeying to Italy to obtain marble for it. Many worshipers of Valentino's memory were bewildered, for movie magazines—the denominational bibles of the fans—claimed thousands of admirers had wanted to build a magnificent temple to Valentino's memory. So why should Gabelleri have to file suit to collect the $950 due him? The court was uninterested in this rhetorical question, and Municipal Court Judge George W. McDill dismissed the case against Ullman but continued it against Alberto Guglielmi.

Hard upon this news, the federal tax collector again got into the act by filing income tax liens against the estate for 1925 and 1926 that amounted to $64,103.63. Betting commissioners were willing to wager that the tax man would collect before Mr. Gabelleri.

These suits certainly saddened George Ullman and the Guglielmis, but Alberto had more on his mind. Poor Alberto had returned to the plastic surgeon and demanded a "pure Grecian nose." This "second" one was not as good as the "first," for it bulged at the tip, was too short, and exaggerated his upper lip. It was suggested to Alberto that the nose would not seem so short if the upper lip were shortened. Alberto submitted and a tuck was made under the nose to pull the lip away from the teeth in a perpetual smile; still, even this was not quite right. In a fourth operation, wax was put into the nose to make it longer, but the wax melted and ran down the sides, which gave Alberto an even more bulbous nose. This one was made longer by snipping off some of the septum, but even after this no one had seemed to find the right combination. The *Literary Digest* for September 21, 1929, concluded on a note of bravery that "a last effort is to be made. A 'seventh' operation is determined on."

By April, 1930, however, the estate had actually accumulated a cash surplus of $800,000, and Ullman filed an accounting with the court to prove he had paid out $551,346. Listed disbursements included advances of $21,616 to Maria and $36,949 to Alberto, though Mrs. Werner had thus far received nothing. Ullman also requested $50,000 for himself for cash disbursements he had paid out of pocket, and for services. He also petitioned to be reimbursed for the $1,800 he had spent to tip police at Valentino's funeral, and the $428 he had paid to the veterinary who had cared for one of Valentino's dogs.

Ullman left his accounts with the court for approval, and turned his attention to the projected ceremonies to be held on May 6 in De Longpré Park in Hollywood, where a statue to honor Valentino would be unveiled. This had been executed by Roger Noble Bernham, a local sculptor, and was the first real achievement of the Valentino Memorial Committee. Furthermore, it would be the first statue of an actor ever erected in a city park. One would have thought that the motion picture community would be wholeheartedly in favor of such a statue, but a number of old-time residents who lived in the neighborhood protested violently to Mayor John C. Porter against any memorial to the celluloid apotheosis of sex appeal. Men and women of little vision, they insisted there was room in the park for but one statue, that of Paul de Longpré, a noted artist of early California. Mayor Porter referred the protest to the art commission; the art commission referred the matter to the park board; the park board solemnly threw the ball back to the art commission; and a compromise was effected. Permission to erect a statue to honor Valentino would be granted, but only if it was not a literal representation of the late star.

Without argument the sculptor agreed to these stipulations and created a four-foot bronze male nude, slightly reminiscent of the later "Oscar" and called "Aspiration." Poised on a globe placed in the center of a small lily pond, the figure's stylized head was lifted toward the stars. It was unveiled on Valentino's birthday, and not a single studio notable attended the ceremony. Several days later, a photograph was taken of the statue, the sculptor and Dolores Del Rio, to prove that at least *one* actress had attended. "Aspiration" was reported to have cost $18,000, and like everything else connected with Valentino, it inspired a lawsuit. As related almost twenty years later by Dean Jennings, "A New York widow named Zunilda Mancini sued the executor of the estate for a rebate on a $5,400 contribution she had made toward the bronze statue. . . . She claimed the statue cost only $2,000, and the courts ruled in her favor."

For twenty years "Aspiration" stood in the park and stoically suffered multiple indignities. Tourists usually disliked the statue because it did not represent Valentino as they remembered him from the movies, and local residents disapproved because they considered its nudity offensive. It has been a favorite target for vandals. Finally, the park department set the statue in a concrete base, which foiled its attackers for almost ten years, but in 1950 the statue was sledgehammered from its base and left flat on its face. "Aspiration" was then braced by steel rods, and concreted more firmly to its base. Nevertheless, it was subjected to a variety of abuses until January 31, 1952, when it was finally stolen. Some time later the statue was found in an empty lot about a block from the park and returned to its base, where it was intermittently daubed with paint or spattered with mud. Two years later, it was again dislodged from its base and in disgust the park department hauled it to a warehouse where, if it could not be seen, at least it would have safe haven.

ACT FOUR: SCENE FIVE

Somewhat more than a month after Ullman had submitted his accounting to the probate court, he was informed by reporters that Alberto and Maria had filed against him charges of mismanagement and fraud. This new action again sought to remove him as executor of the estate, and in partial answer Ullman revealed that an "improper loan" of $40,000, with which he was charged, had actually been made at the request of Maria to Frank Mennillo, identified as one of Valentino's oldest and best friends. Furthermore, Ullman continued, he had exploited two Valentino pictures and this exploitation had not only cleared away the debts but created a surplus of $600,000.

But another portion of Ullman's statement really raised eyebrows:

Instead of losing money for this estate, I converted liabilities into assets, and in doing so I have immortalized the name of Valentino so successfully that I will wager today that all over the world there are thousands of motion-picture fans who do not know that Valentino is dead.

The estate was $160,000 in debt when Valentino died. . . . I had the task of disposing of my friend's personal belongings. He had about $16,000 worth of hardware which he collected as souvenirs; swords, armor and the like. It cost me $35,000 to fix up legends and publicize this stuff, but I sold it for $97,000 and they criticized me for spending this $35,000, too.

Of course, I resorted to some tricks. For instance, Rudy had lots of books, but he had only autographed a few of them, and he didn't have a book mark. I had a mark designed, stuck it inside the covers of his books, which were worth about two bits apiece, and at the sale they fetched about $3.00 apiece and nobody knew the difference and won't until they read the stories you boys will write.

Ullman was determined to fight the case through to the highest courts because he believed, and with just cause, that his skillful uses of ballyhoo had made the estate solvent. If the Guglielmis didn't understand ballyhoo, was it his fault if they were unacquainted with show biz? How could they fail to see, especially now that they were in Hollywood and increasingly familiar with films, how important had been this exploitation of the deceased? But the Guglielmis not only refused to see but on June 5, 1930, they elaborated their charges and added a new one: Ullman had made fraudulent attempts to appropriate money from the estate by a suit to acquire a quitclaim title to certain property held in the name of Rudolph Valentino Productions. They objected to the elimination of this corporation from the estate because ninety-eight shares of stock in the company had been held by Valentino and only two were held by Mr. and Mrs. George Ullman. Their petition to make the production company a component of the estate was looked upon with favor by the court, and Ullman, in an attempt to rid himself of an increasingly onerous and intolerable situation, offered the court his resignation as executor. Judge Stephens accepted and the Bank of Italy filed a petition for letters of administration to take over the management of the estate, whose day-to-day evaluation fluctuated more wildly than a penny oil stock on the Canadian exchange.

Inasmuch as the following month would see the fourth anniversary of Valentino's death, attempts were made to reconcile the differences among all the parties. Joseph Schenck's advice about the advantages of harmony had been ignored, and moviegoers, even judges, were reacting badly to the acrimonious dispute. Legal fees were multiplying at a geometric rate.

What confused and distressed Ullman was that throughout the industry he had been praised for doing the best of all possible jobs, and had actually spun straw into gold. Obviously, a man of his abilities, talents and flair for showmanship and promotion could have done far better; and if he had followed the standard business practice of his contemporaries, he could have stepped away immediately after Valentino's death and left the problem of his estate, its numerous debts and problems, in the laps of United Artists and the Guglielmis. Valentino's estate had consisted of expensive baubles for which the actor had paid too much and received too little, of clothing no sane man would wear and of two houses no rational man would live in. His extragavances were a matter of international record; his cavalier disbursement of money had indeed contributed to his fame. Ullman now realized he should have stepped aside as soon as Alberto had returned to New York and—as Ullman later testified in court—asked, "How large is the estate?" Now, even though he had resigned, he could not block a post hoc judgment of the activities and decisions he had made when he administered the nonexistent and existent estates and—irony!—he would have to budget much of his time, energies and funds to defend a devotion which everyone in the industry agreed had been most unusual.

The final disposition of this marathon court battle, however, was not reached until late in 1932, six years after Rudolph Valentino's death, when Superior Judge Albert Stephens ruled against George Ullman and held that many of the disbursements he had made had been without proper authorization. No matter his good intentions—even to the money he had spent for publicity, which had implemented the value of the estate—he had now to pay the Guglielmis $183,754, plus interest, retroactively, at the rate of 7 percent. But as lagniappe, which Ullman was unable to collect because accounts payable were far in excess of accounts receivable, Judge Stephens awarded him $15,000 for his services as executor. If it was any consolation to Ullman, Judge Stephens denied the Guglielmis' petition for a partial distribution of the estate, and forbade any distribution until all tax claims and lawsuits incurred by the actor in his lifetime had been adjudicated.

New tax liens levied by the federal Collector of Internal Revenue for 1927 through 1930 against Rudolph Valentino Productions totaled $18,175 and those assessed against Valentino personally for 1926–1928 amounted to $67,398. Ullman did not have the sum levied against him by the court, and in 1934 the court ordered retired from his indebtedness to the estate the sums he had advanced to Alberto and Maria, and further adjustments reduced his indebtedness to about $100,000. In 1947, Ullman still owed the estate $92,493, which he further reduced by a payment of $5,663. The suit and judgment, although they were old history, managed to achieve some small headlines when James E. Sheridan, the attorney for Jean Guglielmi, Alberto's son, collected the $5,663 and presented a bill for services for $566. Sheridan had previously received $200, which he had used to initiate a new legal action against Ullman, and when he presented his bill for the additional $566 fee, he was discharged by the dead actor's nephew. Before the case could come to trial, a settlement was made out of court; Mr. Sheridan accepted $325 and was promised a percentage of any further sums recovered from Ullman.

During the days before Christmas, 1947, Superior Court Judge Caryl M. Sheldon approved a new judgment against Ullman for $118,840, and five years later Jean Guglielmi again named Ullman in a superior court suit in which he demanded $160,000, to cover the indebtedness and five years' cumulative interest of $41,108. Morton E. Feiler, the new attorney for the Guglielmis, told reporters: "Ullman keeps Guglielmi posted on his finances and obviously is unable to make good on the judgment. But maybe he'll strike it rich some day." The case taught Hollywood a hard lesson in Nature's First Law of Relatives: deal with a man's relatives, if you have to, when the man is alive; have nothing to do with them after he dies.

The protracted court battle proved, however, only a Pyrrhic victory for the Guglielmis. Evidently their popularity with the film colony was at low ebb, for an attorney retained by Sylvano Balboni, June Mathis' husband, called upon officials of the Hollywood Memorial Cemetery to discover when the Guglielmis planned to remove Valentino's body from the Mathis family crypt. After June Mathis' tragic death in a Broadway theater while she was attending a performance, Valentino's body had been removed from her crypt and placed temporarily in the modest space reserved for her husband.

The cemetery officials referred Balboni's attorney to Alberto Guglielmi. Interviewed by reporter Jack Grant at Metro-Goldwyn-Mayer, where he worked in the section concerned with Italian distribution, Alberto said he had not received any direct word from Balboni or his attorney and "expressed surprise that his own countryman might be forcing the removal of Rudy's coffin." He elaborated:

"When I last saw Sylvano before he went to Italy," Alberto said, "he told me that he hoped it would be a long time before he would need his crypt. He made me feel his generous loan was bestowed in friendship and that Rudy's family was welcome to use the temporary accommodations as long as necessity demanded.

"I hope everyone realized how distressing this situation is to our family. That Rudy has not been buried in his own grave is a matter of deep concern to us. . . .

"Rudy would have been taken back to Italy, had it not been for the urging of executives high in the motion picture profession to bring his remains to California. They wanted him buried in the film capital. June Mathis Balboni kindly offered her own crypt until the estate might be settled and other arrangements made.

"That was six years ago. The estate is still to be finally closed and in its present state of liquidation, it is doubtful whether very much is left. Perhaps nothing at all will be realized.

"Shortly after my brother had been entombed, two movements were launched to build him a mausoleum by public subscription. Each group had separate plans and designs for the final resting place they hoped to erect. I was placed in the delicate position of being unable to participate in either movement. After all, one cannot go campaigning for a fund with which to bury his brother!

"Of course, I was grateful for the interest displayed, but other than suggesting that the two groups consolidate their efforts, I took no active part. Both eventually disagreed on a memorial and disbanded; the several thousand dollars raised was returned to the givers."

Elsewhere in his reportage Grant revealed that "ordinary plots in the Hollywood Cemetery cost from $42.50 to $200."

In good time the Guglielmis arranged to buy from Balboni the crypt in which their brother lay. But this plebeian resting place never pleased Valentino's admirers, and on August 22, 1965, the day before the thirty-ninth anniversary of the actor's death, the Long Beach *Independent Press-Telegram* published an interview with Luther H. Mahoney, a former employee of

Valentino's who revealed his ambitions for an appropriate memorial:

"I'd be happy if I could help to get him a nice place to rest," Mahoney said. "My idea is to build a tomb with black Belgian marble inside with his silver-bronze casket on display. It could then be viewed by the public. Ever since he died and they stuck him in a borrowed crypt it has disturbed me. The unfortunate way they treated his body still haunts me. I'd like to do something about it before I die."

The cash value of the estate had proved a terrible disappointment to both the heirs and its executor. The auctioning of the dead star's effects had netted only a small fraction of what had been expected. Was Valentino really just ephemeral? Did he, as some chose to believe, really occupy a favored place in the love lore of America?

An ironic aftermath came to pass in 1938, when a small film exhibitor paid a pittance for a blind lot of old film negatives discarded by major film companies. Among them he found a serviceable print of *The Sheik,* and he restored the print, had duplicates made, dubbed them with sound and sent them out as a gag. This humorous ploy netted him almost a million dollars.

At that point Emil Jensen, president of Articinema Associates, who years before had purchased the rights to *The Eagle* and *The Son of the Sheik* from United Artists, decided to test a booking at the Little Theater in Washington, D.C. The result was sensational beyond a press agent's most optimistic dream.

The Washington reaction inspired Jensen to distribute both films throughout the country, and to make the films more effective, sound effects and a musical score were dubbed into the prints. Within several months Valentino was once again a top box-office star; and in New York City *The Son of the Sheik* trebled the highest grosses taken in the past seven years at the George M. Cohan Theater. At Chicago's Garrick Theater it did more business than first-run talkies. In Philadelphia the original week's booking was extended to six. And in Cumberland, Maryland, Mayor Thomas W. Koon issued a public proclamation expressing the city's gratitude to the Liberty Theater for booking *The Son of the Sheik,* and giving the local citizenry "the privilege of seeing again one of the screen's great artists in what has been acclaimed as his finest film." Mayor Koon designated the opening day of the film at the Liberty Theater as "Rudolph Valentino Day."

ACT FOUR: SCENE SIX

During the six years of the Guglielmi-Ullman dispute, the major studios had undertaken what they hoped would be a most productive enterprise: an intensive search for a star to replace Valentino. Between 1927 and 1928, the transition from silents to sound had emptied the producing companies' coffers and severely strained their credit ratings. Then came the economic debacle that began on Black Tuesday, October 29, 1929, when over sixteen million shares of stock were dumped on the market at a loss of fourteen billion dollars, to bring the industry to the fine edge of bankruptcy. Financial chaos and national despair demanded an anodyne, and dreams were the RX prescribed by the film studios. Their ability to provide such healing dreams for a pittance enabled Hollywood to weather its financial crises and, to the amazement of economists, showed consistently healthy profits throughout each year of the depression. Once the industry had accomplished the transition to sound, the scramble for new stars was resumed with fervor. Top studio priority was a new Valentino.

For once, if never again, industry economists were in fullest agreement with production executives: motion pictures were produced primarily for women, who made up the largest and most faithful audience, and if this audience's enthusiasm was to be translated into profits, a vocal heavy breather and nostril twitcher would have to be found to replace the sainted Sheik.

Social psychologists and anthropologists were employed by several of the major studios to help them find a hero like Valentino, a man who could be all things to all women. Women had been able to accept Valentino in any role: costumes merely added to his height, boots contributed to his swagger and dancing pumps gave him feline grace. When he kissed a woman's hand he was Sir Charles Lovelace or Don Juan, the Earl of Rochester or Casanova, Launcelot or D'Artagnan—never Uriah Heep, Tartuffe or a John Held, Jr. lounge lizard. When Valentino had kissed a woman's hand her body juices had heated and she shuddered right down to her darling pink little toes. The studios were aware of the specifications; the task was to find the man who fitted them, a man who could persuade a woman to free herself from the inhibitions of the Protestant ethic. Here she was, trapped in a trackless desert without friends or family, by a booted man who carried a whip! What could she do—except submit gracefully?

For a time the social scientists had decided that a romantic hero typical of the thirties might be the answer, a man who had built a railroad, a tower to the sun, but was now out on the streets begging Buddy for a dime. At Columbia Studios the experts had been asked if they thought Clark Gable might be the answer and they rejected him because he had such big ears. The experts were sent home because it developed that Clark

Gable, who was taller than James Cagney and heftier than George Raft, actually looked great in a moustache and undershirt. But no woman ever dreamed of him as an equestrian rover in military breeches, black puttees or a burnoose, who would steal into her bedroom window while she was asleep and carry her off to his tent under an orange desert moon, where he would make her feel so tingly!

On July 19, 1936, *The New York Times* reported:

> Warner's feel that time has come for the return of the Valentino type. Paramount thought so too when they introduced George Raft, but that actor failed to fill the bill and all mention of his resemblance to the great screen idol was dropped. But the Brothers say that was a long time ago and so they are about to introduce Alexandre d'Arcy, a French importation, as Valentino's successor . . . he bears a striking resemblance to the late actor. At one time such an attempt would have been greeted with resentment by the patrons, but an entirely new crop of fans has grown up since Valentino's death and the avid followers of the player are not as avid now. It is to the newcomers that d'Arcy will be directed in the hope that he will capture the fancy of this generation as Valentino intrigued the last.

Little, if anything, was ever heard of Alexandre d'Arcy again, but by some strange confluence of circumstances, in part due to the re-release of *The Sheik* and other Valentino films during the summer of 1938, the revitalized international interest in Valentino could no longer be ignored by the sex-hungry, matriarchal public or by the press who catered to it. *Life* pointed out, in its picture spread of June 30, 1938, that during his lifetime Valentino had become "the romantic dream lover of women the world over. His sleek black hair, his mournful eyes, his Roman nose and muscular torso probably caused more heart throbs than any male who ever lived." Once again the nation's women shuddered to the mystery of his person, reacted with sighs even to the sound of his name. When a reporter queried an attractive miss in the theater lobby what visceral responses she had experienced during her viewing of *The Son of the Sheik,* her reply echoed the conclusions of women a half generation her senior: "Valentino makes Robert Taylor look anemic."

If the ladies gushed, few men shared their enthusiasm. Wallace X. Rowles, a feature writer for the Los Angeles *Times,* tried to explain the "why" of Valentino—his magnetism, personality, mystery—as subversive bunk. He revealed Rudolph Valentino as nothing more than a:

> slick-haired, side-burned, bell-bottom-pants Lothario of a hysterical post war jazz age. Men were still busy talking about the war. Women were trying to forget it. Rudolph Valentino didn't talk war, he talked romance; and talked it eloquently— through the most elegant medium of all time, a motion-picture screen!
>
> And he had a lot of help in his work!
>
> The motion-picture business was just beginning to realize the potentialities of big spending. They gave Rudolph Valentino the finest of clothes and costumes, the most daring adventures, the finest Arabian chargers and the world's most beautiful women to play the part that every woman hoped to play in a man's life.
>
> It is true he looked good at his work; but when you come right down to it, where's the mystery? He had a perfect set-up, didn't he?

The *Times* editor's desk all but disappeared under a barrage of letters of protest. And the studios also received thousands from complaining females scolding them for having been so dilatory: twelve years had passed and the studios, capable of creating past empires, historical personages, even heaven, hell and other fantasylands on order, had been unable to create another Valentino! With all their vast resources it did not seem possible. Or was this part of some gigantic male conspiracy to keep the women of America resigned to men who were something less than demon lovers?

American women rather testily ordered the studios once more to find them another Valentino, a lover with whom they could have the most fantastically sensual of romances, yet who would disappear with the night to leave them inviolate, and still of good reputation and able to endure their heavy-handed husbands.

The interest in Valentino bubbled merrily on. To keep the pot boiling, a biography of Valentino seemed a most likely subject for the screen, and late in 1939 *Pic* magazine invited its readers to help the editorial staff choose a candidate to depict the Sheik. Suggested were Del Casino, a radio singer; Anthony Quinn, actor son-in-law of Cecil B. De Mille; George Raft, now firmly established as a film villain; Paul Vincenti, an Hungarian actor who bore a close resemblance to Valentino; and Emmo Hugo, who in Europe was often called Valentino's double. Between 1939 and 1942, a film biography of Valentino intrigued every studio and independent producer, yet the problem of whom to cast in the lead seemed beyond hope of solution. Moreover, in a community as superstitious as Hollywood, where omens, signs, tokens, the casting of bones, the reading of tea leaves, crystal gazing, tarot cards, palmistry, phrenology and the opinions of soothsayers, conjure women and cross-eyed humpbacks were taken seriously, it was generally considered that the mere mention as a candidate for the role of Valentino was apt to bring on the evil eye or the hard mouth.

Jack Dunn, the young English ice-skating champion who had appeared with Sonja Henie, bore some physical resemblance to Valentino, and shortly a biographical film was announced in which he would star. But Dunn went off on a desert holiday to hunt jackrabbits in celebration, and ten days later died of tularemia. To Hollywood it must have appeared that with absolute ruthlessness from the Beyond, Valentino was protecting his unique place in film history. Moreover, there was another consideration: if an actor were considered for the role and then rejected by the public, the simpleminded producers and studios might think of him as typecast in *that* role. Victor Mature, Ray Milland, Phillip Reid, Don Ameche and Tyrone Power quickly assured everyone how uninterested they were in *The Life of Valentino*, though producer Edward Small continued to herald it as one of his major films. To that actor's great relief, Small decided that the public would not accept George Raft as anyone but George Raft.

In commemoration of the twentieth anniversary of Valentino's death, *The New York Times Magazine Section* published "After 20 Years Valentino Still Wows Them," a résumé of the actor's life and career, almost as *Photoplay* had originated it some twenty-two years earlier. The piece, by Sara Webb, reported that Valentino's films, when shown at the Museum of Modern Art, drew large audiences and that World War II and all its heroes had not diluted his romantic essence. A group of psychologists, confronted with the riddle of Valentino, offered what seemed to them a reasonable explanation: "Valentino believed as genuinely and as unreservedly in romance as did any and all of his followers. Not as a Cellini, a Don Juan or a Casanova, but with a simple-hearted faith that made him consider romance with all its trappings the most important business of life." An attempt was made to compare Sinatra with Valentino—for Frankie had seemed to satisfy the love hunger of millions of women whose men were away at war—but the comparison was greeted with laughter. Sinatra symbolized something boyish, someone in need of protection; Valentino was a god, the very thought of whom stirred a tidal wave of juicy responses.

That the ultrarespectable and perspicacious *New York Times* had expressed an interest in Valentino was enough to assure Edward Small he was on the right track. On August 3, 1946, he trumpeted that he was prepared to spend a quarter of a million dollars to find the man who would play Valentino, and that the total budget of his projected film was two and a half million dollars. Small also announced he had taken space at Hal Roach Studios and that his casting people had already received more than fifty thousand communications from aspirants, many of whom had sent photographs and motion picture clips for him to judge. For three years Small searched and searched, and still no man could be found who pleased him enough to start the camera rolling. Then a small damper was put on his enthusiasm. In March, 1949, the Hampstead Theater in London revived *The Son of the Sheik,* and though elderly ladies reacted in character, a young woman reporter for one of the London papers expressed what seemed to be the opinion of her generation: "Maybe I don't swoon easy—but he left me colder than a codfish on a marble slab."

Nevertheless, when Gavin Lambert, in an article in the prestigious *Film Quarterly* comparing Valentino and Fairbanks, concluded that Valentino was the better actor and had the more lasting influence, once again Edward Small blew hot. His optimism continued to grow when Dean Jennings wrote a lengthy article on Valentino in *Collier's,* called "The Actor Who Won't Stay Dead." With evident enthusiasm Jennings discussed the Valentino legend, which by now had been incorporated in at least two testaments and voluminous apocrypha, and reported that public librarians were being plagued by a new type of dedicated vandal, who tore anything pertaining to Valentino out of books and magazines.

Authorities at the Hollywood Memorial Cemetery had informed Jennings of the many inquiries still received from women anxious to spend eternity in the same mausoleum as Valentino; some of them had already booked space. And every Los Angeles newspaper, and even those in the surrounding suburbs, had experienced visitations from women who claimed to have borne

Valentino's children. According to Jennings, the count stood at thirty-five, and by 1960 at least two hundred ladies claimed to have been delivered of the Sheik's love children. That all admitted the Sheik's children had been born from one to twenty years after his death did not perturb them. They had become gravid through ectoplasm.

But hot upon the heels of the *Collier's* article came July proclamations to make Edward Small—who by now regarded himself as the official cinema Boswell to the Sheik—simmer. Twentieth Century-Fox announced *The Life of Rudolph Valentino*, starring Tyrone Power, and hard on its heels Jan Grippo, famed producer of the *Bowery Boys* pictures for Monogram Studios, released his plans for *The Return of Valentino*. The first day's shooting would be on August 15. And for authenticity in his version he had retained the services of Ditra Flame, president of the Hollywood Valentino Memorial Committee.

Because both were members of the MPPA, Fox was willing to talk the matter over with Small, but Grippo was not. Therefore, Small threatened Grippo with an injunction and suit. The producer of the *Bowery Boys* was undaunted, and hastily called that popular Hollywood entertainment, a press conference:

> If I continue to be intimidated and harassed by friends of Fox and Small I'm going to take legal action. This is America, not Russia.
>
> They're putting the pressure on me from all sides to try to stop me from making the picture. But I've got the money and the story and I feel Small no longer has a moral priority to the idea because he's been fiddling around with it for eleven years and still hasn't made the picture.
>
> My lawyers have told me that Valentino's story is public domain. Anyone can start filming a man's life three minutes after his death. The trouble comes in getting legal clearances to impersonate people still living who played important roles in the man's life.

I've figured out a way to avoid such evasion [*sic!*] of privacy. If I can't get the few clearances I need, I can do without them.

It won't hurt the story a bit not to include his two wives or members of his family. I've got a trick opening. Then we go back to Italy, his birthplace, and pick him up as a kid of 9. We follow him to manhood, his early struggles in New York and then his stardom in Hollywood.

In reply, Edward Small delivered this to the Los Angeles *Mirror:*

We will start actual filming on "Valentino as I Knew Him" just as soon as it is humanly possible to get all the pre-production elements together. These consist of the finest story we can put together for the best production values, including actual places where Valentino carried on a portion of his life; the best directorial talent and the finest supporting cast we can get.

The anticipated injunctions, suits and countersuits were never realized, for Twentieth Century-Fox and Jan Grippo abandoned their plans when Edward Small presented Tony Dexter to Hollywood as the star of his *Valentino*. At his next press conference Small announced that he had had Dexter under contract for two years, and had had him groomed secretly in every facet of the polished sheen required of any man who hoped to impersonate the Great Lover.

Pre-production filming is now going on with tests of sets, costumes, supporting actors and locations.

In Tony Dexter we have secured a boy who will be a credit to the fine acting career of Rudolph Valentino when he portrays that man's role. He has all of the necessary qualifications.

He has been trained for the past two years by the best experts in this field—Frank Veloz for dancing, Lester Luther

[Shirley Temple's dramatic coach] and, best of all, he has an ability to do a good job.

Briefly, Dexter had come to Los Angeles from Talmadge, Nebraska. His Latin appearance had been noted by several ranking members of the Valentino Memorial Committee, who had introduced him to Edward Small. And now that it appeared there was actually going to be a picture, all branches of the news media took heed and throughout the land those concerned with perpetrating banalities warmed up their typewriter ribbons, as they rewrote hot gospels and legends of Valentino as lover and man. And because this was a serious matter for votaries of the saint and keepers of his shrines, the Los Angeles *Mirror* referred the matter to Joseph Ranald, Ph.D., a well-known palmist. Dr. Ranald charted the palms of Valentino and Dexter and copyrighted his findings in an exclusive article in the *Mirror:*

> [Valentino] was the personification of irresistible sex magnetism. . . . His hand marks reflected an assortment of many strange qualities, both good and undesirable. The semi-circular line (1) at the base of his fingers is the "girdle of Venus." It is not considered a favorable mark in an ordinary hand. In the case of actors and dancers, it can be an asset for creative, rhythmic imagination. His rather shallow heart-line (2) indicated an ulcered and superficial emotion. Most important of all was his sex appeal marking. The star of irresistible sex magnetism on the mount of Venus (3). This means great attraction for the opposite sex. The V-shaped mark (4) on the mount of Luna is a shining mark found in the hands of a successful actor or actress.

But Ranald found Dexter's hand quite different. To the breathless question asked by countless women, the doctor replied that Dexter did "not have the star of sex magnetism in his palm. But he does possess many other favorable markings, including some that contributed to Valentino's flashing success.

Dexter may never incite women to mass hysteria or induce large-scale swooning but he can become an actor of merit."

If women were disappointed, the American male sighed with relief. And if he had never revered Estelle Taylor as a leading actress, he was now indebted to her for certain responses to questions put to her by Reed Porter of the Los Angeles *Mirror*. Joseph Schenck had signed Miss Taylor—who was married to Jack Dempsey—to appear in the next four films planned for Valentino before his death, and during the actor's last weeks in New York, Miss Taylor and her husband had been frequent guests at his champagne luncheons. When the reporter asked if Valentino was a sexy man, her reply was direct and significant. "Honey, I never really noticed. I was married to Dempsey! Yes, he was handsome in his swim trunks, with a towel draped around his neck."

"What kind of person was he?" the reporter asked again.

"He was either morbid, melancholy, or dumb, but I don't believe he was dumb because there were flashes of brilliant intelligence. Those white circles in his eyes made him look sexy. But he was an unhappy man. He never ceased loving Italian food. He sometimes had a garlic breath."

Before Miss Taylor could be attacked as a witch and heretic by the local high priestesses of the Valentino cult, she left for New York, and Reed Porter remained behind to bear the brunt. Almost instantly the high priestesses demanded that he come to see the scarves they had embroidered with Valentino portrayed in cross-stitch, backstitch, French knots and lover's knots; their paintings of him, in all media including lipstick; and china decorated with Valentino as he had been garbed in his most famous roles. One persistent lady telephoned Reed Porter daily, then invaded his office with a copy of *Day Dreams*, which she insisted the *Mirror* reprint immediately, distribute to every purchaser of the paper and use as a circulation builder. *Day Dreams,* she claimed, would make all men brothers and eliminate the United Nations, thus saving taxpayers multimillions of dollars and sending the evil foreigners who infested the United Nations headquarters—which was after all on sacred American soil—back to where they came from.

The local interest aroused by Mr. Porter's articles impelled Ditra Flame to invite the general public to an open meeting of the Hollywood Valentino Memorial Guild. Later, members of the press concurred that it was as uplifting as any gathering at the Angelus Temple when Aimee Semple McPhearson was at the height of her prestige. Several days later, Miss Flame chose one of the hundreds of laudatory letters to show to Mr. Porter:

> . . . I felt that Valentino was standing on that stage with you Tuesday night. It took real courage to share your memories with the public in that overpowering, overflowing audience. That night a majority shared with you and your Guild a sincere admiration for a superb artist and a great man.

Life devoted two pages to "The Great Lover," just to assure its readers that it was aware a film was being made about Valentino, and editorialized again that no matter the role, he was always Rudolph Valentino, the Great Lover, the answer to a dream hidden deep in American women's hearts.

Throughout all of 1950, Edward Small was delighted by the space devoted to his film and the ease with which his press agents had been able to stimulate nationwide concern whether Tony Dexter could portray Rudolph Valentino. Indeed, Small was certain he had achieved his very ambition when Miss Adela Rogers St. Johns—who occupied in the film capital the same position once held by Plutarch in ancient Greece and by Raphael Holinshed in Elizabethan England—decided to dip her pen into chocolate syrup and write an account of Valentino's life for her Hearst readers. But delight became despair when in March, 1951, a month before *Valentino* was to be released, *Pageant* published an article by Sidney Carroll titled "Ghost of the Great Lover," the burden of which was: "Now they've made a movie of the life of Valentino, but who can tell the man apart from all the mush?"

The disrespectful tone of the article infuriated Small and Columbia Pictures, which was releasing the film, but nothing caused them as much anxiety as Carroll's revelation that "Police officials claim that if you look deeply enough into their records of the time you will find this Guglielmi's name there as a petty racketeer and blackmailer." Anxious yes-men assured Small and Harry Cohn, president of Columbia Pictures, of the magazine's unimportance; most people would ignore the article's charge, and even if someone were to get into the police files, they would find nothing. The disappearance of the records from the booking folder had been complete, but Cohn insisted that even the folder should be removed from the police files. He was unable, however, to persuade any of the fat mice around him to volunteer for so dangerous a mission. It was decided to ignore *Pageant,* to mark Sidney Carroll as a fink and to get on with the release of the picture.

On April 14, 1951, Edward Schallert reviewed *Valentino* for the Los Angeles *Times* and said some vaguely kind things about the picture, mentioning the production values and pictorial recreation of the twenties. He was kind to all the supporting players, and even included an oblique salute to Tony Dexter:

> He is about as near to Valentino as the story is an exact duplicate of the Italo-American luminary's life.
> His resemblance comes and goes, fitfully in flashes, and is chiefly aided by the costumes that he wears.
> While his work as a screen performer is faltering and uncertain in some speeches, he has a surprising assurance at others. He has to carry what is essentially a romantic role and sometimes there is a strain to the intimate love scenes.

Because Hollywood had always taken creative license with

history, Schallert did not criticize too stringently the liberties taken with Valentino's biography. But Bosley Crowther, in his April 20, 1951, review for *The New York Times*, stepped all over the film, its producer, its male lead and everyone associated with what was in his opinion one of the worst movies of all time:

> Written as though the script writer, George Bruce, was fresh from correspondence school and acted as though the director, Lewis Allen, was learning the trade, the best to be said for the performers is that they shirk not, neither do they fail . . . [all] descend to absurdities in this.
> What a hopelessly ridiculous romance!

Today *Valentino* is considered a poor picture, even for television's late, late show, whose viewers would dismiss it as greasy kid stuff.

Even the industry began to wonder (as if the picture were its subject's fault) if all the adulation and worship lavished on Valentino had not been undeserved. There were even those who attempted to have the "star" in the Walk of Fame that Hollywood Chamber of Commerce had allotted to Rudolph Valentino relegated to some other deserving old-time actor. The Walk of Fame was planned to extend from Gower to Sycamore Streets on Hollywood Boulevard and along Vine Street from Sunset Boulevard to Yucca Street. When intelligence of this treachery reached members of the Valentino guilds and associations, they wrote long letters to the Hollywood Chamber of Commerce about keeping Valentino's "star" in the pavement. They prevailed, and Valentino's "star" is still located at 1632 Vine Street, just an Arab steed's leap off Sunset Boulevard.

Meanwhile, Rudy's former home, built for Natacha (who in 1934 had married Don Alvaro de Urzaiz, a Spanish nobleman) at 6776 Wedgewood Place in Whitley Heights, was being methodically destroyed by souvenir hunters. The home was located on a right of way through which the Hollywood Freeway would pass, and the owners had sold the land to the state for ninety thousand dollars, promising to move the house to another location. This contract became the subject of litigation but what the defendants had failed to do, vandals were rapidly accomplishing. Tile by tile, shutter by shutter, the house was being dismantled. Tiles from the exterior and interior walls had been wrenched out, and large sections of wallpaper removed. Even sections of the walls had been destroyed to get to the expensive wiring. Carved beams had been removed; a goodly portion of the roof tiles had disappeared; expensive bricks had been dug out of the patio; mirrors had been pried from the walls; medicine cabinets, even toothbrush holders, had been yanked out of the lavish bathrooms, along with plumbing fixtures. In an attempt to forestall further destruction, armed guards were posted, but the souvenir hunters, in their nip-and-tuck race with the bulldozers, had left little for the wrecking crews.

ACT FOUR: SCENE SEVEN

There are still men and women who persist in their enraptured worship of the dead Sheik. One of the most dedicated came to light in 1953, when the Wilcox Street Police Station in Hollywood received a call that someone was about to commit suicide at 5546½ Hollywood Boulevard. The police crashed into the apartment of Rudolph Florentino—née Dominic Giordano—but found him very much alive.

"Nonsense," Florentino protested to the police officers, and to the reporters hard on their heels. "I didn't really intend to kill myself. You see, I'm in love with this girl, and taught her how to tango like Valentino. We had a quarrel and I wanted to scare her. I have too much to live for. All this . . ."

The police officers stared about them in amazement. In the apartment situated over the Apollo Theater was pitched a full-size Arab tent, complete with sand, silken divans, pictures of dancing girls, large posters of Valentino, a life-size portrait of the Sheik, and other memorabilia certain to delight the cockles of all Valentino worshipers. As the police continued their awed inspection of these appointments, even kneeling to finger the sand, which they were assured was genuine and imported from the Sahara, more reporters and photographers arrived. Florentino obliged by changing into his gaucho costume, complete with colorful poncho, Valentino-type suspenders for the dress trousers, full-sleeved shirt with French cuffs, and a gaucho hat whose tie-string was carefully adjusted under his chin. He obliged further by posing before the Valentino portrait with a sword—which the police appropriated, along with a revolver. Florentino elaborated upon his background: he was now a brass welder, but claimed to have been a dancer, a film bit player, a double for the Sheik and a gardener at Falcon Lair.

Among the more treasured memorabilia in his collection, Florentino displayed Valentino's gaucho hat from *The Four Horsemen*, the lute he had played in *Blood and Sand*, a chair from Falcon Lair, and a hookah, taborets and other pieces of Arabic furniture inlaid with tiles and mother-of-pearl, along with a pair of spats and a beret that had been Valentino's, numerous pencil and crayon sketches of the Sheik, and piles upon piles upon piles of magazines, newspapers and scrapbooks, all choked with miscellaneous photographs and clippings of his dead hero.

Along Hollywood Boulevard and its side streets, Florentino is well known in bookstores and costume shops, where he browses for Valentino items and authenticates the occasional piece of wearing apparel offered for sale by a collector hard pressed for funds. There are in Hollywood, and other remote posts of civilization, gentlemen of cultivated refinements who claim to be reincarnations of Valentino, but Florentino dismisses such claims as nonsense. He considers himself to be the dead actor's only *authentic* disciple, for his worship of Valentino is sincere and without thought of financial gain.

In June, 1956, newspapers in Los Angeles and its suburbs were made privy to the happy news that Florentino intended to open his Valentino Memorial Shrine to the public, and he invited the press to cover the opening ceremonies and to photograph them in full before the public was admitted. On June 19, reporters interviewed James Kirkwood at Florentino's Memorial Shrine, where they were told that in 1921 he had been a famous actor under contract to Jesse Lasky, who had offered him the starring role in *The Sheik*. Kirkwood had laughed at Miss Hull's book, turned down an increase in salary to thirteen hundred dollars a week, and Valentino had got the role at five hundred dollars. Valentino had gone on to fame; Kirkwood had lost his importance. But he still considered *The Sheik* to be "a cheap, corny picture."

Meanwhile, the anxious host and busy curator had difficulty dressing in his Valentino sheik costume because he kept running from his bedroom to the living room—which was the museum— to show the reporters various items of apparel, which he insisted they compare with photographs so they could see how authentic was his collection. In addition, he showed them Valentino's cigarette case, with his name engraved on it, a ring that also bore the name, and a black cutaway coat with a label inside the lower breast pocket identifying that it had been tailored for Valentino.

After Florentino was dressed, the press was introduced to a producer from Australia, a press agent from Canada and a bevy of slave girls—some of them middle-aged and of distinguished varicosity—who lounged in their silk pantaloons and breastplates on the sand beneath Valentino's portrait or in the Arabian tent, where other noble effects of the actor were featured. Sand was a distinct inconvenience to the slave girls and filtered into everyone's shoes as Florentino displayed his cobra charms, stemware, wall hangings, slave bracelets, ornate candlesticks and plaster busts of Valentino. And even one of the Sheik's homburg hats. There also was a copy of the 1926 auction catalogue, autographed by Mr. Weil.

Mrs. Mary D. Solarno, president of the Sons of Italy lodge, which was cosponsoring the exhibit, then told reporters: "We will honor the memory that still lingers in the hearts of Valentino admirers without violating any sentiments. We are very conscious of our responsibility and it is with the greatest feeling of humility that we are trying in our humble way to re-create for the generation of fans who have mourned his death all these years—the Valentino legend."

Florentino told everyone the exhibit would be opened the next day without charge. And on the morrow hundreds of elderly ladies, appropriately garbed for the occasion and twittering with rapture, swarmed through the incense-laden museum and exclaimed over each item as Florentino, in sheik's costume complete with slave bracelet, explained that the collection had been his forty-year labor of love. Mint copies of Valentino's *My Private Diary* (published in 1929 by Occult Publishing Company) and Natacha Rambova's *Recollections* were also on display. Nothing was for sale, and several not-so-nice ladies who attempted to pilfer a relic to enshrine in their own cozy little chapels were unceremonially hustled out of the museum.

The exhibit was well received in the community, and even inspired another gentleman to announce plans for opening a Theda Bara "vamp" museum, complete with Turkish corner, in her former home. The Valentino shrine and museum, however, eventually closed its doors and since then Florentino has devoted himself to financing the World Wide Pictures Corporation, which as its first project would remake the Valentino biography "into the beautiful story that it was." Florentino is the ranking, and most zealous, of Valentino's paladins, and waits with patient dignity—his collection still intact, for he will neither rent nor sell so much as one grain of sand—for the world to recognize him.

And in 1956, the same year that Rudolph Florentino opened his short-lived shrine-museum on Hollywood Boulevard near Vine, Castellaneta commemorated the thirtieth anniversary of Valentino's passing. It was the first time Valentino's birthplace had ever acknowledged by genuine public proclamation either the life or the death of its most famous citizen, though he had put Castellaneta on the fan-magazine map.

The mayor decreed a *festa* to honor the prophet in his own country, and prizes were offered for the best window exhibits of Valentino photographs. A requiem mass was recited in memory of the actor, and the mayor acknowledged the town's belated debt. The townfolk actually applauded suggestions for a monument to Valentino's memory; local pride demanded that something be done beyond the plaque installed at the site of his birth some twenty-five years earlier by the Valentino Fan Club of Cincinnati, Ohio. Business leaders also hoped an appropriate memorial might lure American and European tourists to a town seldom included on any itinerary. A Roman sculptor, Nicola Cantore, was commissioned to prepare studies, but these were disapproved and in 1960 a new commission was granted to *Professore* Luigi Gheno, another Roman sculptor.

Gheno spent eight months in the creation of a ceramic figure of Valentino dressed as the Sheik. The figure was of heroic pro-portions—some eight feet tall—and the robes were yellow, red and blue, but for some artistic reason that the sculptor never ex-plained, the face was blue. Picasso, too, had had his Blue Period, and Mayor Semarraro seemed delighted with the work. He ordered a base prepared on Castellaneta's Via Roma, where the statue would be installed, and planned to dedicate it during Easter Week of 1961.

Suddenly, where all had been peace and harmony, there was now discord. Whether it was the statue's blue face that alarmed the populace is perhaps moot, but a dissident group proclaimed loudly that it would resist, if need be with force, any unveiling of this statue. The group insisted that the mayor return the statue to the sculptor, and demand a return of his $2,720 fee. The dispute became so bitter that local members of the clergy refused their cooperation, so attempts to dedicate the statue during Easter Week were abandoned. Undaunted, the mayor refused to yield and planned a new dedication ceremony for September 20, when, he told his constituents, there would be a public banquet and speeches by many government notables. Mayor Semarraro prevailed, and the dedication took place. *Il Messaggiero di Roma,* one of the nation's most respected papers, reported meanly that the cost of the statue, banquet and receptions, plus the cost of transporting Italian motion picture personalities, had amounted to a considerable sum which might better have been used by the community. Besides, the "personalities" who had attended were either unknown or unimportant. In short:

> This belated honoring of Rudolph Valentino represented a hard blow to the treasury of Castellaneta. . . . With the money for the banquet and receptions, they could have bought shoes for the poorest children. With the money for the monument they could have built some public utility, which certainly would have been more useful than a monument . . . and particularly in a country where the people have enough to do to live, let alone find enough time to honor their saints.

The harsh criticism of *Il Messaggiero* compelled the government spokesman to explain hastily that the monument was aimed at representing *all* the emigrants who had left Italy, not merely Valentino himself. "He was for all emigrants, a symbol of success," the representative from Rome explained, and then went on to say that the expenditures had actually been minimal and the area not nearly so poor as the newspapers claimed.

No influx of tourists materialized, and those few who came to view the statue snickered; there has since been a strong movement in Castellaneta to remove it.

In 1961 David Wolper presented an hour-long television special, *The Legend of Rudolph Valentino,* which rather superficially explored the social changes undergone by the United States between 1913 and 1926, and in 1963 *Mondo Cane* was released, a startling color movie whose first scene is devoted to the dedication of the Valentino statue by Mayor Semarraro in Castellaneta. As the camera focuses on a variety of angles of the astonishingly blue-faced statue, a narrator comments on the young men of Castellaneta, who affect long sideburns, intense expressions and twitching nostrils. Many of these young men claim to be related to Rodolpho Guglielmi, and: "In this little farming community in the south, where the soil is stingy, the prospects offered by a movie career arouse far more enthusiasm than those offered by agrarian reform. The nights of Castellaneta smell—not of new-mown hay, but of brilliantine. And the young men dream their favorite dream, with background music, the limpid strains of the tango."

Although shifts in standards, tastes and currently popular fantasies have tended to strip Valentino of some of his rank as a god or saint, he has always been accounted a famous man. On April 2, 1965, the Los Angeles *Times* reprinted an exclusive from the New York *Daily News* announcing that Marcello Mastroianni intended "to portray the title role of Rudolph Valentino in a stage musical comedy, opening [in Rome] next fall. Mastroianni told a press conference: 'As a film actor, I want to do this stage musical as an experiment, just for fun.' Asked if the show would be seen on Broadway, Mastroianni replied: 'Perhaps —if it is a success in Rome.' "

To everyone's surprise, this announcement was a truth rather than some press agent's dream, and on December 12, 1965,

The New York Times published a long interview with Mastroianni in which he discussed the effect the love talk of fans and their psychological demands had upon his virility, or upon that of Valentino or any other cinema sex symbol. "One can't help become a little impotent," Mastroianni said. "But that's normal in actors. . . . Certainly he was a victim. If people tell you you're a great lover, how can you make love with this heavy baggage on your back?"

When the reporter pressed on for the reasons that had prompted Mastroianni to undertake an interpretation of Valentino, the actor explained how he had "wanted to see the celebrated tango of Rudolph Valentino, so I got hold of an old Valentino movie. In my imagination I saw something wonderful! The crazy thing is that in the picture you don't even see a tango. You see a whoosh here and a whoosh there, and it's all over. You don't see anything. There's nothing there. But the public accepted it and the greatest myth grew up. He dances" —Mastroianni searched for the exact comparison—"he dances worse than me." The prowess of Valentino disposed of, Mastroianni continued: "The Americans always showed Valentino as an idiot. I don't agree. Not because he was an Italian and I'm a patriot. But I want to see the real Valentino—to see what's behind the facade. Maybe he *was* an *idiot*. Or maybe they *made* him an *idiot*."

Ciao, Rudy! ("Good-bye, Rudy!") opened in Rome on January 6, 1966, and for three hours Mastroianni cavorted about, the only male on stage with a bevy of thirteen leading ladies. It was scorned as ludicrous even by the gentlest critic, and Mastroianni's performance censured as unskilled, pedestrian and shallow.

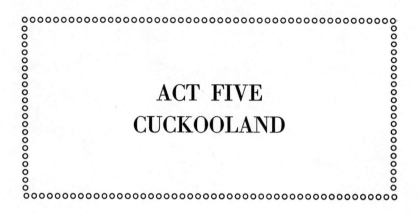

ACT FIVE
CUCKOOLAND

At my alighting, I was surrounded by a crowd of people, but those who stood nearest seemed to be of better quality. They beheld me with all the marks and circumstances of wonder; neither indeed was I much in their debt, having never until then seen a race of mortals so singular in their shapes, habits, and countenances. Their heads were all reclined either to the right or the left; one of their eyes turned inward, and the other directly up to the zenith. Their outward garments were adorned with the figures of suns, moons, and stars, interwoven with those of fiddles, flutes, harps, trumpets, guitars, harpsichords, and many more instruments of music, unknown to us in Europe. . . . It seems the minds of these people are so taken up with intense speculations, that they neither can speak, nor attend to the discourses of others. . . . They are very bad reasoners, and vehemently given to opposition, unless when they happen to be of the right opinion, which is seldom their case.

JONATHAN SWIFT,
"A Voyage to Laputa,"
Travels into Several Remote Nations of the World, by Lemuel Gulliver (1726)

To understand the elevation of Rudolph Valentino from mortal man to immortal god demands an examination of certain significant facets of the American cultural, intellectual and religious character as derived from the New World-Puritan tradition of the seventeenth century. Such idolatry cannot be dismissed or written off as an isolated case of mass arrested development. Rather, it is our earliest example of American social banality that has succeeded where culture and intellect have failed—a banality whose alterations, ramifications and hybrid growths made kin all the peoples of the western world.

There are in the United States today between fifteen and twenty successful spiritualist churches, which, by toning down the spiritist elements in their faiths and beliefs, hope to achieve a standard of respectability in the American religious community as sound as the Puritan Congregationalism from which they sprung. It should be remembered that the Puritans, our most revered ancestral group, gave strong credence to the activities of witches, warlocks, satanists and familiars who inhabited their communities and the surrounding dark gloomy woods and glades. Cotton Mather was one of the influential theologians who believed in the power of witches and the prevalence of supernatural enemies in Massachusetts; and he did his best to prove that the Salem witchcraft trials were honorable offensives against devils and righteous judgments of their human agents. Mather's works number more than five hundred and contain numerous evidences of pathological blindness and stubborn conceit that made it impossible for him to question by even a tittle the worthiness of Puritan theology, predestination, his own election to grace and the community's political distaste for democracy, a heinous form of government offensive to God and theocrats.

The Great Awakening of 1734, as it glorified God and debased man, introduced revivalism and hell-fire preaching to the colonies; and Jonathan Edwards' famous sermon "A Sinner in the Hands of an Angry God" had his congregation begging for mercy as it groveled in the aisles. Yet emotional revivalism with its shrieks, fits and faintings was frowned upon, even by Edwards, and social students of history now believe the revival meetings of the eighteenth century were a primary source of recreation to a lonely people in a primitive and still hostile land. But as settlers moved westward, the established churches and their ministers did not follow on the same mules and wagon trains, and itinerant preachers established their own denominations, offered their own interpretations of the Bible, and by the vigor of their oratory even established some primitive congregations where a "heart" religion was encouraged and a "head" religion abjured. That these preachers were often illiterates, or at most semiliterates, who derided education and the establishment of schools in primitive communities, did not trouble the settlers, for they believed increasingly that education stratified society. School learning, which fostered skepticism, was the source of human misery, and it is no small wonder that in such an atmosphere the supernatural was respected and feared.

The years 1857–1858 saw the second national religious revival throughout the United States and its territories. Characteristic of this period was the camp meeting, where jerks, frothings and talking-in-tongues were taken seriously, and these manifestations of religious ecstasy and visitation by "the Spirit" were normal for the gaining of converts and the reform of backsliders. Again, this form of religion was most enthusiastically accepted in the West, where orthodox theology and trained ministers were considered to be as necessary as a fifth leg on a horse. New western settlers were detached from the traditional past, even from the present, as they forged their future, and they had little association, understanding, sympathy, time or need for formal theology.

After the Civil War, revivalism added a new dimension— personal communications from the beyond between persons who had "passed over" and certain chosen eclectic groups of Protestant Americans. This new dimension split Protestant revivalism in two: one branch still bore a resemblance to fundamentalist religion; the other became pure spiritualism, catholic in its incorporation of pagan faiths and rituals into Protestant Christianity.

In 1917, Edward Clodd, an English critic of spiritualism, wrote an article for *The New York Times,* which recounted the story of Margaret and Katherine Fox, two little girls who lived in Hydesville, New York; they had told townspeople of the ghost of a murdered man who haunted their house and answered questions "yes" and "no" by a determined number of rappings. The children were shortly thereafter exposed as frauds, but not before they had become quite famous and had inspired others to become mediums. Clodd then stated: "As a modern movement spiritualism began in America in 1848. . . . Its inception was in fraud and a tainted atmosphere has clung round it from that time to the present. Its history is a record of the detection and confession, one after another, of a pack of sorry rascals of both sexes, some of whom had been committed to prisons as rogues and vagabonds."

The writer also pointed out that the phenomena of spiritualism were twofold—physical and psychical—and intermingled. Table-rappings and turnings, slate-writing, materialization, mediums floating in the air, and the apparatus of ghosts and haunted houses were physical manifestations easily exposed by trained investigators. "The psychical includes clairvoyancy, crystal-gazing, telepathy, hallucinations and the trance state, and automatic writing. . . . It has much in common with theosophy and Christian Science—twin delusions."

Although the spiritualist believes he is a member of a religious sect, most authorities agree that such groups are best identified as cults. A sect normally has an episcopal form through which its gospel is taught and disseminated, and the traditional physical forms are accredited seminaries and colleges. The cult, on the other hand, seldom possesses a permanent physical structure—although it aspires to and usually promises imposing structures to its faithful—and usually disseminates its gospel from rented stores, halls or theaters. It will move and continue to move from place to place, if necessary, until a salutory and salubrious environment enables it to flourish. Another essential difference between the two is that the sect increasingly tends toward formality of ritual; while the cult, although it encourages informality, insists that its texts and rituals are derived from arcane and esoteric documents predating the birth of Christ or the building of the great pyramids, and were usually written in Atlantis or Mu. Most sects attempt to impress on their followers the tenet that impersonal immortality is superior to personal immortality. Through ritual and seance, cults emphasize personal immortality and the ability of the spirit to communicate and even to return at will to this plane. Sects usually, therefore, possess more status in the community than the most chic or entertaining of cults.

In the last hundred years the American belief in witches has lost ground to other forms of spiritualism, not so malevolent and far more entertaining: spirit rappings, divination by cards, crystal balls, tea leaves, the reading of palms, phrenology, even Ouija board readings. And to these were added a variety of Utopian-communal movements: freak diets, with emphasis on graham crackers, nuts, berries or roots; the emancipation of women to grant them the right to wear bloomers and ride bicycles; and a flux of purification cults that emphasized deep breathing through the mouth, deep sleep and sex as some of the keys to direct communion with spirits in the Beyond. Seances and spirit manifestations are thrilling entertainments that all strata of American social, economic and intellectual life have at one time or another dabbled in. In the twentieth century American spiritualism received an important assist from Sir Arthur Conan Doyle, who fervently believed Sir Oliver Lodge's assertion that the dead could communicate with the living, and to skeptics he suggested as required reading Lodge's *Survival of Men*, Raymond Hill's *Psychical Investigations* and William Thomas Stead's *After Death*. In a 1917 article for *The New York Times*, Sir Arthur also mentioned the biography "of a Judge Edmonds of the United States High Court, in which that eminent lawyer claimed to have kept in close personal touch with his wife for many years after her death."

There is actually a reasonable explanation why southern California has become so favored of spiritualists. It is suggested that all the neurasthenics, neurotics, visionaries, naturopaths, hydropaths, diet faddists, rhapsodists, paranoids, cranks, eccentrics, ravers and those blessed by election to be first in the ranks of the hallucinated somehow received their calls and began their missions along the eastern seaboard, a region that may tolerate such emotional March hares, along with their strange beliefs, but does not offer them a fertile ether for growth. Therefore, these square pegs drift westward, and though in their migration some of the moonstruck die natural deaths, others die violently and still others are certified as mental incompetents and institutionalized, the rest manage to win through, but these are the hardiest. The survivors cross the Great Plains and the Rockies, and as any examination of a topographical map of the United States reveals, there is a continental tilt that facilitates a sliding into southern California. It is not impossible that if these oddballs had been amphibious, they would have entered the sea and continued their westward migration until they reached the mysterious East, possibly India, acknowledged by almost all spiritual cults as the fountainhead of their faith. But the creatures are not amphibious, and once they reach the Pacific there is no place left to move on to.

No state has experienced so consistent a growth in population as California, particularly the region south of the Tehachapi range; and among the thousands who enter the state each and every month, there were and still are a sufficient number of social mutants to bring strength and comfort to the displaced migrant, the lonely pensioner, the rolling stone, or the superannuated couple who refuse to enter a community of senior citizens and become members of such adult kindergartens. Despite the great number of churches of established denomination in southern California, a religious vacuum of broad dimension exists; and it is filled for many of the disassociated by attendance at spiritualist-cult meetings. Furthermore, California law is generous to all cults. Those who wish to found their own "religions" and thereby gain respectability discover the formal process to be simple and inexpensive: no more is required than that three people join together "to sign articles of incorporation and pay a fifteen-dollar filing fee." The rest is a matter of the better mousetrap. Among the more startling and bizarre are: the Agabag Occult Church, whose woman leader favored violet-dyed hair and green eyelids; the Great White Brotherhood, whose members wear yellow robes and worship the full May moon; the Maz-Daz-Lan, led by Ottoman Bar-Azusht-Ra-Nish, who recognized "the eternal designs of Humata, Huata, Hu-Varashta, A-Shem Vo-Hu, A-Shem Vo-Hu." The twenties even saw a growth of The Nothing Impossible Group; the Ancient Mystic Order of Melchizedek; the Temple of the Jeweled Cross; and the Crusade for the New Civilization.

One of the most dramatic health cults that found especial favor in Los Angeles in 1926 was headed by an itinerant from some unknown place, who preached the outlawing of the automobile, insisting that there were several million automobiles and pneumatic-tired trucks in Los Angeles County (the true figure for that year was 559,684 automobiles and 60,340 pneumatic-tired trucks), and each had four tires and a spare, all inflated with forty-five to sixty-five pounds of air, so by simple arithmetic this withdrew from the atmosphere some four to five hundred million pounds of air and explained the increasing incidence of pulmonary, circulatory and cancerous ailments in Los Angeles County. Until such legislation could be passed, this healer offered a course in "filtered breathing," which would enable the student to draw into his lungs more than the normal amount of "thinned out" air and purge it of its deadly impurities. This healer prospered until his death, when his followers hailed him as a martyr and claimed "he had been murdered by the automobile tire."

Then consider the Agasha Temple of Wisdom, founded in the thirties to relay vocal messages from Agasha, an Egyptian priest who lived seven thousand years ago, or, cheek to jowl, the

Institute of Mental Physics and the First Christians' (Essene) Church, founded "to apply the teachings of the Essenes of Syria and Palestine, and the Theraputae or Healers of Lake Mareotis in Egypt." This rich decade of southern California cultism also spawned the Akashic Science Group, which interprets the secret Akashic records for a better understanding of lost Atlantis, and the Temple of Spiritual Logic, which proves how necessary it is to hold all seances in light rather than in darkness. Greater Los Angeles possesses many honorable and distinguished institutions of study and learning: the Westwood branch of its state university, the University of Southern California, California Institute of Technology, Occidental College, Loyola University and the Pomona-Claremont Colleges. But within a fifty-mile radius of City Hall are located the Coptic Fellowship of America, the Institute of Thought Control, the Rose Chapel Psychic Center, the Soul Science Center, the Temple of Soul-Truth and the University of Totology as well. Is further proof required that here indeed is an intellectual center for sociopathic angels to burn the lamp of learning in their pursuit of auditory analgesia, electromatic psychology, spectral decompression, judicial astrology, sciomancy and the orgone orgasm?

And in 1923 and 1924, the discovery and opening of Tutankhamen's tomb and sarcophagus were the inspiration for lurid Sunday-supplement articles whose heavy emphasis was on the ancient curses that caused the death of many of the archaeologists involved in the explorations and "desecrations" of ancient Egyptian and Mesopotamian tombs. It also revealed a rich new lode for the motion picture, which must not be overlooked in any examination of the cults; although the industry would deny this, how else can one consider any organization so deeply dependent on unreality and a variety of dreams that all but staggers the imagination? Where else could one see portrayed so many of the cultists' most important elements: the formalities and rites of devil worship and demonology, vampirism and lycanthropy, necromancy and voodooism, mad scientists and priests of Set, Shedim, Moloch, Belial and Shiva? And though during his lifetime, even when he attended seances and believed in spirits, Rudolph Valentino offered little to the cultists, his death provided them with an overflowing Christmas box of ectoplasm.

In Cuckooland there are many mansions, but we shall visit and observe only those that shelter the indigenous creatures devoted to Valentino: (1) Falcon Lair; (2) spiritualists in direct communication with Valentino, who through his death was firmly established as one of the most prominent morning stars of heaven; and (3) the Lady in Black.

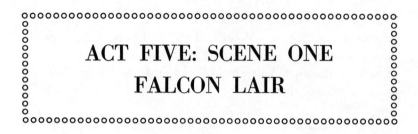

ACT FIVE: SCENE ONE
FALCON LAIR

Although Jules Howard, a New York jeweler, bought Falcon Lair in December, 1926, there is no evidence to show that he ever took possession of the property or lived there. Probably Mr. Howard's bid was never covered by a cash deposit large enough to satisfy the requirements of the court. Occasional actors have since taken up residence there, usually a star of the silent screen. Possibly the occupants temporarily endured residence in the dark, musty house in the hope that the address would again arouse the interest of movie moguls in their faithful but fading box-office attractions but, needless to say, this never happened. Among those in temporary residence was Harry Carey; but he complained of nocturnal clankings and groans, and left for happier quarters. Alberto and his family also lived in the house, but only for a short period of time, because it was uncomfortable and badly in need of extensive and expensive repair.

For almost eight years Falcon Lair stood vacant, during which time a trickle of the meager Valentino assets had to be assigned to its maintenance and taxes, normal household bills and the support of a private patrol to keep the house, walls, gates and garden furnishings from being carted off by simple souvenir hunters, dedicated cultists and uncomplicated looters descended from Egyptian tomb robbers of the first eighteen dynasties. Despite the diligence of such private patrols, the depredations continued, until the Bank of America stepped up its efforts to sell Falcon Lair by offering it with a sharply reduced price tag. But the nationwide depression rendered large, cumbersome houses, situated amid grounds that demanded unusual maintenance, unattractive and impractical purchases. In addition, the sale of a house reputed to be haunted always presents problems: the people who love haunted houses can seldom afford them.

As the house remained unoccupied and Valentino worship became more widespread, caretakers and gardeners soon came to consider the discovery of females lurking in the shrubbery, garages or stables as quite routine; some even managed to gain the house before being apprehended. Most of these dedicated ladies and some dainty young gentlemen risked life and limb to climb over the walls, even seemed content to remain hidden in the stable loft for days on end in the hope of reaching the innermost holy of holies—Valentino's bedroom. Some pilgrims had crass commercial motives, and would anonymously notify newspapers or the police concerning their intentions; usually they were aspiring actors and actresses who hoped to spend a night or two in the master's chamber in order to absorb its essence so they might make a greater contribution to the American screen. Such personal aggrandizement was deplored by the sincerer pilgrims, who were not so easily evicted. Their protestations of love and adoration could become shrill and abusive in-

vective as they fought, clawed, scratched and even bit at those
who attempted to push them out of the main house. Usually they
would stand outside the wrought-iron gates of the estate, where
the women would curse all with an intensity and flow of language
that would have made Wolf Larsen, in the cabin of the *Ghost*,
cringe and turn pale.

There were also problems with gardeners and caretakers, a
series of whom became involved in a simple scheme that earned
them far more than their salaries. With great show of secrecy,
to impress the sincere pilgrim of the risk they were taking, they
would arrange to meet in some unobtrusive place, where they
would part with a small but "authentic" piece of bric-a-brac or
clothing worn by Valentino, which they claimed they had stolen
from the house. Worshipers purchased incense burners, note
paper with Valentino's initials, candlesticks and tapers, cuff links
and salt cellars, neckties and handkerchiefs, and even vials of a
rare perfume supposedly favored by Valentino during his lifetime. Another racket was individual feathers, nicely framed,
which they claimed to have removed from Valentino's pillow.
Caretaker after caretaker was discharged, but each time a lady
appeared at the gates and pleaded for something sacred, and
for which she would pay a good price, a new caretaker would
somehow find himself in business.

The most difficult kind of estate to maintain is an uninhabited
one, and Falcon Lair, which had been valued in 1926 at more
than a hundred thousand dollars, now begged for a purchaser
at any price. Realtors assigned by the Guglielmis or the bank
to sell the property discounted the stories of ghosts and haunts,
but none of them could deny that strange, eerie noises were
sometimes heard in the corridors and empty rooms. Some impressionable realtors, fearful of specters, refused even to show
the property. At last one of the more hardy locked the house
for a week and step by step traced down the spectral sounds
until he discovered that they were produced by a clever mechani-

cal contrivance concealed under the floorboards of a closet. This complex gadget must have delighted Valentino but was unappreciated by most of the real estate fraternity. Occasionally an enterprising realtor, in an attempt to stir up some interest, would persuade one of the Hollywood columnists to run a standard item: Pola Negri planned to return to the United States and had cabled an offer for the house. But if officials of the Bank of America were queried, they had a standard reply: the bank had never been approached by the exotic actress or anyone who represented her.

Year by year the price fell, until in 1934 the house and grounds were appraised at only twenty thousand dollars. When a man named Juan Romero offered eighteen thousand dollars, a sale at that figure was approved by Probate Judge Walton J. Wood. Romero—dubbed a "mystery man" by the local press— was unknown to the Hollywood community, but upon moving into Falcon Lair was identified as an architect, and more important, a friend and admirer of Valentino. He had attended many auctions in Los Angeles and San Francisco, and even traveled abroad, to repurchase furniture and artifacts sold to other collectors during the auctions of 1926. It was his stated ambition to refurbish the house and reconstruct the grounds exactly as they had been at the time of Valentino's death, and later Romero estimated that he had spent more than $150,000 in this endeavor. In addition to the restorations, he constructed an outdoor marble shrine to the memory of Valentino, which was completed in 1939.

Wartime building limitations hampered some of his major plans for Falcon Lair, but in 1943 Romero announced that as soon as restrictions on nonessential construction were lifted, he planned to add a room to the mansion merely to house the armor collected by the Sheik. Included would be a "16th Century Crusader's gauntlet, engraved with the crest of St. George." That the last Crusades, the sixth, seventh and eighth, had been undertaken in 1248 and 1270 did not distress Romero. What difference did two or three hundred years either way really make to a believer? And wasn't it true that the C. B. De Mille historicals were even better than the original events?

During his restoration of the house, Romero achieved a reputation as a party thrower, and had some success in reviving the old tradition of Hollywood gaiety. Briefly, the hilltop became a merry place. The eerie, ghostly sounds amused his guests, among the more prominent of whom was Miss Virginia Hill, the tenant of another house owned by Romero. (In 1947, Miss Hill's close friend, Mr. Bugsy Siegel, was gunned down by a party or parties unknown.) By 1944 Romero had lost interest in Falcon Lair, and had sold most of its furnishings. The continued depredations by sightseers and cultists who believed the property belonged to anyone with an interest or belief in Valentino prompted Romero, early in 1945, to sell the house to Werner Janssen, the symphony conductor, and his wife, Ann Harding.

The Janssens were reported to have paid seventy-five thousand dollars for Falcon Lair, and to have spent thousands of dollars more to redecorate. But they did not enjoy the house, even after the sound-effects machinery was torn out of the closet, and after they had experienced one Valentino anniversary, and been besieged and invaded by hordes of the faithful, who conducted a variety of rites and memorial services that would have delighted Sir James G. Frazer, they sold the house to Mrs. Gerald "Gypsy" Buys of San Francisco. Aware of the obligations and responsibilities inherent in the purchase of one of the most famous landmarks in greater Los Angeles, Gypsy Buys told reporters that she would continue Romero's great work of restoration. Gypsy and her husband spent the summer of 1946 in Europe, where they attempted to locate and repurchase original furnishings, but upon their return Gypsy's joy in the house was diminished because her husband believed himself to be suffering from cancer, or some other fatal ailment. Both were advanced spiritualists, but even their astral incantations failed to make Jerry well. Soon he became convinced that Falcon Lair was aggravating his multiple illnesses and begged his wife to return him to San Francisco. Gypsy believed in the supernatural, but believed even more fervently in her duty as a wife, so reluctantly she closed Falcon Lair. Shortly after she and her husband returned to San Francisco, where they moved into a hotel suite, he committed suicide. An autopsy was performed and physicians discovered that he had never had cancer, or any other fatal disease.

Once more Falcon Lair was on the market, and in February of 1949, Gypsy accepted a deposit from a syndicate of five San Francisco women who identified themselves as "The Group." They agreed to pay one hundred thousand dollars for the house. Mrs. Buys refused to identify the ladies, but the nation was not kept on tenterhooks for an unreasonable length of time. Soon a spokeswoman announced their intent: to make Falcon Lair into a Canterbury, a place of reverence, a shrine where rites to the memory of the Great Lover would be conducted by the high priestesses of "The Group." "For tens of thousands of women," a subsequent proclamation read, "the only inspiration in life is worship of the memory of Valentino." Religious observances would begin promptly at midnight, it developed, after a burst of red, white and blue rockets summoned the faithful to worship. The red rockets would symbolize "passion," and the rockets together would serve as an invitation to Valentino's ghost to bless the services by its presence.

Such a project undoubtedly stirred the enthusiasm of the faithful, but the neighbors reacted as if they had been invaded by Martians. They refused, they said, to have a church in their vicinity, and the City of Los Angeles politely informed "The Group" of a variance in the zoning laws, which approved only single residences in the area. "The Group" was astonished; they had believed Falcon Lair to be in Beverly Hills. And when they were informed that Beverly Hills was even more conservative in its zoning restrictions, the San Francisco ladies told Mrs. Buys the deal was off. Later Gypsy discovered they would have been unable to pay the balance of cash required anyway.

From then on she rejected all propositions made to her by various Valentino cults, including the offer to carry the zoning battle to City Hall. And a few weeks later Mrs. Buys announced the sale of Falcon Lair to an organization with the impressive title The Falcon Lair Foundation for World Peace.

On March 21, 1949, the first day of spring, Robert T. LeFevre, the spokesman for the foundation, moved into Falcon Lair with his wife, two-year-old son and three female members of the foundation, who apparently would help him set up house-keeping. Zoning officers appeared, and in the presence of re-porters LeFevre made several astonishing announcements. He had, it seemed, been the real estate agent who had arranged the purchase of Falcon Lair, which The Foundation for World Peace did not really intend to occupy but would offer as a prize to the person or organization that, in 1949, would bring forward the most effective religious program to foster peace and destroy international communism. In brief, they planned to unify the religions and churches of all the world into a spiritual front able to function *after* World War III, which the group believed im-minent.

"We believe religion, in its broadest sense, is the world's only avenue of escape from destruction. We advocate no particular religion or sect, but believe there is a great deal of good in each of the existing creeds. We believe disaster may be averted by uniting all religious peoples on a common ground of desire for peace and refusal to bow before the onrush of communism."

LeFevre went on to say that the League of Nations had failed and the United Nations "is failing because only material, not spiritual, values are considered important. That's why we're offering all we can, more than fifty thousand dollars, in hope of reviving spiritual values."

Elaborating on the peace prize, which was the sole topic LeFevre was willing to discuss, he explained that three nationally known figures, whom he refused to name, would serve as judges, and only until the award was made would Falcon Lair serve as group headquarters. There was no doubting the sincerity of LeFevre; he had served nearly four years in the Air Force during World War II, had been discharged, in December of 1945, with the rank of captain, and had put his money where his mouth was. He received no salary, only expenses, from a philanthropic group composed of students of peace and comparative religions, who had first met in 1940 but had not incorporated themselves until 1946.

"We chose Falcon Lair as a practical means of getting publicity we cannot afford to buy," LeFevre said at the conclusion of his interview. "The group is not wealthy. Nearly everything we have is going into this one all-out attempt to awaken the world to the danger of war which we expect within a year."

"What will you do when your plan either succeeds or fails?" he was asked politely by a reporter, for everyone was impressed by the young man's sincerity. Visionary he might be; charlatan he was not.

"Get back to selling real estate and make some money," he replied.

Then another reporter succumbed to his training, and asked LeFevre if his group would fire off red, white and blue rockets? Quite properly, LeFevre told the reporters that the interview was at an end.

In the days that followed, he devoted himself to supervising the estate until formal plans for the peace prize could be published. Like previous residents of Falcon Lair, LeFevre had to contend with uninvited sightseers; fanatical trespassers who sought to spend the night in Valentino's chamber; and brass-hided picnickers, who would park outside the main gate, bully their way into the grounds and knock at the kitchen door for some sugar, ice cubes for their drinks or the use of the gas range. Some, aware they were about to make a more formal request, knocked on the front door for permission to use the bathroom. And a wishing well filled with goldfish, which was to inspire contributions for the peace prize, had to be abandoned, because, as LeFevre reported sadly, the metal coins killed the fish. The only well-mannered group to visit Falcon Lair during his occupancy made its appearance in June of 1949, when Archbishop Gordon Safarian I of the Holy Apostolic Church of the First Century led a hundred pilgrims in a candlelight procession up the winding road. In the courtyard the pilgrims signed the Universal Peace Proclamation, prayed and departed in silence and good order. Not so much as a pebble or blade of grass was purloined as a souvenir.

Communications received by The Peace Foundation from various Valentino associations ranged from the pleading to the violent, but all ordered LeFevre to cease and desist in his plans to give away Falcon Lair. Rather, he was to make the estate immediately available to cultists, who, despite the zoning ordinances, intended to establish a church there where interdenominational devotional services (including Hindu, Buddhist and Mayan rites, though without blood sacrifices) would be held daily to worship Valentino. Many of the letters contained direct quotations from Valentino exactly as the writer had received them the night before. LeFevre was even ordered to restore the sound equipment removed from the closet, since with the ear properly attuned, direct messages from Valentino could be unscrambled, translated and relayed by his disciples to the waiting world. Several even suggested that Valentino was really entitled to the prize, since he had preached and practiced love better than any man throughout the ages.

The response to LeFevre's contest had, alas, been minor, and the only submissions of a world plan whereby religion would overcome world communism had been made by "several old ladies, three Italians and a British spiritualist." It soon became evident that The Peace Foundation lacked sufficient funds to meet the mortgage payments, and sadly LeFevre, his family and his helpers disbanded their group, for the world, it appeared, was not yet ready to heed their good message. Falcon Lair stood vacant for almost two years, with only a caretaker in residence. The work was actually too much for one man, and the property ran down, but every day this one devoted attendant fixed a living rose to the lips of the Valentino portrait that still hung over the living-room fireplace.

In November, 1951, Falcon Lair was sold to Robert L. Balzer, a Los Angeles importer of fine groceries and table delicacies. Balzer was also an art fancier, an author and a whilom Buddhist monk who had studied his craft in Tibet. A man of sophistication, taste and imagination, he decided to treat the estate as a setting for appointments appropriate to the architecture rather than as a museum furnished in the atrocious Roxy-lobby style much favored by Hollywood in the twenties, when even the kitchen sink might be fringed. His sole concession to the past was to restore the interior walls to their original light beige. During the process of restoration, more ghostly wiring was uncovered by his workmen; it was torn out. Balzer, too, suffered his share of unwanted guests, and shortly after his improvements had been described in detail by the Home Section of the Los Angeles *Times,* he offered Falcon Lair for sale. Until it could be sold, he rented it for three months to Millicent Rogers, an heiress to the Standard Oil fortune, but Miss Rogers vacated the Lair after one night. She explained her hasty departure to friends by telling them of her fright when Valentino's ghost had stalked her in a lonely corridor.

Balzer then rented the house to Gloria Swanson, who lived there for three months, and in March, 1953, Doris Duke, one of the world's wealthiest heiresses, purchased Falcon Lair for an undisclosed price. She was immediately besieged by collectors, who offered either to buy furnishings already in the mansion or to sell her *their* Valentino appointments, providing she intended to restore Falcon Lair to its original condition. Miss Duke's sole interest in the mansion seemed to be having it occupied by musicians, as her house guests. Joe Castro, a pianist and leader of a small Latin combo group, was one of the more permanent residents until he quarreled with Miss Duke and was banished from the estate, after which it became known that he had been married to her twice. Miss Duke still owns Falcon Lair, but prefers to spend her time in other homes, of which she has a number. She has not set foot in the house for several years.

Time and the slackening of Valentino worship, which has failed to recruit young romantics in sufficient numbers to replace those who have died, have brought peace to Falcon Lair. In addition, the Los Angeles police seem less tolerant than formerly of the cultists who attempt to get into the estate, nor do the Beverly Hills police encourage movie-fan sightseers of any ilk, and they must pass through that city to reach the house. The practice of photographing stars' homes and reproducing them on picture postcards has been discouraged, and as property values continue to soar in and around Beverly Hills, all garish monuments are probably marked for extinction.

The view from Falcon Lair is still remarkable but more so at night, when the twinkling lights of the ever-growing megalopolis extend all the way to the sea. By day, if there is not too much smog, the view can still excite the imagination and inspire thoughts of heaven. An occasional elderly lady of abstracted appearance may ring the doorbell and ask to see the house, usually specifying that Valentino had commanded her to do so. The caretakers find occasional notes in the mailbox that ask if rooms are for rent, even in the servant quarters, or if Miss Duke would be willing to sell the estate to a nonprofit organization short of funds but long on ideals. Once in a while a photographer amid a group of tourists will stop to take a picture, but sightseers who attempt to chip off a piece of the wall as a souvenir are discouraged without ceremony. No attempt is made to stop anyone who wishes to pick up a pebble, a stone, a bit of earth, a blade of grass or a leaf, so long as it is outside the gates. All requests to enter the grounds are refused.

It is only a matter of time before Falcon Lair crumbles under the wrecker's ball, for the site today is worth far more than the house. It could easily be subdivided into at least five lots large enough to accommodate ranch houses, complete with swimming pools. Not one would have the charm of Falcon Lair, yet all would have something Falcon Lair lacked, for Valentino preferred to do his swimming at the Santa Monica Swimming Club, or the beach house of Marion Davies, where he and Pola Negri were often photographed as they frolicked in one of Marion's pools. The rumor, by the way, still persists that Miss Negri may or already has moved into Falcon Lair.

ACT FIVE: SCENE TWO
SPIRITUALISM

During their marriage Valentino and Natacha were strong believers in mediums and controls as well as devoted sponsors of soothsayers, astrologers, fortunetellers and all sorts of men and women who claimed they could communicate with the astral world. So it should surprise no one that most of Valentino's spiritualist friends claim they have communicated with him after he passed over into the Beyond. Inspiration to attempt such communications was certainly nurtured by Louella Parsons, in her column of August 26, 1926, published three days after Valentino's death, which featured an item about Beatrice Lillie and her "harrowing experience of having her automobile turned over on her way home from Jack Gilbert's house Monday night. Valentino had died that day, and that night she had positively heard the dogs at Rudolph Valentino's house groan and howl as if in pain. She said she had been thinking about Mr. Valentino, and as she came near the house she was so upset at hearing the barking of the dogs that she lost control of her motor."

Meanwhile, the New York *Graphic* had already profited by the intelligence it had received from its mediums, who had seen Valentino in heaven, as proved by the composographs, which had increased circulation by one hundred thousand copies. It had also published an interview with Nicola Peccharara, the medium who claimed he had received messages from Valentino demanding that an autopsy be performed on his earthly remains.

And then, on November 25, 1926, with Natacha Rambova as one of its first-class passengers, the *Homeric* had docked in New York City. On the following day *The New York Times* reported that Natacha, too, had been the recipient of

> . . . spirit messages from Valentino, through George B. Wehner, a medium and member of the American Society for Psychic Research, who also was a passenger. She said that Valentino had sent word that he was in the astral plane and longed to be a legitimate actor; that the message did not mention Pola Negri, and that he spoke only "of significant things and those subjects that mean something."
>
> She said that Valentino told of making frequent visits to moving picture theatres where his films were being shown, and that at first he was pleased by the "flattery" of the audiences, but later began to "see through all things," so that movie popularity seemed strange to him. Miss Rambova said Valentino had told her in one spirit message that he had met Caruso in the astral plane. She said she would publish a book on her communications.

There were several dissenters. Miss Pola Negri, for example, "intimated that somebody, unnamed, was publicizing the matter in a way that was 'profane and commercial.' " From her bungalow at the Ambassador Hotel in Los Angeles she said that "spiritualism is a very great and a very serious thing. A message from the other world would be a beautiful and comforting thing to the sorrowing ones left behind to mourn their dear ones. However, it seems to me to be a profanation of the memory of Rudolph Valentino to make public statements like those I have read. I am deeply shocked. In this instance, in regard to my own recent loss, I feel the subject is altogether too sacred to be commercialized and I cannot help thinking that this publicity we have been reading is unworthy of the grand dignity of the great beyond."

And from Chicago Miss Jean Acker voiced her disapproval even more succinctly: "Rudolph Valentino did not believe in spirit messages. He was intelligent, and if he had lived the world would have heard of him in other ways. Even if such messages were received, they should have been too sacred to broadcast."

It is interesting that even a superficial reading of both statements proves that neither Miss Negri nor Miss Acker denied the possibility of such messages; rather, they merely deplored the source, George B. Wehner, and the mouthpiece, Natacha Rambova. If Natacha was disinclined to give strong retort, Mr. Wehner suffered from no such inhibition. The press found Mr. Wehner at his studio on West 152nd Street in upper Manhattan, surrounded by spirit paintings—works of art, Wehner announced, far beyond the capability of ordinary artists. They had been produced while he was in a trance, his mind and being in a state of excogitation, so obviously he alone could not have been capable of creating them. Not a man or woman from the press dared challenge Mr. Wehner or the paintings, for they were indeed fine frenzies.

After their appreciation of his art exhibit, the reporters pressed Mr. Wehner: Had he really communicated with Rudolph Valentino after death? Mr. Wehner answered them and elaborated: Valentino was now governed by two overriding impulses—resentment at his untimely death, for in life the Great Lover had been an egoist, and "pleasure over the tremendous furor which accompanied his lying in state and his funeral."

The great American public—especially that credulous portion of them susceptible to suggestion and anxious to believe in wonders—was intrigued by the controversy and its principals, and it was impressed even more deeply when, on December 11, 1926, Mr. Henry Hoyt, a motion picture director, added his voice to the growing number of believers. Hoyt based his belief in the authenticity of the communications on "his own knowledge of Wehner's medium-like powers, and upon his faith in Miss Hudnut's sincerity." He had directed Miss Hudnut in *When Love Grows Cold*, and one evening after the day's shooting he had dined with Natacha, her mother, Clive Brook and Wehner. After dinner Wehner. had conducted a seance and Hoyt concluded that the medium must have been sincere because "he appeared more like a businessman than a spiritualist." Hoyt added that he knew personally of Natacha's deep and everlasting love for Valentino, "and knowing her sincerity and Wehner's ability, I feel sure that she could get some kind of messages from the other plane."

In June, 1926, *Photoplay* published an editorial that indicted "Hollywood hokum" and the credulous stars who made possible its lucrative harvests. But apparently what had been published in June, 1926, did not hold true in February, 1927, when *Photoplay* startled its readers with an article by Frederick James Smith titled "Does Rudy Speak from the Beyond?" Although Natacha herself was the oracle from which the article sprung, *Photoplay* still felt called upon to add an editorial note "to make clear its position in presenting the so-called spirit messages of Rudolph Valentino. These messages are presented as a matter of news."

And the article was news indeed, for Miss Rambova told Smith that three days after Valentino's death, spirit messages had begun to come through from her former husband, and

George B. Wehner had been the means of transmission. She had been reluctant to reveal anything about them, she said, because she intended to include them in her forthcoming book, whose working title was *Rudolph Valentino Intime*. This work was to have two parts, a recollection of her life with Valentino on earth, and a detailed transcription of his messages to her from the astral plane. However, because she realized that many Valentino fans might never read her book unless they had first knowledge of it through *Photoplay*, she had deigned to make known the answers to certain questions put to her by Mr. Smith.

Is Valentino happy?

Not at first, she replied. At first he had been bitter and angry because he had been taken away at the height of his career. Even the spirit of his mother had been unable to console him. But the funeral had fascinated him. "Rudy, of course, saw his funeral. . . . He was lonely too. He could not reach his friends. . . . He tried to talk to them but they could not hear. . . . Soon, however, the interest of the astral world began to hold him. Now he is radiantly happy, anxious to begin his work there."

Whom has he met?

"He named Wally Reid, Barbara La Marr, and little Olive Thomas . . . [and] Enrico Caruso. . . . Caruso has taken Rudy to the opera and to hear astral concerts. Rudy, too, has met the personal friends with whom we used to communicate by means of automatic writing."

What did they say?

"They have explained the astral world to him. He is slowly coming to comprehend the sublime qualities of the new life about him."

Does Valentino know of the sorrow that swept the world at his death?

"Naturally, he was conscious of the world's sorrow. . . . It tortured him in those earthbound days."

Valentino has referred to the opera and the spoken drama on the other side. Did he tell more of this?

"Opera and drama, sublime things of radiating tones, moods and colors . . . are presented in massive theaters built of thought substance."

Valentino has said there are no movies. Why?

"Because the films are a mechanical perversion of the drama. In the astral world there is nothing mechanical. . . . Mechanism is material and consequently not a part of the astral scheme of things."

What earthly successes does Valentino remember now?

"He remembered all, at first. Rudy wandered the film theaters where his last film was being shown to sorrowing audiences. He walked his old haunts on Broadway, particularly around 47th Street, where he used to spend many hours of his old penniless days. He suffered because his old friends used to pass him by unknowing. Yes, he tried to speak to them without avail. He shouted 'I am Rudolph Valentino,' but they did not hear. It was hard for him to understand. He was just as alive, but in a different vibration. As Rudy has grown in astral knowledge, however, these recollections have lost their appeal. The old glamour of the earth-people is passing. Our world is growing fainter."

Has Valentino any message for his old host of worshipers?

"Yes . . . he wants earth-people to know and realize that there is no death and no separation. . . . He wants them to realize and believe in the beauty of this after-life."

If Valentino were to live again, would he make motion pictures?

"He would try whatever circumstances would permit. He would have to meet the problems of the earth-life."

With this cryptic reply the interview concluded, and Mr. Smith asked Natacha how she could be sure these messages had come from her former husband.

"When we receive a telephone message from another city," she countered, "how do we know who is speaking? From mannerisms, from thoughts, from the topics of conversation. Every

message from Rudy undeniably has carried authentic earmarks."
To further explain, Natacha told the reporter that marriage was
physical and of this earth, but that the spiritual essence of marriage transcended and survived death. She and Rudy had been
spiritually very close, hence the messages. "Rudy was really
psychic. We used to do mechanical writing a great deal. One
of our principal spirit contacts was an old Egyptian who calls
himself Meselope. He gave us psychic lessons and prayers but
never spoke of material things."

Natacha explained that messages had warned her that Valentino would die, but since she believed in reincarnation she had
not grieved. "We come back without memory to see if our
lessons have been thoroughly learned," she continued. "Now
and then we have faint, dim patches of previous existences. I
believe that I lived in previous ages, as did Rudy. Undoubtedly,
we met."

In Hollywood, tarot cards, crystal balls, Ouija boards and
hoodoo powders were complete sellouts, and studio warehouses
reported thefts of caldrons and other bits of hardware associated
with magic. Meanwhile, the world impatiently awaited
Natacha's book, which was first published in England, in 1927,
before an abridged version appeared in the United States. True
to her original design, the first section of the book concerned
Natacha's "Recollections," though most of these were lengthy
accounts and examples of spiritisms in which she and Rudy had
ardently engaged. She cited instances of automatic writing and
of messages received from Rudy's mother, Gabriella Guglielmi,
and how they had first established rapport with Meselope, the
ancient Egyptian, and Black Feather, with whom Rudy had had
so many interesting "powwows." Indeed, Valentino had been so
fond of Black Feather that he had had himself photographed
in Indian headdress and beads, and Black Feather had signaled
his approval by puffing out a contented message on his peace
pipe. And Natacha now revealed that the black feather on the

title page of *Day Dreams* was in memory of Rudy's spirit guide
Black Feather, and that Meselope himself had dictated one of
the poems!

(*To M.*)
The serenade of a thousand years ago,
The song of a hushed lip,
Lives forever in the glass of to-day,
Wherein we see the reflection of it
If we but brush away
The cobwebs of a doubting faith.

There was more that was revelatory, for Natacha called attention to the true authorship of "The Gift-Book" (James Whitcomb Riley); "The Love Child" (Lord Byron); "Gypsies"
(Robert Browning); "At Sunrise To-morrow" (Elizabeth
Barrett Browning); and Rudy's favorite, "Glorification," had
actually come from the astral pen of that good gray poet Walt
Whitman.

The second section transcribed eleven messages, all of which
she had received after Valentino died. The very first message
informed her of Rudy's meeting with "that great spirit who has
helped me to find myself in these new surroundings and who is
teaching me to understand the realities of being: the spirit of
H.P.B." To the uninitiated Miss Rambova explained that the
initials were those of Helena Petrovna Blavatsky, founder of the
Theosophical Society. If so—and who could prove otherwise?—
Valentino was being tutored by one of the truly formidable
teachers of all time.

Born in Russia of a distinguished military family on July 30,
1831, Mme Blavatsky had had an undisciplined childhood, and
even as an adolescent she had been given to frenzies and hallucinations. Much of her younger years are still clouded in mystery
and any log of her travels is open to dispute, although she
claimed to have studied theosophy in India and Tibet. But in

1858, while living in Paris, she was converted to spiritualism and took avidly to the study of spirit rapping. Later, she traveled throughout western Europe, England and the United States, where, without false modesty, she proclaimed herself a medium, and in 1875 told her followers that certain ancient Egyptian mystics had ordered her to found a society. The Theosophical Society would be dedicated to the study of ancient occult religions, and their influence on later generations. Theosophists described heaven as a place of exaltation, but claimed there was no hell. They also favored but did not demand celibacy and vegetarianism, and, like Unitarians, considered Christ to be only one in a company of great teachers. Whatever psychic demonstrations Mme Blavatsky performed in 1884 for the English Society of Psychical Research on a London visit may have been deemed unsatisfactory by its members, but in her time she impressed William Butler Yeats mightily, as William York Tindall noted in his *Forces in Modern British Literature* (1949): "On Blavatsky's arrival in London in 1887, Yeats visited her and was permitted to smell spectral incense, hear spectral bells. Following her advice, he placed the ashes of a rose in the receiver of an air pump, reduced the pressure, placed the apparatus in the moonlight, and watched all night for the ghost of the rose."

Mme Blavatsky was described by Valentino as being so radiant he was almost blinded by her presence, and through her he had met Hindus of great learning and wisdom. In an aside to Natacha he explained how distressed he was that Alberto and Maria were disputing his inclusion of "Auntie" Werner in the will. "They were my little family. Why should they not share and share alike? I hope God will let my way be seen to be the fair way."

In other messages Valentino described his method of communication with George Wehner, and also dealt in detail with the intellectual Chautauquas he had attended to increase his knowledge a hundredfold. He also described theaters, stage activity and performances, and concerts and operas he had enjoyed in the company of Caruso. In fact, Caruso had himself sung in an opera called *The Journey of the Soul*. Matters of astronomy were disclosed to him by Mme Blavatsky, and he received instruction in healing from Florence Nightingale herself, though why, since there was no physical illness in heaven, there should have been need of that was not explained. He was also taking dancing lessons from Vernon Castle, who discoursed with him about the various levels of dancing, claiming that the lower ones "hinder[ed] the soul's progress."

Heaven was wonderful; Luther Burbank had approached Valentino, introduced himself and explained his surprise, when he first entered heaven, to find no birds or insects there. Pollination was accomplished in a way that dispensed with the birds and the bees, as was later detailed to Valentino by John Burroughs and John James Audubon. And earthbound musicologists, as well as sheiks and Shebas, were fascinated by Valentino's next revelation, which sounds not unlike the origin of the rash of go-go joints that were to plague later earthlings:

> There was music—jazz—and a great deal of dancing, good and bad. There was no restraint whatever. People did exactly as they chose. Some sang at the top of their voices. Some shrieked madly. Some flung themselves into the most grotesque postures—sort of solo dances, one might call them. Others told all kinds of stories of drinking and of various vices, for the purpose, I was informed, of exciting their desires.
>
> Whenever people reached what appeared to be the height of their wildest frenzy, they trooped off, in great mists of dull red colour, brown, and reddish orange, earthward, to gratify through human beings their frantic desires. Having no longer physical bodies of their own, they are forced to use the bodies of others still living upon earth. H.P.B. has told me that earth-

people reached and attacked by these earth-bound souls find their own desires and appetites, quite unaccountably to them, literally sweeping them off their feet.

She says their sensations are greatly magnified as they enjoy not only their own but the added sensations of the influencing entities. Now I can understand the realer [*sic*] reason for perverts of all kinds—habitual drunkards, drug addicts and degenerate persons; all of them weak, evilly controlled people.

In conclusion, Valentino described meetings with Charles Frohman and Clyde Fitch, then revealed to Natacha that Pola Negri, Charles Chaplin and Doris Kenyon were mediumistic, and could easily develop these talents if they so chose, though he was rather disappointed in Jimmy Quirk of *Photoplay*.

During the time my body lay on view in New York, I went to his office several times. I always liked Jimmy and I tried to make him realize I was still alive. I touched him. I thumped on his desk. I shouted in his ear. But Jimmy just could not seem to hear. He is too surrounded by a wall of the hard-and-fast facts of everyday life to be easily reached psychically. Yet Jimmy's impressions of people are usually right. Somewhere within his complex lingers that psychic spark which, under certain conditions, might be fanned into a flame.

In his eleventh and final message, Valentino discussed science, which heaven's servants thought "too strictly classified; too mechanically, too materialistically labelled," and at last told Natacha:

> The force is weakening. I must go.
> Good night, Natacha, good night.
> Rudy

Reviewers who received copies of *An Intimate Portrait* from Hutchinson and Company, its English publisher, stood in such awe of its contents and were so convinced that their earthbound pens could not give to it the justice and breadth of vision it deserved that they ignored it completely. But the book received wide word-of-mouth attention and one braver American, Walter Lippmann, in an article for *Vanity Fair* called "Blazing Publicity; Why We Know So Much About 'Peaches' Browning, Valentino, Lindbergh and Queen Marie," acknowledged the volume *en pocas palabras:* "And as for the recently published memories of Rudolph Valentino from the spirit world, even the most trusting smile as they read eagerly about his love life there."

An Intimate Portrait became the first testament of the spiritualists who were to rally around Valentino, and it inspired a plagiarism of pamphlets all more or less derivative. From as far away as Texas, in the twenties hardly an intellectual or spiritual oasis, one appeared asking *Is Valentino Communicating with Mortals?* The answer, of course, was yes.

In Hollywood the book inspired a special service at St. Paul's Presbyterian Church, where the sermon was entitled "Valentino's Spirit Returns," and at Paramount Studios certain extras, clerical help and caretakers who claimed to be extraordinarily sensitive, reported they had seen Valentino's ghost haunting the vicinity of his dressing room or had come upon it in the wardrobe department searching the racks for the costumes he had once worn. Press agents who suffered uninspired voids could now get a plug published merely by giving their clients' opinions of the work, which became more important to the Hollywood flack than even a dictionary.

Less inspired literary mystics began to publish cheap pamphlets of ecstatica and broadsides reportedly received by them direct from Valentino, and several of these gurus even had the temerity to challenge Miss Rambova's book as phony. One shaman challenged her to a debate by seance, the contest to be held any midnight of Miss Rambova's choice in the Hollywood Bowl, where before a full amphitheater each would speak to

Valentino and through amplifiers the spectators could hear direct from the Great Lover's mouth whether or not, as Miss Rambova claimed, he had been happily married to her. Sports figures and the betting gentry perked up and wondered if the Polo Grounds might not be a better choice for the match.

Although earthlings loved the book because it was a Baedeker to heaven and also described Valentino's life on a higher plane, studio heads became increasingly worried. Was their industry, which had suffered major scandals of the body, now to be indicted for one of the mind? Studio heads met with Will H. Hays, film czar in charge of morality, and together they held several quiet meetings with James Quirk. Quirk finally suggested that *Photoplay* publish an article about occult fakery in which he would name the major fakers who preyed on the industry, though he might also have to mention the names of some stars, directors and producers. An attempt was made to convince him that there was no need for such specificity, but Quirk realized he had come up with a hot article indeed, and refused to compromise. If the industry wanted his help he was willing to grant it, but names would have to be spelled out.

In the December, 1928, *Photoplay* the feature article was Harry Lang's "Exposing the Occult Hokus-Pocus in Hollywood," which was subtitled, "The Truth About the Strange 'Psychic Guides' Who Influence the Destinies of the Stars—It's a Great Racket." The article was a bombshell, for Lang did indeed name names. Among the more favored of the dozens of occultists in Hollywood was Dareos, formerly butler to a Hollywood star who had often consulted a Pasadena medium. Soon enough Dareos came to realize that there was more profit in ectoplasm than in ushering guests into the star's parlor, and he set up in prophecy for himself, though in the telephone book he was listed as a psychoanalyst.

On my mother's side [he told Lang] I come from the

English peerage. One of my relatives, you'd be surprised if I told you his name, but of course I can't, is a British governor-general. I was born in California, but I lived for a long time in the East and in Europe. My people thought I was going to be a lawyer, but I didn't want to. It was in 1916 that I first took up psychic work. I was in Coronado, walking up the Pike with some society girls. We went into a fortuneteller's tent and, before we came out, I had told his fortune instead of him telling me mine.

But how had Dareos established himself in the motion picture colony as one of its foremost seers?

"Through Norma Talmadge. I met her through a Mrs. Bush, who brought Norma to me. I read her and later was invited to her home. And the nice things she said about me spread my fame among the movie people.

"I've read Gilbert Roland and Joseph Schenck. Mr. Schenck comes to me quite a bit. . . .

"Chaplin—I predicted his mother's death. I predicted the scandal in his life, and said that he'd come out of it O.K., and he has. I predicted Thomas Ince's death. . . ."

[This has been corroborated by a number of film people who were present at the gathering at which Dareos foretold that Ince would die on the water.]

". . . and there's Tom Mix. Tom Mix should be careful. I predict that Tom Mix will be ruined if he's not careful. If he doesn't watch out, some day a bolt will strike him like lightning out of the blue!

"Mae Murray—I told her she'd win her lawsuit, and that she'd have a baby. And, by the way, there are whisperers who say that it isn't her baby—but they lie. That's most certainly her baby!"

Warming to the interviewer, Dareos provided even more startling information. "Pola Negri—I told her she'd never marry Valentino. I warned her against companionship with Valentino; I told her he was too romantic a type to bring her complete happiness. I remember how she cried in my office."

Among the stars mentioned in *Photoplay*'s exposé were Joan Crawford, Eric von Stroheim, Virginia Valli, Constance Talmadge, Billie Dove, Florence Vidor, Mabel Normand, Claire Windsor, Olive Borden, Jetta Goudal, Eleanor Boardman, Richard Dix, Richard Arlen, Eileen Pringle, Anita Stewart, Ralph Ince, Ramon Navarro, Corinne Griffith, and Lupe Velez.

The article discussed at length Valentino's interest in spiritualism, but added little in the way of new detail. It also reproduced a schematic drawing of the Wanda Tipping Table, invented by Grover C. Haffner, an accomplished osteopath. Haffner was making a fortune from his improvement on the old Ouija board—35,000,000 of which had been sold at the peak of its popularity. The *Photoplay* piece was much discussed in Hollywood but failed to accomplish its purpose. The gullible among the stars and picture people on the way now knew where to go, and they were not slow in going. The business of the Morganas and Merlins increased, and soon hundreds and hundreds of astrologers and palmists, phrenologists, life readers, fortunetellers and clairvoyants, cartologists and cartomancers, crystal gazers, mediums, hypnotists, prophets, necromancers, psychologists and numerologists, and just plain kooks, packed their gear and took off by bus, car, train or thumb. In Hollywood the weather was more pleasant, the living easier, and those who really counted had richer pockets and simpler minds.

In the meantime, an old Valentino pet declined and on February 2, 1929, a grave Hollywood dispatch announced, nationwide, the death and burial of Kabar, one of Valentino's favorites. The Doberman had been one of those whose howling, as reported by Louella Parsons, had so "frightened Beatrice Lillie that she ran her car off the mountain road and fainted. . . . With the peculiar intuition credited to dogs, Kabar was aware that something serious was wrong with his master. And his howls . . . could not be appeased."

Miss Rambova's book had discoursed on animals, explaining much about them to earthlings:

> Such animals, with their beginning of soul development, often have keen sight of things in the astral. Dogs, cats, parrots, horses and elephants often clairvoyantly see spirits. And spirits are often able to influence animals to accomplish seeming miracles. What power is it that guides a horse and rider through the blinding terrors of a blizzard? It is the guiding hand of the rider's guardian spirit leading the psychic horse onward to safety.
>
> Why do dogs often howl before the death of some member of a family? Is it just coincidence? No. It is because the dog's psychic faculties sense the subtle change that is commencing in the physical organism of the person who nears the hour of change; and that change, the mysterious loosening of spirit from body, gives off a peculiar vibration which startles and alarms the dog.
>
> Henry Watts says this death-vibration may be seen as colour: mauve-grey. It may also be heard as a sound: a continuous, low, sighing whistle. And it may be smelled as an uncannily permeating odour.

Kabar's funeral, though hardly as elaborate as his master's, had much going for it and he was buried in a cemetery for dogs of noted lineage, that had recently been dedicated in the San Fernando Valley. A hundred thousand dollars had been spent to make this pet cemetery one of the most lavish in the land, for it included a chapel, crematory, monument plant, embalming laboratories, casket shop, day-and-night hearse services and floral shop. Kabar's costly headstone bore the simple epitaph:

KABAR
Rudolph Valentino's Dog
Born in Alsace, June 20, 1922
Died January 17, 1929

European spiritualists, meanwhile, were also active, and early in 1929, one of the more prominent of these, a Hungarian teen-ager in training for a career as an actress, unburdened herself to her disciples about Valentino's unhappiness over the small turnout at the second anniversary of his death. Valentino, she said, was also in despair that the international guilds and associations devoted to his memory had failed to erect a suitable monument to honor him. As if the young mystic's message of distress had been received loud and clear in Hollywood, that year the whole character of the memorial service at the crypt began to change. The movement had passed through its missionary phase, and though no film personalities of any consequence showed, among the fluttering ladies was one of true psychic prominence, Mrs. Cora MacGeachy, a lady Natacha Rambova had credited with being a medium much favored by Valentino. But though more than half the people gathered at the crypt believed in astral communication, and a three-piece ensemble played pleasant but derivative melodies composed during trances in gypsy tearooms, Valentino refused to speak.

At this time Paul Ivano, in what amounted to heresy, denied Valentino's interest in the psychic to an interviewer and said the Great Lover had not been a priapic Italian, and that actually his main interests were centered on eating and sleeping, for he had small reserves of nervous energy and sleep was essential to his well-being. Ivano's statement was deemed downright seditious, and thus ended 1929, with nothing really important happening so far as the spiritualists were concerned, unless a materialistic body was interested in some footling nonsense about a disturbance in the stock market.

In 1930, Harry T. Brundidge, author of *Twinkle, Twinkle, Movie Star!* recorded an interview with George Ullman in which it was explained that Valentino and his business manager had agreed upon a "code," to be used to communicate between the "worlds" if one died before the other. Thousands of letters and telegrams had been received by Ullman from people who claimed to have established communication with Valentino, but not one included the secret password.

"Those who are familiar with the Valentino of the screen and the Valentino who was the public idol, will find it hard to believe that this self-assured young man who was inclined to be shy and timid was a strong believer in the supernatural," said Ullman. "When I became associated with him in 1922 I soon learned that he and his wife Natacha were interested in something supernatural, but it was not until later that I learned it was what mediums call 'automatic' writing and 'spirit writing. . . .'

"Hundreds of the letters which continue to pour in are from mature women who claim to be in touch with Rudolph," Ullman continued. "Some claim he is their lover, and visits them regularly. Others assert he is trying in vain to get into communication with former friends on earth. Then there are the persons who say he is trying to relay 'messages' through them about the disposition of his estate. Look at some of the letters which have been addressed to me on this general subject of Rudolph and his affairs."

Invited by Ullman to view this category of unabashed, passionate letters, Brundidge did, marveled, and published a few samples. One of the better ones was from a lady in Douglas, Arizona, who wrote: "I have been spending the nights in the desert with Rudy and I am enclosing a message he has written you." In a rather poor imitation of Valentino's hand, the message from out there read: "George—I am using automatic writing to reach you. What is the matter that you refuse to communicate with me? I want to come home, George, for I am oh! so lonesome. June [Mathis] is with me and she, too, is lonesome. It is dark out here and we are afraid. Please, George, get in touch with me through this medium. Black Feather asks it also."

Day by day the national interest in Valentino was nurtured

by groups of astralites who used this continuing interest to amalgamate and expand their California activities. A new spate of pamphlets was distributed, exhorting all believers in communication with those in the Beyond to cluster around Valentino, who by his nature and psychic activity was tuned in to the beliefs that they all honored. Only one thing more was necessary to establish the new religion—a straight out-and-out newspaper acknowledgment (by a journal of importance published outside an asylum) that communication with Valentino was not only possible but had been established and authenticated. To the delight of the spookish clergy, this acknowledgment became a reality in 1931. On February 17, 18 and 19, the Hearst press syndicated, on the first pages of its newspapers, three feature articles concerned with such mediumistic communications with Valentino, written by R. T. M. Scott, Chairman, New York Section, American Society for Psychical Research.

In the first installment, a later communication established with Valentino through George Wehner was fully detailed. Mr. Scott related how Ruth Roland, a prominent screen actress, a stenographer and a reliable witness, had been present in a large studio at a special seance attempting to contact the spirit of the Great Lover. After medium Wehner went into his trance, the spirit of Valentino's mother spoke through his lips (in English) and informed everyone in the studio that her son's spirit would be pleased to communicate with them. Then Valentino greeted the assembly and gallantly asked that Ruth Roland speak with him. The actress found her tongue, responded pleasantly, and Rudy said he greatly enjoyed chatting with her again, since it had been some time since they had last talked.

Ruth replied it was indeed strange, even sad, to be in communication again with her good friend, whose flashing eyes had woven a lasting spell around so many feminine hearts, and Valentino modestly answered, "Very strange."

Miss Roland then put twelve prepared questions to Valentino:

Does a person on this earth need to be psychic in order to communicate with a person who has died and does such a communication have to pass through a medium?

"I would say that anyone in the earth, who desired to communicate with one who had passed over, would have to be psychic to get a communication. And what was that about a medium?"

Does such a communication have to pass through a medium?

"It would not because the person getting the communication would be his own medium. He would be psychic. Psychic means sensitive. Such a person would have to be psychic enough to feel the vibrations."

If you had lived, would you have gone into the talkies?

"I think I would have because I had a good voice—or so people said. I used to sing, although I did not have a trained voice. I even made several records. I think I sang one time something about pale hands—'Pale Hands Beside the Shalimar.' It wasn't a success, but I believe it would have sounded well in the talkies. I would have loved to have gone into the talkies."

What is the relation of man and wife in the spirit world? Are they together, or aren't those things important?

"I think it is very important, the relation of man and wife in the spirit world. It all depends on what they meant to each other. If there was great love between them, then most certainly they are united, because you cannot sever love in reality. It is all that lasts. If they did not love one another, but were bound by legal or earthly ties, they may find themselves free from one another at death. If either the husband or wife had injured the other, they would be bound together until they had worked that out and had come to a harmonious understanding."

Is one immediately cured after death of the disease from which he died?

"In a certain sense most decidedly, because the disease is left off with the physical body, but the mental conception of that disease may remain with the spirit after passing into the astral plane for some time. In that sense, the spirit might be earth-bound in the vibration of the disease.

"I have seen many instances of that where some spirits seem to suffer from the effects of a disease they had on earth. But that doesn't last very long unless the disease made a strong mental impression."

Do people ever return to this world as ghosts, perhaps?

"It would all depend on what people call ghosts. I would say yes. The earth-bound spirits return as ghosts. People see apparitions of them. Very often, haunted houses, they are drawing the ectoplasmic force to their astral bodies—drawing the atoms of ectoplasmic force from some human being."

Can you communicate with anyone as you like, or must you be sent by a higher power?

"I cannot communicate with anyone I like because there are many obstacles. I have gone to some of my old friends, stood beside them, touched them, but to no avail. They were not sensitive enough to feel me. Others I have reached almost immediately.

"Sometimes those I am used to coming to are shut to me through some depression which makes it impossible for me to get down to the level to which their spirits have dropped. I am not sent by any higher power. I go because I want to talk to someone or because I love them."

Are you thoroughly settled in your present sphere, or will you move on to other places?

"I am not settled at all. I don't know how long I shall be in this sphere, where I am constantly learning things that are spiritual. I know I shall progress to higher planes. I know also that there are things I can only learn in the earth world before I can progress to higher planes. I think I shall come back to the earth world before I can ever go to higher planes."

You mean to be born over again?

"Yes. The earth is the schoolroom of the soul, the lowest class, the kindergarten. You cannot get away from it until you have learned all the lessons in it."

Who is, in your opinion, the greatest film star today?

"That is a difficult question because people are great in different fields. I do not think anyone has reached Charlie Chaplin's place in comedy. Gloria Swanson is a great artist in her line of work. Also there is that Swedish artist, Greta Garbo. Her husky, throaty tones are wonderful for expressing emotion."

Have you ever returned to haunt your house in Hollywood?

"Yes. I have returned, but not for the purpose of haunting it. I have returned to walk around the place and live again the old days in memory. It is the same as when you sit in a chair and think over past days. When we think of a place we are there immediately. In living the old days over again, I have gone to that house and wandered through the rooms, thinking of the old happiness and sorrows. Sometimes people have heard me walk around and have felt my presence."

Had you any premonition that you were going to die?

"Yes. I was in an awful mental state. I felt a breaking up of things. I had the feeling that nothing material mattered very much and so I let go of myself. The premonition took that form."

How did you die? Was there any justification in the rumors of shooting or poisoning?

"That is very difficult for me to answer because it involves a great many people. I will say that—I did not die a natural death. I am not going to divulge any names. I have no desire for revenge, contrary to the opinion most people might have. I do not wish to have any suffering come to them . . . more than will come to them through natural causes. We cannot do wrong without suffering the consequences. . . . I think I would relieve them—if I could."

Fan-magazine editors and publishers were well aware that their readership was, for the most part, the same as that of the Hearst papers. A healthy circulation demanded that it emulate and improve upon a good thing when one became evident, so in April, 1932, *The New Movie Magazine* published an interview with Roger C. Peterson titled "My Strange Experiences at Valentino's Grave." Peterson, an attendant at the Hollywood Memorial Park Cemetery, had kept a diary in which he described the many anguished women who prostrated themselves at Valentino's tomb and wept hysterically about their all-consuming passion for the departed Lover. His diary was critical of the souvenir hunters who had torn or snipped buds and ribbons from the floral offerings left at the crypt, and he described how he had collared vandals attempting to chip pieces of marble from the face of the crypt.

Once he had found two women who were attempting to pry loose Valentino's bronze nameplate, and despite their tears and pleas for clemency, for they had been inspired by love, he had marched them to the administrative offices of the cemetery. A cemetery attendant has to be a man of considerable equanimity, but on September 30, 1927, Peterson's calm was shaken. A woman, he wrote, "came to the mausoleum today with the wildest delusion yet. She claimed she was about to become a mother and Valentino was the father of her child. This, thirteen months after his death. The woman asked for permission to have a cot placed before Rudy's crypt, where she might remain until her baby was born. She went up to the cemetery office, and somehow or other they got rid of her." Later, Peterson began to notice an increasing influx of occultists, and wondered to his diary if there was "a convention of spiritualists around here somewhere." But the spiritualists were mostly quiet women and though some effected odd dress, they made no attempt to steal souvenirs or mutilate the face of the crypt, because, as they told Peterson, they were in direct communication with Valentino.

What materialistic possession could compete with their ability to speak at will with the Master?

In December, the first of many mediums sought to hold a seance at the crypt; Valentino himself, she explained, had ordered a pioneer to cross the continent to perform this ritual. Quite impressed, Peterson informed the bright-eyed lady he would not object to the ceremony if it was conducted quietly, decorously, and ended before the time he had to lock the doors of the mausoleum each night. But as an afterthought he added that she had best check it out first with the management. She agreed and went into a trance, and moments later a series of knocks was actually heard from the crypt! The medium began to run in circles, shouting, "Hear! Hear! He knocks! Rudy knocks!"

This attracted a number of other persons, who agreed that they heard the strange knocking. In awe they shivered; some fell to their knees. Something of a skeptic, Peterson felt called upon to conduct his own investigation. He climbed up into the mausoleum and discovered a large bird, a yellowhammer, that somehow had managed to get in and was flying about in a panic, banging against the windows. Peterson opened a window and the bird escaped.

Several months of quiet passed, then an elderly representative of the softer sex appeared with a bouquet of staggering size. As she knelt before the holy crypt, Peterson heard her cry out: "At last, Rudy, at last I have come. Your spirit has led me on, ever on to view your final resting place. Rest, dear heart, rest." Ever the gentleman, Peterson helped the overwhelmed communicant to a chair and brought several large vases for her flowers. While she recovered her composure, she told Peterson "how Valentino's spirit had come to her as she lay ill on a hospital cot in a southern city. Valentino whispered that she would get well immediately, but she must make a pilgrimage to his tomb before she could find happiness." Her health had been restored; she had made the pilgrimage. And now she had found complete happiness, the happiness of at last seeing where her beloved's mortal remains rested.

In 1937 Peterson published a book, *Valentino, the Unforgotten*, which he dedicated to the spirit of Rudolph Valentino. In the preface he noted that the publication of the article about him in *The New Movie Magazine*, five years earlier, had brought him "a flood of correspondence from people all over the world," and that his replies to these thousands of letters had occupied his evenings for five years. To read Peterson's book is a disquieting experience. The tales he recounts of those who visited the tomb, and the descriptions of their behavior, read more like a compendium of case histories provided by some institution. Women hid in the mausoleum, chained themselves to wrought-iron fixtures, moaned, wept, wailed, gnashed their teeth, rent their garments and became catatonic. Bereft of all sense and propriety, other vestal communicants lay supine, raised their arms and parted their limbs as if awaiting fulfillment, wiggled and wriggled to the crypt, kissing its face or pressing their ears to the cold marble, crying out that they heard Valentino speaking to them. Husbands arrived to drag their wives home, and one irate gentleman of little patience insisted that he was going to name "the ghost of Valentino as corespondent."

The book also contains an analysis of a specimen of Valentino's handwriting by A. Henry Silver, a well-known graphologist, and Dr. Juno Kayy Walton, a numerologist, provided a numberscope for Valentino. Paul Foster Case, identified as a writer and lecturer, supplied an astrological analysis. All are interesting and informative. And in passing, Mr. Peterson noted that a Miss Emma Leutgeb of Salzburg had entered into correspondence with him. He had dispatched to her photographs of the crypt and Falcon Lair, and in turn she had sent photographs of a room in her home dedicated to Valentino's memory. Pictures and souvenirs were arranged tastefully in glass cases, and her collection was considered notable and first rate. European magazines had reproduced it many times. Miss Leutgeb seemed deeply concerned about a story, which had gained considerable circulation throughout Europe, that Rudy's remains had been removed to potter's field. Mr. Peterson assured the good fräulein that this was not so.

Peterson included as well a prose poem by Mrs. Mary E. Palmer entitled "A Tribute from the Mothers of the World to Rudolph Valentino."

In 1935, another apostle of the new religion, a Danish lady named Marchen Jorgensen, migrated to Hollywood. She called herself a concert pianist and an actress, but these achievements were secondary to another extraordinary talent. Miss Jorgensen was an astral typist, and whenever she went into a trance she was moved by occult powers to the typewriter, where she rapidly tapped out messages from Rudolph Valentino. Like the other sacerdotalists, of the new religion, Miss Jorgensen quickly built up a following, but her newspaper coverage was soon overshadowed by an event of even greater significance—Germany tore up the Treaty of Versailles, an act that led eventually to World War II. To meet the challenge of a global war, even before it was drawn into it, the United States geared itself to mass production. This wiped out unemployment, and once America got in, the national effort was geared to compel the Axis powers to accept unconditional surrender. These were lean years for the new religion, but after a number of them, the war was finally over. To all members of the Valentino cult this was the signal to get out of their workaday overalls and into their spiritualist robes to start the cult moving again. Full employment had made for full wallets; now was the time to reap a bonanza.

The cultists, in Hollywood at least, were roughly divided into two groups—those who oriented their services around the actual crypt, and those who attempted to communicate with Valentino through mediums, though there were a few who kept their days *and* nights busy and exciting by joining the many activities undertaken by both. The latter group was led by Mrs. Carol McKinstry, who used whenever possible the facilities of Falcon Lair, generously provided by Gypsy Buys. They received by far their greatest share of the public attention, however, after Falcon Lair was put on the market, for inasmuch as Gypsy could offer no guarantee that the next occupant would be of the faith, she granted the solace of one last seance supreme. Thus it came to pass that on May 6, 1948, the anniversary of Valentino's fifty-third birthday, thirty spiritualists gathered together for a superhappening at Falcon Lair.

Heralds had spread the news to reporters and photographers, who were urged to come, witness and marvel. The press harkened the call, and on the appointed evening the spiritualists, in their robes and gowns of thaumaturgy, gathered in the den of the famed hilltop mansion, where Mrs. Buys offered baked meats, sweetmeats, flagons of ale, wine and stronger spirits to medium and newsman alike. Most of the press, men of little faith, suspected the seance was an inspiration of Edward Small's publicity agents, but a representative of the producer denied this vehemently, saying that Mr. Small intended to keep *his* film "dignified."

Carol McKinstry, solemn and regal, was very much in evidence in a full-length dinner dress, a sweeping cape with a lining of contrasting color, and elaborate jewelry dazzling enough to catch the eye of any mortal or wandering apparition. Suddenly Mrs. McKinstry closed her eyes, breathed deeply and exhaled slowly to signal a dramatic hush. "Rudy is here," she announced, her eyes still closed, "with a message for Gypsy Buys. He says don't despair, just keep faith."

Mr. and Mrs. Buys perked up visibly. This was good news

indeed; did it mean they were going to sell the house without trouble? There was then a lull during which Jerry Buys took the reporters and photographers on a tour of the manse. A highlight was the huge fourposter bed that he identified as having belonged to Valentino. A brash young reporter, unawed by the surroundings, insisted upon referring to it as "a great sack for a really great shack-up." But the tour was cut short because it was time to begin the seance, and everyone returned to the den to be presented to the Venerable Lokanatha. Clad in a yellow toga-like robe and elaborate sandals, the Venerable One merely acknowledged with a modest smile the homage paid him by Mrs. McKinstry, Mr. and Mrs. Buys and several other cultists.

"I caught the monk in Tibet," Jerry Buys whispered to the gathered reporters. "He's on a word-fast tonight and will not speak. He's on a word-fast in the interests of world peace. But soon he's going on a lecture tour. Today he was downtown among the people, but his feet are too sacred to touch the sidewalks so I had twenty beautiful girls spread their long hair for him to walk on. It made a wonderful newspaper shot."

Several photographers present wondered if the lady spiritualists gathered around the Venerable One might be persuaded to kneel and reconstruct the morning rite, but Mr. Buys doubted that the Venerable Lokanatha would be agreeable. "The monk comes from Brooklyn," he whispered after an iconoclastic reporter informed his colleagues that the Venerable One's real name was Salvatore Cioffe. "His family is Italian. Some of his relatives are dignitaries of the church, so we cannot mention his family name."

Considerable mental pressure was then exerted upon Mr. Buys to permit the seance to begin, since a number of mediums seemed unable to restrain themselves and had begun to moan and lament that the vibrations they were receiving from Valentino, who wished to appear, had become impossible to endure. Jerry Buys agreed, and at a signal from Mrs. McKinstry, a circle was formed and two servants brought in a large chair with a birthday cake on the seat. The lights were dimmed, "Happy Birthday" was sung and two infrared bulbs were quickly screwed into lamps for photographers who might wish to take spirit shots if Rudy decided to cut the cake.

Eyes closed, brow furrowed in deepest concentration, Lokanatha sat in silence as the other mediums clapped their hands and chanted in singsong: "Valentino, Valentino, we desire to contact you. Valentino, Valentino, we are the friendly ones. Valentino, Valentino, we desire to contact you." Suddenly several mediums began exclaiming that they saw Valentino, and reporters began asking the fortunate ones to describe the Great Lover. But strangely there seemed to be differences concerning this, for some saw him in a blue robe and smiling, and others claimed he was dressed in desert garb and glowering. One medium, trembling as if consumed by the ague, insisted the robe was white, and still another that Valentino was wearing his gaucho costume. Before the argument became too bitter, a lady medium shrilled that indeed it was his gaucho garb, and that Valentino had just invited her to tango. Curtseying with more verve than grace (she had been nipping generously from a little flask that she had filled at the bar), she joined Valentino on the floor—literally—but when she bent backward (possibly Rudy's attention was elsewhere) she hit the floor with a resounding thump. A sentimental chorus of lady mediums wept with her.

But the spotlight was not hers for long, because at that exact moment another medium shivered himself out of a trance to announce that Rudy was directly in front of him. "He's seated inside an electric bulb, which glows with his presence. But the bulb is made of ice."

The assembled sighed in awe, the reporters scribbled busily in their notebooks, and photographers started shooting like crazy in hopes of getting an exposure of Rudy inside the electric-light bulb. Urged to continue, the rapt medium obliged. "A light is shining through to bathe Rudy as he sits and looks down at the sole of his boot. And on the boot is inscribed 'My love is like a red, red rose.' "

As the Los Angeles *Daily News* reported the next day: "One medium, evidently confused by the tugging and hauling exerted on the spirit world by the galaxy of believers, said she saw Louis B. Mayer riding on a white horse, but this passed without confirmation."

With the proceedings on the verge of chaos, the Venerable Lokanatha brought everyone to heel by simply raising his right hand, which the assembly interpreted as an order for silence, along with his blessing. The assembled quickly regained their composure, restored the folds in their robes and concentrated again on the birthday cake.

"I see Rudy's dog! It is a noble beast," someone said suddenly.

Several others began to snap their fingers and to call out a variety of doggish names, including Buster, Tige and Here, Dog. "Kabar. That's the dog's name!" another announced in triumph. "Kabar is licking my face!"

But this animal lover almost immediately lost his audience when another, a lady, stamped her feet for attention and rose to proclaim that while everyone else had been concerned with the dog, Valentino had dictated a poem to her. It took little urging to get her to recite it, while the medium who had been licked by Kabar did what he could to upstage his colleague's act. Loudly he ordered Kabar to stand on his hind legs and to perform tricks, all of which he applauded loudly. But in a moment Mrs. McKinstry crossed the circle to whisper in the ear of the Venerable Lokanatha, who again raised his hand in blessing, then gestured toward a draped window. Many later swore they had seen Kabar leap through the closed draperies and the window, though the window glass remained intact. The lights were then raised and the lady medium proceeded to read her poem, which lauded the beauties of Falcon Lair. Only the reporter of *The New York Times* was unimpressed, for he noted that "the lines neither rhymed nor scanned, the only one worth repetition being the closing phrase: 'Why do you sing so loud and badly?' "

The poem had not been much of a success, and it was evident that the skeptical reporters and photographers, who insisted they had seen nothing, needed better proof that Valentino *was* present. Five of the most omnipotent then seated themselves in a smaller circle around a table, placed their hands on its top and attempted to levitate the heavy piece of furniture. They managed to move the table from side to side, but one leg always remained on the floor as they panted and strained. Meanwhile all the faithful chanted:

> *Raise the table, raise the table,*
> *Raise the table, Rudy dear.*
> *Raise the table, raise the table,*
> *Raise the table, Rudy dear.*

When even this failed, one of the levitaters explained "that the vibrations weren't correctly neutralized and it was useless to proceed further." So the table was retired and the lights dimmed and then everyone inhaled ecstatically after Mrs. Mc-Kinstry, the most important of the memsahibs, announced that the odor of desert perfume was filling the room. Some of the spiritualists began to roll their heads and babble as if under the influence of some other hallucinatory agent. And shortly the conduct of everyone became increasingly ecstatic and disorderly. Some began to twitch, sing and whirl like dervishes, while others imitated nautch dancers. One of the more extroverted ladies began to cooch about, and the irreverent young reporter who had referred to Rudy's bed as a sack forgot himself and began to clap his hands, whistle shrilly and shout, "Take it off, doll! Take it off!" His colleagues, many of them by now quite sodden with drink, felt as if they had been hit on the head with the old Howard Theater.

For all intents and purposes the seance was now over, and as Mrs. Carol McKinstry stood in front of the fireplace, over which hung a painting of the Sheik, candles were lighted in silver candelabra. In her hands she held a manuscript and when the house lights were dimmed, save for the candles, Attila von Sealay, a Hollywood portrait photographer, took her picture with infrared film.

When Mr. von Sealay later developed the film, a strange ball of light showed on the painting in the region of Rudy's heart, and a shaft of light from it appeared to point toward the manuscript held by Mrs. McKinstry. The Los Angeles *Herald Express* reproduced the photograph and interviewed von Sealay about it. "A remarkable coincidence to say the least," commented von Sealay, "since the manuscript, a novel of spirit life, was purportedly dictated to Mrs. McKinstry by Valentino through clairvoyance." The photograph was then submitted to experts, who suggested that the ball and beam of light were probably caused by light reflected from the painting but von Sealay thought otherwise. So did Mrs. McKinstry, and the photograph ended up as one of the more sacred objects in the Valentino cult of love.

Numerous accounts of the seance appeared in local and distant newspapers, most implying that the gathering had been pure bedlam, though others considered this an understatement. Mr. and Mrs. Buys were shortly visited by several angry representatives of the city, who had come at the request of the owners of surrounding property. Mrs. Buys promised to be a good neighbor and indeed permitted only one other seance the following year, after she had sold the house and she and her husband were about to return to San Francisco. Again the seance was conducted by Carol McKinstry, with Rudolph Florentino, garbed as a sheik and representing the Sons of Italy, acting as her attendant. Reporters did as bid and informed their readers that the costume worn by Florentino had belonged to the Great Lover, and it was hoped that this would serve as "an added touch to help persuade the film idol to return to his earthly residence." Before the seance began Mrs. McKinstry gave readings to the guests as Florentino hovered behind her, entranced, as she explained how important was the reappearance of Valentino to "thousands of lovelorn women whose only inspiration in life is the worship of his memory." At the conclusion of the seance, at which little of shattering impact occurred, Mrs. McKinstry announced a personal message from Valentino. "Rudy is here with a message for Gypsy Buys. He says don't despair, just keep faith."

It was several months later that Gerald Buys committed suicide.

In 1952, Mrs. McKinstry published her life's work, *The Return of Rudolph Valentino*. She had begun it in 1927, when she had astonished all Hollywood by announcing that since his death Valentino had occupied himself by dictating a screenplay to her. She had submitted *A Warning from out the Ages*, but not one of the studios had shown sufficient breadth of vision to recognize the treasure offered them. Determined, however, to give the swine another chance at the pearls, the two of them had undertaken a rewrite—for approximately twenty-five years.

The background of Carol McKinstry is impressive. In about 1921, she began her career in Binghamton, New York, where she founded and presided over the Universalist Spiritualist Church. During her residence there she lived in the old Corby castle, later purchased by George F. Johnson, the shoe manufacturer, who in turn left the castle to the county as an orphanage.

Carol McKinstry believed that the mysterious Otranto in which she lived intrigued Valentino's spirit and induced him to visit her first on the night of December 7, 1926, when they became fast friends as he discussed with her the American film, how it could be improved and what he believed would be the ideal story for the screen. Mrs. McKinstry was no fool; in her experience she had met spirits who were impostors, who had attempted to pass themselves off as the shades of important men and women. Therefore, she demanded some positive identification, and Valentino promised to provide it the very next night, when through her he would produce a screenplay that bore "the stamp of my personality."

True to his word, Valentino appeared the following evening and began dictating a screenplay entitled *A Warning from out the Ages*. His rapid dictation confused Mrs. McKinstry, so she covered her eyes with a black blindfold, the better to envision the scenes described by the spirit turned writer. But this created a problem, for she wrote uphill and downhill and could scarcely cross her *t*'s and dot her *i*'s. Mrs. McKinstry worked with Valentino for many months, during which he urged her to make their collaboration known. This Mrs. McKinstry did, even to informing the studios which actors and actresses Valentino wished cast in the screenplay. The studios, however, failed to purchase the completed work, but Mrs. McKinstry was not dismayed, for heathen, pagans and lip-service Christians seldom honored the literary inspiration of God, or His saints and prophets.

Early in 1927, Mrs. McKinstry moved her family to Washington, D.C., where she was ordained a full-fledged minister of the National Spiritualist Association by Fred W. Constantine, secretary of the New York State General Assembly of Spiritualism. Ordained to the ectoplasm, she threw herself with fervor into the work of the Longley Memorial Church, but also devoted herself to rewriting the screenplay with dialogue, since by this time talking pictures had come into being. A sad interruption to the work occurred on the morning of April 29, 1931, when the Reverend Carol McKinstry was arrested for telling fortunes without a license. She refused to plead guilty to the charge, for she would not be considered by the district commissioners in the same category as fortunetellers, then took her case into the courts and succeeded in winning an acquittal. Spiritualists acknowledge it was her dauntless courage and heroic efforts that bestowed upon them all the rights and privileges due an honorable faith; however, for the next five years court battles demanded all of her enormous energies. Valentino understood and did not resent this interruption of their collaboration, but on July 8, 1936, his spirit appeared to ask when they might begin work again. He also warned of the imminent death of Thomas Meighan, whom he had chosen as the lead in their moving picture.

Work was resumed, and the revision of the screenplay was completed in the fall of 1938. An actress, Miss Helene Vanderpoole Sinnott, helped Mrs. McKinstry to correct the spelling and the punctuation, and in general put the script into its final form. But the studio executives in far-off California did not hear opportunity, even when it knocked again. They were, alas, little men.

Carol McKinstry had resigned from the Longley Memorial Church in 1932, and in June of that year founded the Spiritualist Church of Psychic Science, which received its charter from the International General Assembly of Spiritualists; she maintained the connection for more than eight years. At that point, Mr. Perry McKinstry, her husband, suffered a stroke and she brought him to California to convalesce. But before she left, an undaunted Mrs. McKinstry, still in collaboration with Valentino, had begun to expand the screenplay into a novel. The first draft was finished in 1941, since Valentino, even as in life, proved to be a perfectionist and insisted upon rewriting chapter after chapter. By 1951, he informed Mrs. McKinstry that he had shown their work-in-progress to Shakespeare, Milton, Sir Walter Scott, James Fenimore Cooper, Louisa May Alcott,

Mrs. E.D.E.N. Southworth and Elinor Glyn, and in rare unanimity each of these literary giants had agreed the work was now ready for the world to see. Happily Mrs. McKinstry entered into correspondence with publishers, for it was her dream to use the enormous profits from the book to found the Valentino Memorial Church of Psychic Fellowship in Hollywood.

When she began to submit her manuscript to New York publishers, she included words of goodwill from an in-this-world critic, a Dr. Hereward Carrington, who beneath his signature identified himself as "Noted Researcher, Author, Lecturer, Scientist and World Recognized Authority on the Subconscious." Dr. Carrington recommended "Mrs. Carol McKinstry [as] a woman of integrity and sincerity," but even with this prestigious puff, and the undeniable fact that the work had been authored by the world's greatest lover, Mrs. McKinstry had to settle for a local vanity-press publisher. And as if an intellectual conspiracy prevailed, the book was ignored by the literary journals and those critics in whom the American public blindly put their trust.

The book deserves full discussion, for in the foreword, Valentino himself speaks:

Hail All! I, the spirit of Rudolph Valentino, greet you from the plane of my soul existence. Not from a great distance, as you might suppose, but closely interwoven and intermingling with the one upon which you are now functioning.

Although the names of the characters and the time and place differ, the novel actually consists of parallel stories whose characters and situations are similar. Thus Jack Ardath and Yohanna, the Arab dragoman, are one and the same; Corrine, Jack's sweetheart, is also Iris, the wife of Yohanna; and Ruth Daniels, an American artist, is likewise Leila, daughter of the sheik.

Jack and Corrine, who are childhood sweethearts, plan to marry. One day Jack and his father, both of whom work for the railroad, encounter the president and his dark-haired daughter, Ruth, who discreetly passes a card to Jack inviting him to visit her. Ruth is an artist and wishes to paint Jack as Apollo, but the sessions in her studio are also devoted to activities that make Jack a willing slave of illicit passion. Terribly smitten by Ruth, yet feeling guilty, too, Jack loses interest in Corrine, whose broken heart causes her to waste away. The prescient reader knows that Ruth will soon tire of our Jack, but he doesn't; and he abandons himself to the wildest joys of pure lubricity, which he imagines is love. Meanwhile, poor faithful Corrine is not far from death's door, and Corrine's mother, and even his own, beg Jack to return and plight his troth. But Jack is torn between two loves: one pure and innocent, the other tempestuous but so thrilling! Exhausted by his indecision, he falls asleep, "and with sleep [came] a dream and the remembrance of another life lived and loved in a day and age of long ago."

The reader now finds himself with Yohanna, and his blond Arab wife, Iris, who have just arrived at an oasis. Yohanna and Iris are quite happy, and very much in love with each other, until they learn that the local sheik, who has been planning a business trip across the desert, is unable to embark because his dragoman, or business manager, has suddenly become ill, and the other dragomen, believing the illness to be an evil omen, refuse to serve in his place. This superstitious ignorance incenses the sheik, who threatens to put them all to death, until Yohanna volunteers to lead his caravan across the burning sands. Iris is not happy about this; she's alone in a strange land. But Yohanna tells her she will be doing a fine thing by permitting him to leave her, for this will save the lives of the other men. Iris is almost persuaded, until she learns that the sheik's daughter, Leila, is going along for the camel ride, which sends Iris into an utter funk. Needless to say, Leila gets to Yohanna the first night out, and oddly she, too, is an artist whose pitch is that she wants to paint Yohanna's picture.

It is worth noting that in both stories the hero is a potent passive who is led astray by dark-haired women, both ready to cast him aside once they've enjoyed him. The reader is enchanted by much florid imagery and strong dialogue in the Arabian section.

"Yo-hum," the Sheik sighed audibly, "uprouse ye, children! 'twere time all honest folk were abed and thieves a-prowling."

Time passes, and Yohanna and the caravan return to the oasis. After much philosophical and religious discussion between Yohanna and Leila, and after she has introduced him to every delight advocated in Sheik Nefzawi's *Perfumed Garden,* she boots him out of her tent. Yohanna is sick with remorse, for on his return, his manservant, Saleem, informs him that Iris and her *mata* have gone into exile, and are determined to die in the desert. Sadly Yohanna realizes his mistake, and leaves in search of his true love, but when he finds her she is dead. . . .

Jack now awakens and swears a mighty oath. "Mother of Moses! . . . that was no dream! But what was it?"

Jack's dream, or whatever it was, has taught him not to repeat the mistake he made when he had been Yohanna, so he returns to Corrine, who has recovered sufficiently to marry him and bear his child. But the Three Fates—Clotho, Atropos and Lachesis—decide to interfere and, nudged by Clotho, Ruth Daniels decides to paint a portrait of the lovely son of Corrine and Jack. At first Corrine is thrilled. But when she is introduced to the artist and realizes who she is, she draws herself up proudly and denounces Ruth:

"I am Mrs. Jack Ardath, the wife of the man you painted as the Greek God Apollo—and this is his child. You may be a great artist, Ruth Daniels, but I know you to be a shameless, heartless, soulless, indecent woman. You nearly ruined both his life and mine—and you couldn't paint my child if you paid me a thousand dollars a sitting."

Such a tongue-lashing by an inferior compels Ruth to whip up a diabolical plot to kidnap the dear little one of Corrine and Jack. Her Hindu manservant, Chandra, balks at such villainy, but at last undertakes her instructions, paying one of the professional kidnappers to see that no harm really comes to the boy. At last the dastardly deed is accomplished, and when Ruth looks into a magic potion brought to her by the versatile Chandra, she sees the lad sitting on the railroad tracks as a steaming, snorting iron horse roars down the rails toward him. The sight is too much for Ruth and, overcome by remorse, she takes poison. If only she had known that Jack was driving the locomotive, and—through the telescope he always carried with him—would sight the obstruction in time! Turning the controls over to Jocko, his fireman, he clambers down the steaming, straining engine, and at the risk of his life, from the cowcatcher just over the thundering rails, scoops up the "wee-trespasser" in the nick of time.

Am I going too fast for you?

That night the little family rejoices, wonders grimly who could have kidnapped their son? Who might have wanted him dead? Fear clutches their hearts as they realize it could only have been that vengeful doxy Ruth Daniels, and they shudder, for now they will be safe nowhere, not even, Corrine says tremulously, "if we move to Kalamazoo!"

However, the morning newspaper carries headlines about Ruth Daniels' suicide and, soberly moralizing that money does not make for happiness, Jack and Corrine embrace.

The tale should now be at an end, but no, the reader is now transported to Limbo, where Ruth Daniels has been forced to take up residence since she took her own life. There she is revealed in serious dialogue with her manservant, Chandra, who, as the perceptive reader may have surmised, is not really a manservant at all, but a Hindu mystic and scholar of sacred lore. He implores her, before he returns to his beloved India, to rescue other souls lost in Limbo. And Ruth replies, "Real love never sins, nor loses its way, Chandra. Lest you forget, I remind you: Love was before the light began—when light is over, love shall be."

The tale inspires awe. Could Valentino, whose earthly compositions were all written by literary ghosts, have suddenly acquired real literary skills in the great Beyond? To answer this burning question, Mrs. McKinstry showed the manuscript to George Ullman, who read it and wrote her in 1940: "The substance of his message is more profound than his language to life, but his development can certainly be extremely marked during the years since he left us."

Mrs. McKinstry included this deposition at the end of the book:

A WARNING FROM OUT THE AGES
A
Psychic Consignment
from
Rudolph Valentino
by
The Reverend Carol E. McKinstry

To the public at large, I do hereby certify that this script titled, "A Warning From Out The Ages," was received through my clairvoyant and clairaudient faculties and scribed by my physical penmanship from the spirit of Rudolph Valentino.

REVEREND CAROL E. MCKINSTRY
1342 Gallatin St., N. W.
Washington, D.C.

Washington, D.C.
  Subscribed and sworn before me this 9th day of
January, 1939.
(Seal)

William Oppenstein
Notary Public
Commission expires Aug. 15, 1940

Notwithstanding Ullman's recommendation and this strong
legal manifest of authenticity by an important public official,
the motion picture industry still chose to ignore the work. But
what could be expected of former trumpet players, furriers,
glove manufacturers and their nepotic relatives? And if Carol
McKinstry's work was ignored by literateurs, it was enthusiastically hailed by the spiritualists. In a frenzy of vibrations
they attempted to raise funds to produce the film themselves,
for Mrs. McKinstry told her followers that she had discussed
this with Valentino and he had been so touched, so moved, he
had wept. Enthusiasm and courage never flagged, but dollars
in sufficient number could not be raised.

Mrs. McKinstry despaired because she was mortal, but, being
mortal, understood how difficult it was for those who had neither
the gift of sight nor the faith to believe in what they were
unable to see or touch. There was still work to be done, and
Mrs. McKinstry continued to meet with those of the faithful
who had not lost courage because her book had failed. They
helped her carry on the good work and her sibylline pronouncements gave them faith. Valentino would yet return to usher in
the World of Romance. And when her "Wednesday Nights"
outgrew her little apartment on Carleton Way, she rented a room
in the Masonic Temple on Hollywood Boulevard, next door to
the Paramount Theater and just across the street from Grauman's Chinese.

The services conducted by Reverend McKinstry were simple
and dignified. She would appear in a vintage-twenties evening

gown, which in its day had been quite beautiful, and perhaps a long black satin cape and a Hindu headband. In lieu of an invocation, Mrs. McKinstry would begin with a meditative poem, with occasional responses from her congregation. A voluntary contribution entitled a communicant to ask three questions, to be written on small slips of paper, folded and initialed. These were collected by an assistant and Reverend McKinstry would then reveal the question without seeing the slip of paper, and answer it. Her eyes were always closed during this part of the ceremonies, and occasionally she might call out that some spirit had come to visit them and sent regards to a particular person in the audience. These meetings were never as interesting as those held by Mrs. McKinstry in her own apartment.

In a recent letter, a man who attended several of these "Wednesday Nights" on Carleton Way remembered that:

> McKinstry would start the sessions with a recording of Valentino singing the Kashmiri Song, which was rather worn and scratchy. Between the living room and the dining room hung a little glass wind chime from which was suspended a small cardboard obelisk, one side of which was painted red and the other green. Sometimes, during a seance, the wind chime would shake violently and McKinstry would cry: "Oh, Rudy's here!" and we would all turn to the chime. She would then ask questions which could be answered by "yes" and "no" and the obelisk would rotate from "green" to "red," sometimes whirling strangely until it finally settled on one or the other.

Carol McKinstry died in September, 1963; she was in her seventies and had never seen her dream fulfilled, for she had begun losing her position of eminence in 1952, after her book had failed so miserably. That year—1952—there seemed little strength left in the official ranks of the spiritualists devoted to Valentino; Americans of the fifties tended more toward barbecues and color television sets, and when they did worship, it was at the altars of the young gods and goddesses of television.

But the torch borne by the Valentino cultists was never extinguished; its weak flame was merely taken from the hands of the spiritualists and for some years to come would be carried by the Lady in Black, who headed the other branch of the new religion.

ACT FIVE: SCENE THREE
THE LADY IN BLACK

Noted actors and actresses died before Valentino and important ones have died since, but no other star has ever been accorded the international honor of an annual commemorative service on the day of his death, and certainly no other ever inspired an adult cult of worshipers complete with clergy. This deification and worship of Valentino are wondrous but understandable.

True, the commemorative service of 1927 attracted only about two hundred of the faithful, and no important movie mimes or film executives were among those gathered together to honor the dead star. In 1928, there were even fewer of the faithful, but 1929 saw an increase in attendance and the strong fervor, expressed without embarrassment, made the press look forward to 1930.

The press had not hoped in vain; 1930 was a vintage year,

for "Aspiration" was dedicated in De Longpré Park as part of the annual commemorative service. And at the anniversary observance a year later, headlines were not concerned with rites conducted at the crypt but with the person of a lady dressed in black, complete with veils that completely hid her features, who made her first public appearance in De Longpré Park to grieve and pray in silence as she knelt before "Aspiration." Although this mysterious female was unaccompanied, local newspapers had been tipped off, and reporters and photographers rushed to the park for interviews and explanations. However, the Lady in Black—as she was dubbed by the press—maintained silence, rejecting all bribes to reveal her identity, and answering all questions with a cryptic shaking of her veils, eluded reporters by escaping in a waiting limousine of compatible black.

In New York City, the *Graphic,* sensing another circulation builder, went to work to uncover her identity—an undertaking in which it was not alone. The *Graphic* prided itself on having the world's most complete file on Valentino, and a knowledge of every woman he had ever known in Europe and the United States. But all were unable to identify the Lady in Black, and her identity remained unknown until 1938, at which point she had proliferated to Ladies in Black, for there were times when as many as a dozen claimants appeared, either at the crypt or at the site of "Aspiration." It became impossible to tell them apart since all maintained their silence—even when confronted by their spurious sisters. And just when it began to appear, in 1938, as if she might join the Easter Island statues as one of mankind's unexplained mysteries, Russell Birdwell, one of Hollywood's foremost and most imaginative publicists, revealed that the Lady in Black had actually been his invention.

In his early creative career Birdwell had produced three films: *Street Corners, Main Stem* and *The Only Normal Man in Hollywood,* the last featuring a normal but misanthropic hermit who fled the bright lights and tinsel of Hollywood for the idyllic solitude of the Hollywood Hills—and a lady veiled in black. Birdwell and his cameraman had searched the area for interesting outdoor shots and one day had come upon "Aspiration" in its lily pond. He had decided that a dramatic vignette could be evolved about a mysterious woman who mourned Valentino, and a five-dollar-a-day extra was clad in weeds and instructed to approach "Aspiration" and mourn silently until the scene ended. After the film was completed, a narration was dubbed in (Birdwell was also the narrator) which explained that the mysterious woman appeared annually, just before the sun set on the day Valentino had died. A local student of literature might wonder if perchance Birdwell had ever read Nathaniel Hawthorne's "The Minister's Black Veil."

Some years later, Birdwell gave up films and returned to the newspaper field, where he found employment with Hearst's Los Angeles *Herald Express*. To his astonishment, he was called in by his editor, James H. Richardson, and ordered to do a feature story on the Lady in Black and, if possible, to discover her identity. Dutifully, like any good reporter, he went to De Longpré Park and to his surprise discovered not one lady in mourning, maintaining a silent vigil at the statue, but another as well. A little investigation revealed what had happened: the extra had so enjoyed the role created for her by Birdwell, the attention of spectators and all the press, that year after year she had rented the same costume, purchased her own flowers, hired a getaway limousine and gone through the same act with embellishments of her own invention. Of course, she rather resented her imitator but what could she do? Birdwell had not patented the role; there was no law against any nut dressing up in black and getting a lot of cheap publicity by mourning Valentino.

Each year newspapers would look forward to the anniversary of Valentino's death to discover whether the Lady in Black would again appear. It was on August 23, 1937, that the second Lady in Black appeared at Valentino's crypt. As reported by the Los Angeles *Times*, "She, too, wore unrelieved black, was veiled and silent as the one who had mourned the dead each August 23, each Christmas, and each Easter for years. She, too, knelt in silent prayer before the flower-banked plaque that reads: 'Rudolph Guglielmi Valentino, 1895–1926.' And she also disappeared quietly before anyone could find her name or the reason for her visit."

To the disappointment of the press, the two failed to meet in direct confrontation. The first Lady had brought red roses, the second had deposited a more formal wreath on the crypt, and for days thereafter the press speculated widely. In 1938 both again made their appearance, and Russell Birdwell broke his silence. But the explanation was ignored by the faithful, the sensation seekers and the curious, even the press, because the myth and its mystery were far more entertaining.

In 1939 there were three and in 1940 the drama of the services at the crypt was heightened by the appearance of Jean Acker and five, possibly six, others. Miss Acker was the star that year, however, for it was the first time she had visited the crypt. She carried a huge bouquet of cut red rosebuds, Rudy's favorite bloom, and she placed her floral offering in a vase in front of the crypt, meditated silently and left without comment "except to say that she had wanted her visit to be as quiet as possible, explaining that she had called cemetery officials to learn if all the photographers had departed." There is no record of the reply to Miss Acker's queries, but a photographer of the Los Angeles *Times* happened to be there and Miss Acker posed most graciously.

Before Miss Acker's arrival, another of the Ladies in Black had appeared at the cemetery gates at six in the morning, an hour before the gates opened officially. This early bird, who had arrived by taxi, was garbed entirely in black, including a veil, but wore white-rimmed sunglasses—evidently to assure her privacy and make her appear inconspicuous—under her veil. Leo Rosten noted, in *Hollywood* (1941), that the wearing of sunglasses provided "a solution to the movie star's dilemma who yearned for anonymity on the street but not so complete an anonymity he [or she] would fail to be recognized." Such novel blinders concealed the identity, yet attracted attention; they identified the wearer as a movie star, but which movie star remained secret. When waitresses and extras took up the fad, however, Hollywood became a baffling morass of celebrities.

The cemetery gates were opened at seven and the sunglassed Lady in Black placed a basket of mixed roses at the mausoleum door, lingering only long enough to cooperate with photographers. She posed as often as requested but refused to reveal herself, and when the mausoleum was officially opened at eight she disappeared. The Los Angeles *Times,* which covered Miss Acker's visit fully, and carried a photograph of the Lady in Black in her spectacular white-framed sunglasses, also reported the appearance of five others. The article reiterated that the Lady in Black had begun as a publicity stunt, but no one seemed to care.

A delightful aside is that some reporters for a number of large eastern newspapers had been celebrating their exile too strenuously the night before and, so badly hung over the next morning as to be unwilling to venture into a Hollywood cemetery, they solved their problem by dressing one of their playmates in the appropriate costume and, in the privacy of their hotel suite, took cheesecake photographs and sent them on to their papers with imaginative accounts of doings at the crypt.

Also worthy of recording in this 1940 memorial celebration was the delivery of a dome-shaped floral piece complete with a picture of Rudy dressed as a sheik. A taffeta ribbon stamped with gold letters bore the legend "Rudy from Ditra."

Ditra proved to be Ditra Flame, the leader and guiding

spirit of the Valentino memorial groups in Hollywood, but not the wearer of the white-rimmed sunglasses. In 1941 Miss Flame did appear as a Lady in Black. Our entry into the war diverted many women into essential industry, but a sufficient number was left to assure at least a dozen, and sometimes as many as two dozen participants in the rites of love at Valentino's tomb and in De Longpré Park between 1942 and 1945. Most of these were uninspired, imitative in their showmanship, and reporters allotted most of their coverage to Ditra Flame and the one who had distinguished herself in 1940 by wearing white-rimmed sunglasses. On November 10, 1945, this lady was stripped of her anonymity when she was identified by a banner headline in the Los Angeles *Herald Express:* LADY IN BLACK TRIES DEATH.

She was identified as Marian E. Wilson, whom Valentino had known as Marian Benda, the Follies beauty he had taken to the fatal Warburton party where he had collapsed. Marian, recently divorced from Dr. Blake H. Watson of Los Angeles, had taken sixty-eight sleeping pills. Before lapsing into unconsciousness, she had been discovered by her cousin, Perry Combs, a former runner-up for the title of Mr. America, and rushed to the Santa Monica Hospital, where her stomach was pumped out and her condition pronounced "fair."

When Marian recovered sufficiently to be interviewed by reporters, she made several startling announcements: she was the sole original authentic Lady in Black, and the only one who had the right to the claim since she had known Valentino *intimately*. How intimately? Intimately enough, she assured the reporters; in 1925 she had married Valentino in New Jersey. The marriage had been kept secret, though she had borne him two children. The first, a daughter, still lived in England, and the second, a son, had been raised in Italy, and undertaken military service in Ethiopia where he had been killed. These were sensational disclosures, so the reporters scurried to George Ull-

man's office for a statement. Ullman listened and denied there
had been any such marriage.

"Rudy dated her from time to time, but I'm sure there was
no marriage. As for her having a child by Rudy, there are
thirty-five women who advance that claim. I believe that had
Valentino married her, I, occupying the position I did in his
life, would certainly have known of the event. He squired her
about New York on a few occasions, but their relationship was
both short and formal."

Ullman's denial did not discomfort the attempted suicide, who
clung to her story: she was Valentino's widow and the only
mother of his children. She swore she had married Valentino
in France. When reporters pointed out that she had first said
New Jersey, she retorted that sixty-eight sleeping pills taken at
one time could confuse anyone. They had been married in
France after she had been introduced to Rudy by Ben Ali
Haggin, a Hollywood promoter, and though reporters continued
to be skeptical, readers seemed to be interested, so the reporters
dug deeper. Neighbors were interviewed, and one and all agreed
that Marian had told them about her marriage, and that their
pretty redheaded neighbor had made these claims while sober.
She had even sworn to this on the Bible, and her eyes had
neither rolled nor glittered, which seemed sufficient evidence of
sincerity and veracity.

She was released after she had spent one day in the hospital,
and en route to the home of friends in North Hollywood, granted
another interview, in which she denied being the Lady in Black.
However, she would not retract her claim to the name Mrs.
Rudolph Valentino; she had been the third and most beloved
wife of the silent screen's greatest lover. "I suggest you look up
the records in New Jersey," she told newsmen, and when another
newsman reminded her about France, Miss Benda continued as
if he had not interrupted: "Valentino and I were married in

1925, but I never told anyone, because I was afraid the knowledge of a third wife might disillusion the millions of movie fans who adored him. 'When you belong to the public, you are the servant of their whims and illusions,' Rudy often told me. 'You must give them what they pay for at the box office and a married great lover doesn't somehow measure up to their demands.' "

Asked to explain why the marriage had been kept secret after Valentino's death, Marian replied that she had never revealed it because "of the shameful way Hollywood exploited the tragedy. Our daughter was born just before Rudy died. She lives with friends in the British Empire and has never been to this country."

Reporters, like old ladies, are inclined to be prying and not above using their fingers in tallying up certain important intervals of time. If they accepted Marian's statement as true, Valentino had not only been a singularly unusual man in his marriages, for there was strong belief that he had never consummated either, but also singularly unusual in his bigamies; he had married Natacha before his divorce decree from Jean Acker had become final, and if Marian was telling the truth, he had married her before Natacha had received her French divorce. In any other community, reliability is tied to facts and figures, but this is not necessarily true in Hollywood and its suburbs, where the average movie fan cannot conceive of any great emotion or staggering event being meaningful unless it is accompanied by appropriate thematic music. What Marian claimed was intriguing, mysterious, romantic, and certainly fitted the life pattern of a Great Lover. A Nietzschean *Übermensch* would never have been restricted by the mores and folkways of modern western society. Furthermore, despite the conflict in dates and places of marriage and ages of the children, there was the testimony of the neighbors, good simple people without guile. They believed her, and added to this was the corroborating testimony of Perry Combs, who swore that Miss Benda "had married Valentino and had for almost two decades appeared at his mausoleum on each anniversary of his death."

Marian Benda's marital history was indeed interesting: she claimed, after she had been widowed by Valentino's death and had mourned him a respectful length of time, to have married Bill Wise, a golf professional, and still later married Baron Rupprecht von Boecklin, who had settled $230,000 on her after their divorce, in 1934. In 1941 she had divorced Dr. Watson. Marian then decided she had had enough of matrimony; and to keep busy had established a dog kennel and a model agency. Both occupations were sensible and sane, and seemingly kept her in sound financial circumstances. In digging through their morgues, reporters discovered that Marian had arrived in New York in 1924, from Oklahoma City. With her beauty, she naturally had gravitated to the theater. There she had met William Benda, creator of the famed Benda masks featured in the Ziegfeld *Follies*, and shortly thereafter Benda announced he had found the perfect model for his masks. He asked Marian to change her name for professional purposes, and within a year she became one of the most famed and highest paid of the Ziegfeld beauties. In 1927, Mayor James J. Walker had named her "Miss New York," and included her in the official party to greet Charles Lindbergh upon his return from Paris after his famous nonstop flight. Who could say that so famous a beauty had not married Valentino?

After Miss Benda's recovery she was besieged by clairvoyants and spiritualists to join *their* groups as a follower, or if she preferred, even as a high priestess, but the former showgirl refused all such offers. Firm in her belief that she was Valentino's third wife and the mother of his children, she preferred to mourn him as a true widow should—alone. Despite her previous denial of ever being a Lady in Black, Marian showed up again at the Valentino crypt on August 23, 1946, an appearance that received even more attention than had her second attempt at suicide, again by sleeping pills, on April 19, 1946. On January 21, 1947, Marian once more attempted suicide and was found unconscious in the room of a hotel where she had registered as Mrs. J. O'Brien. She recovered consciousness at Los Angeles General Hospital, received standard medical treatment and was released to the care of friends. She then retired into obscurity and reporters noted that in 1947 and 1948 she was not among the "celebrities" at Valentino's crypt. She escaped the newspapers' attention until March 29, 1949, when she was the subject of a hearing before Superior Judge William J. Byrne. The week before, she had once again attempted suicide, this time by slashing her wrists; a psychiatric report, with recommendations for her care, was being prepared for Judge Byrne.

The hearing was held in the hospital ward and Miss Benda presented a pathetic appearance. Without makeup, her dark-red hair unkempt, and dressed in the ill-fitting nightgown that is hospital issue, she could hardly be visualized as one of the most famous of Ziegfeld's former showgirls. Judge Byrne read and evaluated the report of the hospital psychiatrists, weighed the findings and ordered Marian Benda committed to a mental institution, where she would be treated as a county ward. For Marian was penniless; of the $230,000 received in her second divorce settlement, and the $25,000 she received as alimony after her divorce from her third husband, nothing remained.

By the end of 1951, Marian Benda was judged sufficiently recovered to be released, and took an apartment in Beverly Hills. That her release had been premature soon became evident, for in May of that year she took another overdose of sleeping pills. Again she was processed through hospitalization and released. A year and a half later, Marian—now forty-five and of a faded appearance, but still insistent that she was Valentino's widow and the mother of his children—was arrested on a narcotics charge and jailed at Lincoln Heights. By this time the police realized she had become addicted to sleeping pills, and she might not have been removed to jail had she not fought the orderlies at the Hollywood Receiving Hospital. Her last arrest occurred on November 23, 1951, and a week later Perry Combs forced open the door of the furnished room where she had moved after her release from Lincoln Heights Jail and found his cousin dead. It had taken her almost six years to determine the number of pills necessary to accomplish her death. What had caused her emotional and mental deterioration has never been established, but it is not perhaps rash to suggest that at some time after Valentino's death, when she had insisted that Pola Negri was not Rudy's true love, she had come to believe more and more that Valentino had loved her and would have married her if he had lived.

The death of Marian Benda removed her from the Hollywood scene, and from the crypt in the cemetery and the pedestal of "Aspiration" in De Longpré Park. But her death did not significantly diminish the number of Ladies in Black, for she had not been their acknowledged leader even while she lived. That honor had long been accorded Ditra Flame (pronounced Flamay), who had combined her career of public mourning with vigorous leadership of the Hollywood Valentino Memorial Guild, where she was the moving spirit behind an organization that occasionally made slight alterations in its name but never in its purpose. Actually, Ditra Flame built her claim on solid ground, and by 1947 was ready for her role as the Supreme Leader of Marathon Mourning.

On August 23, 1947, after some years as just another anonymous Lady in Black, Ditra arrived at the crypt at 12:10 P.M., the exact hour and minute of Valentino's death twenty-one years before. Clad in a black dress with white sleeves and an unveiled white hat, she carried a sizable bouquet of marigolds and asters. After shedding her anonymity and positively identifying herself as Ditra Flame, she entered the cul-de-sac where Valentino's body lies in the Mathis family crypt, and made the first of her weighty pronouncements: "I knew him years ago," she said. "I've been keeping the vigil since 1926." Miss Flame then removed a mourner's veil from her purse, draped it over her white hat, lowered herself into a chair beside the vault and obliged everyone by posing for photographs. "I am president of the Hollywood Valentino Memorial Guild," she confided to the press. "We keep alive his memory. I have one of the most extensive Valentino picture collections in existence."

After the photographers had completed their shots, Miss Flame rose from her chair, doffed her veil and prepared to offer her flowers. Since there were red dahlias in the vases attached to the face of Valentino's crypt, she tastefully arranged her marigolds and asters in receptacles attached to neighboring vaults. "In fact we plan to open offices in Hollywood this fall and eventually to erect a shrine to honor him—a place for meditation. The motto of the Guild is 'Vita brevis, ars vivet aeternum—'Life is short, art lives forever.' "

Ditra then completed her reverences and announced that she would spend the rest of her days in her study, at work on *her* book. In 1948 Miss Flame arrived at the memorial park in a taxi; in 1949 she was driven there by a chauffeur in a standard black limousine. That year she affected heavier mourning; her head was swathed in a thick black veil held in place by a chin strap, the only touch of color to relieve this sobriety being a coronet of satin roses worn over her veil to match the bouquet in her arms.

Gleefully, because they enjoyed stirring a little trouble into the rites, reporters informed Ditra she had not been the first Lady in Black to appear. Earlier, Ida Smeraldo, who had identified herself as a native of Castellaneta, had kept an hour-long rendezvous before the crypt and left a funeral spray of gladiolas and asters. Also, a representative of the English Valentino Memorial Guild had left urns of red and white carnations. But Miss Flame ignored these warnings, for her faithful had earlier advised her that both had been received indifferently by the spectators. Everyone's spirits perked up visibly when Miss Flame removed the flowers already in the vases, flung them to the four winds and replaced them with her satin roses. She signed several autograph books and returned to her limousine, where her chauffeur had been passing out handbills announcing a Valentino memorial program to be held by the Guild at eight that night. Ceremonies would include a showing of *The Son of the Sheik*.

As Miss Flame drove off, another car approached, skidding to an abrupt stop. A policeman on special duty at the mausoleum hurried over to interrogate the driver, because Miss Flame had reported to the press and the authorities several threatening phone calls warning her not to visit the crypt. But the car proved to be friendly and presented reporters with sheet music of a song entitled "Candlelight," composed by Ditra and with lyrics taken from a poem by Rudolph Valentino dedicated to Ditra Flame. The publisher of this musical opus was Whimsy, Ltd., and the distributor, Lady in Black Publications. The back page carried information about Miss Flame's plan for a memorial, the Valentino Memorial Wedding Chapel, "dedicated to the memory of the twentieth-century symbol of romance—Valentino."

Ditra's appearance at the crypt, the threats of bodily harm, her new song and the memorial services on the evening of August 23 were all so successful that they prompted Reed Porter to include an interview with Ditra Flame in the series he was doing on Valentino for the Los Angeles *Mirror*. His interview with Ditra appeared on August 26, 1949, and is quite remarkable.

. . . on the day of his death in 1926, she was a girl of 18. At 10:10 A.M., which would have been 12:10 in New York City, she sat down in Sanford, Colo., where she was visiting with relatives, to write to her mother in Bakersfield, Calif.

She put pen to paper. "Dear Mother," she wrote. . . .

SUDDENLY, THE WORDS THAT WERE APPEARING ON PAPER WERE NOT OF HER CREATING.

Her hand and pen were writing them but they were not her thoughts. This was what she found had been written:

"I am free. My epitaph unwritten by the hand of man is found and you have found it. For this accept my deepest appreciation—from here on SEE."

Suddenly the room in which Ditra sat was filled with an overpowering perfume, unmistakably oleander. Ditra and her aunt, who had then come into the room, searched for a broken perfume bottle but none could be found. Then suddenly Ditra remembered! Oleander was the flower Valentino had loved above all. Later that day Ditra learned of Valentino's death in New York. His spirit had immediately communicated with her, and since that sad but wonderful day Ditra Flame had had "frequent contact" with Rudy. Before Porter left Miss Flame, she gave him a poem "written by the Great Lover," which she wished to share with readers of the *Mirror*.

TO A PRESSED FLOWER
How beautiful you were in your fullness.
How sweet your perfumed breath.
How many people can recall your fragrance?
They only see you as you are now—
Your petals faded and your perfume lost.
How easy it is to forget beauty
Once it has passed from before your eyes.

Each year Miss Flame's Guild presented a memorial tribute at which she presided. No admission was ever charged, although love offerings were welcomed. At a typical service Miss Flame might wear a regal, flowing black velvet gown, with a Valentino locket at her throat and a silver crucifix on her girdle. The evening would be opened by readings from the manuscript of her book, *The Miracle of Valentino,* followed by stereoptic projections of Valentino in his various roles. Then there were usually performances by singers and dancers, metaphysical pantomimes and interpretative ballets, the music composed by Ditra Flame but inspired by the Great Lover.

In 1950, local and national media commented on the annual services at the cemetery and Guild Hall but only the Los Angeles *Times* bothered to report Alberto's visit to the crypt. He had left floral offerings in the urns, which Miss Flame had removed and replaced with her own sixteen roses, to commemorate her sixteenth birthday, when she had received a heart-shaped locket marked simply "To Ditra from Dolpho. Always remember this day."

The next year, 1951, marked the twenty-fifth anniversary of Valentino's death, and noble and wondrous ceremonies had been planned. But to the extreme annoyance of Miss Flame, she was confronted by two young Hollywood hopefuls who had arrived early at the crypt, where they were making a strong attempt to steal the show. John Wayne Caler, an eighteen-year-old drama student who aspired to Valentino roles, and Josee Metrick, seventeen and also a student of the drama, had dressed as gaucho and Spanish flamenco dancer respectively. It is always difficult to compete with youth, especially when it is brash, but Miss Flame was equal to the occasion. For she appeared with a dozen red roses, a single white rose and a draped oil portrait executed by Ray Richards of Valentino as the Sheik. Another disciple bore a small bronze bust, which he gave to Ditra after the portrait had been hung and unveiled.

It was indeed a banner year. After John and Josee left, additional Ladies in Black had put in an appearance, and even Tony Dexter had stopped by. "Right off the set of his next picture!" a studio man announced proudly to the reporters. But even more notable was a Swiss yodeler and spiritualist,

Amana Tannerose, who delivered herself of some strong phil-
ippics against "insincere persons" before she launched into a
spirited description of how she had met Valentino ten years
ago "up there." She had been introduced to him by no less a
spirit than Omar Khayyám. Amana asked for permission to
sing, and when it was refused, sang anyway—"In the Sweet
Bye and Bye."

Miss Flame fainted, but not before she testily removed some
flowers another woman in black had set in the two vases flanking
her idol's tomb. After being revived and regaining her composure, she sighed and said, "I know they'll say this was a
publicity stunt. But it really isn't. I really was overcome with
it all." As she departed, a song plugger passed out copies of
"Candlelight."

The following week Alberto Guglielmi and his son Jean demanded "an end to the disgraceful display which takes place
annually at Rudy's tomb," and warned "that legal steps would
be taken to prevent a repetition of the slapstick such as was
exhibited last Thursday." They had actually consulted an attorney, who believed they had cause for action. "Fainting spells,
black veils, limousines with chauffeurs and sheik costumes are
certainly out of place at the tomb. We have always kept in the
background, but even on the anniversaries of Rudy's death, the
family has not been able to pay its respects at his tomb because
we would have become involved in the degrading carnivals that
take place there."

Ditra Flame must have agreed, because at her next anniversary appearance at the crypt, she emphasized, "I was the original Lady in Black, and for many years I came to mourn quietly.
Then a lot of phonies started coming." Although Ditra made
her statement about "phonies" loudly enough to be heard by
everyone, a Lady in White refused to go away. To whose who
had not met her the year before, she introduced herself again
as Amana Tannerose, and revealed to a conventicle of reporters

that her mellifluous name had been bestowed upon her in the eleventh century by Omar Khayyám, whom she had not seen again until nine hundred years later, when he had introduced her to Rudy. Amana then informed the reporters of the thrilling spirit visit she had had from Valentino at seven in the morning the previous day, during which he had asked her to announce to the world that he desired peace proclaimed among nations. His parting words had been: "Farewell, my friends—peace prevail within your souls."

By 1953, a number of the Valentino cults and cultists were either dead, dying or on the verge of being dispersed. The 1951 sale of Falcon Lair to Robert Balzer, and his resale of this holy shrine to Doris Duke, had put the Lair beyond the reach of cultists. Also contributory was the failure of Carol McKinstry's vanity-press book to arouse interest at the studios, as well as the bitter squabbling among cultists, after the book failed, as to whether Valentino had *really* written it. It revealed a chink in the orthodoxy that had previously united the ranks of the faithful. Besides, the people with fervor, those who make the best cultists, had suddenly become interested in flying saucers and their elaborately uniformed grotesques. There were still Valentino evangelists in Hollywood who attempted to recruit new members from such groups as the defunct Kingdom of Yahweh, Mankind United and the Great I-Am cults, but such cultists usually offered their energies to some other, more respectable metaphysical organization, such as The Self-Realization Fellowship, whose gentle leader, Paramhansa Yogananda, had died in 1952. Others, feeling the passing of time in their bones, transferred their allegiance to the Townsend-George McLain elderly movement, or something similar, which strove to make aged pensioners economically important.

The danger was evident to the dedicated Valentinoites in Hollywood: If the influence of their headquarters continued to decline, some distant missionary group might overthrow the

Hollywood leaders and move the seat of worship elsewhere. Who would be left to keep the annual vigil at the crypt? Who would be left to communicate with Valentino and comfort him in eternity, where he wept because romantic epics of the desert had degenerated into what the studios, and even a cynical public, called "tits and sand" movies? So 1953 was a year of decision for Valentino's dwindling number of followers. Ditra Flame exhorted her faithful few, and those of rival groups, to join her in proving the strength of their faith. At two minutes before the appointed hour of noon on the next anniversary, a limousine rolled up to the portals of the mausoleum, a chauffeur in black uniform opened the door and Miss Flame, confident that her appeal had been heard and taken to heart, made her grand entrance. To her dismay, no more than threescore of the faithful had assembled—if one chose to include the troublesome Lady in White.

Still, the ceremonies had to go on, so Ditra adjusted her veil and the folds of her black dress and, with two dozen red roses in her arms, entered the marble halls and hurried to the alcove where the body of the Great Lover rested in the Mathis crypt. Quickly Miss Flame arranged her roses in the twin urns on the crypt and stepped back so the photographers could take her picture beneath a stained-glass window. Noonday sirens began to wail, and Miss Flame lifted her veil to begin her eulogy.

"Ladies and gentlemen, we are here to honor the memory of a great artist."

She read firmly, and with conviction, pausing occasionally to finger a rosary that dangled from her left wrist as she compared Valentino with Byron and Caruso, in whose immortal company he rightly belonged. "To many he was only an actor with grease paint on his face. But to others, he was the epitome of romance. He wanted his name to ring around the world, and to awaken love."

As the Los Angeles *Times* reported the event, it held elements of true human sadness: "Ditra Flame then distributed her remaining roses among the crowd and went back to her waiting limousine with the demeanor of one who had accomplished a mission."

But even Ditra Flame realized that the flame was burning low, and this most prominent of Ladies in Black, this most faithful of Valentino cultists, agreed that this would be the year of her farewell. However, before she retired from the scene, leaving the field wide to fakes, starlets and kooks, Ditra determined to make her farewell as a Lady in White. True to her resolve, she did appear in white, with a blue cape draped over her right shoulder. In the company of George A. Harris, vice president of her ailing Guild, she charged that the occasion for her annual pilgrimage to Valentino's crypt had become tarnished, and sensationalized by people who were far from couth. As a result, she had decided to surrender her life to God because He needed faithful servants in this world of crisis. "Rather than weep for those who have departed," she said, "let us weep for lost souls." Ditra had joined the Rose of Sharon Evangelical Ministry, and under the auspices of that organization would continue her labors.

After Ditra's farewell appearance, the Valentino memorial services lost their zing; the pageantry and pathos of former years had departed with her. True, on every anniversary of Valentino's death, the Troupers, the Masquers and Benevolent Thespians, several Italian organizations and those who still claim to represent important Valentino associations or guilds continue to make an appearance. James Kirkwood usually delivers the eulogy for the Masquers, and Belle Martel speaks for the Troupers and Benevolent Thespians. In 1959, a new Lady in Black appeared at the services and her presence was reported by the Los Angeles *Mirror,* but newspaper photographers were uninterested, and did not bother to photograph her. Rather, the press noted that most of the old regulars who had appeared during the first twenty years of services were now gone. Only a handful remained. Some reporters conjectured that the faithful of years, no longer present, were with Valentino in his great tent in the sky from which they looked down upon Hollywood Memorial Park. Edward F. O'Connor, Jr., of United Press International, concluded that at some future time, a " 'mysterious lady in black' might show up again and if unmasked, she might even turn out to be a teenager."

To all intents and purposes the Lady in Black was finished, and no more mention was made of her until January, 1961, when Paul Coates of the Los Angeles *Mirror* devoted two columns to Ditra Flame. As Coates organized his material and reported Miss Flame's statement, she had been one of the mourners who had filed past Rudy's bier when he lay in state at Campbell's Funeral Church. Although in past years reporters had counted the number of blossoms Miss Flame carried and found their number varied, Coates reported that "FOR HIM, she always took thirteen roses—a dozen red ones and one stark white."

Coates, by the way, agreed with Miss Flame's contention that there had been a Lady in Black *before* 1930, when the next had sprung full grown, like Minerva from the brow of Jupiter, out of the fertile imagination of Russell Birdwell. By this time, however, no reporter or Hollywood historian disputed Birdwell's creation. It had lived more than a full generation and by fission split to become two, then four, then eight, then as many as the population could support, enjoy or tolerate. Nevertheless, Coates reported that "In black dress, black stockings, black shoes, black hat and heavy black veil, [Ditra] made the daily journey to the star's crypt at Hollywood Memorial Park Cemetery for nearly three years after his death." If true, it is quite odd, for Roger Peterson, whose cemetery assignment was the mausoleum that housed the Valentino crypt, identified the original Lady in Black as "very poor. . . . Her husband left her several years ago with a small child to support. She earns all she can by doing housework of the hardest sort. . . . I knew she would like to meet Alberto, so I made a point of introducing them. When I told him how she came regularly to bring flowers, he thanked her graciously."

Miss Flame was also reported by Coates as being "a concert violinist and pianist," but the lady never cited dates or the sites of her performances or how they were received by the public and musicologists. Now that she was again in Los Angeles, she told Coates about the resumption of her private visits to Valentino's tomb; she went there in simple dress and at such times as she could be certain of a private and uninterrupted communion with the Great Lover. Miss Flame also told Coates that she had first met Valentino "at the home of mutual friends." However, earlier, on August 24, 1950, when Miss Flame was interviewed by the Los Angeles *Examiner,* she told the press that she had "met Valentino in 1919, when he was an unknown in a Valencia Street rooming house." And in 1949, when she had been interviewed by Reed Porter of the Los Angeles *Mirror,* she had neglected to mention a journey to the Funeral Church to view Rudy lying in the Gold Room.

After their first meeting in 1919, as described by Paul Coates, Ditra explained how they had become fast friends, and that Rudy had called her Sorellina, which meant "little sister." "It's true that we used to hike together in the Hollywood Hills. Sometimes we'd sit on the hillside and listen to concerts at the Hollywood Bowl. We'd sit there listening and looking at the stars."

It is here that Miss Flame's lovely tale of friendship with the Great Lover falls apart, for the Hollywood Bowl presented its first concert in 1922, a busy year for Valentino. He made *Beyond the Rocks* and *Blood and Sand;* married Natacha on May 13, and was jailed for bigamy; acquitted of the charge, he had gone to New York to quarrel with Jesse Lasky, Adolph Zukor and the producing company to whom he was contracted; he had initiated his lawsuit against Famous Players-Lasky, and remained throughout the latter half of 1922 in the eastern part of the United States. One must reject, quite seriously, Miss Flame's claims to close sodality, through her devotion as a cultist is beyond dispute. One must doubt it as seriously as Hollywood Boulevard regulars doubted the assertions of the creature who in the forties haunted the Boulevard from Highland Avenue to Vine Street, claiming to be Valentino's bastard.

These days the bronze vases of Valentino's crypt are usually filled with flowers, and mausoleum attendants say such bouquets are brought by several elderly people, but most often by a devoted lady who claims to be a former housekeeper and drives in from Santa Monica three or four days a week. In the *Film Quarterly* article in which Gavin Lambert compared and contrasted Douglas Fairbanks and Valentino, he concluded that Valentino's influence and impact had been the more important. If so, the irony is that Valentino occupies a simple crypt in Hollywood Cemetery's Cathedral Mausoleum. Adjacent is the Sunken Garden Monument, with its reflecting pool at least fifty feet long and proportionately wide, surrounded by gentle green slopes and appropriate foliage. At the far end, on a raised pedestal, is the magnificent marble sarcophagus of Fairbanks. Behind it is a marble wall in which is set a bronze bas-relief profile of Fairbanks, along with the dates of his earthly stay. This is the sort of monument to the departed that movie fans and cultists believe appropriate for a star.

The crypt occupied by Valentino is one to which any mortal might aspire. It is not good enough for Valentino, for there still are annual services for him attended by strange beings and publicity-seeking starlets who can afford only press agents and publicity men of impoverished imaginations—without flair for *shtick*—and who visit the tomb only after they have first notified the newspapers and industry trade papers. They are ignored, which might be as Valentino would have wished it. For never, in any message supposedly sent by him through a spiritualist, did he approve of the goings-on at his crypt.

In 1965, Richard Arlen delivered the eulogy at Valentino's crypt and Ditra Flame returned in ordinary dress. She might never have been recognized had she not spoken and beseeched the fifty or so teen-agers gathered there out of curiosity to revere and worship the memory and ideals of Valentino. But it was difficult to hear her over the giggling and the snap of bubble gum.

EPILOGUE

The lease held by Valentino as a god or saint of a Palace of
Love at the end of the Rainbow Bridge with its fine view of the
Hereafter was effectively canceled in April, 1964, when *Playboy*
featured Peter Sellers on its cover in the dress of the Sheik.
Sellers wore the burnoose, robe, vest and other accouterments
of the Great Lover. On the forefinger of his left hand was an
effeminate ring, on the right hand a ring that featured the
Playboy Bunny. Staring soulfully at Sellers, but with anticipa-
tion, is Karen Lynn, garbed as a slave girl. Under the photo is the
caption: "Oh, Rudy, I'll be your slave if you'll let me see your
April issue . . . and the wild parody of movie lovers by Peter
Sellers!"

Inside the magazine, Sellers mimed José Ferrer as Toulouse-
Lautrec; Francis X. Bushman as Ben Hur; Bela Lugosi as

Dracula; James Stewart as Destry; Cary Grant in *Notorious;* and Groucho Marx. Once again he portrayed Rudolph Valentino as on the cover, his eyes resembling hard-boiled eggs as he swoops Miss Lynn off her feet, and is about to carry her into the innermost recesses of his tent.

Even if Mastroianni's *Caio, Rudy!* had been an international hit, it is doubtful whether Valentino could ever be recanonized or stimulate the adulation he formerly inspired. Succinctly, Valentino doesn't "grab" today's teen-ager. For the question asked almost a quarter-century ago—could Sinatra replace Valentino as the American sex symbol?—was neither outlandish nor unperceptive. Even the shallowest investigation reveals that the average age of the male American sex symbol is becoming younger and younger. Sinatra was replaced by Marlon Brando, who was replaced by James Dean, who was replaced by Elvis Presley, who was replaced by Tommy Sands, who was replaced by Fabian, who was replaced by the Beatles, who were replaced by . . . ? And so it goes, on and on.

The American listening and viewing audience—or at least that significant portion of it financially responsible for the success or failure of records and concert appearances of current popular stars, either adenoidal or *castrato*—is conditioned to react with ecstatic delirium only at the sight, sound or gyration of boy or girl vocalists still adjusting to puberty. True, there is a sex type that is devoted to the ideals and practices of modern romance, but this ethnic type resembles neither the cavalier, the suave gentleman of the drawing room nor the yachtsman clad by Abercrombie and Fitch. The courting dress of this new sex type is a combination of far-out costume tailoring and successes achieved by rummaging through a city dump to find the worst, seediest and most outlandish apparel. Both genders affect fright wigs and Spanish boots with baby-doll heels. In appearance the new male sex idol is childishly primitive, unscrubbed, wildly coiffured, often with a Chinese beard, and there is neither subtlety nor masculinity in his AC-DC approach to sex. His mating dance is not a tango but an exaggeration of pelvic movements, grinds, bumps and thrusts to simulate love as it is practiced by young, screaming Yahoos.

Sex is no longer worshiped through its images as an ideal, and an adult male can no longer generate the excitement of the old matinee idol. Furthermore, the worship of sex idols, usually found today in the ranks of teen-age rock 'n' roll singers who yeh-yeh "I luhv yuh," is an added dimension of the anti-intellectual attitude that the American adult has been able to pass on —seemingly as his *only* significant bequest—to his children. In *The Great Audience* (1950) Gilbert Seldes observed: "The closer a man approaches the status of an 'intellectual,' the less capable he is of coping with timetables, supermarkets, the weather, laundry, babies, and all the other trifles of daily existence; and the more certain he is to be first baffled and then enchanted by a pushing teen-ager whose glandular attractions he considers signs of abstract intelligence until the end of the sixth reel."

Not too long ago, when Valentino was accelerating the heart action and increasing the blood pressure of the female, she saw herself, in her mind's eye, before their luxurious tent pitched under a desert moon sipping a champagne cocktail. Today the squealing female adolescent—dressed in pink hair curlers, a halter, blue jeans and dirty feet—sees herself in her optimum vision of romance in the back seat of a convertible in a drive-in theater under a smog-filled sky, chomping on a pizza and sniffing airplane glue, the better to appreciate an orgiastic movie that stars Hysterical Hector and His Hysterectomy Five, who are all narcissistically in love with their own acne. "I want to take you in my arms" has become, as electric guitars plunk their way into young America's heart, "I whonner hol' yer han'." Finally, to plight their troth, the adolescent driver will permit the jill of his choice to join him in a contemporary ceremony of fidelity: together they will hold up a liquor store.

Even the facade of maturity has been destroyed: poetry, agility and vigor have been banished from the screen. All the old gods are in their twilight; therefore Valentino is not the exception to this rule. The baroque religion of flamboyant filmdom has been destroyed; its temples have been cleared away to become parking lots. It is difficult to cheer and hail the new faith, which prefers to worship a mop-headed Peter Pan rather than a slick-haired Sheik.